Walter Feinberg's Democratic Vision

SUNY series, Horizons in the Philosophy of Education
David J. Blacker, editor

Walter Feinberg's Democratic Vision
Classic Writings on Public Education

WALTER FEINBERG

Edited by
BRYAN R. WARNICK

Cover credit: Courtesy of Walter Feinberg

Published by State University of New York Press, Albany

© 2025 State University of New York

All rights reserved

Printed in the United States of America

No part of this book may be used or reproduced in any manner whatsoever without written permission. No part of this book may be stored in a retrieval system or transmitted in any form or by any means including electronic, electrostatic, magnetic tape, mechanical, photocopying, recording, or otherwise without the prior permission in writing of the publisher.

Links to third-party websites are provided as a convenience and for informational purposes only. They do not constitute an endorsement or an approval of any of the products, services, or opinions of the organization, companies, or individuals. SUNY Press bears no responsibility for the accuracy, legality, or content of a URL, the external website, or for that of subsequent websites.

EU GPSR Authorised Representative:
Logos Europe, 9 rue Nicolas Poussin, 17000, La Rochelle, France
contact@logoseurope.eu

For information, contact State University of New York Press, Albany, NY
www.sunypress.edu

Library of Congress Cataloging-in-Publication Data

Names: Feinberg, Walter, 1937– author. | Warnick, Bryan R., 1974– editor.
Title: Walter Feinberg's democratic vision : classic writings on public
   education / Walter Feinberg ; edited by Bryan R. Warnick.
Description: Albany : State University of New York Press, [2025] | Series:
   SUNY series, horizons in the philosophy of education | Includes
   bibliographical references and index.
Identifiers: LCCN 2024042829 | ISBN 9798855802269 (hardcover : alk. paper) |
   ISBN 9798855802283 (ebook) | ISBN 9798855802276 (pbk. : alk. paper)
Subjects: LCSH: Education—Philosophy. | Public schools—United States.
Classification: LCC LB14.7 .F45 2025 | DDC 370.1/2—dc23/eng/20250117
LC record available at https://lccn.loc.gov/2024042829

Contents

Acknowledgments   vii

Part I: Introducing Feinberg

1   Introduction   3
       Bryan R. Warnick

2   Autobiographical Essay: The Construction of a Social
      Philosopher of Education   23

Part II: Paying Attention in the Study of Education

3   Educational Studies and the Disciplines of Educational
      Understanding   45

4   The Discourse of Philosophy of Education   65

5   A Role for Philosophy of Education in Intercultural
      Research: A Reexamination of the Relativism-Absolutism
      Debate   77

6   Critical Pragmatism and the Reconnection of Science
      and Values in Educational Research   95

7   The Conflict Between Intelligence and Community in
      Dewey's Educational Philosophy   121

8   Critical Pragmatism and the Appropriation of Ethnography by Philosophy of Education: Critical Pragmatism and Local Understanding   137

9   Fixing the Schools: The Ideological Turn   149

Part III: Public School: A Democratic Vision

10 The Public Responsibility of Public Education   177

11 The Idea of a Public Education   191

12 Culture and the Common School   219

13 Uncommon Identities: Hard Cases   239

14 Affirmative Action and Beyond: A Case for a Backward-Looking Gender- and Race-Based Policy   265

15 Faith and the Pedagogical Limits of Critical Inquiry: Toward a Generous Reading of Religious Schools   303

16 On Public Support for Religious Schools   325

17 Reconciling Liberalism and Pluralism in Religious Education   341

18 Religious Education in Liberal Democratic Societies: The Question of Accountability and Autonomy   345

19 An Assessment of Arguments for Teaching Religion in Public Schools in the United States   373

20 Toward a New Progressive Educational Movement   385

Notes   403

Reference Bibliography   425

Index   431

Acknowledgments

Chapter 2: Originally published in *Leaders in Philosophy of Education: Intellectual Self Portraits*, ed. Leonard J. Waks (Rotterdam: Sense Publishers, 2008), 63–80.

Chapter 3: Originally published in *Educational Studies*, 10, no. 4 (1980): 375–91. Used with permission of Taylor and Francis; permission conveyed through Copyright Clearance Center, Inc.

Chapter 4: Originally published in *Critical Conversations in Philosophy of Education*, ed. Wendy Kohli (New York: Routledge, 1995), 24–33. Reproduced by permission of Taylor and Francis Group.

Chapter 5: Originally published in *Teachers College Record* 91, no. 2 (1989): 161–76. Copyright 1989 by Teachers College Record: www.TCRecord.org

Chapter 6: Originally published in *European Journal of Pragmatism and American Philosophy*, IV–1 (2012): 1–20.

Chapter 7: Originally published in *Educational Theory* 19, no. 3 (1969): 236–48.

Chapter 8. Originally published in *Studies in Philosophy and Education* 34, no. 2 (2015): 149–57.

Chapter 9: Originally published in *Issues in Education* 3, no. 2 (1985): 113–38.

Chapter 10: Originally published in *Journal of Philosophy of Education* 25, no. 1 (1991): 17–25. Used by permission of Oxford University Press and the Philosophy of Education Society of Great Britain.

Chapter 11: Originally published in *Review of Research in Education* 36 (2012): 1–22. Copyright 2012 by the American Educational Research Association; reproduced with permission of the publisher.

Chapter 12: Originally published in *Journal of Philosophy of Education* 41, no. 4 (2007): 591–607. Used by permission of Oxford University Press and the Philosophy of Education Society of Great Britain.

Chapter 13: Originally published in *Common Schools/Uncommon Identities: National Unity and Cultural Difference* (New Haven: Yale University Press, 1998), 158–89. Copyright Yale University Press.

Chapter 14: Originally published in *Teachers College Record* 97, no. 3 (1996): 362–99. Copyright 1996 by Teachers College Record: www.TCRecord.org

Chapter 15: Originally published in *For Goodness Sake: Religious Schools and Education for Democratic Citizenry* (New York: Routledge, 2006). Reproduced by permission of Taylor and Francis Group.

Chapter 16: Originally published in *Teachers College Record* 102, no. 4 (2000): 841–56. Copyright 2000 by Teachers College Record: www.TCRecord.org

Chapter 17: Originally published in *Religious Education* 108, no. 3 (2013): 241–44. Used with permission of Taylor and Francis; permission conveyed through Copyright Clearance Center, Inc.

Chapter 18: Originally published in *Education and Citizenship in Liberal-Democratic Societies: Teaching for Cosmopolitan Values and Collective Identities*, ed. Kevin McDonough and Walter Feinberg (Oxford: Oxford University Press, 2003), 385–413.

Chapter 19: Originally published in *Religious Education* 109, no. 4 (2014): 394–405. Used with permission of Taylor and Francis; permission conveyed through Copyright Clearance Center, Inc.

Chapter 20: Originally published in *Dewey and Education* (New York: Routledge, Taylor and Francis Group, 2018), 103–26. Reproduced by permission of Taylor and Francis Group.

The editor gratefully acknowledges permission to reprint these papers.

Part I

Introducing Feinberg

1

Introduction

BRYAN R. WARNICK

For more than fifty years, Walter Feinberg has been one of the foremost analysts and interpreters of education in democratic societies. The papers collected here are intimately tied to the story of the American experiment in which they are embedded. The reader will find a philosopher of education who is responsive to the specific problems and debates facing the national community. Feinberg is not just theorizing in the abstract; instead, he directly addresses the pressing economic, political, and cultural problems of the times. Feinberg can be seen responding to the Vietnam War and the divisive conflicts of the 1960s, to the economic and social concerns of the 1970s and 80s triggered by the specter of Japanese competition, and to the emergence of the religious right. Likewise, he responds to the controversies about multiculturalism in the 1990s and to the pressing questions of identity in the 2000s. The great debates over educational policy—from affirmative action to school choice to school prayer—all receive probing analysis. To read Feinberg's published papers is to reexperience national history through an educational lens.

This does not mean that these papers are of a merely antiquarian interest. Nor does it mean they are of interest only to American readers. Quite the opposite. Part of the reason for their continuing relevance is that the problems Feinberg addresses have never completely gone away; in fact, some continue to loom, as large as they ever have. Questions remain over religion in public schools and affirmative action, over parental rights and multiculturalism. The questions he asks are relevant to any society that takes democracy seriously. Everywhere, we wonder what it means to be a community as cultural differences multiply and polarization intensifies. We wonder about the role of public schools in an increasingly privatized society. Feinberg's engagement with the problems of his time and place—his careful analysis, his important distinctions, his normative arguments—remain every bit as relevant today as they were in the decades and locations in which he writes.[1]

An even deeper reason for the continued relevance of these papers is that they offer a model for the serious study of education, particularly in the field known as philosophy of education. This area of study is characterized by a wide diversity of perspectives and approaches, a diversity that can be both bewildering and invigorating. Students often question where they can find clear examples of excellence. Feinberg's papers provide a highly instructive model for how to do philosophy of education, and how to do it well. This keen responsiveness that Feinberg demonstrates to pressing social and educational problems of his day (rather than being obsessed with, say, interpretive questions of Plato or Foucault, or the endless analysis of concepts such as "education" versus "indoctrination") is one thing students can learn from these papers. But even more than that, Feinberg's papers model a philosophy that *pays attention*. These papers reveal a writer who pays attention to the latest developments in philosophy and in the world of ideas more broadly—readers will find Feinberg in conversation with many key contemporary philosophers and educational thinkers. But this work also attends to the little details of schooling, to the depths of different perspectives, and to the ever-changing legal and policy landscapes. It attends, that is, both to the details of specific empirical circumstances, in addition to the more traditional landscapes of philosophical imagination and argumentation. As Feinberg pays attention to the world in this way, he models a productive way of doing philosophy of education.

In this introduction and in the collection of papers that follows, then, I discuss two aspects of Feinberg's thought that are worthy of consideration. First, I talk about his distinctive way of studying education, particularly his way of doing philosophy of education. This approach attends to the multiplicity of modes by which philosophers can achieve a better interpretive understanding of the world around them. Feinberg shows how this interpretive approach is fundamental to the traditional normative work of the philosopher. Second, I look at the substantive arguments of the papers, focusing on what they have to say about education in a pluralistic, democratic society. These arguments are as relevant and interesting in today's world as they were when they were written. Finally, I hope to suggest that there is a deep connection between Feinberg's way of studying education and his normative vision of democratic schooling.

Paying Attention: A Democratic Approach to the Study of Education

This attention to the empirical has led Feinberg to be something of a pioneer in the practice of what he calls philosophical ethnography. This is an approach that does not so much pretend to be an exacting social science, but to simply learn from the world, to improve one's understanding of how others see the world, and to thereby grasp a vision of underexplored educational possibilities. Before philosophy answers the question "What should be done?" it must first answer the question "What is going on?" and "How are things being understood?" Feinberg's method begins with this general ethnographic stance, but with focused questions relating to a particular educational question of dilemma. Feinberg, starting with philosophical questions, proceeds with an anthropologist's thirst for observation and conversation, surveying the landscape of experience and meaning surrounding the question before determining the direction in which to travel.

Feinberg reports that he learned in his graduate training the importance of rich and detailed understanding and of paying attention in sympathetic ways. His mentors encouraged him, when studying another thinker, to articulate the best restatement of that philosopher's position before trying to identify problems. "The emphasis on teaching was reinforced by the message that we earned the right to criticize a position only after we have represented it fairly," he writes. "The ideal was to represent an argument in a way that was even stronger than the original" (see "The Construction of a Social Philosopher," p. TBA). Feinberg took this insight about reading philosophy and democratized it. It is important to give this this sympathetic reading not only to philosophers, but also to the teachers, students, and everyday citizens who comprise the educational community of concern. Philosophical ethnography tries to uncover the constellation of possible reasons for why people believe and act as they do. It is not only descriptive, but also partly reconstructive. It not only finds what people think and feel, but also tries to imagine such reflections in their most convincing light, to find the most powerful articulation of their positions. In this way, the philosopher learns from empirical study in a way that supplements normative theorizing. Only when the relevant voices are heard in their clearest and most persuasive way can new educational possibilities emerge.

In his paper "A Role for Philosophy of Education in Inter-Cultural Research," Feinberg describes this attitude as a kind of "haunting," that is, as a sort of anthropological ghost that should disturb philosophers who seek universal principles, whispering questions about what they may have missed about others in their understandings of problematic situations. The ghost demands cross-cultural respect, and this often makes it difficult to avoid cultural relativism, reducing moral values to cultural norms. Feinberg does not think he can answer this question of relativism in the abstract, but finds pathways forward in certain practical situations, such as in teaching situations where teacher and student come from different cultures. "Practice," he says, "belongs neither to the philosopher not to the anthropologist" (p. TBA). As a teacher reads the situation, different forms of cultural respect present themselves. The teacher might leave things alone or show restraint in offering judgment, depending on the situation, or the teacher might use cultural difference as the basis for a productive educational encounter. If something about the other voice seems odd, this should promote deep reflection. This reflection, however, should not just challenge our own values and assumptions about ourselves, but also our interpretative methods. The philosopher may begin "by questioning our interpretation" of the seeming cultural oddities—maybe what seemed odd is a misunderstanding. There are countless ways our understanding of others can go awry. The anthropological ghost reminds us that great care is needed.

Beyond anthropological-style inquiry, there are various tools available to help refine the quest to better interpret social realities. One of the most powerful tools resides in the humanities, which Feinberg describes as vehicles to travel into the experience and reference frame of another. What makes the humanities unique is not their content, but how they provide windows to glimpse the ways in which people see the world. They expose a world of interpretation, allowing us to think about our own thoughts as we better understand the experiences of others. A poem, a history, a painting, a scientific theory, a philosophy—these can all be part of the humanities to the extent that they are studied humanistically, that is, studied in a way that helps us understand different human experiences and perspectives on how to see the world. With the humanities comes a sort of humility, a realization that there are ways of viewing the world that are "credible" other than our own. One way of understanding Feinberg's approach to philosophy of education is to see him as furthering this humanistic approach to the study of education, centering the interpretive task of understanding others as the primary task to philosophy (instead of, say, discerning metaphysical truth). The humanities, in fact, are a certain way of paying attention to the interpretative framework of others. The study of education is inescapably humanistic.

History, of course, also plays an important role in all of this. These papers show the need for philosophers of education to pay attention to historical events and narratives. For Feinberg, there is philosophical value in understanding how ideas emerge. Philosophers need to ask about the social, economic, and political conditions that gave birth to educational policies and practices—who has benefited from all this, and why? The failure of many philosophers to consider the significance of history in shaping educational norms led Feinberg to become disenchanted with the analytic approach to philosophy of education. It also led him to question celebratory stories of public education that viewed public schools in glowing and uncritical terms, as paeans to enlightened progress and democracy. As part of answering the question "What is going on?" we need to ask, "Who benefited as practices were formed?" All of this must come before the question "What should we do now?" This emphasis on the historical and the critical aligned Feinberg (in the eyes of some) with revisionist historians who cast a skeptical eye on the history of American education, interpreting schools as vehicles simply of oppression and exclusion. While Feinberg does indeed find value in this critical historical gaze, the difference is that Feinberg believes philosophy plays a role that goes beyond criticism.

A key lesson from these papers is to attend to the "outsiders," the hidden and marginalized. The attention to outsiders was present in Feinberg's thought from early on. In his dissertation on John Dewey and Bernard Bosanquet, Feinberg had noticed a tension in Dewey's thought between a national need for coherent citizenship and a promotion of scientific inquiry. He became keenly aware of the fact of cultural pluralism, the fact that modern liberal democracies are complex amalgamations of groups with sharply contrasting belief systems. In his earliest articles on John Dewey, Feinberg draws attention to a report that Dewey wrote for the US government during the First World War that illustrated the tension, and the way Dewey tried to resolve the tension in practice. In that 1918 report, Dewey doubted whether the Polish minority population in Philadelphia could be trusted to be loyal to the United States, and he advocated for its surveillance and control. Other scholars have subsequently interpreted this as an aberration of Dewey's thought, a blind spot in the application of his own democratic theory. Feinberg, however, argues that Dewey's failure to live up to the ideals of participatory democracy in the "Polish Study" is not a personal failure, but a deeper flaw in his social philosophy. In pursuit of technological progress, Dewey's philosophy could not quite cope with the existence of groups that seemed indifferent to democratic institutions or antagonistic to the expression of values shaped democratically. Feinberg criticizes Dewey on this point: democracy is not neat and tidy, it must accommodate groups with vastly different beliefs, and it must even "protect the rights of undemocratic groups" (p. TBA). In the end, Feinberg concludes that Dewey's evolutionary account of ethics is based on an oversimplified notion of social coordination, agreement, technological development, and scientific inquiry.

Feinberg's analysis of Dewey began to shape his general approach to knowledge, ethics, and education. Dewey wanted to formulate a theory of social intelligence that was "naturalistic," that is, that did not involve the invocation of controversial and non-testable metaphysical principles. For Dewey, human intelligence is aroused when communities face common problems, problems that can be recognized by all, and debate ensues about "what to do," with each person providing a perspective about the desired solution. The solutions that face the test of questioning and experience give "objectivity" to ethics. Ethical principles are justified only insofar as they help us to work together and harmonize our actions, to increase our coordination and cooperation, in response to the problems of living. Feinberg complicated this view by pointing out that even the process of identifying common problems or framing them in the same way is not something that we can so easily assume. People coming from different traditions and having different experiences will find different things problematic. There are no "common problems" that we can collectively subject to the lessons of experience. This complicates Dewey's notions of social intelligence.

Feinberg believes that only by taking seriously the situation of the outsider—say, the Polish-American population in Philadelphia—can the philosopher develop the necessary conceptual tools to recognize and then address the tension between intelligence and community, which Dewey failed to acknowledge. It is in response to the challenge of the outsider that throughout his work Feinberg urges the adoption of key distinctions: between non-democratic groups versus anti-democratic groups, between government tolerance of such groups versus government support for such groups, between government coercion of such groups versus government encouragement of such groups to change, and between the governmental responsibility to educate versus a parent's right to guide their children's development. These distinctions are critical to discussions about democratic education, and Feinberg employs them regularly as he engages with ongoing educational concerns. These philosophical tools were formulated precisely because Feinberg takes seriously the outsider. The lesson is that those of us who consider ourselves philosophers of education have a responsibility to project ourselves in and sympathize with those in a minority position. This attention is a key theme of Feinberg's work across the decades. The technical philosophical tools are used to help us pay attention to the swirling cacophony of voices within democratic communities, particularly to the voices that are not often or easily heard.

To further understand Feinberg's approach to studying education, a good way to start is to look at his conception of education. Feinberg agrees with those who see education in terms of social and cultural reproduction, of "maintaining intergenerational continuity—that is, of maintaining its identity as a society across generations and even in the context of many possible and significant changes" (Disciplines of Educational Understanding," p. TBA). Education as a scholarly field, then, would be defined as the study of the methods and institutions by which a culture regenerates itself. The study of education is the critical investigation of these processes of social reproduction. In particular, it is the study of the sort of the knowledge and skills that constitute unique forms of vocational and social life, and of the "knowledge codes" that arise as some forms of knowledge are deemed to be of higher status and more valuable than others. It will need to critically engage with these value structures. This suggests that the study of education is not simply a descriptive task; it will always involve ethical judgments. It will need to ask what about a society is valuable to reproduce, given the scope of possibilities and the limitations presented by practice.

This vision of the study of education finds expression in Feinberg's particular notion of pragmatism as it relates to educational research. Feinberg is a critic of attempts to eliminate discussions of value in the study of education. Against the fact/value dichotomy championed by positivistic researchers, Feinberg endorses a form of inquiry called "critical pragmatism." Like pragmatism, critical pragmatism holds that the function of research is to address pressing social problems through ongoing inquiry and open discussion. As a culture regenerates itself, the pragmatic process requires the sharing and reshaping of experience through both individual and collective actions. Pragmatism becomes "critical" when, among other things, it attends to the role of power in the shaping and sharing of experiences. Whose problems are taken seriously in cultural regeneration? What voices are silenced and why? The study of education, then, must bring to light the unexamined biases of the processes of socialization. It looks at what is taken as the "common sense" of day, the logic of past practices, the unchallenged assumptions of social science, and seeks alternatives. Education research, as a study of social reproduction, must pay attention to value judgments.

As a branch of educational research, educational philosophy also cannot escape a focus on the specifics of institutional schooling. For Feinberg, philosophy of education, in fact, gains its very identity, its reason for being, from the existence of formal institutions of educational practice, largely schools. True, there are many philosophical questions related to education that one could ask apart from schools (What is the nature of knowledge?, What is childhood? and so forth). But these are questions that belong to the traditional branches of philosophy. Philosophy of education is an institutional philosophy, for Feinberg. It is concerned largely with the questions faced by institutions and practices that are explicitly charged with social reproduction. A question like "Who should control schools—parents, democratic communities, or professional educators?" is not a canonical philosophical question. It depends on the existence of institutions to give meaning to the question and to make the question matter. This is why philosophy of education is historically and rightly tied to schools of education instead of departments of philosophy. True, schools interact with many other aspects of culture, and an analysis of schools must also attend to these things. As a discipline, however, philosophy of education will always be grounded in the work of schools.

Feinberg's paper "Fixing the Schools" exemplifies many of the notable characteristics of his attentive approach to the study of education, particularly from a philosophical perspective. As he surveys and evaluates documents of school reform, one can find him situating them in historical context, using a critical approach by emphasizing structural considerations, attending to anthropological observation and interview data, and focusing on institutional schooling, all within a project that is infused with philosophically informed value judgments and normative assessments. When Feinberg wrote the paper, there had been a spate of reform proposals, signaling that the nation was in a moment of transition. Many of the reform proposals were blaming schools for alleged poor US economic performance, particularly vis-à-vis competition from Japan, using alarmist language and predicting national catastrophe. In this article (and later in his book *Japan and the Quest for a New American Identity*), Feinberg places these reform documents, particularly the 1983 *A Nation at Risk* report, in historical context and within a much richer understanding of Japanese schools. While sympathetic to the more measured and moderate policy reform ideas of his day, Feinberg also finds that the lack of attention to structural issues of poverty and racism to be troubling. In short, he criticizes these reports for failing to attend to the realities of schools, to their histories, and to the cultural and social structures in which different school systems are embedded. This paper exemplifies a philosopher who *pays attention*, bringing a range of tools to examine pressing educational questions and initiatives.

School: A Democratic Vision

The continued relevance of Feinberg's papers resides not simply in exemplifying a process of paying attention in a democratic way but also in the insight it provides about normative educational questions in democratic societies. Questions such as: What society should we be trying to produce? What do democratic schools look like? What problems do educators have a responsibility to address? With these questions comes a set of educational problems with which the philosopher of education must grapple. Unlike many revisionist historians who focus only on the shortcomings of public schools, Feinberg recognizes a key role for a common, public education in a democratic society. Indeed, a democratic society regenerates itself precisely through *public* education, a type of education that initiates students into an awareness of their shared collective fate and that fosters a willingness to work with strangers to shape the future. Given Feinberg's interest in the outsider, there is a particular concern for how public participation can occur across lines of cultural difference in a pluralistic society. There are three themes that emerge under this general topic area: diversity and the common school, national identity in historical context, and religion and the democratic public.

Diversity and the Common School

Feinberg is dissatisfied with the idea that public education can be successfully defined in terms of state funding, government control, or universal access, and instead wants to discuss the democratic aims that make public schools truly "public." The distinction is a normative one. Public schools have an explicit obligation to promote citizens who both care about democracy and work together to enhance it. A public school, in the normative sense, helps students gain a sense of themselves as part of a public, that is, as having a collective identity as well as an individual identity. When a public education is successful, students should come to care about the good of the commons as well as that of their individual selves.

Feinberg makes a distinction between the "common good" as economists employ the idea and the "public good" as educators should employ the term. The common good is simply the sum of all individual goods, added together as individuals seek their own happiness. The public good refers to a notion of good that is shaped as people encounter one another as they live together, as they deliberate and learn from each other, and as they construct a vision of the social good that transcends the summed total of the individual desires. Market forces can sometimes effectively promote the "common good" by maximizing the satisfaction of individual preferences, but they do not ask people to come together to reflect, deliberate, and learn from each other. They do not ask people to change their individual preferences in light of what is best for a community. In a market, desires may be satisfied; in a public, desires may be transformed through deliberation. Public school is a location for this transformation from separate individuals into a public. A public school does not require for its existence that people agree about everything related to education. It requires a willingness to change and grow together. This shared life requires transparency, generous benefit of the doubt, and skills of cooperation and deliberation. Public schools are places that nurture these interactions.

Even in a diverse society, Feinberg believes it still makes sense to talk normatively of a public school as a "common school," at least in some sense. A common school is common because it allows for shared experience and commitments. To be sure, there are versions of common schooling that should be left behind, namely, the version that posits schools as promoting one culture as superior to others and coercing students to fit into that singular mold. Formulating a better version, Feinberg argues, requires abandoning the concept of "culture" that treats it like an object that exists apart from people, that people retain as a sort of possession. If, instead, we stop thinking of culture as an object to possess, but rather as a process of meaning-making, then a better version of a common school becomes clearer. When schools serve public ends, they engage in a process of "culturing." That is, they become places where students come together and participate in shaping the collective meanings that will help them live together. The common school is forward looking. Instead of building a national identity around a preexisting vision of cultural life, it will ask about what students can *come* to have in common rather than forcing them into a preexisting box. It will help students learn to construct visions of shared lives with those around them. When the school is built around this vision of culture—culture as a process of collective meaning-making moving toward the future—the common school can then be seen for what it is: an essential part of constructing a truly democratic public.

National Identity in Historical Context

The fact that public schools, as Feinberg envisions them, have a forward-looking mission and that they need to be sensitive to emerging forms of meaning-making, does not obliviate the complexities of history. History plays a key role in reinterpreting the common school's mission in pluralistic societies and in providing the material—both physical and narrative—to shape a shared future. A pluralistic society, as was noted, is constituted by many groups that have different values and systems of meaning. Scholars, political figures, and activists differ about the stance democracies should adopt toward these different expressions of culture. For example, some want different cultures to live separately, with separate schools serving their particular needs. Others hold that schools should impose a single, unified, national culture and demand allegiance from all. Others believe that schools can and should remain culture-free and neutral, while teaching tolerance for cultural difference. Others believe that cultural differences are essential to human autonomy and identity and that school should celebrate cultural differences, but within a context of cultural gathering within public schools. We are presented, then, with a question: Should schools actively recognize and promote certain cultural identities, should they remain neutral and teach tolerance, or should they try to forge a unified national identity?

Feinberg argues that history holds an important key to answering such questions. The history of different groups and their incorporation into the mainstream allows us to see the value of different responses to the demands for recognition, including demands for educational autonomy or public support for different cultural expressions. Some groups joined the national culture more willingly as immigrants, while others were subjugated or brought here as enslaved people. Systematic, multigenerational discrimination and oppression create a cultural "debt" that a majority owes to some groups but not others. In such cases, public schools have a duty to support the cultural groups that have been under persistent and systemic attack. This can take the form of special recognition in the curriculum, the observance of certain holidays and special times of remembrance, assistance with student groups and language programs, and perhaps even public support for separate schools dedicated to furthering the interest of the oppressed cultural group.

This idea of cultural debt plays a role in Feinberg's specific defense of affirmative action policies. Feinberg urges us to resist the temptation to transform affirmative action programs into programs that focus only on economic deprivation, moving away from race-based to entirely class-based assistance programs. While programs for those in poverty are vitally important, economic circumstances are not the only barriers to equality. There also exist structures of meaning that need transformation. Legacies of race-based oppression have structured the self-understanding of the oppressed. While external opportunities for all underrepresented groups are important, for example, there also must be an *internal* transformation in how the oppressed see themselves and how they perceive the opportunities that are available to them. For example, if a young person never encounters a doctor or professional who "looks like them," then it will be difficult to imagine a professional medical career. Feinberg argues we must work "simultaneously," addressing both the inner and outer dimensions of the legacy of oppression.

The focus on economic inequality alone also does not address the obligations that society incurs to members of specific historically oppressed groups. The history of the treatment of some groups involves "historical crimes of such egregious nature that special obligations have been created for the larger society" (p. TBA). Certain groups, like

African- and Native Americans, have been exploited for centuries, all in service of building the wealth and capital of the nation. This must be repaid somehow. Calculating which groups are owed a cultural debt, deciding who should pay it, and determining how the payment should be made are all complicated issues, to be sure, but not issues from which a society can be excused. Paying the debt must involve overturning the racially stained scripts of dominance and submission that have persisted for generations. Focusing only on economic deprivation, while important, is not sufficient. As in other areas, as we try to sort out what justice requires in a pluralistic democracy, Feinberg shows how history can reveal important distinctions. The particular experiences of social groups matter a great deal; not every group can be treated the same.

Religion and the Public

Religion, and religious education in particular, present a particularly thorny set of dilemmas for liberal, pluralistic democracies. Religious schools are often thought to be outside the realm of public accountability, as they recognize different forms of authority than do public schools. In such schools, different priorities and values might be emphasized, some of which may be in tension with democratic values. Religious schools may favor ancient texts over science, obedience over free expression and individuality, centralized authority over consensus, or exclusivity over inclusivity. Religious schools often force democratic societies to confront the tension between the values of liberalism and the values of pluralism. On the one hand, pluralism recognizes the wide variety of human beings and emphasizes that there cannot be one model appropriate for all people. This implies a tolerance for other ways of living, and this includes a tolerance for different forms of education. Pluralism would advocate allowing parents a great deal of discretion over how they raise their children. Liberalism, in contrast, holds the values of freedom and equality in high esteem and emphasizes the need for individuals to choose their own way through life. This implies that children be taught about a variety of different ways of thinking and be given the skills to evaluate and criticize the options presented to them. This includes being able to criticize the beliefs they are being taught by their parents. But what happens if a religious school, chosen by parents to foster parental beliefs, does not encourage liberal values? This would seem to bring pluralism and liberalism into direct conflict.

Feinberg approaches this question in several ways. The first is to understand "what is going on" in religious schools. Feinberg approaches religious schools with that spirit of sympathetic understanding that exemplifies his approach to philosophy. Through philosophical ethnography, Feinberg recognizes that, indeed, there are a number of pitfalls that religious education presents. Sometimes the doctrinal mission of imparting dogma, for example, interferes with a pastoral mission of nurturing youth (think of a teacher in a conservative tradition with a queer student). Feinberg also finds, however, that religious educators often navigate such tensions in creative ways and that religious education is often not as closed and indoctrinatory as secular critics assume. Religious traditions can be seen as a multivocal conversations that may change with time rather than as holders of a unitary, static dogma. Religious education also can promote some goods that a secular education may have more difficulty advancing, for example, "a heightened [student] awareness of their responsibility to an intergenerational community" ("reconciling liberalism and pluralism," p. TBA). This suggests that religious schools may have something positive to contribute to democratic societies. Religious education, then, is not *necessarily* anti-democratic or opposed to public values. The potential of religious education can be more fully realized with the assistance of philosophical pragmatism, which suggests different ways of thinking about religious truth. Pragmatism would emphasize, for example, the role of religion in constructing community identity rather than revealing a metaphysical reality. Belief in the ultimate truth of one's own religion does not preclude acknowledging that other religions can also have truth in this pragmatic sense and respecting them for it.

Beyond the potential of religious schools, Feinberg probes the question of whether religious schools should have public support and whether religion should be taught in public schools. For Feinberg, an essential feature of public schools is that they are accountable to citizens. Public schools should give citizens a place to talk about, and experiment with, the meaning of democratic citizenship. It is a place to debate the ways that future citizens should be shaped. The public schools should reflect whatever rough and provisional consensus emerges from this ongoing discussion. Public schools are supported through public funds partly because they are presumed to be accountable to this consensus. To be sure, some religious families may strongly object to this consensus, and such parents should indeed be permitted to send their children to private religious schools. To exercise this right, though, they must now pay for their children's education in addition to paying taxes to support public schools for other children. Some have claimed that this is unjust, a form of double taxation. Feinberg argues that such families are not being treated unjustly. Such families, in effect, trade the financial support of the state for the freedom to leave the consensus. Moreover, the alternative, which would mean forcing citizens to financially support specific forms of religious instruction with public funds, would be even more problematic. The traditional arrangement, where public schools are supported by public funds and regulated by the government, while private religious schools are privately funded but largely exempt from such regulation, can be politically justified, even if it is not always democratically ideal.

Religious schools raise the issue of parents' rights to make educational decisions. Feinberg is sympathetic to the idea that parents have a good deal of discretion in directing the education of their children. There are at least two issues, though, that limit the rights of parents: self-esteem and the public good of critical reflection. Some forms of education can destroy student self-esteem and inhibit the ability of students to think critically about their interests. In those cases, the state may have a responsibility to step in and protect the interests of children. While all teachers can fail at their responsibilities to protect these interests, religious teachers who want to nurture self-esteem and critical reflection might face difficulty if they work under conservative doctrinal frameworks. At the very least, Feinberg argues, teachers in such cases can be made aware of creative strategies to foster these goals *within* their doctrinal frameworks and also be reminded of their responsibilities to share certain types of information (for example, about sexual health) regardless of those frameworks. With respect to religious schools, Feinberg points out that they function best in conjunction with strong systems of public education. At their best, public schools promote the tolerance, understanding, and acceptance that make religious diversity (and thus religious schools) possible.

The notion of the pubic also plays a role in Feinberg's analysis of whether public schools, for their part, should teach religion. There are several arguments for including religion in public schools, many of which Feinberg believes are shallow or deeply misguided. Nevertheless, he holds that religions do provide powerful visions of the good life and that students should be exposed to such visions if they are to intelligently consider and revise their own conceptions of the good. In Feinberg's view, this exposure is a critical component of a liberal, democratic public education. In addition, instruction in religion is helpful in constructing a democratic public. In a pluralistic society, people will need to create shared meaning across their differences and to recognize a shared future. Citizens must overcome misconceptions about each other, and this requires some knowledge of different faith traditions. A humanities course focusing on religion is of great assistance in building the democratic public that Feinberg envisions. This idea speaks to his earlier work detailing the civic power of the humanities to help human beings to understand different interpretative frameworks—to recognize that they themselves have an interpretative framework and to be able to read the frameworks of others with both empathy and historical awareness.

Democratic Citizen/Democratic Researcher

Feinberg's chapter "Toward a New Progressive Educational Movement" returns to Dewey's "Polish Study" and to the issues there that motivated his early work. This time he reflects on the study with an eye toward his own development as a citizen and researcher. He initially understood Dewey's mistake with the Polish study in terms of a technical issue of philosophy, a logical problem of the tension between community and technology. Feinberg reflects that he, himself, was caught up in a social imaginary of hope, optimism, social cooperation, and trust, hallmarks of the progressive mentality of the earlier twentieth century (the imaginary that Dewey was also working under). With the Vietnam War, Watergate, and the failures of the 1954 *Brown* decision to create an integrated society, Feinberg's mentality transformed into a social imaginary of suspicion. In this imaginary, social cooperation, particularly between government and academia, was deemed a "co-option" of philosophy into an unjust system. It was with this shift that the Polish Study took on a new meaning for Feinberg—Dewey, the champion of democracy, had been "co-opted" into the War Department. The study became newly relevant to Feinberg as a cautionary tale about American democracy rather than serving as a technical problem in philosophy. Feinberg frames his own journey, and his own realizations about the workings of power, as exemplifying something important about his own education, both as a democratic citizen and democratic researcher. To be sure, the Deweyan vision of democracy focused on community, novelty and diversity, and experimentation could and should be maintained. It needed to be informed by the social imaginary of suspicion, however, which includes beings savvy about the workings of political power. Dewey's pragmatism needed to become "critical" through this new social imaginary. With critical pragmatism as a model for civic engagement, democratic education should help students critically examine their own social imaginaries. They should confront the unfair distribution of resources, creatively imagine new social possibilities, and gain the skills that promote political agency and individual fulfillment. On an even deeper level, young citizens should also be aware of how their own interpretations of the world, and the interpretations of others, are influenced by their different social imaginaries. As Feinberg's own journey through these imaginaries as a researcher suggests, democratic citizens should be able to read sympathetically the social imaginaries of others while also being aware of the limits of their own.

Conclusion

The notable characteristics of Feinberg's papers include an exemplary responsiveness to the specific problems facing the national community. This is not a philosophy of the ivory tower; this is a philosophy of the messy street. It is a philosophy that pays attention to the shifting contours of society, ready to read the indications of social change and to interpret the educational implications of these changes. There is consistent emphasis on listening to others to understand "what is going on" before moving on to "what to do." This approach to philosophy of education provides a compelling model for anyone who wants to think deeply about education. In addition, within the selection of Feinberg's papers presented here, there is a helpful body of arguments and analysis, engaging with enduring questions of education. The arguments about the nature of a public education, about the place of religion and cultural difference in public education, and about the direction of educational policy all deserve serious consideration when considering the contemporary problems and enduring dilemmas of our democratic landscape.

Of particular interest behind Feinberg's body of work is a compelling vision for what it means to be a democratic citizen. The task of public schools is to create such citizens. These citizens will share a sense of shared fate with those around them. They will identify with the good of the community and not just their individual good. They will cooperate and compromise. They will be flexible and change as they learn about others. They will understand the workings of power and the appearances of oppression. They are, above all, reflective. They listen to the voices of those around them, reflecting on the different interpretative frameworks, using the best tools of understanding that they have, and adjust their actions in a responsive way. They are makers of meaning with those around them. Feinberg's philosophy of education, focused on listening and reflective action, is the research equivalent of the democratic citizen.

This Volume

This volume contains papers selected to show the breadth and depth of Feinberg's work. The paper that follows this introduction in Part I, "The Construction of a Social Philosopher of Education," is an autobiographical statement describing how Feinberg understands his own work, the major themes that he sees, the values that he finds behind his approach, and the process by which it is all developed. The volume is then organized into two additional sections. The papers in part II have been selected to illustrate Feinberg's approach to the study of education and to philosophy of education in particular. These papers discuss the nature of education and explores what it means to study education. They discuss the role of philosophy and history of education within the broader scope of educational research and introduce the notions of philosophical ethnography and critical pragmatism. In these papers, one can find exemplified Feinberg's particular notion of *paying attention* to context, to history, and to the voices and perspectives of others. All the elements of Feinberg's approach are exemplified in his engagement with educational reform as displayed in his paper "Fixing the Schools: The Ideological Turn." Part III moves from how Feinberg studies education to the results of his inquiries, particularly as he pays attention to the problems of public education in a democratic society. Feinberg carefully conceptualizes his notion of "public education" and its relationship to democratic ideals and then confronts the quandaries of social choice, cultural diversity, affirmative action, and religion in education. In these papers, he keeps the aims and purposes of civic education in a pluralistic democratic society in the forefront. All of this comes together in his essay "Toward a New Progressive Education Movement" to round out the papers. While I have separated the question of how Feinberg studies education from the substantive questions he studies, these questions are, in practice, inseparable. Indeed, the process by which Feinberg studies education is deeply related to the view of democratic education that he champions.

2

Autobiographical Essay

The Construction of a Social Philosopher of Education

Introduction

At the time I entered Boston University (BU) as an undergraduate in the late 1950s, all juniors in the liberal arts college were required to take two semesters of philosophy, and I selected a course from Peter Bertocci who had a reputation as a stimulating demanding teacher. Bertocci was an exciting undergraduate lecturer and addressed issues that I had privately pondered without guidance in high school about the character of truth, and the difference between truth and illusion, about the nature of the good life and the "real" meaning of success, about the existence of God in a world where evil can thrive. By the time I decided to major in philosophy the Department was expanding its orientation beyond its original Personalism, which developed out of the Methodist tradition, and now included in addition to Personalists, Marxists, Pragmatists, Existentialists and Positivists.

BU had traditionally been strong in the history of philosophy and philosophy of religion, and during the 1950s professors like Peter Bertocci, John Lavely and Richard Millard joined with Professors in the College of Education to develop a role for the Department in philosophy of education. They secured funds from the Federal Government for graduate students in philosophy who wished to focus some of their work on education. I had been dissatisfied with my own high school education, feeling that it emphasized the importance of grades and getting into the right college to the neglect of something deeper, and I was pleased when I was offered one of the three Fellowships.

Learning to Be a Philosopher

In graduate school I learned how to address the questions of others and began to take small steps towards formulating my own questions by interrogating the arguments of established philosophers. We were taught that an internal criticism—one that took an argument on *"its"* own terms—had priority over an external one—a criticism that took an argument on *"our"* own terms. I do not recall being told really why this insistence, nor do I recall questioning the assumed boundaries between external and internal, or the relative authority this gave to the text over the reader—all considerations that might be raised today. Nevertheless the priority was an important component of our training and it communicated a deep respect for the works of historical and contemporary thinkers. It required that we work hard to suspend our own perspectives and initial judgments as we tried to enter into the systemic thought of philosophers.

This training was not much different than that of many others who graduated with a Ph.D. from philosophy departments in the US in the mid-1960s in philosophy, but it was very different from much of the work that I saw in College of Education, where certain views were taken as definitive, and others judged by how well they measured up to an assumed standard. Ironically much of Dewey's writings seemed to me to be used in this way, and I had trouble with a couple of the instructors in the College of Education when they took offence when I challenged aspects of Dewey's work. Sadly the philosopher of openness had become for some the prince of dogma and the "anti-dogmatism" that Dewey advanced took on a dogmatic quality.

There were also gaps in the BU philosophy curriculum, and some important works in modern philosophy were slighted. For example, while I had seminars in Quine, Whitehead, Hegel, Alexander, and Bergson along with the rationalists, and empiricists, BU did not offer a seminar in Wittgenstein or Austin and it had very limited offerings in the growing area of conceptual analysis. Moreover, while we were expected to cut our philosophical teeth by close textual readings of the "historical" greats, there was little opportunity to explore some of the contemporary issues, or the concepts used to describe them. Hence while I was trained well as expositor and critic I was not encouraged to explore issues of the day philosophically.

For example, while the Free Speech Movement was beginning, and while the civil rights marches had already begun, there were no seminars exploring issues of speech, even as it was developed by Austin, and the idea of a philosophical seminar examining issues of race was unheard of—even though BU's now most famous alumni, Martin Luther King, was then leading the Civil Rights movement. I was fortunate that later in my graduate career I received a Fellowship in the interdisciplinary Human Relations Center where, under the leadership of Kenneth Benne, a prominent philosopher of education who had studied under Dewey, many of these issues were topics of consideration. Ironically, the one issue that concerned Benne most directly—homosexuality—remained unspoken until decades later, but at the time, no one asked and he didn't tell.

At that time the distinction that is now common between teaching and research universities was less developed. However, if there had been such a classification BU would have been viewed as a teaching university. The Graduate Program in philosophy stressed teaching and every Ph.D. student was expected to take one course in teaching philosophy before completion. And, while I thought it might be nice to publish something at some later time in my career, my efforts and my thoughts were focused on studying philosophy in order to teach it at the college level. The emphasis on teaching was reinforced by the message that we earned the right to criticize a position only after we had represented it fairly. The ideal was to present an argument even better than the original, and some like Richard Millard did a masterful job of advancing different positions over the students' attempts to puncture them.

Graduate seminars involved explication and critique with students sparring with the professor over the internal coherence of the text. For me the pedagogy served three purposes. First, it provided a first-hand understanding of significant texts and a familiarity with the complex structure of a philosophical argument. Second, it helped to hone my own critical skills, and to gain some ability to address arguments on their own terms and third, as my own skills developed, I began to overcome my own painful shyness, and to develop a higher level of self-esteem. Self-esteem, not to be confused with over-confidence, is critical to any intellectual work. It is the sense that you have the capacity to improve on your latest effort and that a single mistake is not a sign of an inability to improve. Because self-esteem requires the ability to recognize one's own errors, it is very different from over-confidence in which errors are overlooked or their significance minimized.

However, the pedagogy requires a shared understanding that critique and argument are not intended to diminish students, but to engage them in an intellectual quest. Many philosophy students do understand this, but as I was to learn when I began to teach in schools of education, where a kinder, gentler climate seemed to prevail, it is not universal and should not be taken for granted, and if this shared understanding is not present, blunt critique can be counterproductive.

The pedagogy was limited from another standpoint. It was, in education jargon, heavily teacher-centered with the instructor explicating the texts, the students raising issues and the instructor responding to further explicate or defend the text. Hence discourse flowed from text to teacher to student to text, to teacher, to another student, etc. It rarely, if ever, flowed from student to student or from student to text to student. The method was Socratic in more ways than one. The student dialogued with the teacher (Socrates) but only the teacher was acknowledged as the repository of Wisdom. When I began teaching I found this to be a foreign approach for many students in education, and needed to adjust my pedagogy considerably.

The pedagogical style of the philosophy department was complemented by a friendly, but formal ambience. I do not recall ever passing a philosophy professor without being pleasantly greeted, but greetings were formal, Mr. Feinberg, Dr. Millard, or Professor Lavely, etc. (While the faculty at BU had hired one woman just before I left, it was, like most philosophy departments, dominated by white men, although there were some outstanding women graduate students.) The Human Relations Center, which I will discuss shortly, was governed by a very different pedagogy and a much more informal ambiance.

During my senior year, I took a course with Marx Wartofsky in American philosophy. Wartofsky, a Marxist and a Jew could not find an academic job after graduating from Columbia in the early 1950s because of the Red Scare, until he was hired by the then President of BU, a Methodist minister, Harold C. Case. Wartofsky was an enormously talented person, an accomplished violinist who spoke a number of languages and had worked as a machinist while biding his time during the McCarthy era. Given my own background—Jewish with both parents originally from New York—and given that my own political socialization began in grade school when my mother's cousin, James Wechsler, the editor of the then liberal *New York Post*, was interrogated on Television by Senator McCarthy, it was easy to relate to Wartofsky.

I had entered Boston University with a vague idea of attending law school as one way to effect social change. While I hardly knew James Wechsler, his experience before the McCarthy Committee, together with the army McCarthy hearings were for me lessons in the abuse of power. I followed the hearings intensely, began to buy the *Post* when I could get a hold of it at the newsstand at Harvard Square, read the editorial pages and, mostly left, columnists. While I was still in public school I had ordered the record of these hearings and tried to figure out the subtleties of certain remarks or innuendoes.

My encounter with Wartofsky, and later Kenneth Benne a professor in philosophy of education, suggested that I might be able to pursue both my interests in philosophy and my interests in social change together. Both had come to BU under unusual circumstances. As I mentioned Wartofsky had been hired by Case after his black listing from other Universities for his earlier political activities while Benne had been fired from University of Illinois after he was outed as a homosexual and then hired by BU. When he came to BU he was ill and stayed with Case until he recovered.

Benne was an amazingly creative and energetic man who used his training in philosophy of education and pragmatism to inform his pioneering work on organizations and small groups. Likely without McCarthy witch hunts, Wartofsky would have remained in New York, teaching at Columbia, NYU or CUNY, where he went after retiring from BU and if it were not for the homophobia in Champaign/Urbana, Benne, who Dewey in his letter of recommendation to Illinois[1] described as the most talented graduate student he had had in decades, would have remained at Illinois to help develop what at the time was fast becoming the most prominent philosophy of education program in the country. Ironically, because of the courage and integrity of President Case, I was the beneficiary of two witch-hunts. After the three years I was given a fellowship in the Human Relations Center to work with Benne.

BU was always seen as a poor relation to its counterpart across the Charles, but it is somewhat ironic that while Harvard, the bastion of liberalism, was hiring "the best and the brightest"—Kissinger, Bundy, the architects of Vietnam, the Methodist Minister who served as President of BU, was hiring, much to my later educational benefit, homosexuals and

Marxists, as well as renegades from Soviet oppression in Eastern Europe. (Wartofsky once told me that in his job interview Case asked him to tell him *everything* about his political activities. When he was finished Case thanked him and explained that he wanted this information so that if he were ever asked whether he knew of Wartofsky's past when he hired him, he could answer that he did.)

Although Wartofsky kept his politics out of his teaching much in the same way most of the BU Personalists left their own religious views out of the classroom, I began to get the idea that philosophy might be more than an intellectual exercise and might well have a role to play in improving people's lives.

The rich mix in the department—Personalists, Existentialists, Pragmatists, positivists, and Marxists—was the result of the academic openness of Case and of those Personalists in the Philosophy Department who had followed its founder, Borden Parker Bowne (1847–1910), in their willingness to entertain unpopular views. (At one point Bowne was the object of a heresy trial by the Methodist Church.) Sadly, after I left and after the University hired its first non-Methodist Presidents and later, with philosopher John Silver as President, this climate of openness was severely strained.

Having been socialized into this formal atmosphere of the Philosophy Department, the informal ambience of the Human Relations Center was very disconcerting. Here everyone regardless of rank—students, secretaries and faculty—was called by their first name. It took a considerable amount of time before I could call "Dr. Benne" by his first name and he never suggested that I do so. However, that was the norm and so I went out of my way to avoid calling him anything for a year or so, but later I conformed to this non-conformist climate and called him Ken. The pedagogy practiced in the Human Relations Center was also a stark contrast to that in the philosophy department. Instead of the professors occupying center-stage, here they faded into the background as students engaged with one another. The object of study was the interactions of the group and too much intervention on the part of the professor would interfere with the dynamics of the group.

I still maintained formality when in the philosophy Department until the day I received my Ph.D. when I also received a license to call my philosophy professors, Peter, Dick, John and Marx. I now understand that the difference in ambience is more than simply a matter of personality, although it was that as well. It was related to the different ideas about the purpose of education and the role of scholarship in the two fields. Although I tend toward the informal with my students, I have come to appreciate (or perhaps overly romanticize) the way the use of formal titles can enable work to continue with students and colleagues even when personal relations get bumpy. Nevertheless, I have come to prefer the style of the Human Relations Center, not that of the Philosophy Department. However, it is often useful for me to recall just how difficult it was to enter into an informal mode with my professors, especially when I am working with more traditional students from Korea or Japan. There is a lot more that could be said about each of the two "styles" and the assumptions about the goals of education and the understanding of autonomy that they rest on, but for a student studying philosophy of education it was useful to experience them both.

The Human Relations Center was involved in applied social science research about organizational change. Among its major activity was the running of T-groups, a practice modelled after the work of Kurt Lewin and pioneered by Benne and a few others. The T-group was supposed to be a laboratory in human relations and democratic leadership where the facilitators, as they were called, took a nondirective role and created opportunities for members of the group to reflect upon the dynamics and interactions among them. The members of the groups came from a variety of backgrounds, business, education, religion, but almost all were liberal in their orientation.

While I had reservations about the philosophy behind the T-group idea, and questioned whether it could work under conditions of unequal power, I found the groups personally rewarding. They provided insight into some of my own characteristic ways of responding in group settings and provoked certain adjustments. For example, I tended to hesitate or not to advance a hunch for fear of being wrong. Part of this came about because of family history where "mistakes" could be lamented for a lifetime, but part came from the philosopher's caution to get the argument right. The T-group ideal is that truth is approximated best through engagement and dialogue, and that hunches need to be expressed if the idea is to work. This is especially true when many of those hunches involve the meaning of the gestures, involuntary expressions, postures or ideas. The same situation may also apply in schools and classrooms where the written text delivers only part of the picture.

The two fields served different needs, but both were important in my development. Philosophy—austere, distant, rational, systematic, and intellectual—was useful for a young scholar trying to hone his analytical skills and gain intellectual confidence. The Human Relations Center with its commitment to social justice and its direct involvement in schools, churches and the civil rights movement, and the discourse that it encouraged across disciplines, grounded my studies in philosophy and provided a practical outlet for it.

By the time I entered the Human Relations Center, I had written a Masters' thesis on Hegel's concept of property.[2] The thesis was an examination of the nation state as an institution for liberal ideals. At the time, the status of German philosophy in the United States was very low, and Hegel was completely out of fashion in most high prestige departments. One reason was that a stigma on anything German carried over from the War Years, but another was the growing influence of analytic philosophers who disparaged the German system builders as obtuse, meaningless and philosophically irrelevant. Wartofsky, along with the Personalists went against this trend and, for different reasons, had a deep interest in German philosophy. Thus both encouraged this project.

When a draft of the thesis was completed, Wartofsky returned it unmarked, except for three words penciled in red at the end—"opaque, turgid and completely incomprehensible." Even though it was a thesis on Hegel, himself, pretty opaque, turgid and, at times, incomprehensible, coming from Wartofsky these marks were not meant as high praise. (Thirty-five years later I thought of the perfect come back—"Come now Marx, surely you must know that if it is opaque it cannot be *completely* incomprehensible." Yet by that time he had passed away.)

Since this was also a time when my father became sick and had to give up his small store, I questioned whether I should continue in graduate school, but having few options stayed and spent the summer rewriting the thesis. When it was finished Wartofsky sent it over to his former teacher, Herbert Marcuse, then at Brandeis, who asked to see me and praised the work very generously. The visit was short, but very important and helped validate my growing sense of competence. I have shared Wartofsky's response to the draft thesis with my own graduate students when they get discouraged about their progress hoping that it can help them understand graduate education is a process where honest but painful criticism serves a productive role. I try to be careful, however, to make my own criticisms less caustic and more detailed than Marx's had been, and rarely write in red.

The thesis on Hegel helped to shape the issues that would define much of my career. In Hegel's own work, and especially in those who followed him on the left. I began to glimpse a tension in liberal thought between the concern for some kind of national coherence and identity and a concern to allow friction and to acknowledge differences. While Hegel presented this tension in terms of Civil Society, he believed that it was reconciled by the emerging modern state. Some years after my thesis was completed, I began to see the tension in cultural terms and to relate it to problems of schooling in liberal, democratic societies.

In my dissertation,[3] I attempted to address this problem through a comparison and analysis of the work of a British Hegelian, Bernard Bosanquet and John Dewey. Bosanquet argued that the state is a natural outgrowth of human development and not, as the liberal tradition would have it, the artificial result of a contract that arises out of a state of nature. It should thus not just serve to resolve conflicts, but to harmonize human needs and desires. As such Bosanquet argued that the state is the condition for the ethical fulfilment of the individual.

Although Bosanquet advanced his argument before the Third Reich made a mockery of the idea of the state as the ethical fulfilment of the individual, I thought that there were elements in the argument that were worth salvaging and that Bosanquet could be seen as providing not a political program that would subsume the individual to the state, but rather a standard by which to judge the state where the flourishing of the individual would be a measure of its goodness. Dewey, while much more circumspect about the role of the state, shared with Bosanquet a concern to harmonize human interest and desires through voluntary associations. The state was important in constraining the adverse indirect consequences of private acts and, through education, in encouraging the development of new interests and associations. While I thought Dewey's understanding of the state was superior to Bosanquet's because it provided for the development of individual interests and associations, I was critical of his ethical theory and this criticism was to shortly play a large role in both my reassessment of Dewey and of philosophy itself.

Early Career

When I finished my degree I had a choice of entering a philosophy department or teaching philosophy of education at Oakland University, in Michigan. I chose Oakland, a new dynamic institution aided in its founding by the cooperation of labor and industry. I felt that it would allow expression to both my philosophical and practical bents. Oakland was founded with the participation of both Walter Ruther, the former Head of the automobile workers and Matilda Wilson, an heiress to the Dodge motor company fortune, and is located just outside of the industrial city of Pontiac. The idea was to provide a first class liberal education for the children of workers and first-generation college graduates. The appointment came at a time when most intellectuals and many leading politicians believed that education alone could solve the nation's racial problems and lift people out of poverty, and Oakland was an expression of that hope. At Oakland I worked with two colleagues Henry Rosemont and Marc Briod, to establish a tutorial in the city of Pontiac. The tutorial was one of the few places where students at the University could interact with African American inner city children. It survived riots of the late 1960s and was still functioning many years after I left Oakland for Illinois in late 1967.

Very early one Saturday morning toward the end of my first year teaching at Oakland I received a call from the Chairman of the Department of History and Philosophy of Education at the University of Illinois asking if I would be interested in coming there for an interview. Although Illinois had perhaps the most renowned program in the Country, having been socialized in a philosophy department, I knew only two things about the University—that it had fired a biology professor for advocating free love and it had a famous classicist on its faculty who was a member of the John Birch Society and who accused Dwight Eisenhower, a moderate Republican president, of being a front for the Communist Party—I was not inclined to go, but I told the Department Head that I would talk to my wife and I asked him to call in a few days. Having lured my wife to the heartland of Michigan, I was uncertain how she would react to the prospect of moving to Champaign/Urbana, cities that as provincial Bostonians, neither of us had heard of before the phone call.

By the time the Chair called back, however, we had spoken to Rosemont, who had been an undergraduate at the University of Illinois, and he advised me to accept their invitation for an interview. I spent a day on Campus, much impressed by its quad, the fantastic library, and many of the people that I met, and at the end of the visit I was offered the position and a couple of weeks later, I accepted it.

Graduate students and faculty today would see this entire procedure as odd and much of it would now be illegal. I never applied for the position, I had not published, and I was not asked to teach a sample class or to give a paper. Although the actual reason Illinois approached me is unclear, it is likely that Ken Benne or Richard Millard, my undergraduate honors advisor, both of whom had close friends in the Department, had been asked to recommend someone, and that they recommended me. Often when the issue of affirmative action comes up today in my class I used this experience to shock some students into an awareness of just what white privilege meant, how invisible it can be and how much it can be taken for granted. Given that by and large *only* other white males were in the pipeline, it is almost impossible to tell what a truly open search might have secured.

The University of Illinois

During my first year at The University of Illinois, Martin Luther King was assassinated, and race dominated the discussions in my class. Two events stand out. The news of King's assassination came as I was teaching an evening course and many in the class were stunned, but one older white student muttered to me after I dismissed the class: "he got what he was asking for!" The other event involved an African American who, a couple of years after the assassination, had been appointed as the first Black Principal of one of the elementary schools in the area, and told me that in his desk was a bible that had been donated by the KKK in 1948. Even though Boston had lots of racial tension, especially around bussing, I was still stunned to confront these issues in such a direct and raw way.

One of the things that is difficult to comprehend these days is the fact that there were almost no African American students on campus, and also just how much that absence was taken for granted on the even the most liberal of Northern campuses. People who would decry forced segregation in the South often did not even take note of the absence of Black students at their own universities. At Oakland we thought we were doing a good deed by bringing white Oakland students into the inner city and not until our Christmas party did it hit me that all of the tutors were white and all of their pupils were Black. When I arrived at Illinois there were more students from Taiwan on Campus than there were African Americans. Moreover, there was not one Black faculty member in the Education College, and I believe that there were only two in the entire university. There were, however, at least two graduate students, one of whom, James Anderson, is now my Department Head and another, who came a few years later, Mildred Griggs, recently served the College as its Dean. However, at the time few seemed to notice this absence or see it as a problem.

Protest and Change

As a consequence of the assassination and the riots that followed, the University agreed to admit 500 additional Black students by the fall. I proposed to my College that we develop a consciously integrated "Alternative Teacher Education" program (ATEP) that provided students with small seminars and coordinated their freshman courses together with an early in-school experience. In ATEP we worked with students to accommodate them to the requirements of the University while we introduced them to the world of schools. The program was organized around small seminars. The instructors worked on reading and writing skills and connected the student's assignments to their classroom observation in the public school. Of the 500 Black students admitted to the different programs in the University, the retention and graduation rate among the hundred or so students in this program was by far the highest.

Scholarship and Research

During my involvement with ATEP I began to do the research for my first book, *Reason and Rhetoric*.[4] At first I saw this work as paralleling the work in my dissertation and drawing on the largely philosophical concerns that were addressed there. My dissertation focused strictly on philosophical texts, exploring as good philosophy graduate students might, the meanings, arguments, ambiguities and contradictions that I found in Dewey and Bosanquet. However, I also later read a report Dewey had written during World War One and submitted to the War Department on the Polish community in Philadelphia.[5] The report, marked confidential questioned the loyalty of the leaders of the community and suggested that the government keep a close surveillance on them, proposing such illiberal ideas as government infiltration of their membership. I was both bothered and puzzled that until this time the study had been overlooked by virtually every Dewey scholar, including me, and this was so even though it was described in the then most authoritative bibliography of Dewey's works.[6] I also began to see this event in light of the more abstract criticism that I had made of the conflict between intelligence and community in Dewey's ethical theory.[7]

In reflecting on my oversight, and why I had not given more significance to this episode earlier, I began to question aspects of my philosophical training, and some of the pedagogical assumption it entailed. For example, close textual reading, exposition and internal criticism assumes that meaning of the text remains stable over time. Yet in the case of my reading of Dewey, subsequent historical events and understandings began to influence what to count as the "meaning" of the text. The war in Vietnam certainly influenced the fact that the Polish Study came into focus as part of the Dewey canon and this in turn illuminated parts of his other works. While writing my dissertation, I was largely interested in the *philosophical* works of Dewey, and his study of an American Polish Community was not philosophy in the usual sense of that term. It did not lend itself easily to the form of internal criticism I was taught to prize. Yet that internal criticism was important allowing me to see this study as a result of an important ambiguity in his ethical theory. And, it brought many other issues into play—what is the appropriate line between truth and power, scholarship and effectiveness, National unity and cultural identity—themes that would enter into my later work.

Prior to the Vietnam War many on the progressive left were largely unconcerned with cooperation between the university scholar and the National government, with many liberals believing that there was a progressive and benign quality to such cooperation. They believed, with some justification, that in many areas, such as Civil Rights, the Federal government must serve a crucial partner in advancing a progressive agenda. I shared this assumption, and thus initially ignored the citation and quite full description of this work that was published in the definitive Dewey bibliography mentioned earlier. Given the assumption about the benign quality of cooperation with the national government I likely dismissed it as rather unremarkable.

Vietnam altered my consciousness, and so Dewey's involvement in this episode took on a larger significance. The change was not in Dewey, however, but in a social norm and in my view about how much citizens ought to trust their government. Dewey rightly held that moral norms are human creations that have proved useful to the evolution of the species, but the Polish study was a dangerous violation of those historical lessons, made easier because [. . .] his moral theory was less sensitive than it might have been to the way coordinated government power could be abused in the name of an important cause.

Still, the close reading and internal criticism of Dewey allowed me to view the Polish study in a wider context and to see both benefits and costs of his evolutionary conception of ethics. Dewey's evolutionary view of ethical theory placed the highest value on coordination and cooperation and in his view the Poles were not adequately cooperating in the war effort. Yet the view of ethical development as increased coordination placed pragmatic limits on the development of a moral vision that could have constrained his understanding of the rights of Poles in the United States and his willingness to recommend to the War Department that it intrude on them. The other side of this, however, is that his evolutionary view of ethics does allow for growth and development in our collective moral understanding, and it is this growth that allows us to now reflect back and to question Dewey's engagement with the War Department on ethical grounds.

I became interested in the fact that Dewey scholars, myself included, had ignored this involvement for so long. It was only when Vietnam provoked protests about government and academic co-operation that the spot light focused on his involvement with the Polish Community. Reports of government infiltration of anti-war groups during Vietnam were foreshadowed by Dewey's report to the War Department on the loyalty of Polish American Americans. Certainly Dewey's involvement exemplified my criticism that his moral theory limited the scope of moral vision, but it also eventually led me to see both an evolutionary and a tragic quality to much moral deliberation.

The Vietnam War marked a change in the zeitgeist and in the way the rights of members of minority groups is understood. The melting pot ideal, once the default position of liberal theorists, has given way to a more refined understanding of the significance of cultural identity. And while we can only speculate, I would like to believe that had this understanding been available to Dewey in the way that it is to us that he would have conducted his study more openly and drawn different conclusions. Certainly, as Kevin McDonough and I have pointed out, the philosophy of liberalism has taken a different turn since Dewey's time and is developing more awareness of the importance of cultural factors to individual development, a move which we call affiliational liberalism.[8] However, if this speculation is correct it also reinforces Dewey's views about the potential evolutionary quality of ethical ideals, and allows that there can be progress in our understanding of social justice.

Philosophy of Education

Unfortunately, and in violation of his own critical spirit, Dewey had become an icon for many educators. His influence on philosophy, however, had already waned by the 1950s to be replaced by the analytic school and shortly after, a number of American and British educational philosophers began to follow the analytic movement. The model for education was actually laid down by Charles Dunn Hardie in his 1942 book,[9] but Hardie's book came out during the war and did not receive any significant attention in the United States until it was republished in 1960. Hardie applied the then new method of analytic philosophy to education. His concern was not to reform education directly, but to bring clarity to the muddle that he thought often passed as meaningful discourse about education. After the war, this movement was led by people who were educated in Departments of philosophy and included, among others, Israel Scheffler at Harvard, Richard Peters at the London Institute of Education and Paul Hirst at Cambridge. They were joined by newly minted Ph.D.s in some of the high profile programs in education such as the University of Illinois and Columbia Teacher's College.

This period was marked by considerable collaboration between Departments of philosophy and some of their colleagues in philosophy of education and it was marked by considerable intellectual vitality. New journals were initiated, and bright graduate students were attracted to the field directly out of undergraduate college. The changes were visible in the Philosophy of Education Society (PES), where the older ways of classifying philosophies of education—essentialism, pragmatism, perennialism, reconstructionism, etc.—were dismissed by the young Turks as too broad, too vague and too uncritical. Within perhaps ten years the analytic style of doing philosophy came to dominate PES and it remained in control until the early 1980s, when a series of different voices began to be heard and the influence of Marxism, feminism and post structuralism was felt.

While the analytic movement helped establish the academic legitimacy of philosophy of education, the field moved away from the work of schools becoming increasingly distant from the immediate needs of educators. Although I was attracted to its rigor I felt that it failed to explore the larger social context of education and thus had a largely quietist influence on the field. If I had been dissatisfied with the justification that Dewey provided for education reform believing as I did that it was both theoretically and practically flawed, I was even more dissatisfied with the possibility that the analytic tradition provided. At its best, it seemed to leave everything as is, in the belief that all our problems were the result of linguistic muddles. Caught between a naïve optimistic belief in progress and a similarly naïve linguistic reductionism, philosophy of education seemed paralyzed. Some analytic philosophers of education, such as R.S. Peters,[10] tried to smuggle a normative perspective into their analysis of language (in this case Kant), but Peters' attempt to marry analytic philosophy and Kant was transparent and unsuccessful.

One of the mistakes of the analytic movement was to act as if concepts had an independent existence and that one could thus understand them by mapping out the conceptual terrain in which they are imbedded (as, for example, with the analysis of the concept of indoctrination) or to show how a concept is used given certain conditions (Austin). Missing was a history of the development of the concept itself, and an understanding of how that history influences the debate over education. An example is the concept of "racism." The concept first appeared in the middle part of the twentieth century as an appendage to a Webster dictionary. Yet here its meaning referred largely to the attitudes of people of different white nations towards one another. "Racialism," a rather benign term, was more often used to describe the attitude of whites toward blacks and "racism" had to wait decades before it was fully born, and used to counter the racist reproduction process and the social "scientific" explanations—racial differences in IQ; cultural deficit—that served to reinforce it. The development of the concept of racism, in contrast to the earlier and morally neutral concept, racialism, allowed the discourse to explore institutional patterns rather than just individual attitudes. The analytic movement largely ignored the birth process and took concepts as born fully formed. Yet when the history of a concept is considered educational philosophy [it] can reach beyond itself and engage with concepts developed by other disciplines as they influence the debate about the direction of social reproduction.

I began to develop this insight in my 1982 book, *Understanding Education*[11] where I argued that educational philosophy had a critical agenda—to use philosophical analysis to critically examine the educational consequences of the ambiguities and taken for granted normative assumptions of social science and their educational research programs. For example, I analyzed the claim "IQ tests measure intelligence" and showed why that claim is ambiguous and how that ambiguity is used to promote a conservative social agenda. In addition, *Understanding Education* offered a positive task for educational philosophy and proposed a conception of educational study where its object would not be reduced to fit into some other field such as psychology or sociology.

I proposed that education as an institutional practice involves the conscious reproduction of skill clusters, or roles, and forms of intersubjective understandings. Together these produced a more or less coherent social identity. The role of educational scholarship, as I saw it, was to probe processes of reproduction so that it would be possible to evaluate the hierarchies that resulted in relation to the functions they served or the opportunities that they disregarded. Given this view, then the practice of educating had a normative aim—to enable students to become critically aware of the ways in which skills are clustered and common meanings are produced to shape a shared identity. The practice of educating thus involves not only the reproduction of skills and identities, but also the development of a critical consciousness that should enable students to be mindful of a given social arrangement. The corollary for educational research, as my colleague Eric Bredo and I argued in our *Knowledge and Values in Educational Research*,[12] was to develop research programs that highlighted these constraints and opportunities and thus fostered critical engagement.

Following the publication of *Understanding Education* I became interested in examining specific instances of social reproduction and as a result in some of my work I began to incorporate specific observations and interviews as a part of my discussion of social issues. Sometimes I used these interviews to create virtual dialogues between different participants in the social reproduction process. At other times I used them to probe the limits of understanding across cultural and religious boundaries and to probe the appropriate responses to these limits that are available to those who are committed to a liberal conception of justice. Broadly speaking the earlier studies[13] focused on inequality and the more recent ones on identity. However, there is no single point where one receded and the other became more dominant and I continue to address issues of equality.[14]

The transition from a focus on inequality to a focus on identity came in my study of the relationship between Japanese schools and the practices of Japanese industry. I began the study in response to the claim made in the early 1980s that American schools are responsible for the decline in American industry and in the loss of its competitive edge, especially to Japan. While the claim itself is obviously simplistic (as proof, witness the decade long recession in Japan in the 1990s) it was an occasion to explore just what schools reproduce when they function in radically different societies, such as Japan and the United States. The result was an extended essay on the philosophies of individualism and communitarianism and the way in which they are incorporated into schooling and work in the two countries.[15]

While I use the term philosophical ethnography[16] to describe these studies they are not to be confused with the more descriptively comprehensive studies of anthropology. "Ethnography light" is perhaps a more accurate qualifier. For example, I visited but did not live in Japan; the observations and interviews were not as extensive as they would be if conducted by a professional ethnographer, and they begin not with the question "what is going on here," but rather with a focal concern such as in a recent study of religious schools, *For Goodness Sake*[17]—"how do these educators understand the relationship between religious instruction and moral education?" Moreover, the focus is always some normative issue and the immediate object of these ethnographic studies is to engage participants in a philosophical discussion that will illuminate the reasons for their educational decisions, and will probe other possibilities. While the method has its limitations, it is an important tool for philosophers of education to use when appropriate and in this age of social engagement where the idea of a single, hermetically closed thing called "a culture"[18] is no longer appropriate and where engagement across different normative frames of social reproduction is increasingly common a philosophical "ethnography light" method will be a needed tool for philosophers of education.

My Recent Work

When Dewey reported on the Polish community, he was concerned about the incorporation of a non-democratic group into a democratic society. He seemed here, in contrast to the tone of much of his more theoretical writings, that democracy justified extraordinary means of incorporation, including government surveillance. Whatever one may think about Dewey's role in this event, the question of the relationship between the larger society and its subgroups—cultural, religious and others—remains one of the most important issues for modern philosophers of education to address, and these concerns continue to be the focus of my most recent scholarship, from my defense of affirmative action[19] in *On Higher Ground* to my argument that public schools have an obligation to some cultural subgroups to enable them to maintain a cultural identity; in *Common Schools/Uncommon Identities*,[20] to the exploration of the idea of affiliational liberalism in the introduction to Kevin McDonough and my anthology, *Citizenship in Liberal-Democratic Societies*; to my examination of the conflict between pluralism and liberalism as it is expressed in religious schools in *For Goodness Sake*. In these works I explore the roots of philosophical liberalism and argue that considerations of race, class, religion, gender and sexual identity are consistent with the liberal educational ideal of promoting individual growth and autonomy. In my two most recent works, *For Goodness Sake* and "The Dialectic of Parental Rights and Social Obligation"[21] I show how the public's interest in social justice and equity, the child's interest in an open future and autonomy, and the parents' interest in advancing their own children's life chances and shaping their religious beliefs can be reconciled.

The Future of Philosophy of Education in a Global Context

Most of my work has been done within a North American and specifically US context. Even the work in Japan was undertaken with educational reform in the United States as the primary concern. Yet today in an ever shrinking world, flattened out by rapid transportation and instantaneous communication, in a world in which a sneeze in an elevator in Hong Kong can initiate an epidemic in Toronto, where a half an ounce of pressure on the return key of a computer can send a billion dollars flying at the speed of light from one part of the world to another with thousands of jobs following it; where a seed designed in a laboratory in Illinois can be developed in China and save thousands of lives in the Sudan, where a movement begun in India can inspire a letter on rights issued by a minister sitting in a Birmingham jail and where that letter can lend sparks to a revolution in Johannesburg and Soweto, in such a world we have no choice but to address the aims of education and the process of reproduction not just as citizens of nations but as the planetary species with the recognition that we alone have the responsibility for survival of all life that dwells here, with us.

The problem for new philosophers of education in addressing and shaping norms of intersubjectivity will be to do so in ways that extend individual identity globally without destroying the sense of self so often associated with being located within a specific place and with belonging to a coherent community. To address this challenging problem, philosophers of education will not be able to draw solely on the material and inspiration of one nation or one intellectual tradition, but will need to function as normative ethnographers, translating one community to another while engaging the forms of understanding and norms that are imbedded in each.

When the new philosophies of education are written some will not be from the standpoint of the nation state with clear national boundaries, with singular cultural and linguistic preferences and sharply defined loyalties. Rather they will be written from the standpoint of a citizen in an ever-interdependent world one where childhood represents the emergence not from dependence to independence, but as Dewey thought from dependence to interdependence where education involves learning to reconstruct self and desire conscious of finite resources and of other peoples.

Part II

Paying Attention in the Study of Education

3

Educational Studies and the Disciplines of Educational Understanding

The young Marx concluded his theses on Feuerbach by boldly proclaiming that hithertofore: "Philosophers have only interpreted the world . . . the point, however, is to change it." Fortunately for Marx this thesis did not have to be approved by a committee of educational philosophers before it appeared in print. Had it required such approval Marx would have been seen as an unreconstructed generalist and told that he lacked sufficient commitment to the intellectual pureness of the singular disciplines that form the proper basis for educational thought.

It is more likely, however, that long before such an embarrassing situation arose, some friendly faculty advisor would have taken the young scholar aside to inform him that one-liners like these are not acceptable to educational philosophers, and that given his inadequate commitment to disciplinary purity there would be little point continuing in philosophy or even changing fields to history, economics, sociology, or any of the other disciplines that form the core of educational thought. For the point indeed is not to change the world, but to know it. And in order to know it one must be able to reflect upon it through the concentrated lens of a single discipline. Generalists with missions would be well advised to study educational administration and to seek a career as a school principal or superintendent. A new suit, a clean shave, and a more winning smile would be necessary, but beyond these requirements, and a few courses in finance and interpersonal relations, he could easily manage the intellectual demands of the field. Of course, if he still maintained scholarly aspirations he could, if he insisted, consult a member of the American Educational Studies Association, a group which, as one colleague described it, presented a retreat from the study of education by the pure and respected disciplines and a home for the older foundationists who were uncomfortable with the world of high specialization and research.[1] The mocking displeasure which marked this last piece of advice would likely have given Marx reason to pursue it further. For Marx's thesis on Feuerbach was not motivated by a drive to maintain the purity of a discipline, but to weld a bond between the theoretical and the practical spheres of human activity, a motivation which was later to be shared in their own way and with a different emphasis by Dewey and the foundationists who followed him.

This fantasy is meant to signify the central dispute in educational studies, a dispute which has been expressed many times in different ways, but which can be captured by a single question: Is the understanding of a practical activity such as education best approached by modeling inquiry after the established disciplines, or is there something about the object of educational understanding itself which cannot be captured by any single discipline or even by adding together the insights of many disciplines? Each side of this dispute has its advocates, and it is an issue which has been raised in more than one of the allied disciplines. On one side of the issue stand the traditional foundationists who believe in an integrated course of study in which the insights of various disciplines have been sifted and sorted for that which speaks to the practical work of schooling. On the other side are those who believe that to subordinate a discipline to some unquestioned end, such as the improvement of schooling, is ultimately to distort its insights and to turn it into a tool of propaganda and ideology.

Among these latter scholars, it is said in criticism of the traditional foundationists that their work is tied too closely to the concern of immediate practice. It is said that they have been unable and perhaps unwilling to look critically at the relationships between schooling and other more powerful institutions, and thereby to see the crucial ways in which schools are bent, shaped, and molded by dominant interest groups. It also has been said that they have watered down the insights of the disciplines by looking at the past from their perspective in the present. It is said that they have served as apologists for the public schools and have given educational scholarship a bad name. Now whether or not what has been said is accurate will depend upon particular cases, and I do not want to take up these in this presentation. There is good reason to believe, for example, that many traditional scholars have not ignored problems of racism and discrimination, but that they have placed an unwarranted faith in public education to correct these evils.

Whatever one may think of this debate, whatever side one may support, there is little doubt that recently the older form of scholarship has been in retreat, and that the current emphasis placed on methodological rigor within a discipline has spirited new insights and helped redirect the educational debate. Historians have shaken us from the belief that schools were always the bastions of equality and freedom that many believed them to be. Economists have forced us to consider the powerful influence that the nature and distribution of work has on the nature and distribution of education. Some scholars have confronted us with strong evidence to the effect that a person's social class background still has an influence on advancement, an influence that mutes other factors such as talent and ability. And philosophers have carefully distinguished such concepts as education and equality, setting the stage for discussions about whether a purportedly educative activity is meeting the standards that these terms imply.

In light of these disciplinary achievements one can reasonably ask if there is anything that can be said for the older generation of foundation scholars, for those who believe that educational scholarship, perhaps because of its relation to practice, but perhaps for other reasons as well, was in some fashion unique and required an understanding to which disciplines might contribute but which they could not override. This question can be joined by looking first at the criticism as it has been developed in one field—history.

It has been said, at least among the circle of educational historians, that the older scholars relaxed their objectivity and let the past speak not for itself, but for the present. The history of education, it is said, became the prehistory of the undaunted movement towards a comprehensive compulsory system of public schooling which served to instill the values of equality, freedom, and human rights into the consciousness of a new generation of Americans. It was thus the gloss of the present that guided the understanding of the past and hence distorted it.

For the historian, the charge of presentism described here seems to be the most biting of all. Yet presentism is a charge pressed against many but admitted by few. The old foundationist is said to be guilty of presentism because of an unswerving commitment to the public school. The older generation of pure historians, the Bailyns and the Cremins and the Curties, are said to be guilty of presentism because, writing under the background of the Cold War, they presented an image of American society in which democracy had learned to exist peacefully with an ever expanding role for the expert, and that in providing such an image they also provided a justification for the power and the glory of the expert society. Similarly the newer revisionist writers are said to be guilty of the same presentism because, in their concern to address the issues of racism and discrimination, they perceived the educational past as a prelude, an unbroken continuum which has reached its nadir in the present. In doing so, it is said they have helped to undercut the very basis of public support which the schools so desperately need—a conclusion which, of course, brings us back to the charges that were made against the older foundation scholars.

What are we to think about this cycle, about this strange dance of the historians in which each must gesture to the purity of the discipline before addressing education through concerns that have been informed by present conditions? Might one not begin to think that perhaps the activity of education is so intricate a part of the human enterprise that our understanding of the past is largely initiated because of our uncertainty about the present? And, might one also think that where one stands in the present will influence what is seen of the past and also the way that it is interpreted? Ironically, historians have not overlooked this insight either. Presentism always belongs to someone else. One person's presentism is another's unique framework and individual values, values which generate historical description, but about which the historian has little to say.

Presentism is not a problem. It is a condition. The problem is when the interpretation of the past is put forward without any reasonable consideration of obvious and alternative interpretations (the kind of consideration which should be second nature to philosophers) and when it is assumed without question that ideas and events had the same meaning for those who lived in the past as they do for those who are writing about them from the present. The dangers of educational history are these and not any abstract sin called presentism.

If educational history runs the danger of failing to provide alternative explanations, of indelicately mixing facts and values, of confusing exposition and interpretation, and of embedding criticism within description, educational philosophy may be said to be endangered in a different way. While philosophers may have provided us with clearer understandings of such important concepts as indoctrination and equality, they have failed to consider the historical context in which such concepts took on importance. The concept of equality of educational opportunity, for example, is often treated in the abstract without consideration given to its relationship to the development of technology, the changes in the structure of work, the breakdown of an older more stable rural structure. The idea of human rights is analyzed without due consideration given to the need to maintain an active and articulate public to serve as a check on government, an idea which clearly formed an important part of the context for the early discussions about human rights in the American experience. As philosophers have ignored the historical context in which these concepts were developed, so too have they lost the practical significance of the concepts that they have undertaken to address. Thus, in examining the idea of human rights they have often failed to ask whether or not such rights are sufficient to sustain a public in an age in which great disparity in wealth coupled with advances in communication technology have made the manipulation of the many by the few all too possible.

Because of their belief in the integrated nature of educational studies, it was easier for the older foundation scholars to recognize, as a fundamental plank of educational scholarship, the premise that history needs philosophy and philosophy needs history while education needs and alters them both. What is more questionable is the belief that schooling is the best vehicle for integrating these and other studies.

The recognition that educational scholarship is not exclusively defined by public schooling and that not every past educative relationship is best understood as the prehistory of universal, compulsory schooling is one of the key intellectual factors that marks the shift between the older and the newer scholarship. Yet as attempts are made to shift the focus beyond the public schools, it has become increasingly difficult to maintain the integrated nature of educational understanding. We can see this difficulty in the implicit split that has occurred between philosophy and history. Hence, as historical studies have expanded beyond the public school, they have brought about new interest in the areas of child-rearing practices, working class socialization, and other fields which have been conceived broadly as cultural and social transmission. However, philosophers, in attempting to clarify our understanding of the concept of education, have distinguished it from related but different concepts, such as indoctrination, training, play, and from most other activities which can, in contrast to the work of the historians, be broadly classified as *merely* cultural transmission. Therefore, as history has moved in one direction, some philosophers implicitly have denied that that direction is still the study of education. Thus, if it were once the case that the public schools provided too narrow a focus for educational studies, it is now the case that there is no single focus, and the success of each of the disciplines has further split them apart.

It might be said that this new found pluralism is a good sign, a signal of the maturity of educational studies and a recognition that different disciplines are designed to do different things. All this may be granted, but one question still remains to be answered: What is it that makes a study a study of education? As we have seen, some historians have an answer to this puzzle. The history of education, they say, takes as its domain any institution or practice which is concerned with cultural transmission and socialization. Yet it is important to understand that the concepts of cultural transmission and socialization have themselves been borrowed from other foundational areas and that there are important aspects of the educational relationship which they leave out, allowing only the ingenuity and common sense of the historian to bring them back into consideration. Most important, in their emphasis on habit formation and fixed belief systems, these concepts leave out of consideration the entire question of human knowledge, and are unable to account for the development of new cultural forms.

If it is knowledge that such concepts have left out of the picture, it is knowledge which the philosophers have included with vengeance, often reifying it with such passion that only a graduate of some of the better Ivy League liberal arts colleges could truly be thought of as educated. Some philosophers have paid so much attention to the forms of knowledge and have spent so much time justifying the liberal arts curriculum,[2] that they have forgotten just how well most people are able to function simply by understanding the basic rules of social interaction, rules which the behavior of other individuals and the arrangements of dominant social institutions reinforce daily, providing all of the evidence needed to stamp such knowledge with the philosophically prized label of a *justified true belief.*

There is one movement in education which does have potential for reunifying educational studies. It is a movement which has had some influence in a variety of fields, including history, economics, sociology, curriculum studies, and even, but to a lesser extent, that laggard discipline, philosophy. This is the movement which emphasizes the reproductive role of education. However, while most of the recent studies on this issue have treated social and cultural reproduction as but a finding of empirical research and have not been concerned with clarifying the domain of educational understanding, I would like to consider it as the domain of educational studies itself. That is, I believe that education is best understood by recognizing that one of the functions of any society is that of maintaining intergenerational continuity—that is, of maintaining its identity as a society across generations and even in the context of many possible and significant changes, and that it is the activity and institution of education, both formal and informal, which carries on this function.

This insight is not new but is shared by Plato, Dewey, Marx, and other traditional scholars. Yet to suggest that social reproduction is the appropriate object for educational research is not to say, except in very general terms, what it is that is being reproduced, or what it is that should be reproduced. It is only to provide, in general outline, an idea of what educational scholarship seeks to understand. In order to bring the object of social reproduction more clearly into focus, I want to look at an example of a study in which social reproduction is also central, but not as the focus of educational research, but as the finding of the educational researcher. I refer here to Bowles and Gintis' important work, *Schooling in Capitalist America*.[3] In this study, Bowles and Gintis see as one of the major limitations on American educational reform the role that schools are expected to serve in reproducing the relationships of production that are so important in the maintenance of a capitalist society. Such things as the hierarchical character of schools, the different personality traits of children from different social classes and in different curricula, and the relative immobility of certain classes within the society are explained in terms of the function these serve in maintaining the capitalist relations of production.

The point about this research that is important to take note of here is that it is intended not simply as a neutral empirical analysis of the relationship between education and production in capitalist society, but also as a critique of those relationships. And this is to Bowles and Gintis credit. However, the question that I want to explore is: What is it besides the relationships of production which is being reproduced in the society such that Bowles and Gintis can expect that their analysis will be taken as a critique rather than as a neutral description of the way the educational machine works? Let me provide an example in order to illustrate this puzzle and then we can move on to exploring the major point further.

In the British Broadcasting Corporation's television series, *Upstairs Downstairs*, which follows the life of an upper class family and its servants from about the turn of the century to the Depression, there is an episode which takes place during the boom times of the 1920's in which one of the servants, Frederick, decides to take leave of the household and pursue a career in the movies. The butler, Hudson, the bearer of traditional culture, is deeply disturbed by his underling's announcement and tries, unsuccessfully, to dissuade Frederick from his decision.

Now, what is going on in this exchange is a clash of world views, one in which the value of a career is being pitted against an older ideal of station and place. For Frederick, a career in the movies represents the possibility for individual growth and riches, for personal reward, and recognition. For Hudson, it represents the breakdown of the traditional structure and the wrenching of a person from an environment of mutual service where self-identity is achieved through serving and being served by a visible household community.

Frederick's decision is to Hudson both imprudent and foolish. It represents a challenge to Hudson's sense of rightness. For Frederick, however, careers rightfully belong to all who have the drive, the skill, the intelligence, and the daring to grab them. They are the prizes which await the talented who are willing to venture outside of the security of the household. Hudson's is a world not of equal chances but of mutual service, one in which the ideal of "my station and its duties" still has meaning. We know that Hudson's world was in the process of breaking down and that it had already crumbled for the majority of British workers whose station had been transformed into a position in the wage/labor force. Even those upstairs felt this breakdown. For some, like Georganna, it was expressed in a purposelessness that at times crossed over into decadence. For others, such as the head of the household, James, it eventually led to a recognition of his own violation of the norm of mutuality and hence, to suicide.

Through all of this, Hudson persists as the bearer of the culture to the bitter end. But what he is left with is a distorted picture of the way the social world is and the way it works. Yet, does Frederick's flight from service to pursue a career in the movies represent a truer picture than Hudson's? And what are we to say about the moral justification of Frederick's decision? Frederick is not heard from again, and so we can only guess at the answers to these questions. It would not be too difficult, however, to understand Frederick's decision as one in which the idea of mutual service had turned into the horror of a dead end job, and where the only service remaining was to stand witness over a decaying corpse. The vigor of life was to be found elsewhere. It was to be found in the idea of growth brought from the new world and transplanted in the old. To take leave of that world of mutual service was not, as Hudson perceived, to violate life's moral boundaries. It was to recognize and to support a new morality, one in which talent, vigor, risk, and ingenuity are rewarded *without limits*.

Given this clash of world views, we can now ask, How is it that *Schooling in Capitalist America* can be understood as the critique that Bowles and Gintis intended it to be? For surely, Hudson would not understand it as critique, or at least not the critique that the authors intend; rather, it is Frederick's moral vision, one that accepts the empirical and moral view of equal opportunity found in liberal thought, which allows the description given in *Schooling* to work as a critique. Given Frederick's world view, *Schooling* can show that his vision is as listless and moribund as Hudson's. In other words, in order to critique liberal society, *schooling* must rely upon the fact that the moral consciousness of that society has been reproduced in the intuitions of its members. Frederick represents a moment of this reproduction.

This analysis is useful in order to point out the major features of education as social reproduction, and to display the aspects of social life that an educational system strives to reproduce. First, there is the reproduction of skills or, which for reasons which will soon become clear, I call skilled clusters. Second, there is the reproduction of consciousness which includes an understanding of the rights and privileges associated with the legitimate exercise of a given skill cluster. Every society will have some arrangement whereby it strives to reproduce these two aspects of its life across generations. And even where more critical forms of education are undertaken, they will involve a reflection upon these primary moments. Yet the reproduction of skills and the reproduction of consciousness are not divorced from each other but are connected in a number of ways that provide rich areas for both social change and educational understanding. Here, I want to sketch a few of these connections.

The study of education is to be understood as the study of the aims and processes of social reproduction as reflected in the practices of institutions and individuals. Insofar as education is concerned with developing the skills for operating upon and making sense of the world, that is, insofar as it is concerned with work and consciousness, it is concerned with knowledge. This thin model of knowledge is intended to provide us with a way to focus upon the processes and aims of education as social reproduction and is not intended to respond to issues about the nature of true knowledge or to assess formal criteria of verification. It is, however, intended to move beyond a naive conception of socialization or transmission, a conception which is unable to capture and explain the development of new patterns of social activity. Rather, it directs us to take seriously the point of view of the social participant in order to later arrive at the point of view of the social analyst and critic with all of the refinements about knowledge that those terms imply. The idea here, however, is to put aside the question of real or true knowledge and to examine what is *taken* as real knowledge by a given culture, and to investigate the routes by which it is obtained. In order to illustrate these relationships, let me begin with work or the reproduction of productive skills.

Every society has certain ways in which some skills are clustered together into a particular social role and whereby other skills are excluded from that role. The fact that most recent criticisms of education have neglected this simple fact has meant that challenges have been directed only at the fairness of the selection and allocation process and not at the structure that generates the positions that are allocated. Nevertheless, skills can be clustered in different ways. For example, it is intuitively possible to think of the various traits associated with healing as clustered in a number of possible ways, some of which may be consistent with our own ideas about the health professions and others which may be quite alien to our conceptions. For example, physicians in the United States may prescribe drugs but are unlikely to dispense them, although they are not prohibited from doing so. Pharmacists are expected to fill prescriptions. They are prohibited from prescribing them. Surgeons cut people for a living but they are not expected, as they once were, to cut hair and trim beards. And doctors today are expected to heal only people. To call a practicing physician a good horse doctor is not a compliment to her, although it certainly would be if said of some veterinarians. Thus, work takes on its distinctive character within a society partly as a function of the kinds of skills that are clustered together and the range of objects over which they are expected or not expected to be exercised. These are the factors of scope, and they determine where the boundaries of one kind of work ends and another begins.

In addition to scope factors there are level factors which differentiate the roles within a given field and help us to understand the variations in status which attach themselves to different occupations within a field; hence, I return to an earlier example. Physicians generally only prescribe medicine, but they are not *prohibited* from dispensing it. Pharmacists, on the other hand, have no more right to prescribe than the patient. They can *recommend* non-prescription medicine, but are prohibited from *prescribing* prescription medicine. They normally act on order from physicians, and the institutional assumption is that the activity of prescribing is beyond their trained capacity. The educational system of a given society, whether formal or informal, functions to distribute such skill clusters and thereby establish or maintain the work relations in a society.

Now, let's turn to the reproduction of consciousness. Consciousness is not, incidentally, intended here to suggest merely a set of attitudes or personality characteristics, such as active or passive, initiatory, or conformist, as Bowles and Gintis suggest. Rather, attitudes are a function of perceived social relationships and thus imply a specific set of understandings about social practice, a set of understandings which, when attitudes are stable, is verified daily by the activity of individuals and the structure of institutions. Thus, along with the reproduction of skills is the reproduction of ideas about the ownership of knowledge and of the rights and responsibilities of those who possess certain forms of institutionally granted knowledge. The reproduction of consciousness is the other side of the reproduction of skills. It is the factor which, as a general rule, enables the clustering of skills into specific roles and the clustering of roles into specific classes to persist relatively unchallenged in a stable society. And, it is also one of the crucial factors which must change if any significant alteration of the skill cluster and the society is to be effected.

We can speculate that the reproduction of consciousness serves to maintain a given distribution of skills, in a number of ways, from providing acceptance of the fairness of the institutional routes by which the present cluster of skills is developed and licensed, to teaching people to respond appropriately to the trappings which symbolize that a person may rightfully exercise a given skill. Such trappings include the traditional garb of the witch doctor or the wig of the barrister or the blood-stained robe of the surgeon worn in the sterile setting of a hospital. We may also speculate that a change in consciousness will accompany a re-distribution of skills in similar ways.

While specific consciousness will, granted individual variations, attach itself to the exercise of specific skill clusters (I call these frames), the reproduction of the general social consciousness will entail a more or less stable and institutionally enforced consensus about the level of knowledge which is appropriate to each role and will define the categories of general roles, such as manual laborer, professional, white collar worker, etc. Moreover, the general consciousness will entail beliefs about the consequences of a group having access to more knowledge than is thought appropriate for it. As one Englishman wrote, arguing against the development of charity schools in the 18th century, "If a horse knew as much as a man, I should not like to be its rider." Jensen provides a contemporary example of this by implication, as he spells out the kind of knowledge which is appropriate for children with different scores on I.Q. tests.[4]

In any society in which there is a hierarchy of roles, the institutional reproduction of consciousness will strive first, to develop in each individual an acceptance of his or her own position, and second, an understanding and acceptance of the way in which that position relates to those above and below it. This is a major condition for stability, and it would hold whether a society approaches a situation of zero mobility across generations or a totally random distribution of positions across generational lines. The institutional interest of stability requires not only that individuals in one social position know how they are to relate to those who occupy positions above and below their own, but also that they accept the general principles governing these relationships. Without such an acceptance, each felt violation of the relationship would be an occasion for challenging the general distribution of skills and the privileges and responsibility accompanying it. Thus, along with an understanding of the activities appropriate to a given role, institutional means are developed to provide a generalized awareness of the reasons for developing intellectual efforts in one direction rather than another and for distributing knowledge in a given way.

Societies can often be related to and distinguished from each other in terms of the pattern of intellectual development that is encouraged and in terms of the reasons that are provided for maintaining the established pattern. These form the *knowledge code* of a given society, and the identity of a single society over time often can be traced in terms of the conflicts that arise within an established knowledge code and the changes that take place in the pattern of development and distribution.

Formal education, with which traditional educational scholarship has largely been concerned, can be understood as a consciously designed and institutionalized system of instruction which functions to establish or maintain a given knowledge code and to further the patterns of intellectual development associated with it. The concept of a knowledge code is intended here to suggest the fact that education involves not only learning certain skills, but also learning other factors which are associated with possessing such skills. We learn, for example, what is high and low status knowledge, and we also learn how to identify, either through manner, mode of expression, dress, or physical environment, the different values that are placed on those with different modes of knowledge. Moreover, we learn the range of activity over which a person with a certain level of knowledge is to be granted authority. The knowledge code itself is to be understood as an interrelated body of arguments and beliefs about the importance of a certain set of information and skills, a body which is ideally coherent and which serves to propel intellectual energies in one direction rather than another.

To say that a knowledge code is ideally coherent is not to say that it is without inconsistencies or that it provides the most adequate explanation for all experience. It is simply to say that the inconsistencies will be taken as signs of the limitations of present understanding, rather than as signs of the inadequacy of the body of arguments and beliefs. An obvious example of such a code is the categories of knowledge that are recognized and ranked by a systematic body of religious beliefs which has implications for the conduct of everyday life and the governance of the society.

Yet knowledge codes are fragile because they must be expressed through the ordered working of different skill clusters, and they must be understood through the significance provided by different frames. For example, the efficiency expert, carrying with him the knowledge code of the scientific-technological enterprise, orders skill-clusters and performances on the shop floor in ways that best meet the goals of the enterprise. He perceives and eliminates unnecessary movements; he perfects old ones and adds new ones and thus serves as the embodiment of the knowledge code. What he fails to perceive as significant and what he cannot order are the swaggers with which these movements are performed, or the sneers and snickers with which his presence is greeted by those whose movements are being ordered.[5] Yet it is the swagger and the sneers that are signs of a different frame, one which understands the knowledge code, but does so in a different way and with a different sense of significance. And it is the swagger, the sneer, and the snicker which are the outward signs of a frame that is shared among the workers. These signal the presence of a culture which is antagonistic to the prevailing knowledge code and which contains the potential for developing a new code and, hence, for effectively challenging the established one.

Formal educational systems offer protection for knowledge codes that are threatened by a number of different kinds of situations. Among these are situations in which the conditions of work and family life are no longer thought able to accommodate the instruction of children towards an acceptable level of consciousness, such as the shift from small farming to large industries, or an increase in the number of families that are perceived to be antagonistic to a favored code, such as some cases of immigration. Moreover, threats can arise from within the code itself, as, for example, when the items within the code become too diverse, unwieldy, and inconsistent, thereby threatening to destroy the coherence of the code and, thus, the authority of those who possess it. This kind of threat often accounts for the movement of professional areas away from apprenticeship forms of training and towards training within a formal university structure where knowledge is no longer reproduced in the activity of the master, but rather in the systematic form of a textbook. Hence, for example, the shift from the law as carried on in the accumulated decision of individual judges to the law as contained in textbooks and journals, and transmitted within the university.[6]

In addition to protecting an established code, formal institutions serve other functions as well. They are used to seal the end of a dispute between experts about a given issue within an accepted code and to communicate an image of smooth and unbroken progress within the code. Science textbooks, as Thomas Kuhn points out, typically neglect the weight of the counter-arguments that were proposed prior to a theory's general acceptance and under-emphasize the strong features of counter theories.

Formal institutions are also used to crystallize the development of new codes as, for example, when one country colonizes another or when there is a shift in the mode of leadership and power within a country, say from religious to industrial. Formal systems of education are used to ensure that the skills that are perceived to be effective in meeting defined social needs are preserved from generation to generation. Preservation is accomplished by providing a setting for the transmission of skills that are defined as especially important and which are thought to take considerable amount of time to learn. Protection for such skills is often provided by preparing the general public to recognize them as important, to consent to the provision of special incentives for their continuation and development and to believe that their development requires rare and specialized abilities. Finally, formal institutions can be used to shift certain forms of knowledge from the local community to larger, more centralized institutions, and to reduce as well as to augment the skills needed to perform a given task.

Thus, the study of formal education is but one aspect of the study of social reproduction in general. Formal institutions arise at specific times in specific places to perform specific functions in relation to the reproduction of specific skills and the reproduction of a specific consciousness.

Having provided some idea of what I take to be the domain of educational understanding, let me return to two themes which have been identified with the older group of foundation scholars—the integrated nature of educational studies and the relationship between theory and practice. Given the perspective of hindsight, it is not difficult to see that these themes were connected too closely to a belief in the liberating possibilities of public schooling. But, the themes themselves can be extracted from any particular set of beliefs. I will begin with the question of the integrated nature of educational understanding.

The important point about the integrated nature of educational understanding is not the particular way in which various disciplines might decide to cut up the conceptual domain of education. Rather, it is that by recognizing that there is a reasonably clear domain for educational studies, the nature of the disciplines and their problematics are altered in a similar direction. A clearer understanding of the domain provides educational studies with a more coherent research program regardless of the particular discipline through which it happens to be articulated at any given time. Where any particular study may begin is influenced by the discipline and background of the researcher. However, all of the studies would be designed to inform us about the nature of the knowledge code of a given society and the way in which that code is processed by different individuals and groups, through different frames and with different implications for the reproduction of skills and the reproduction of consciousness. For traditional pedagogical research, this means that typical problems of teaching and learning would be examined not only to decide upon effective methods of teaching, but also to understand the way in which a given knowledge code influences our understanding of pedagogical ends and means. For example, it would mean that learning theory and research would try not only to account for differences in achievement, but also to account for how those differences influence the way in which various groups of youngsters come to understand their own role in the larger scheme of things. It would examine the way in which knowledge in the classroom is defined for different groups of students and the influence that this has on their self-understanding—on their understanding of the kinds of people and learners they are, and how this understanding may or may not facilitate their later acceptance or rejection of their social role. The integrative quality of educational studies also points beyond the classroom and suggests that the body of research in education should attempt to understand the transmission process in the context of an examination of the knowledge code of a given society and the relationship of different individual and group frameworks to that code. Thus, while the school, because of its contemporary influence on transmission, often may be seen as the focus of such studies, it does not define their problematic. Rather, schooling itself is to be understood as a longitudinal system which functions to initiate people from different backgrounds and with different frameworks into some aspect of a prevailing knowledge code. Just which code and which aspect of the code must, of course, be determined by empirical research. What is important here is the way in which the school interacts with these other frameworks.

Schooling, however, is but one of many starting points. For example, educational research could also proceed by attempting to understand the process by which different frames intersect and are reproduced and modified in a new generation that is in the process of coming to understand its social world. Rather than beginning with the school or with the various intellectual debates about appropriate knowledge, researchers could begin with the family or with members of a particular social role or class and attempt to understand what is to count as appropriate knowledge for children of that group. They could then begin to study the changes that this framework undergoes as other institutions, such as schools, join the reproduction process. Finally, they could begin to examine the way which certain frameworks are related to the material conditions of a group and the way in which alterations in these conditions influence the particular manner in which frameworks are reproduced.

For example, many small shopkeepers have, over a period of time, experienced a dramatic change in their own self-understanding and esteem, a change which they identify with shifts in the power relation between the large corporation and the small businessman. Hence, some small businessmen, who now believe that they serve as but a conduit between the corporation and the media-conditioned buyer, recall a time when the customer looked upon them as a buffer who could advise about both price and quality. In our own terms, these retailers view themselves as people whose license *as knowing* a specific and important area has been usurped, and they resent both the corporation for its usurpation and the customer for failing to understand how his or her own best interest has been denied by media manipulation.

These perceptions, which, on a descriptive level, are consistent with a radical framework, often melt into a more conservative one on the level of prescription where law and order and fewer government "handouts" may be proposed as the solution to the problem of contemporary life. Given this particular framework, the educational researcher would be interested in knowing how it is altered when attempts are made to reproduce it in a newer generation growing up in the context of other more powerful frameworks and whose first-hand experience has not been developed out of the historical context of a personal relationship relatively unmediated by corporate and media control.

Given the paradoxical nature of the initial framework, there are a number of possibilities ranging from complete rejection to complete acceptance of the older framework. It must not be thought, however, that these frameworks are to be understood simply on a political level. Each, for example, has its own way of interpreting the setting in which fundamental human values are to be applied. There are, for example, different rules for truth telling that developed with each.[7] For the traditionally minded retailer, truth telling may be appropriate when customers give evidence that they are able and willing to listen. Otherwise, silent complicity in the interest of a sale and, of course, of the corporation may be accepted as an appropriate norm. Within the corporation, truth telling may be appropriate when it involves a strictly technical question or when the potential truth teller will not be perceived as violating the more acceptable norm of corporate trustworthiness. Here the setting largely determines when and to whom the truth can, with impunity, be told. Thus, certain truths can be told to superiors but not to subordinates, and others can be shared on a private level and may even be universally but privately acknowledged as true. However, it would be thought untrustworthy to share such truths in any of the more public settings, such as committee meetings, even with those who already know them. Within the corporation, these rules are known and acknowledged with different degrees of commitment, and other rule structures may, from the corporate point of view, interfere with the smooth application of the rules. Some people may place a higher priority on personal loyalty than corporate efficiency, while others may insist that certain higher principles have priority over corporate rules. Still others may accept the rules but be inept at knowing when to apply different ones, and substructures within the organization may have different sets of priorities.

The process by which the transmission of subordinate frameworks influences the way different groups come to relate to the dominant rule structure is an area that educational research has only begun to explore. However, to capture these various frameworks and the process of their reproduction and alteration would be but one task of educational scholarship. Equally important is to understand the process by which such frameworks are established and maintained or diminished, and the way in which the material conditions of different groups influence their frameworks. For example, the paradoxical framework of the small shop keepers might be understood in terms of their fragile condition in contemporary society and the fact that their survival depends upon maintaining at least minimally good relations with the corporation and a competitive advantage over each other.

An integrated notion of educational studies would be concerned to understand the aims and processes of social reproduction as it occurs within different settings at different times and through different frames. It would be concerned to understand how dominant and subordinate frameworks interact with each other to produce generational variations in work and consciousness, and it would attempt to identify the possibilities for progressive changes in light of the restraint of historical factors and contemporary material condition.

It is this last point which brings us to the second theme of the foundationist's concern, the relationship between theory and practice. For ultimately, educational scholarship as the study of social reproduction molds the disciplines because it recognizes that value considerations cannot be divorced from the way in which reproduction is understood and that the researcher is a product of a certain set of values that have been socially reproduced. The concepts used, the problem studied, and the factors highlighted are to be understood in part by an understanding of the prominent values and concerns that dominate both the society and the researcher who dwells within it. Thus, educational scholarship requires a degree of reflection which some other areas do not, and it requires an ability to capture values which influence the direction of education but which are often concealed in the descriptive posture of social science research.

Yet, educational understanding requires more than simply the reflection upon, and identification of, a set of values. It requires, as the foundationists recognized, the articulation and assessment of those values in the realm of practice in which only some of them can be realized.

It requires, however, that this be done without losing sight of the larger goal of human liberation. For it is at the intersection of the ideal with the possible that practical activity is judged. As Marx observed "men make their own history, but they do not make it just as they please. They do not make it under circumstances chosen by themselves but under circumstances directly encountered, given and transmitted from the past." In other words, we are both bound by past forms of reproduction and creators of new ones; and to forget this simple fact as we attempt to understand the educational process, past and present, is to misconceive the nature of that enterprise, to inevitably distort our perception of it, and to run the risk of misdirecting it in the future.

Acknowledgments

I am indebted to Eric Bredo, Rupert Evans, Richard Franz, Ernest Kahane, Philip Steedman, and Jeffrey Tank for their comments on earlier drafts of this manuscript. I am also indebted to members of the Philosophy of Education Division of the Department of Educational Policy Studies at the University of Illinois for listening and responding to an earlier draft.

4

The Discourse of Philosophy of Education

Maxine Greene situates Philosophy of Education within the discourse about rights, self, rationality and power and provides an analysis that emphasizes deconstruction and renewal. In developing this narrative she raises the most important issues that contemporary philosophers and philosophers of educators must come to address—how traditional (Western) conceptions of rights can be mobilized to generate renewal without reinforcing hierarchy and domination. To put the problem slightly differently: How can the liberating features of the language of human rights be maintained while avoiding using the concept of rights—developed by white, Western, bourgeois males—to lord it over others who have not yet reached the stage of development where they can appreciate the wisdom of the Enlightenment tradition? Although Greene echoes Cixous's ambivalence regarding this conception of rights and the "inalienable" self that it attaches to, she also shares, I think, correctly, Cixous's reluctance to abandon the concept completely.

Given this dilemma, Greene believes the principal role of philosophers of education is to find a way to "expose the inadequacies (and the racism, and the sexism) in so much of the discourse without disposing of the texts themselves." The texts are patriarchal expressions of communications "lightly constrained by rules of logic, linearity, and (on occasion) a range of technical controls, limiting the free flow, imaginative, and spontaneous conversation that characterizes healthy and productive human relationships. Rights talk interrupts the discourse and is patriarchal to the extent that, in doing so, the father in *To the Lighthouse* becomes the interpreter of reality and the final arbiter of truth.

It becomes colonial when it "has not only imposed a 'right' way . . . ; it has in many cases deformed, belittled . . . what has been considered 'undeveloped,' implicitly regressive."

In addition to the philosopher's task of exposing the inadequacies of language without disposing of the text, Greene proposes an additional task for philosophers. True philosophy, she tells us, quoting Merleau-Ponty, "'consists in relearning how to look at the world.' . . . 'Learning how to look' (certainly for educators) may mean learning how to reflect with others upon intersubjectivity itself . . . The philosopher's obligation may involve enabling all sorts of persons to think about the ways they direct their attention, the vantage points they take, the naming, the caring, the concern."

Deconstruction serves as an important tool for engaging in this reflection by revealing the hierarchical binary relations that provide the framework for much of the discourse on Philosophy of Education. In disclosing how much of our thinking is governed by hierarchical binaries such as white/black, male/female, cognitive/affective we have taken an important step in, as Derrida puts it, "*overturning* of the classical opposition and a general displacement of the system." In this way, Derrida, according to Greene, believes that we can "overcome the privileging of the logos and the systematized, the abstract and the universal."

The obligation to relearn how to look at our world—in Merleau-Ponty's terms—is carried on as an intergenerational, as well as an individual project; when it takes on generational proportions, it suggests the role that Philosophy of Education may play in this enterprise. Greene accepts Hannah Arendt's idea that education is the commitment we make when we both provide the material, spiritual, and intellectual support that enables our children to "undertake something new" and at the same time "prepare them in advance for the task of renewing a common world." For Greene, this means that Philosophy of Education serves, among other things, as a reminder of the traditions within which our lives are woven while at the same time reminding us that the vantage point which that tradition provides is, like all vantage points, partial and incomplete. In this recognition, Philosophy of Education provides the release for imagination and for opening "vistas on what might be, what is not yet." Hence, Philosophy of Education is involved in self-development and self-formulation which requires attending to the silences in our own tradition and our own history and therefore breaking through that aspect of the Enlightenment tradition that has served to subordinate women, people of color, and non-Western peoples.

These insights are not just academic or abstract, but have a profound impact on schools and other educational institutions. They are responsible for many of the demands to establish schools that serve a single ethnic or racial group or a single gender. Both the Corporate School and the New Concept School, private schools serving African-American students in the Chicago area, have received high praise not only for the academic achievement of their students but for instilling a strong sense of racial pride rooted in African and African-American ideals. Researchers have praised all-girls schools for the self-assurance, assertiveness, and sense of competence that they nurture. Other institutions have also been influenced by the rejection of the Western-centered philosophy that has dominated our thinking for than a century. Museums must reexamine entire displays developed when the savage/civilized binary was taken for granted as the appropriate framework in which to show the *progress of man*.[1] The imperative that Greene describes is already taking place. Part of the problem for philosophers of education is whether a field more accustomed to academic argument and conceptual analysis has a role to play in the important changes that are encompassed by Greene's observations. I will argue that there is an important role for Philosophy of Education to play, but in making this argument I will need to complement Professor Greene's conception of the field itself by bringing another discourse into focus.

Greene's placement of Philosophy of Education within an intergenerational context is valid: an important task of educational scholarship is to examine the factors involved in intergenerational reproduction and disruption.[2] Philosophy of Education serves as a reflective analysis and evaluation of the intergenerational reproduction of knowledge, skills, and sensibilities.[3] Contemporary philosophical discourse about education should be located within the context of the discourse about rights, self, rationality and power. However, I want to suggest that the discourse Greene describes need not constitute Philosophy of Education, at least as presently conceived. It could simply reflect a philosophical discourse about education (this is but one feature of the discourse of Philosophy of Education). Another side is a discourse about institutions that are intended to educate. The term school can be used to indicate such institutions, but in doing so it is important to remember that formal schooling is but one representation of such institutions. *Schooling* is used here to indicate institutions that take on intentional or expected educating functions, and discourse about such institutions grounds the field of Philosophy of Education as much as the discourse about rights, power, and self.[4]

Without the institutions and practices that are explicitly intended to educate, the profession of Philosophy of Education as we know it today would not exist. This is not to say that there are not educational problems that can be dealt with philosophically without necessarily referencing institutional practices. Questions about the nature of knowledge, the character of teaching, the nature of moral education and virtue need not be addressed in relationship to any ongoing institutional practice. However, when they are addressed in this way they can be situated within a standard philosophical discourse such as epistemology, philosophy of mind, and social philosophy. This discourse takes on the characteristics of Philosophy of Education when it is informed by or centered on institutional practice.

Hence Philosophy of Education is institutional philosophy. It is a reflection on the aims of actual organizations and the practices of established institutions that are involved in some official or semi-official way in educating people. It is for this reason that courses in Philosophy of Education are not usually found in philosophy departments and it reflects the fact that the organ of Philosophy of Education—the Philosophy of Education Society—arose out of the efforts of a group of educators.[5] To remind us that Philosophy of Education has something to do with schooling—a reminder that Greene, whose work in schools is legendary, does not need—is not to say that each and every issue philosophers of education address must bear immediately on the work of teachers. Issues of educational policy as well as evaluation and goals may be quite indirectly related to classroom practice but are certainly important concerns for people in the field of Philosophy of Education. Nor is it to say that schools must be accepted as the best or most appropriate sites of learning. Arguments for de-schooling are important and provocative—although not especially convincing—and they certainly have a place in philosophical debates about the kinds of institutions that educate. Arguments about de-schooling are philosophical when they seek careful reflection on existing practices and the framework of institutional discourse, and they count as Philosophy of Education because they are truly about schools. It is not to say that Philosophy of Education is not often well served by people whose graduate degree is in philosophy rather than Philosophy of Education. It is simply to observe that a philosophical discourse about education that is informed by the practices of schools and other educational institutions is a discourse in Philosophy of Education. In this sense of the term, Philosophy of Education is somewhat more like scholastic philosophy than it is metaphysics; and it has a practical goal—the improvement of the institutions through which the activity of educating is advanced. Unlike much of scholasticism, however, Philosophy of Education does not begin the discourse by ruling out reformation or revolution.

This is not meant as an essentialist definition of Philosophy of Education, but a description of the actual practices that are presently identified as Philosophy of Education and it identifies a role that is recognizable both by those within the field and those outside of it. To the extent that it serves as a definition, it does so through recognizing that definitions perform certain functions in relation to ongoing practice and that they are not completely separable from the institutions which sustain the practices. There is a real sense in which Philosophy of Education is what philosophers of education do when they see themselves doing Philosophy of Education. However, this operational definition should not be taken too far, for if philosophers of education did not relate their discourse to an ongoing institution there would be very little to distinguish their discourse from other forms of philosophy that are concerned with rights, power, self, or that attempt to understand knowledge and the possibility of its transmission. In this sense, Dewey was probably wrong when he equated all philosophy to Philosophy of Education. True, Philosophy of Education asks most of the interesting questions of philosophy, but it answers them in relation to on-going institutional practice.

To describe Philosophy of Education in this way is to acknowledge the importance of the history and practices of the Philosophy of Education Society and to embrace the concern that R. Bruce Raup expressed in its founding to improve "teaching in the Philosophy of Education in schools for the education of teachers and in other educational institutions."[6] Whether or not Raup overemphasized the importance of teachers colleges for Philosophy of Education—and I think he did—the more important point is the need to situate the field at the intersection of two discourses—one philosophical and the other institutional. Teachers colleges and schools of education make the latter discourse more likely and more easy to sustain. It is not, however, the only possibility.

The conception of Philosophy of Education that I have offered, partial as it is, delineates the activities of philosophers of education from the work of philosophers, even those with explicitly educational concerns. The difference is not only in the nature of the work itself but in the discourse within which the works are situated. That the work of a philosopher of education is situated within a professional discourse about the existing practices of schools or other ongoing educating institutions is reflected in the standards used to evaluate work in the field. The philosophical community is rightly concerned with the rigor and originality of the argument, a concern which philosophers of education should also share. However, the community of philosophers of education must also be concerned to reflect an informed and up-to-date awareness of the actual work and issues of the schools or of policies and research that pertain to contemporary educational practices. This does not mean that people who are identified as philosophers will not on occasion write articles or books that are informed about school practice. Nor does it mean that philosophers of education may not sometimes be poorly informed about the activities of schools. The point has to do with the expectations of the field rather than with just how well someone inside or outside of the field may meet those expectations. Or, to put the matter slightly differently: A philosopher who makes mistakes about school practice may still meet the standards of good philosophy. However, a philosopher of education who is consistently uninformed about educational practices and research is failing to meet the standards of the field.

The different discourses in which philosophy and Philosophy of Education are situated have an influence on the way in which the concerns of education are explored. Nevertheless the two have a good deal in common. For example, both philosophers of education are likely to address such fundamental questions as what counts as education, how education can be distinguished from indoctrination, training and the like—questions that were popular among the last generation of both analytic philosophers and philosophers of education and which remain important questions. This common ground is reflected in many of the common texts and issue that are shared by both fields. Plato's discourse on justice in *The Republic*, Rousseau's discussion of freedom in *Emile*, Dewey's reframing of democracy in *Democracy and Education* and R. S. Peters's exploration of the aims of education are likely to be treated in classes taught by both philosophers and philosophers of education. Moreover recently, the influence of feminism, Marxism and postmodernism is being felt within both the philosophical community and the field of Philosophy of Education and has added to each a new concern about whose interests are served by different conceptions of knowledge and different assigned aims.

Philosophy of Education departs from a philosophical interest in education in the high level of interdependence between the work of empirical educational researchers and the work of philosophers of education. Philosophers of education must both mine the findings of empirical traditions to understand the constraints and possibilities of human development and, as practitioners of institutional philosophy, they must critically analyze the extent to which methodological frameworks may reinforce institutional practices that arbitrarily restrict educational discourse. It is at this point that the rights discourse and the institutional discourse intersect.

Institutional philosophies such as Philosophy of Education or Philosophy of Medicine have a complicated relationship to the practical knowledge that is carried on within the institution itself. In the Philosophy of Medicine, the philosopher does not need to be able to perform the technical work of the nurse or the physician or to share the same knowledge base. She does, however, need a working understanding of the organization and structure of healthcare, the availability and benefits of certain kinds of treatment, and a general conception of health and disease. If, for example she was concerned with a just distribution of healthcare, she would need to know the relative benefits, say, of introducing a new water treatment plant in Third World countries as opposed to the development of a new open heart surgical unit. Each has its costs and its benefits, but in many countries the former is likely to service the needs of the vast majority of a population, while the latter benefits only the few who are wealthy enough to survive to the age where heart disease becomes a serious problem. Both the philosopher of medicine and the philosopher of education need, in Greene's phrase, to be able to imagine other arrangements. This imagination, however, is but one stage in a larger process. They must have the philosophical tools to evaluate present practices against alternative possibilities. In these evaluations, conceptions of justice, fairness, autonomy, and independence must begin to inform the existing institutional standards.

Within institutions the meaning of concepts is established through their historical use. The feminist critique of rights that Greene draws upon is powerful precisely because the institutional history of this term is mixed, serving both liberationist, and non-liberationist goals. When institutional meanings are confronted by feminist and other critical scholarship, the historically encrusted meanings are reconstituted as objects of discourse and criticism to be held up against more honorific understandings. Moreover, as Greene notes, deconstruction provides an instrument for revealing frameworks of domination and subordination and overturning—to use Derrida's phrase—"the classical oppositions."

Although deconstruction may encompass critical method and philosophy, it is at best a moment in the Philosophy of Education. In Philosophy of Education, the exposure of institutional meanings provides a promissory note that the possibility of reconstruction will be considered and that serious attempts will be made to reconstitute meanings in new and non-dominating ways. To enter this phase of institutional philosophy, it is important to expose the limits of deconstruction by asking what purpose we might wish to, as Greene advocates, "practice an *overturning* of the classical opposition and a general displacement of the system." What is the reason to bring to consciousness such oppositions as "white/black; male/female; cognitive/affective; literal/figurative" if not because we operate under some notion that certain voices and certain purposes have been wrongly silenced. Yet deconstruction itself is silent when it comes to the question of reconstruction.[7] This is a silence that Philosophy of Education cannot share.

Maxine Greene poses the dilemma of reconstruction eloquently:

> This differs considerably from a conception of objectively existing frameworks in which we can somehow ground a normative order of consequence for young people in our schools. Yet it remains difficult to set aside our commitments to theoretically-grasped principles like freedom, justice, and equality. Similarly, for all our familiarity with the problematic of the "Enlightenment Project" (Horkheimer and Adorno 1972), we are still drawn to idealistic renderings of reason linked to progress and to humanism. They continue to draw us towards them, either as regulatory norms or unrealized possibilities. In a moment of shattered frameworks and alternations between skepticism and hopelessness, they seem to glow in the dark as reminders of what might be, and of what is still to be achieved.

Reconstruction requires that the floating skepticism that energizes the deconstructive project yield some reminders—as Greene puts it of "what is still to be achieved." Such reminders can be found by examining feminists' and deconstructionists' insights and by exploring the larger project which supports these insights. Greene's skepticism of skepticism provides a way to reveal the nature of this project.

When Derrida speaks of overturning the classic oppositions which have much "to do with the way we think and speak" and I would add, feel and act, he is not just proposing a random rejection without any direction in mind. Because the overturnings are of systems of dominance and subordination he clearly seeks a world where, if these hierarchies are not eliminated altogether, they are at least not taken for granted and allowed to exert a decisive but subliminal influence on our structures of discourse. Similarly, when feminists reject the ideas of dead white men, they are not rejecting their ideas just because they are old or because they came from white males. They are rejecting them because they sense that there was woven into their expression a system of privilege which has been perpetuated through and alongside of the ideas. They do not accept the view that the ideas can be separated from their expression. Instead, they hold that the way a person lives is connected to the ideals he expressed. For example, the fact that Jefferson continued to hold onto his slaves during his lifetime, tells a good deal about the conception of rights that he had in mind when he authored the founding documents. Without identifying this system of privilege as the object of deconstruction's skepticism, it is simply impossible to understand why we should overturn this opposition rather than that one; or, why we should worry about overturning any opposition whatsoever. And without similarly identifying this system of privilege as the object of feminists' concern, we are simply relegated to a behavioral paradigm where the difference between being silenced and being quiet is erased. Yet if these are indeed the core projects of these two movements, there is every reason, as Greene affirms "not to set aside our commitments to . . . principles like justice, freedom and equality." The object is in fact to see them for the role they can play in liberating dominated groups while also understanding how they have been sometimes used otherwise. This may very well mean not an out-of-hand rejection of the writings of white males, but a renewed exploration in order to understand both the possibilities they helped to articulate—often as oppressed subjects themselves—and the avenues they blocked as they expressed themselves through the images, norms, and conceptual distinction of their own period and gender. The project also requires the resurrection of ideas of woman, native peoples, people of color, and blue-collar workers whose words were less likely to be provided a public forum.

For philosophers of education concerned about classroom activities and relations, it is very important to be clear about the direction one is taking and the principles that are being supported.[8] As a pacifist, a person may indeed agree that gay people should not be discriminated against in the military—because they believe that discrimination anywhere is wrong. This need not, however, be taken as supporting the military. Similarly, take a teacher who is concerned about the tendency for the boys to dominate the classroom conversation. For this reason the teacher tries to call on girls before boys, to encourage reluctant girls to raise their hand and to teach boys to be patient while a girl is speaking. Consider the different reasons a philosopher of education might give for viewing this *bias* in favor of the girls in a positive light. One reason might have to do with the cash value assertiveness plays in our society. The adage "children should be seen and not heard" just is not good advice for raising children—whether girls or boys—in late twentieth century America. Yet to advance assertiveness for this reason is not to overturn a classical opposition, but to affirm an existing and widespread social value—the value of assertiveness. A philosopher of education who is not wild about assertiveness may, like the pacifist, support the activity for other reasons, say, women have an equal right to good jobs and income and in this society they need to be assertive to secure them. Another likely reason is that children learn more when they engage in active discussion in class, but as a general principle this seems incomplete. Children learn more when they are active participants in a *good* discussion. And a good discussion involves people seeking clarity and truth while they are also concerned about the quality of the relationships that enables the search for clarity and truth to continue in a reasonably unthreatening atmosphere.

There are at least two compelling reasons for the concern about silencing. The first is that people who want to speak have a right to do so and if others systematically monopolize the conversation, this right is being denied. This reason has very little to say about the quality of what is said, but it has a lot to say about the way in which traditional rights doctrines can be used to advance progressive agendas. Systematic silencing in school can be a special and most serious violation of such a right because of the long-term consequences it entails as girls learn eventually to silence themselves.

This reason for objecting to the systematic silencing of girls is an example of how our sensitivity to rights actually guides critical scholarship.

Granted, it calls for a more extended discussion of rights and the way different groups are advantaged and disadvantaged in learning to exercise them. Yet the discussion cannot begin without some awareness of what it means to have a right and when it is appropriate to equate the inability to exercise a right with its violation. A second reason for concern about the girls' silence is that they likely have something important to say and that the silence denies everyone the benefit of their insights.

Although there are at least two reasons for concern about the silence, they mandate considerably different institutional responses. There is a vast institutional difference between the right a person has to speak and the concern that a person be heard. The first is often therapeutic activity—an activity that is undertaken because of a personal deficiency and as a step on the way to something else. The second is a way to promote clarity and truth-seeking by assuring that as many different perspectives can be considered in a deliberation.

Philosophers of education have a stake in the way this distinction is developed because they are engaged in a practice that is centered on the improvement of educational institutions. And, while removing silences—whether for reasons of rights or for reasons of truth—is likely to improve the lives of children, education is advanced when the former also serves the latter.

An important feature about institutions and practices as far as Philosophy of Education is concerned is that they constrain discourse in certain ways that transcend simple logical possibilities. Discourse here entails intervention in ongoing activities. To become conscious of an institutional practice as a practice (rather than an unchangeable act of nature) is to force a decision about whether to endorse the practice through allowing things to be, or to intervene in a way that will change the practice. In the arena of Philosophy of Education arguments are framed within the context of existing practices and possibilities. Historical and social factors must be accounted for and taken into account. Here, ongoing practices exist in a way that constrains action and provides the framework for normative discourse. Philosophy of Education reflects on existing practices as they relate to schools or other educative institutions. Such reflection is most importantly about the aims of those institutions as they are embedded in practices.

5

A Role for Philosophy of Education in Intercultural Research

A Reexamination of the Relativism-Absolutism Debate

For the last few years, I have been examining the educational implications of a new Japanese-managed factory growing out of a cornfield in the Midwest. Because the study requires that I learn something about the characteristic responses of Japanese people, there are times when, like an anthropologist, I must announce my status as a novice learning about a new culture. Yet I am more than a novice learning about a new culture; I am also a novice learning about how to learn about a new culture. It is this learning that I want to consider. I want to ask how a person brought up in the web of understanding of one culture can incorporate the understandings and, if necessary, evaluate the practices of another culture. Hence, this article is not only about my own attempt to understand some aspects of Japanese society; it also is about my attempt to grasp how I am coming to understand Japanese society.

The project has also led me to consider the role of philosophy of education and its relation to other disciplines and other ways of knowing. In grappling with issues of intercultural understanding, I have come to a reconsideration of the role of philosophy of education. Here I undertake this reconsideration through an exploration of the issue of relativism and absolutism.

My Relativism-Absolutism Problem

In my study the issue of relativism has arisen in a number of ways. Take, for example, two of the most traditional parents in the study. When my Japanese translator and I interview the wife alone, she talks so much that we have difficulty interrupting her to ask a new question. Conversely, when we interview her husband alone, we are unable to elicit more than the briefest response. Yet, when they are together, and especially when they are with school authorities, he always initiates the conversation while she but nods her head in agreement with him. Moreover, when they walk, he always leads and she follows a few paces behind. Now if I were to ask them what all of this means, they would tell me that it is the wife's way of showing respect for her husband. Yet as a Westerner privileged to a politically progressive, rights-injected, individualistic view of human behavior, I know that this description is wrong. Subordination and domination is what is important here, not respect. If when I talk to the wife alone, she continues to insist that she is just showing her husband respect, my Western wisdom would let me know that we have here a rather serious case of false consciousness. The woman is accepting a subordinate status on the basis of ascribed characteristics alone. Yet is our Western wisdom really adequate to understand this non-Western convention? Their behavior is extreme for modern Japanese society, but it does represent an important feature of the role of women, which from an American point of view is quite properly described by the word *subordination*. In her book *Geisha*, Dalby mentions that, for the most part, young Japanese women are not encouraged to speak freely with men, and that Japanese wives are dependent on their husbands for their economic base.[1] Outside of the home, Japanese wives still have little independence and power, and there seems to be little ideological momentum for changing this. While Dalby attempts to place this position in a positive light by noting the unusual authority that Japanese women have within the home, she grants that it is not a role that would fit modern Western standards of liberation.[2]

The school provides another instance for viewing the problem of *cultural* relativism and absolutism. Recent critics of American schools have pointed enviously to the study habits and test scores of Japanese children. Yet the other side of this is that the Japanese child not only spends six days a week in school, but frequently studies for two or three more hours a day in a cram school to prepare for the high school or university entrance examination. Many children then return home to a private tutor. After the session with the tutor is over, they turn to their homework assignments. The primary reason for this effort is to gain access to a prestigious high school and university, thereby opening the doors to a job in a large corporation or a government agency. Those who pass the examination into prestigious universities receive a good deal of respect and are granted positions of high prestige and income. Yet even friendly critics of the Japanese system say that the examinations emphasize rote memory and a good deal of trivia. While *we* might question whether these are appropriate criteria on which to judge social worth, students who fail the exam tend to blame their own lack of effort. Perhaps the oddest thing about this struggle is that once entrance to the university has been attained, the competition is essentially over. As difficult as it is to gain access to a prestigious university, it is equally difficult to flunk out, and many students spend their years in the academy recuperating from the struggle that led to their acceptance.

Understanding Dependency in the Japanese Context

In observing these aspects of Japanese society, I am not at all confident of my ability to describe them. One of the ghosts in my machine, the philosopher wanting some basis for transcultural judgment, insists that these are examples of exploitation on the part of the successful and false consciousness on the part of the unsuccessful—at least among those who stand willing to accept their fate and blame themselves for it. People seem to be complying in the appropriation of their own labor against their own interest. Yet another ghost, the voice of anthropologist, whispers that descriptions like these are simply examples of Western chauvinism and of our, or my, inability to take other cultures on their own terms. The voice of the anthropologist grows even stronger when I begin to consider the writings of the noted Japanese psychoanalyst Takeo Doi in *The Anatomy of Dependency*. Using his own response to American society as a mirror to help him understand the Japanese concept of *amae*, Doi writes of his earliest experience in the United States:

> [One] thing that made me nervous, was the custom whereby an American host will ask a guest, before the meal, whether he would prefer a strong or a soft drink. Then, if the guest

asks for liquor, he will ask him whether, for example, he prefers scotch or bourbon. When the guest has made this decision, he next has to give instructions as to how much he wishes to drink, and how he wants it served. With the main meal, fortunately, one has only to eat what one is served, but once it is over, one has to choose whether to take coffee or tea and—in even greater detail—whether one wants it with sugar, and milk, and so on. I soon realized that this was only the American's way of showing politeness to his guest, but in my own mind, I had a strong feeling that I could not care less. What a lot of trivial choices they were obliging me to make—I sometimes felt—almost as though they were doing it to reassure themselves of their own freedom.[3]

Doi wrote this not as a Japanese anthropologist intent on throwing light on the strange customs of Americans, but as a psychiatrist working to uncover some of the deeper aspects of Japanese culture and personality. His own response to American society is to be taken as a mirror reflecting for him something that is a key to understanding Japanese society. The concept of *amae*, which the translator tells us refers to the feeling that all normal infants at the breast harbor toward the mother, is the key to this understanding. It is described as the "desire to be passively loved, the unwillingness to be separated from the warm mother-child circle." In short, *amae*, which Doi sees as a characteristic drive of Japanese personality, could be appropriately described as the quest for dependency.

Yet if Doi's reactions are key to understanding Japanese society, do they not also serve in a disturbing way as a key to understanding my own, characteristically American, reaction to Japanese society? If I want to judge what I see and hear as instances of subordination, domination, exploitation, and false consciousness, then have I not simply brought into play a Western standard of freedom and independence, one that may not be applicable to the Japanese?

Doi's work is frequently cited in commentaries on Japanese society and seems to be accepted by many experts both inside and outside of Japan. Yet one need not endorse Doi's understanding of Japanese society to see that the concept of *amae* provides us with an important specter for educational and philosophical thought. Suppose that there were a society like the one Doi seems to describe as Japan. Suppose that in this society a driving force was the individual's quest for dependency. Suppose that many of the words in this society indicated values that are familiar to us but that where our language gives a certain value concept a positive tinge, theirs would give it a negative one. Similarly, where a certain behavior, attitude, or practice would be described negatively in our language, it would carry positive overtones in theirs. Hence, for example, words like *manipulation, indoctrination, paternalism,* and so forth, all of which communicate to us an unwarranted infringement on liberty, would be seen by them as describing appropriate and possibly praiseworthy behavior. Similarly, words like *independent, autonomous, free choice,* and the like—words we take as describing highly regarded acts—would, in their culture, carry a hint of disapproval. Doi himself does not carry his analysis of Japanese culture this far. Moreover, while he does explore the various ways in which the Japanese language provides a positive indicator for the presence of *amae* and negative indicators for its absence, it is unlikely that English and Japanese map so directly onto one another that one would stand as a mirror image of the other. Yet we could imagine a people inspired by the slogan "inequality, paternity, and dependency."

I use words like *suppose* and *imagine* in the above passage because the ghost of the absolutist in me is whispering that freedom and independence are not just culturally specific values, and that I will not find the slogan "inequality, paternity, and dependency" any more likely to inspire a crowd of Japanese than it would a crowd of Americans. Yet again I hesitate, for even if the Japanese own concepts like domination, subordination, and exploitation, if Doi is right they surely do not apply them in the same way that I do. This hesitation, this thesis and antithesis without resolution, is a part of the problem I am trying to address. Why do I not play the role of the social scientist and get on with the task of defining, classifying, measuring, correlating, and reporting the behavior? If I did not think that there must be something wrong with the value system I hear Doi describing as belonging to the Japanese, I would not be hemming and hawing as I am. This hesitation, this hemming and hawing, may eventually lead to a new, perhaps a better, reading of Doi, but for now I want to try to follow the implications that the first reading holds for cultural understanding and to examine this reading in terms of the issue of cultural absolutism and cultural relativism.

Philosophical and Anthropological Commentaries

Traditional disciplinary stereotypes are useful in locating this issue as the conflict between philosophy and anthropology. Of course stereotypes are limited in value and these labels will not tell us anything about the arguments and commitments of particular anthropologists and particular philosophers. They do, however, point to the concern for capturing the texture of a culture, and for refusing to judge all societies by standards of so-called Western logic or morality that we find among many anthropologists. They capture too the concern to establish the legitimacy of a universal system of logic and moral principles, to reach for an Archimedean point by which to judge different social systems, which some philosophers have felt important.

MacIntyre's Refutation of Relativism

One of the latest attempts to defend the philosopher's point of view is to be found in MacIntyre's presidential address before the Eastern division of the American Philosophical Association (APA). MacIntyre raises the example of a person who is a full member of two premodern language systems as a way to illustrate the problem of transcultural evaluation. In this example, the language systems carry different and conflicting cosmological, psychological, social, and legal assumptions and hence, to choose between them, as MacIntyre's character must now do, is to choose between different ways of life and different ethical systems. The problem involves the dilemma of having to choose by employing standards and criteria that are implicit in one system but not the other and vice versa. Hence, without an alternative system, there is no possibility for a neutral and impartial decision.

MacIntyre tries to find a way out of the dilemma by suggesting the possibility of learning a third language, which, as he describes it, would be such that its "everyday use does not presuppose allegiance to either of the two rival sets of belief . . . or, indeed, so far as possible, to any other set of beliefs which might compete for allegiance with these two. And secondly, it must be able to provide the resources for an accurate representation of these two competing schemes of belief."[4] MacIntyre proposes that because modern languages developed out of the clash of different value systems, they thereby transcend the values and commitments embedded in any premodern system. They thus comprise good candidates for the neutral linguistic point of view. While MacIntyre ultimately rejects the view that modern languages can in fact transcend the kind of dilemma he depicts, he clearly leaves the impression that they do constitute an advance over the premodern systems between which his indecisive linguist is trying to select. In other words, the implication is that while his linguist is not able to choose among his original alternatives, by discovering a modern language, he has already transcended the need to choose.

According to MacIntyre, we transcend relativism because we are able, through a modern language and the form of rationality that it provides, to reflect on its possible inadequacy in a way that the primitive cannot. In other words, a tradition that can conceive of its own value in a relative way and holds out the possibility for its own replacement has transcended relativism.[5] Such, according to MacIntyre, is the tradition that we belong to. Because I am able to recognize that my own cultural tradition may meet its match someday in a superior tradition, I have thereby established, however temporary it may be, the superiority of my own tradition and have thereby transcended relativism.

However, even if we were to find that MacIntyre's characterization of language is correct, and even if we accept his view that a vision of a far, far better alternative than the one we know establishes the one we know as far better than all the windowless systems that have been, we are still left with a variant of the relativist's dilemma. To return to our original example, surely modern-day Japanese is not a primitive language. It has arisen from a number of different linguistic bases, and has developed a philosophical tradition. Clearly, many of those who speak Japanese are able to envisage a time when their own traditions may no longer work and must be transcended. Indeed, regarding this latter point, one might even say that with the massive and conscious transformation of Japanese society after World War II, such a transcendence was no longer just an abstract possibility. To generalize the point, if MacIntyre's transcendence works when we compare modern with primitive systems, it does not work when we compare modern systems with one another, and here the problem of relativism is still unsolved. Because MacIntyre is unable to address this problem, his approach remains, from a hard-liner's point of view, soft on relativism.

The Tangled Web of Relativism

The other side of this issue, the one provided by our stereotypical anthropologist, is no more satisfying than that offered by our stereotypical philosopher. This anthropologist takes caution too far and concludes that because all groups do not share the same values, there is no ground for comparison or judgment at all. In his study of the Ik, an impoverished people living in the mountains between Uganda, Sudan, and Kenya, Turnbull tends to take this course. In his preface, Turnbull warns against what he views as ethnocentrism.

> In what follows, there will be much to shock, and the reader will be tempted to say "how primitive . . . how savage . . . how disgusting" and above all, "how inhuman." The first judgments are typical of the kind of ethno and ego-centrism from which we can never quite escape, however much we try, and are little more than reaffirmations of standards that are different in circumstances that are different. But the latter judgement, "how inhuman," is of a different order and supposes that there are certain standards common to all humanity, certain values inherent in humanity itself, from which the people described in this book seem to depart in a most drastic manner.[6]

Turnbull rejects this idea of common human values and concludes his preface with a personal note that the study has "added to my respect for humanity and my hope that we who have been civilized into such empty beliefs as the essential beauty and goodness of humanity may discover ourselves before it is too late."[7] He then goes on to describe a people who, having lost their source of livelihood, their hunting grounds, have grown callous, neglectful, and sadistic. These people refuse to care for their own children, sending them out to fend for themselves after they are three years old, and they experience none of the expected feelings of loss or separation. If the child dies, there is no one to bury it, no one to cry, and no one to mourn. Those who are not clever and quick do die, usually from starvation. Turnbull thus describes a people who have lost their capacity for kindness, affection, compassion, hospitality, generosity, and industry. In his words, "The people were as unfriendly, uncharitable, inhospitable and generally mean as any people can be."[8] He explains this by remarking that these qualities are no longer functional for the Ik. They do not have the time for "such luxuries" and must employ more basic survival strategies.[9]

Yet Turnbull is really not able to maintain this strictly relativistic point of view and it is not difficult to read between the lines and feel his anger against an international system that, under the banner of progress, has wiped out the Ik's hunting ground, reducing them to their primitive, animal-like existence. He is quite explicit in warning that if progress is able to do this to the Ik, it may soon do the same to us.[10]

One may or may not agree with Turnbull that given the environment of the Ik, both their behavior and their values—or lack of values—are appropriate. Yet even if we agree that the behavior is appropriate to the environment, most people would want to add that the environment is inappropriate for any member of the human species. If what they want is what they get, then we need to question why they want in the way that they do. Indeed, given his own framework, Turnbull can see better than the Ik that behavior they take to be quite natural is in fact environmentally and ultimately politically generated. Without this insight, the Ik lack the intellectual resources needed to develop the desire to change their own behavior. Yet, given Turnbull's description, it would be a perfectly appropriate desire to develop.

If we are uneasy about using our own concepts and set of causal understandings to describe the Ik, it is because we are aware of the extent to which Western colonialism is responsible for their condition, and we do not wish to again impose an outsider's set of categories on them. Even though the modern concept of colonialism has now been infused with the understandings of oppressed peoples, however, the Ik, having lost their own history, are not likely to approach this explanation. Our uneasiness arises then not because we are torn between the Ik way of understanding and our own. It arises because we are caught between two different ways of understanding, each of which is familiar to us and apparently foreign to the Ik.

Exploitation or Western Chauvinism

Now why do I feel uncomfortable about providing the same kind of analysis of the Japanese treatment of women? Does it not warrant a judgment of exploitation, chauvinism, and false consciousness? I may not even have to stray too far from some internal Japanese interpretations in order to approach this judgment. Take, for example, Sawako Ariyoshi's *The Doctor's Wife*, a novel describing the struggle between a wife and a mother-in-law for the affection of a famous eighteenth-century Japanese doctor.[11] The novel appears to be an acknowledgement of the fact that the treatment of women in Japan is a simple case of exploitation. Moreover, the competition between the wife and the mother-in-law to sacrifice themselves in order to become guinea pigs for the famous doctor's dangerous experiments appears to be Ariyoshi's way of acknowledging the fact that false consciousness accompanies such exploitation. Perhaps, though, I am still reading the novel with my Western eyes. Perhaps Ariyoshi simply wants to valorize the largely overlooked role that women within the household played in the development of Japanese science and culture without conveying the larger ideological message about exploitation and false consciousness that my Western sensitivities insist on receiving. Indeed, my hesitation arises because of this concern that my search for general categories of judgment will lead me to overlook that which is specifically Japanese. My hesitation—that is, my straightforward, unphilosophical hesitation—reflects the currency that Japanese culture holds for an uninitiated Westerner. It reflects an awareness of the complexity and richness of Japanese art, language, industry, and tradition, and it expresses the concern that looking with a Western eye will leave little room for understanding the Japanese on their own terms.

Yet my philosophical reflection tells me that the fact that Japanese culture has a large amount of currency should not necessarily lead to the conclusion that exploitation is an inappropriate concept for understanding the treatment of women in Japanese society. My philosophical reflection warns me that I am in danger of justifying the means by its end, by some grand cultural bonanza of Kabuki and Toyotas. Nevertheless, Ariyoshi's novel is useful for understanding the source of my hesitation. It is not just the women's self-destructive competition for the admiration of the doctor and his aloof indifference that makes this novel interesting. It is also interesting because of the background knowledge that Dr. Seishu's experiments, around which the historical novel is developed, led to the use of anesthetics (fifty years before their use in Western medicine), opening up the possibility of treatment for breast cancer and other previously untreatable ailments. It is this kind of background knowledge that leads me not to discard the concepts of exploitation or false consciousness but to want to apply them with delicacy, care, and openness. It is this textual richness my anthropologist ghost fears the philosopher will overlook, but it is the possible injustice of the process that my philosopher ghost worries that the anthropologist will ignore.

The role of women in Japan, and the acceptance of that role by many men and women, is problematic to us precisely because of the awareness we have of the achievements of Japanese culture. We want to know how a culture *so* advanced on *so* many of our own scales understands itself when it departs from our notions of progressive behavior. Hence the label *exploitation*, because of its implications about independence, becomes a way of acknowledging a discrepancy in our perception of Japanese culture, while the concept of *amae*, because of its suggestion of connectedness and dependency, presents an opportunity to interrogate the concept of exploitation. Because the concept of exploitation implies a limitation on choice where one is forced to act in the service of another, it stands in a contrasting relationship to *amae*, where one expects the other to voluntarily act in one's own behalf. It is because of this expectation that the agents expect their own choices to be happily limited by another.

From outside of the debate, the contest between the anthropologist and the philosopher, between the relativist and the absolutist, is easily declared a draw. Philosophers will point to the anthropologist's inability to maintain a consistent relativistic standpoint. They will see the anthropologist's failure to acknowledge the problems involved in allowing two contradictory ethical judgments to be equally valid, to be further proof of the dogmatic character of the anthropologist's antidogmaticism. Similarly, the anthropologist will find the inability of the philosophical community to agree on a single system of ethics as further proof that all forms of absolutism are unstable.

To call the debate a draw will not, of course, bring the conflict to an end, but it can provide a somewhat different framework for approaching the issue of relativism. The debate has been cast within the framework of pure understanding, where issues are addressed as strategies in an argument, not as guidelines for action within a culture. In other words, practice is hypothetical practice brought in as a way to shoulder part of the burden of the argument for or against the relativist position. The anthropologist would rather not have to worry about seemingly clear instances of evil, a Hitler or Stalin, preferring Zunis and other small, isolated social groups, groups more often threatened than threatening. The philosopher is more likely to use examples about Hitler or Stalin in order to preserve concepts of good and evil without needing to add "evil from my culture's perspective" or "from their culture's point of view."

Nevertheless, despite the array of practical examples that relativists and their detractors bring to the argument, decisions about how to conduct practice are not the reason for the debate. The anthropologist wants to understand other cultures and, in doing so, clearly finds our own normative apparatus to be an impediment. The philosopher wants to understand the nature of normative principles and judgment, and, in doing so, finds our own normative intuitions tested by alien ones. True, the issue of cultural relativism is important to both of them, but not for the same reasons. It is the crossroad on which they meet while pursuing different objects of understanding. In both cases, however, the point of the debate is a question about understanding. In the one, it is a question of how we are to understand other cultures; in the other, it is a question of how we are to understand the normative claims of ethics, aesthetics, and the like.

Situations of practice, like educating, ground the issue of relativism around specific activities, not around global questions of the merits of one culture over another. In practical activity, we are not choosing among whole cultures, but rather are making selective decisions about certain aspects of a culture.

Relativism, Absolutism, and Practical Life

Philosophy of education involves reflection on the purposes and procedures of a practical activity and it has an interest in improving practice. Thus, philosophy of education alters the point of the debate. The question changes from how to understand, to how to act. With this question in mind, the philosopher of education recasts the debate between the pure philosopher and the anthropologists by examining the framework of practice and its characteristics.

To put the matter differently, within philosophy of education, the problem of cultural relativism arises when judgments about the appropriateness of a specific practice must be made, such as when two cultures are brought together and when members of one are given the task of instructing members of the other. The issue of relativism is taken as a *real* problem only when there is a belief in the value of the learning that is to form the object of the instruction and where there is a conflicting recognition that the student's culture is also viable and holds different values and beliefs. The issue arises when situations are encountered in which the values held by the two cultures are such that to teach an appreciation of the values and practices of one endangers the values and practices of the other, and where some set of values must be taught. Moreover, the condition for the recognition of the problem of relativism is a situation in which the teacher stands as a representative of one cultural traditional and the student stands in a different tradition, and where each tradition is held in reasonable regard.

For example, to some American teachers working with Japanese children in an American school, the analysis of *amae* provided by Doi would be disturbing because of two mandates that are said to be appropriate guides for the practice of teaching. The first obliges teachers to *respect* other cultures and accommodate the special needs of culturally different children. The second obliges them to develop in children the traits of independence and self-reliance, and to do so by allowing as much individual autonomy as is consistent with levels of maturity and classroom order. It is because Doi's analysis suggests that these goals may conflict, at least in the case of an American teacher and a Japanese child, that the issue of relativism becomes a felt problem for the teacher, and an appropriate issue for philosophy of education.

For the philosopher of education, the solution is to be found in neither the anthropologist's nor the philosopher's alternative. Teachers cannot put aside their own reflective categories in order to render equal respect to all cultures, and educational philosophers cannot assume some impossible standard of cultural neutrality in trying to evaluate the teaching act. Yet respect for members of other cultures will not allow us to assume that the values we just happen to learn in our own family, school, and community are the universal standard by which every other culture should be judged.

Practice belongs neither to the philosopher nor to the anthropologist. Philosophy of education requires a different approach to the issue of relativism. This approach takes the anthropologist's call for pure cultural understanding as an expression of the concern that cultural differences, if possible, be respected. It takes the philosopher's quest for absolutes as a concern to understand the basis for determining whether or how respect should be given in a specific instance. Because it is grounded in practice, philosophy of education requires an analysis of the different conditions in which respect is granted and the different forms that respect can take. What follows is an effort to provide such an analysis in the context of my recent experience with Japanese culture.

Forms of Respect

Within the context of practice, respect for other cultures may arise for different reasons and be expressed in different ways. First, I may respect a culture even though I realize that the life it represents is not one that I would recommend. My respect is given when I realize that this other culture supports a landscape of values I can understand and appreciate.

Laissez-Faire

In some cases respect may require that I take a laissez-faire attitude toward the education of children by the community. It may require that I stand aside and enable the community to establish the mechanisms for the perpetuation of its own form of life without interference from the outside. For example, when we respect the desire of the Amish to educate their own children, it is because we accept the values of care, craft, and devotion their way of life represents. We understand that while theirs is not the only way to express such values, it is an appropriate one. Yet we also recognize that theirs is a fragile culture, one easily endangered by the thunder of choices that our own life-style presents. In this situation respect requires that we allow the Amish to educate their own children knowing that some choices will not be offered and that some child's potential, as we judge potential, will not be fulfilled. Yet leaving them alone is, in this case, the most appropriate form of respect that we can give.

Respect as Constraint

There are other cases in which we may know very little about a culture, where we find the landscape of values hazy and difficult to discern yet still feel that respect is warranted. In this situation respect arises out of two considerations. The first involves a recognition of the importance of culture in the construction of identity and personality. The second involves a general understanding that some cultural practices are tied together in such a way that changing one may create disturbances among many, and it also involves an awareness of the fact that we do not know enough about *this* culture to identify its critical practices. In the absence of specific knowledge about a particular culture, the hesitation of teachers to interfere with specific cultural practices may be taken as a form of respect arising out of this more general knowledge about cultures as such. For example, teachers working with children from certain Native American groups are sometimes told not to demand that the children look them in the eye, since the children's culture takes this as a sign of disrespect, not honesty. When the teachers agree to adjust their practice so as not to interfere with this cultural norm, it is likely that they do so because of their general understanding about the relationship between personality formation and culture. In this case respect takes the form of a constraint that the culture places on the teaching act. The teachers adapt their practice so as not to interfere with certain cultural norms. This is different, however, from cases in which the values of the culture determine the goals and content of instruction, or where the role of the teacher is, as with Freire's pedagogy, to help give voice to the culture. In one, respect involves a constraint on the teaching act. In the other, respect serves to determine how to constitute the teaching act.

Respect as Cultural Encounter

Our encounter with *amae* is different from these other situations. When we decide to leave a culture alone to educate its own children or when we allow another's cultural norms to constrain our own behavior as teachers, we need not doubt the value of our own conception of education. The issue with *amae*, however, is not whether we should act to effect our understanding of good education. Nor is the issue whether we should impose our norms on a culture that we know little about. Rather the issue is what we are to take as constituting a sound and reasonable notion of personhood and thereby of education. As we examine the process through which this issue is encountered, a third form of respect becomes apparent—one that places many of our own cultural values under scrutiny.

Because we already hold Japanese art, industry, language, and tradition in generally high regard and because our reading of Doi suggests that our two societies hold such radically different conceptions of the good, we may feel a need for a radical act of self-reflection, one that makes problematic our own values of individuality and independence. Yet these values serve as the foundation for many of our own most basic understandings and judgments, and to question them requires that we challenge more about our own form of life than just our appraisal of Japanese culture and personality. It would require, for example, a reappraisal of many of our taken-for-granted judgments about rights and personhood. Moreover, since these values are themselves the foundation of our judgments, we would seem to lack a platform from which to examine them. It is wiser to begin our reconsideration by focusing on a feature of our judgment that is more self-contained. We would do better to begin by questioning our interpretation of Doi's treatment of *amae* rather than puzzling about the value of our own standards.

Some misreading of Doi's concept of *amae* actually does seem likely. I have tended to interpret *amae* on a political plane paralleling and contradicting our ideas of freedom, autonomy, and independence. Yet on reconsideration this reading seems inappropriate. It is unlikely that we would find in Japan the cultural evidence that would support the view that dependency is a political quest of the Japanese. No serious political party will truly advance itself on a slogan calling for "inequality, dependency, and paternity." No cultural critic will write a book lamenting the escape from dependency. No children will appeal to their inherent right to be dominated by their parents and no newspaper will chide politicians for failing to consistently manipulate the population. The idea that we are working with a political concept does not make sense. There is no network of social or political activity—no easily projected expectations that could be observed in Japan—that would serve to support this view. Dependency cannot be a political quest in Japan in the way that freedom is seen as a political quest in the United States.

To understand the concept we would do well to remember that Doi is a psychoanalyst, not a political theorist, and remembering this we might do well to restrict our thinking about *amae* to the interpersonal realm, to view *amae* as a drive, a fundamental motor force of behavior in the way that Freud understood libidinal forces. If this is the proper view of *amae*, then there may well be a connection between it and other forms of dependency. However, rather than viewing the connection in terms of a denial of freedom, we now should perhaps come to view it in terms of the overarching trust that we might place in someone who we believe will always act out of care and concern for our own well-being. *Amae* would then be understood not in terms of a negation of a goal such as freedom, but rather as an assertion of a relationship of care. When we know that someone cares for us completely, we need not deny our freedom, but we may feel no need to affirm it in order to assure ourselves that we still hold on to it. We may even reveal our childlike qualities of playfulness and irresponsibility with the understanding that, at least in this setting, we will still be accepted. This interpretation seems consistent with Doi's reaction when he thought that perhaps his American hosts provided so many trivial choices in order to assure themselves of their own freedom. Perhaps when *amae* prevails, such continuous assurance is not required.

If *amae* is to be understood as a basic psychological drive, then we should be able to find a sensible connection with our own experience, our own wants and longings. When we do touch base with the concept of *amae*, we will do so, as Doi suggests in his critique of Western psychoanalysis, by announcing needs that we feel but often fail to acknowledge.

Yet, if we have gone this far in our reinterpretation of the concept of *amae*, and if we have found something promising in Doi's critique of Western psychoanalysis, will we still be able to hold on to our own standards of judgment? Is interpretation the only issue that is at stake? Here it seems to me that respect takes a different turn. As we explore the meaning of *amae*, our own values become vulnerable to interrogation. Doi provides not only a critique of psychoanalysis as it developed in the West, but also an implicit critique of the ideal of independence that serves as the telos of the psychoanalytic process—as the goal, as psychoanalysis sees it, for all normal forms of development. Doi speaks of the overemphasis in psychoanalysis on self-reliance and of the indifference he noticed among analysts toward their patients' sense of helplessness. He speaks of Freud's neglect of expressions of infantile desire for love and attachment. He mentions the distortions that arise in understanding when the foundation for identity is located in the separation associated with the Oedipus complex while overlooking the need for tenderness and the quest for attachment that precede it. If we were to succeed in developing our own sense of *amae*, then we would become sensitive to features in our own culture that facilitate or block its expression, and when these were absent, we might find ourselves appealing to the need for *amae* in the same way that we appeal to freedom or equality. In this case, *amae* would serve to challenge some of the standards we use for judging normal development.

The case I have just elaborated provides a third way of thinking about respect. Unlike the situation where the other culture served to constrain the teacher's behavior, here the other serves as an active guide to a newly constituted behavior. Moreover, we can use the concept of *amae* to help us see some aspects of Japanese education that are often overlooked by Western observers. The gentle relationship between Japanese adults and children, along with the sense of mutual caring and responsibility that teachers in Japan develop with some success among young children, become perhaps more important than the high test scores of Japanese children. These new observations may become important in reformulating our own conception of teaching.

It is ironic that as we elaborate the concept of *amae*, finding new interpretive ground on which to build our understanding of Japanese society, we come close to one aspect of Western feminism. That is, we approach those forms of feminism that have stressed a philosophy of care. Yet it is still difficult to ignore an important difference between the two, for along with a philosophy of care is feminism's insistence that the public realm be open to all and that the role of caretaker no longer be distributed on a gender-specific basis. To hold on to this principle is to open the door to a political analysis of the role of the Japanese household in supporting their corporate economy. Of course, the way the conflict between care and opportunity is resolved in each society will become the material out of which new patterns of identity will evolve.

It is in this kind of encounter between cultures that a third form of respect emerges. Here the other serves to reflect one's own interpretations and standards, providing a foundation for reconsidering the commitments and goals of the educational process itself. It is not the mimicking of the other that this third form aspires to nor is it the molding of the other according to one's own norms. Rather, each provides for the other a reflective moment on which conceptions of education can continue to develop. In these moments philosophy of education can articulate the notions of personhood involved in different educational practices, and it can provide the conceptual material needed to consider new and emerging identities.

Acknowledgments

Appreciation is expressed to Charles Blatz, Eric Bredo, Cheiko Fons, Reiko Hattori, Taiji Hotta, Frank Margonis, Ralph Page, Alan Peshkin, to the students in my research seminar on Japanese education, and to the students and faculty of the Philosophy of Education discussion group at the University of Illinois. This research has been aided by the Japan/U.S. Friendship Commission and the University of Illinois, College of Education, the Bureau of Educational Research, the Department of Education Policy Studies, and the University of Illinois Research Board, as well as by an International Program and Studies Hewlett Grant. This was presented as the Philosophy of Education Society presidential address for 1989.

6

Critical Pragmatist and the Reconnection of Science and Values in Educational Research

Meaning and Nonsense: A Review of the Basic Tenets of Positivism

A brief review of the familiar idea of positivism and post positivist revisions will help to ground my argument. For the positivist there are but two types of meaningful statements. Those called "analytic" are true (or false) by virtue of conformity (or non-conformity) to a definition. "One plus one equals two" and "all bachelors are unmarried men" are common examples of analytic statements. Those called synthetic or empirical statements are those that are true (or false) by virtue of conformity (or non-conformity) to experience. "There is one bachelor in this room" and "The Chinese population is over a billion people" are both synthetic statements. For the positivist therefore scientific statements are a form of empirical claim and as such they need to be verified, in principle, by some directly observable or some inferred event that is directly observable. There are differences within positivism about the status of the object of knowledge and whether scientific claims actually mirror reality, or simply record information and try to describe patterns. By allowing only empirical and analytic statements to be meaningful it discounts value claims relegating them to what it would call *mere* preferences—like whether you prefer chocolate to vanilla—or to ejaculatory sounds like a sigh or a chuckle. They are like the kind of noise that people make when they are perhaps overly stimulated. In a clever play on words these are labeled "non sense"—signifying both meaningless gibberish and assertions that have no sense content.

Post Positivism

Many post-positivists agree with the critics of classical positivism that the claims that propositions are meaningful only if they can be subject to verification through experience, is too strict and too neat. Too neat because as Imre Lakatos (Lakatos 1970) has shown, scientists will often protect their pet but immature and potentially productive theories like a hawk protects her immature chicks, using non-rational as well as rational weapons to ward off real threats. For Lakatos the emotional element has an important function in enabling new theories to develop while they are young and vulnerable to criticism by older, more established ones. Traditional positivism is also too strict because as Quine (Quine 1953) has nicely shown, any theoretical claim, even those of logic and math, is always open to challenge. For Quine this also holds even for direct observation, like pointing (Quine 1960, 1–26).

The recent history of philosophy of science has been one of relaxing the standard of what is to count as science, first from the idea of verification advanced by A. J. Ayer (Ayer 1936), to the notion of falsification provided by Popper (Popper 1959), to the notion of the progressive nature of an overall research program as developed by Lakatos (Lakatos 1970). The affinity of each of these approaches is that they focus on the activity that occurs in the laboratory or in the field and they model the scientific enterprise in general after a certain image they have of physics (Habermas 1971). And, much like the earlier positivists, they discount the place of values in science, as anything but motivational.[1]

Because historically positivists tend to see physics as the quintessential science it has developed a reputation for preferring physics-like research. Controlled field experiments along with statistical analysis and probability statements are thought to be as close as one can get to the certainty of physics. Economics and some forms of psychology such as behaviorism have been favored as close to the real thing, while much of anthropology has been dismissed as not scientific enough. Yet this is somewhat arbitrary, and much that appears as scientific in the social science has a peculiar self-confirming quality (Chomsky 1959). Some are concerned that to take physics as the model of science and apply it to the human sciences must leave out much that is unique to human beings.

Positivism and Pragmatism on Science

As a way of understanding science, positivism has a number of competitors, of which pragmatism is one. Yet pragmatism would find much that is useful in randomized field study and quantitative analysis. It is useful to recall that John Dewey often saw the social sciences as an immature science where he saw the natural sciences as already developed (LW 12). While this observation could have many different implications it is most likely that a pragmatist like Dewey would applaud the appropriate use of randomized field experiments. However, he would contextualize them within a value infused understanding of the world.

The quarrel between positivism and pragmatism is not over the usefulness of certain methods. It is about whether it is reasonable to determine the appropriate method independently of the problem it intends to address. For someone like Dewey, positivists are too restrictive in this matter and too willing to prescribe beforehand what can and what cannot be counted as good science (LW 13).

An important element of that quarrel is about the role of values in research and whether values claims can be addressed in rational and objective ways. For the pragmatist the positivist's understanding of value claims as meaningless or as ejaculatory utterances is a big mistake. As Dewey nicely points out, even an ejaculatory utterance like child's cry has meaning and demands a response. Hence it cannot simply be dismissed by reclassifying as nonsense (LW 13). To put this somewhat differently, a positivist and a pragmatist may find themselves at some stage of a project recommending the use of a randomized field study. However, they will likely differ, as I will show shortly, over what should come before and after the randomized aspect of the study, in how the terms are defined and how the findings are reported.

Values and the Relationship Between the Researcher and the Researched

To be anti-positivist in the pragmatic sense is then not to be against field studies or measurement, or zealously for qualitative research. It is simply to calibrate the research enterprise in a different way by being more open to the interplay between valuing and knowing, between reporting and measuring. This involves a self-reflective understanding of the way different ways of reporting data can influence subsequent behavior.

The image of the relationship between researcher and researched, or in Dewey's terms, the knower and the known (LW 16), is not one of distance and detachment where the knower, as Nagel describes it, surveys the known from the point of view of nowhere (Nagel 1986), and where description has no influence on the behavior of the described. For the pragmatist this self-reflection about values is a critical part of the research enterprise, especially where social research is concerned. Knower and the known are interconnected, and values influence the definition of initial concepts, the methods selected to investigate problems and the language used to report results. A community of inquirers is important to pragmatists not just to verify conclusions but also to enable researchers to become self-conscious about their own values and how they influence the research process. Historically, pragmatists like James and Dewey have embraced the potential of a variety of methods of inquiry.

An Example of the Implications of Positivism and Pragmatism for an Important Contemporary Educational Issue

A few years ago the city of Chicago initiated a policy that requires public schools be closed if their students' tests scores fall below a set minimum for a certain number of years. When they are closed the students are sent to other schools with different teachers and administrators. This policy is in line with the Federal guidelines mandated in the No Child Left Behind legislation first initiated during the Bush administration. The assumption driving this policy is that poor test scores mean poor teaching and that poor teaching signals inadequate administration (de la Torre and Gwynne 2009).[2] However there is an additional story that needs to be told.

As more schools closed, student violence, including murder, increased. Local activists, including some teachers, believed that there was a connection between the closing of schools and the increase in violence. They pointed out that the effect of the policy was to mix together students from rival gangs in the same schools and it required that more students walk to school and cross rival gang territory. The increase in violence has not just impacted gang members. Non-gang members and even honor students have been attacked and some killed. These activists believe that the initial policy wrongly assumed poor test scores necessarily means poor schools, and that the side effects of school closing were never fully thought out.

The activist's concern is about policy, but it has even wider implications about the conception of research that supports the policy. Given that statistical studies have alerted the community to the increase in the murder rate, the problem is not with statistics as such, but with the way values were incorporated into the research project to begin with and with the failure to consider local definitions of a "good school." Most likely safety would have been quite high on any local person's list of the qualities of a good school.

For the pragmatist the definition of a good research must take into account different kinds of values and different levels of understandings, local as well as bureaucratic ones. Unlike some critics of testing and randomized controlled experiments as such pragmatists would not a-priori reject the use of standardized tests in large school systems. Many pragmatists would allow that well designed tests could serve as one important reporting tool among others. However, the pragmatist would be reluctant to allow tests scores alone to define what it means to be a good or a failing school. Pragmatism's commitment to a communal approach would lead it to endorse a consultative research process to define and address educational needs.

For the pragmatists both local and expert understandings are important. Local agents add depth to the understanding of a particular school and its environment; experts provides context showing, for example, how one school compares to others in certain kinds of environments. Chicago is now working to incorporate these two forms of understanding as experts work to identify more closely students who are at risk for violent engagement and as community members employ their understanding to try to reduce that risk.

The Calibration of Facts and Values in Research

The radical fact/value dichotomy proposed by positivism is problematic for the pragmatist to the extent that it dismisses discussions about values as meaningless, or to the extent that it allows some values to dominate the discourse by passing as "facts."

Consider, for example, the difference between a research question that asks about the death rate in Nanking in 1938 and another that asks about the murder rate in the same place during the same time. Researchers can answer both questions in ways that accurately meet the positivist standard, but one requires a much fuller understanding of the situation than the other.[3]

The real danger of the positivist fact value/dichotomy is not that it rids education of values, but that it creates a value vacuum, which is likely to be filled by unquestioned procedures that automatically determine the fate of a school community. The effect is to reproduce the values of the most dominant groups, and help their values masquerade as facts. An example would be the way IQ tests are normed to produce a Bell Curve and thereby create tests that always rank people as smart and stupid according to that same curve, albeit now expressed in numbers, hence reinforcing the impression that intelligence is a linear, one dimensional product.

To be against positivism in a pragmatic way is not to be against testing and measurement. It is to be concerned about narrowly calibrating the researchers' radar so that some reasonable concerns are excluded as "*just* opinions" and others are allowed to pass by as *hard* "fact," subject neither to challenge nor inquiry. In contrast Pragmatism, especially of the more critical kind, allows that fact are vested with values and potentially can always be deconstructed and the values they conceal can be unveiled and re-evaluated in light of new considerations.

For the positivist good educational research requires that researchers restrict themselves to what are assumed to be testable tasks, such as determining ways to increase the rate of growth of human capital development. Under this conception philosophy is limited to policing research so as to determine in this narrow sense whether or not it is scientific. If its claim can be empirically tested it is scientific, and it is "good science" if the conclusions are verified or falsified by the well-structured experiments or observations. Here the critical distinction is believed to be between the refined knowledge of the expert and the unrefined understandings and values of local actors. But this distinction can create problems.

For the pragmatist the problem with "experts" occurs when they assume that they know the *problem* better and in the same way as those experiencing it. For the pragmatist the subject has a special relation to the problem that should not be ignored. To take a simple example, a person knows his or her own tooth ache in a special way even if she does not know what caused it or what can cure it. For the expert to dismiss this knowledge as unimportant is to dismiss the subject as emotionally impulsive, narrowly self-interested or conflicted with other subjects. This in turn creates a view for the subject of the experts as cold, unengaged, and ignorant about local needs and concerns. For the pragmatist, given these different relations to the experience, there is a need for collaboration in defining a problematic situation and addressing it.

For the pragmatist, good educational research arises out of human needs and serves to improve the conditions of real people. One of the tests of good research is whether it takes into account a wide range of values and whether it ultimately serves both to improve the situations of people and to provide them with the intellectual tools to help them reflect on their own interests and to address their own future need. This entails the following starting points:

1. Value claims are not meaningless.

2. Local understanding may be incomplete but not inherently defective.

3. Conflicting value claims can productively be viewed as an invitation to a conversation and the beginning of an inquiry.

4. Expert knowledge can enhance that inquiry.

5. Education as the transfer of the means for continuing growth and development is at the heart of good educational research.

6. The inquiry process should leave those affected in a better condition to handle their own future difficulties.

While pragmatism acknowledges that specialists have developed methods of refining knowledge, it also allows that local actors enjoy a privileged position in terms of the depth of experience. Yet without the other both may lack the conceptual tools required for changing the situation for the better. Local actors may have the insights but lack the wider perspective and the tools that long lasting change requires. Experts may have the tools but lack the local insight needed to apply them effectively.

Specialized methods can be especially helpful when local understandings are unclear, when conflicting interests block further inquiry, or when there is an inadequate understanding of the wider context or historical factors that favor one view over others. They can also be helpful when conventional power and status gets in the way of inquiry. In these cases experts can be helpful in opening up paths for new experiences by generating new understandings. Local understandings are critical, however, in locating problematic situations, developing working hypotheses, defining initial terms and judging the adequacy of general solutions for individual cases. They are also important in exposing the prejudice or unacknowledged interests of the expert.

Two Other Alternatives: Absolutism and Relativism

Two other alternatives vie with pragmatism in the modern world. The first is absolutism as represented in the richly textured, highly nuanced, but often confused work of Alasdair MacIntyre who seeks resolution to value conflicts by appealing to the Aristotelian and neo-Thomism traditions. The second is neo-relativism often associated with post-modernism. MacIntyre (MacIntyre 1981) rejects positivism and allows, with pragmatism, that values are to be taken seriously. He holds that value expressions are meaningful because they are connected to a certain kind of practice like science, art, sports, family life, etc., and as such, they are verifiable. For example, given a knowledge of a practice, say like basketball, we have little trouble identifying a good defense from a mediocre or poor ones. Hence, once we understand a practice and the tradition in which it is embedded, we should have little difficulty appraising value judgments about that practice. However, although MacIntyre often implies that some traditions are more worthy than others, he offers few tools through which a tradition can be critically examined, save through its capacity to resolve internal contradictions. Yet, very complex, rich traditions are likely to have significant contradictions whereas some simpler, yet shallow traditions may be free of contradictions.

MacIntyre's model depends on a radical separation between different traditions, and only when contradictions can no longer be resolved can a tradition be evaluated. In contrast pragmatism is willing to acknowledge that the world is often messy and solutions to problems may be partial, at best. MacIntyre's is a neat and tidy world where we should always know, at least in theory, just what practice we are engaged in, what tradition it is a part of and what standards should be used in judging its performance. In real life, however, there is often uncertainty about what kind of practice we are engaged in and what tradition it belongs. Pragmatism is able to acknowledge this fact: MacIntyre is not.

Any parent who has had to confront a conflict between the responsibility to their children and their responsibility to their job runs into the same issue on a personal level. What practice am I engaged in—worker or parent? And to what tradition do I belong? Under one tradition a mother should not even be working and thus should feel extra guilt if she has a job outside the home. Under another, as a woman she should have the same right to employment as a man and thus is justified in feeling extra resentment if she is denied this right just because she is a mother. MacIntyre writes as if he has answers to these predicaments, but he does not. He simply fails to acknowledge the push and pull of different roles and the overlapping of different traditions and presupposes a coherent, settled, isolated tradition as the norm.

The failure to provide a convincing account of absolutism is relevant for the assessment of pragmatism. Because pragmatists reject absolutism in its various forms, it is thought that it must embrace an arbitrary relativism where power and wit determine what can pass for truth. The critics however fail to distinguish here between truth with a small "t" and Absolute Truth with a capital "T" where the term carries with it a kind of divinely guaranteed certainty.[4]

For the pragmatist a true claim is one that stands up to rigorous tests and has the status of a warranted assertion. Certainly some future test may come along that *de-warrants* the assertion, but this only calls into question whether any reasonably justified claim to truth is immune from modification. It does not equate warranted claims with arbitrary claims that people accept simply because they are forced or tricked into doing so. Indeed, one of the main goals of Dewey's philosophy of education and its emphasis on science and experience was to create a population that would guard against the acceptance of arbitrary claims. Sometimes neo-pragmatists like Richard Rorty have fueled this criticism with quips like: "Truth is what our peers will, ceteris paribus, let us get away with saying" (quoted in Bredo 2009, 442), but the broader import of this for most pragmatists, including Rorty, is that our understanding of truth is always subject to revision.

For the pragmatist the emphasis is on truth (small "t") as an instrument for engaging the world. We understand the limits of our truth claims not just through the way others respond but also as the world pushed back to tell them and us "you do not have it quite right." Other people are an important part of this but they are not the only part. Often when they reject our truth claims it is because they quite rightly see just how firmly the physical and social environments are pushing back. Rorty does not miss this point, and when he does acknowledge it, his pragmatism seems in evidence.

Experience, not guile, is the arbiter. For Dewey and for Peirce when the world pushes back it helps us to decide whether a belief should continue to serve as a guide to action. This is why for Dewey, "true" and "false" are not quite the right terms. Rather a claim is "warranted" or not depending on whether it seems a sound guide for action. Whatever our motives for affirming a claim, it may be status, stubbornness or power, the verification of the claim—however tentative—will depend on the evidence available to support it, and the role it plays in developing possibilities for new experience. T (t)ruth, including moral truth, is prospective for pragmatists and grows.

Moral Invention: An Example

There are many examples of the way in which moral knowledge grows but the debate over euthanasia can serve as a brief example. Here one side holds that mercy killing is murder, clear and simple, while the other believes that intense and chronic suffering justifies aiding a person in accomplishing a self-willed death and that not to allow it is simple cruelty. Some traditions, including Catholicism, have helped lay the ground work for a partial reconciliation of these views by drawing a distinction between taking active steps to *kill* someone, such as administering poison, on the one hand, and *letting a person die*, by say removing life support systems, on the other. While this moral invention certainly does not solve all the issues regarding mercy killing, it does help in those cases where patients need life support systems if they are to continue living.

Another moral invention along this line has been developed in response to an ever-improving capacity to enable vital organs such as the heart and lung to continue functioning by mechanical means. Here a refinement of the concept of death allows that a person may be declared dead if there is no brain activity even if other vital organs, such as the lungs and heart are still functioning. In these cases the pragmatist joins with the absolutist in seeking a resolution that is respectful of the traditional view, but she joins with the relativist in providing more flexible interpretations of established dogma. Sometimes these innovations come from within a tradition as, for example, when the Catholic Church decided that not all lending was usury and redefined the concept as human exploitation in general (Feinberg 2006). At other times the innovation may be initiated from outside a tradition in response to some general need. A good moral invention is a way of resolving the absolutism of tradition with the flexibility of relativism. Of course invention does not always end controversy, but it points in a productive direction that allows apparently dead ends to be reviewed for possible paths of escape.

The Pragmatism and Values: Or, How Does the Chicken Get Across the Road?

There is a famous paradox by the ancient Greek philosopher Zeno that describes the plight of a chicken that is trying to cross a road. According to Zeno, before the chicken can get across the road she must cross the halfway point and before reaching the halfway point, she must cross the halfway point to that point and so on. Since there is always a new halfway point the only conclusion that we can draw is that the chicken could never begin to cross the road. Now, ask a pragmatist to solve the paradox and the answer to how the chicken could even cross the road likely will be a rather simple: "one step at a time and with an occasional forward flutter."

Just as this response dismisses the problem as a mere exercise for formal logicians and beginning philosophy students to puzzle about, the pragmatist would provide a similar response to the positivists' understanding of value claims. Chickens have no problem crossing roads (assuming no traffic) and people have no problem understanding and coming to terms with value claims, assuming sufficient information and an openness to the possibility that, under certain circumstances, they may have to revise their own standpoint.

The interesting things about values are the ways people argue about them, explain why they believe one to be better than another, and arrange their lives according to them. Not only that. They also test their goodness. There's a prospective aspect here that checks desire as, for example, when someone asks: "Is my desire for cigarettes good for me?" Surely value claims are not meaningless. People fight, negotiate, compromise over and cooperate through them all the time. So, if positivists can't find an appropriate way to understand the significance of values other than dismissing them as a modern version of Zeno's paradox, then so much the worse for positivism.

The pragmatist is more in tune with intuition and everyday practice than the positivist, more open to judgment of better and worse than the relativist, and more willing to eschew the ideal for the acceptable than the absolutist. In the abstract of course there is nothing about the logic of this response that must convince the positivist, except that it speaks to life; not simply to logic.

Pragmatism rejects the fact/value dichotomy as an artificial ontological distinction. Facts without human interest do not have a reality of their own. Facts are the outcomes of inquiries. No inquirers, no facts. And values do not exist independent of the means to realize them. Hence, it is an illusion to speak of either fact or value independent of human interest and it is also an illusion to hold the view of many religions that there is some ultimate end to human life above and beyond the strivings of human beings.

Essences, even in MacIntyre's watered down formulation as virtues inherent in a practice, simply do not exist, except as constructed through and by human experience and reflection. Virtue is a socially approved quality of human activity as refined over time; and "tradition" is simply a shorthand way of describing the codification of these virtues across generations of human beings. To reify tradition in the way that MacIntyre does is to obscure the fact that any one person may shape their life within, across or beyond recognizable traditions. It also leads us to look backwards rather than forwards and to assume that the tried and true is always best even when new experiences are encountered. In doing so MacIntyre's absolutism ignores the fact that some forms of conduct viewed now as virtuous may be subject to radical revision in the future.

In contrast, for the pragmatist, the requirements of even a simple virtue like honesty change depending on circumstances. Honesty requires one thing when, say, deciding whether to tell the clerk he has given you too much change when you are right in the store. It requires another if you notice the small amount of extra change after driving miles to your home. A virtue like honesty also requires discretion in when it should be applied. If your uncle tells you that he really wants your honest opinion about the poem he has just composed it may not always be the best course to tell him that you think it should be shredded and burned, even though you do think it should be shredded and burned.

Values in Science

Pragmatists reject the radical positivist idea of value-free science and point to various ways values interpenetrate science. On a practical level value issues are present in critical debates about what kind of science will be funded. Will it be big science that requires billions of dollars to build say a huge particle accelerator, or small science that requires say a few thousand dollars to investigate many different projects, say like the health issues in fast food consumption?

On the theoretical level values are involved in decisions about which theories to adopt. For example at the time in which the heliocentric theory of the universe was first proposed and until Newton developed his theory of gravitation, there were serious problems that the heliocentric theory could not adequately address. Perhaps the most embarrassing was the question of why the earth did not lose its atmosphere as it traveled around the sun? This problem simply did not exist under the earth-centered theory where the earth stood still. Moreover, the earth-centered theory was able to explain many of the successful predictions first proposed by the heliocentric one. Ultimately the latter was accepted not just because of Newton's answer to the puzzle about the atmosphere, or because the heliocentric theory could not provide explanations for the newly observed celestial phenomena, but also because it was a simpler theory, one that was more aesthetically pleasing. It also proved more productive as well. This meant that it was able to generate new and confirmable predictions and not just to explain them after they were confirmed.

Values also enter into science whenever a decision is made about how to define or classify something. Water is H_2O only when it enters into experiments or other similar activity. Otherwise it is a thirst quencher, vodka chaser, or drought stopper. Values are even more obviously implicated in social "facts." It makes a big difference whether the study of group behavior is called a "crowd" or a "mob." These differences may go quite deep into the foundational logic of science, complicating something as fundamental as the identity principle, A=A. Take the following example, which counters both the logic of identity and the positivist's definition of analytic as true by virtue of definition.

Premise:

Major premise: all bachelors are unmarried (true by definition).

Minor premise: all the men in car A are married (empirical claim).

Identity qualifier: all men in car A are the same men as in car B.

Question: are all the men in car B married?

Answer: no, because car A was in Massachusetts, which recognizes same sex marriage, and car B crossed the state line into Rhode Island where same sex marriage is not recognized. Now clearly clever logicians can neaten this so that the apparent inconsistency disappears, but in doing so they must acknowledge the value-laden feature of a factual claim like "there are six married men in this car."

On the Objectivity of Values

One of the intuitive appeals of the positivist understanding of the relationship between facts and values is the view that facts are simply out there to be discovered and therefore are essentially objective whereas values are somewhere in-here—in my heart or in my mind—and are thus inherently subjective.[5] Further it is thought that when we decide something on the basis of *the facts of the case* we are being fair, whereas when we decide matters on the basis of values we are deciding matters subjectively and hence we are *arbitrary*. Hilary Putnam, a modern pragmatist, rejects these associations (Putnam 2002). First, he rejects the out-there-ness of facts and the in-here-ness of values.[6] Second, he rejects the essential objectivity of facts and the essential subjectivity of values and third he rejects the distinction drawn between factual judgments as fair and value judgments as arbitrary.

Because Putnam is one of the most logically sophisticated contemporary pragmatists, it is worth spending a moment examining his position. Putnam lists some of the value norms that go into deciding the worth of a scientific theory. These include: epistemological norms used in judging the merit of scientific theory such as coherence, consistency and the like; aesthetic norms such as simplicity, the beauty of theory and its internal perfection. There are also moral norms that determine whether a scientific experiment is worth performing no matter how much knowledge it yields.[7]

Social science often conceals moral judgment by re-labeling common sense terms. Intelligence becomes "IQ," punishment becomes "negative reinforcement" and reward is transformed into "positive reinforcement." To the extent that this relabeling allows for a reasonable and systematic reconstruction of common sense understandings it can be very important.

However, to the extent that it rejects common sense experience it can be destructive.

For Dewey and Putnam labels such as "cruel," "just," or "brave" have an objective standing in that they appeal to evaluative standards as developed and shaped through the needs and common sense understanding of a community. In that sense an observer could take a sample of behaviors that the community labels brave and provide a reasonable reconstruction of what these standards are and how they are applied. Moreover judgments of standards change depending upon changes in the environmental, the social conditions, and are influenced by the development of new knowledge and understandings, an insight which is at the foundation of many important novels (Coetze 2000; Ishiguro 1989).[8]

One of the mistakes the positivist makes involves an unstated assumption that when something is rational and objective it must result in agreement (Dewey himself sometimes fell into this position, especially when extolling the virtues of "the scientific method"). This is the basis of the positivist's mistrust of value disputes as meaningless.

For Putnam value differences and moral commitments are rational not when they insist on agreement but when they leave an opening for repudiation. For example, if someone is committed to justice and equality but then always acts in ways that benefit her own race, then she needs to re-examine what she means by justice.

For Putnam, we do not need agreement to live in same moral world but we do need to respect differences. For Dewey there was a slightly different emphasis to the objectivity of values. He believed that ultimately coordination of action—both on the individual level, as I coordinate my hand with my mouth when I eat, and on the social level, as individuals coordinate with one another in pulling on a heavy object with a rope,—would serve as a measure of value. Yet the more prominent side of Dewey is quite consistent with Putnam. For both of them values become *valuable* through a process of criticism and evaluation (LW 13). For both the emphasis is more on process than product, more on ends in view rather than ultimate ends.

To the positivist the researcher is thus like a neutral umpire who just calls things as they are. For Putnam the relationship is more complex and values inform the research process at every stage. For example, values may indicate what the researcher counts as successful intervention. In medical research, for example, what to count as a cure may be different depending on the age of the patient. For older men with prostate cancer, medicine that slows the progression rate in half may be as good as surgery which removes the prostate all together. If not a cure in some conventional sense such medicine might be preferred to surgery, considering side effects and estimated longevity. Here "cure" may be defined either in terms of eliminating the cancer or improving quality of life.

Values also enter the picture in determining the appropriate restraints on scientific studies. The famous Milgram (Milgram 1963) experiments at Yale that tested people's willingness to obey authority, even when doing so went against their own conscience, came under heavy criticism for deception and for placing the subjects under severe stress. This criticism was one of the motivations for the development of a new moral invention, the requirement of informed consent, where researchers have to explain the level of danger or stress that subjects might experience and get their written consent to perform the experiment.

In addition values enter into scientific work in decisions about threshold levels. For example, one of the factors involved in the Challenger space probe failure which killed all aboard was the way the company, Morton Thiokol, in cooperation with the space agency set the burden of proof. At the time, the burden was placed on those engineers who thought a launch was unsafe. They had to prove *their* case. Since the O rings had never been tested under the exceptionally cold temperature expected for the launch no one could say for certain what would happen to them, and so the mission was launched. An alternative threshold would have required the burden of proof be placed on those who thought that it was safe to launch. If this could not be shown then the mission would have to have been postponed but lives saved (Davis 1998).[9]

Neo Positivists and Pragmatists on the Calibration of the Fact/Value Continuum

Neo positivists would likely have little problem acknowledging that values do in fact play these roles in research but would then argue that there is a line between science and non-science and when values enter the picture the line has been crossed. However, for the pragmatist, this is less a problem of demarcation, as the post-positivists would call it, and more an issue of calibration. The model advanced by positivists calibrates the research enterprise in a way that defocuses attention from value concerns as if they were not really important for the conduct of science. Questions like "who is framing the problem?" and "who is defining the terms?" are not easily placed inside the post-positivist's radar, and hence there is little inclination to examine the goodness of the initial frames and definitions. This results in part from equating rational deliberation with empirical, testable studies, and then joining with the relativist in allowing that all else is opinion. Of course there is a legitimate concern behind this, one shared by pragmatists as well, that the researcher's private values not drive the findings of the research. There is good reason to distrust the tobacco company "scientists" who, on the basis of a missing chemical link between smoking and cancer, declared cigarettes had not been shown to be unsafe.

For the pragmatist the argument about whether values belong in science is unproductive. Rather research needs to be calibrated so as to provide room for exploring the implications for human well being. The researcher should be open to inquiring into the consequences of a certain way of framing a problem and to the benefits one or another way of framing can provide for different groups. The fact that this calibration entails valuation does not require that values override science, say in some Lysenko-like program. It simply means that pragmatism opens up value claims to rational deliberation.

While pragmatism is friendly to experimental and statistical research, it calibrates its idea of good research in a way that can capture the unstated values that implicitly drive the conducting and reporting of research findings. And part of the job of pragmatism is to then open up these values for inspection and to engage people in discussions about them. That specialized experts have a crucial role in research goes without saying (LW 2), but the fact that values are embedded in different aspects of a research project means that there is considerable room for local actors to interrogate the findings. One of the functions of scientific and professional education for the critical pragmatist is to teach researchers how to be mindful of value issues and how to engage the public in productive discussions regarding the value implications of their work.

Pragmatism certainly endorses the usefulness of statistical and experimental research. For example this research has been invaluable in understanding the importance of class size on the improvement of reading in the United States (Mosteller and Boruch 2002). Yet when used alone and without the insight of practitioners it is limited in understanding why this is the case. In some instances these factors may be fairly obvious.

Smaller classes mean that teachers can spend more time with each student and can isolate and treat his or her specific problem. Sometime this may be quite simple. A youngster who had trouble keeping up with the class in singing from a written songbook may have only to be shown that in Western music the convention of reading stanzas of songs differs from the convention of reading lines in a storybook.

Sometimes a problematic educational situation is more complex, as revealed for example in the studies of Ray McDermott (McDermott 1993) who, through hours of recording classrooms and observing video tapes, shows how a teacher and the poorest reader in the class unconsciously work together in a kind of dance that assures the student is never embarrassed by being called upon to read, but also assures that she is never taught how to read. As a pragmatist would point out, tests may be useful in helping to determine the reading level of a child, but McDermott's research shows other issues that may need to be addressed if reading is to improve. For a pragmatist research methods are tools. The best methods are those most likely to help understand and address the problem at hand.

One of the important contributions of pragmatism is to connect science to common sense to refined methods of inquiry. As Dewey wrote in his *Logic*: "Scientific subject matter and procedures grow out of the direct problems and methods of common sense, of practical uses and enjoyments, and react into the latter in a way that enormously refines, expands and liberates the contents and the agencies at the disposal of common sense" (LW 2, 71–72). Science then adds to common sense by opening up new ways to understand relationships and possibilities. It expands judgment based on previously constricted experience and provides new tools that aid thought and action.

Consider, for example, the simple but obvious ways in which common sense grows. Take the historical evolution of a *common sense of* direction from pointing; to "here/there"; to "left/right/front/back"; to "North/South/East/West"; to "degrees of longitude and latitude"; to the technology of triangulation used in global positioning systems or the directional instruments and concepts used in space travel. Each stage has expanded the possibilities for navigation and an early advance becomes the common sense of a new one. As science moves beyond the latest innovative sense of direction and it gets reincorporated back into a new and expanded common sense of direction. The old sense is not discarded—we still point and we still say "here" and "there"—but is rather augmented. Even astronauts in space with the most advanced navigational equipment at their fingertips will still *point* to a wrench and say "See that over there. Could you bring it here?" The big insight of pragmatism then is that science creates new conceptual and technical instruments that can then serve to liberate common sense, not trespass over it.

The Contribution of Critical Pragmatism

Critical pragmatism allows that everyday understanding is sometimes inadequate *in defining* a situation as problematic, especially in cases where power or experience is unequal. Here common sense may simply accept the situation as a fact of life. In these cases critical pragmatism encourages a dialogue between refined research and everyday understanding about the systematic silences that often mark subordinate or oppressed status.

Critical pragmatism thus supplements traditional pragmatism by highlighting those situations of inequality where local understandings may be systematically silenced or unrecognized. This means a greater sensitivity to the historical relations between groups where unequal power or experience results in the domination and systematic silencing of the one by the other. Here the primary need is not to resolve a predefined problematic situation—in Dewey's terms—but rather to provide discursive structures that will give voice to the dominated group, thereby enabling its members to *identify* certain situations as problematic. For example, feminist researchers have observed classes in which girls are called upon much less frequently than boys, partly because boys raise their hands more often and more vigorously than girls. One practical suggestion has been for teachers to wait longer before calling on a student and to encourage girls to speak out.

For the critical pragmatist the goal is not to police research so as to purify it from value claims, as the positivist would do. Nor is it just to link research to common sense understanding. It is to also give expression to those private, isolated, serially undergone experiences of marginalized group members by exploring the historical inequities that render them publicly inexpressible and unrecognized. This requires familiarity with the conditions that silence some people as well as of the potential avenues and organizations that can give them voice. Critical pragmatism is aligned with traditional pragmatism and especially with the ideas of Dewey, but whereas Dewey starts inquiry with recognition of a problematic situation the critical pragmatism may begin an inquiry with the awareness that oppressive social structures can sometimes silence the expression of values or render their expression incoherent or inappropriate. This was often the case with adolescents where their emerging individual sexuality was often unacknowledged by schools, leaving many teenagers to feel isolated and perverse.

The awareness of the unarticulated aspects of problematic situations brings with it a consciousness of the significance of subgroup identities, or, of groups of people, whether minorities, teenagers, women, gays or bisexuals, who share common yet unarticulated needs. This recognition is one of the important distinguishing factors between traditional and critical pragmatism.

Historically in the United States much of the traditional pragmatist's early educational efforts involved the inclusion of *individuals* through assimilation and an educational process that sometimes involved disengaging the individual from a subgroup identity (Feinberg 1975). Today much of the effort of critical pragmatism involves increasing the recognition of oppressed groups and their members, with considerably less emphasis on assimilation (Glaude Jr.). Nevertheless, in contrast to the positivists who tend to dismiss value claims as meaningless or redundant, pragmatists, both traditional and critical, see differences in value utterances and conflicts as an invitation to a conversation and inquiry. In this sense, value differences for the pragmatist are not to be dismissed as matters of opinion with the conclusion that they are not subject to inquiry, but as moments for pause, and humility in the awareness that other forms of life and other modes of reason are valued.

Critical pragmatism is concerned with repressed needs and silences resulting from systematic, long-standing and severe inequalities. Like traditional pragmatism it acknowledges the link between local experience and refined knowledge but it takes one step back from the traditional pragmatist and wants to know how each is constructed, especially in situations of systematic, historically generated political, social and economic inequality.

Critical pragmatism allows that there are situations where inequality has been so ubiquitous that it has been bred into common sense understandings at all levels and that here there is a strong disconnect between the local experience of inequality and its local expression. In these cases, critical pragmatism looks for the silences that block expression and analyzes the history of common sense and its construction in order to understand how it serves to perpetuate systematic inequality. In these cases philosophy can help educators become aware of ways that they unreflectively endorse values of inequality. And it can help researchers understand how they can serve to develop new understandings. Its goal is to enhance critical reflection within the arena of common sense, and to use this understanding to develop new research projects.

Critical pragmatism needs to be distinguished from critical theory in its various Continental forms. It does not assume, for example, the hermeneutics of suspicion, typical of the French theorists like Foucault (Foucault 1965, 1970) or Bourdieu (Bourdieu and Passeron 1977);[10] nor does it assume a priori that one form of ideal discourse fits all, as with Habermas (Habermas 1968). Critical pragmatism is open to whether there is a problem that needs to be addressed and it is also open regarding what might count as a reasonable resolution of that problem. It does not begin by assuming, as dogmatic followers of Freire do, that oppression is at the basis of all educational differences, although sometimes oppression is indeed the critical factor. Nor does it begin with the belief that all problems can be reduced to distortions in communication, although this too is sometimes the source of the problem. Nor, on the other side, does it assume that the problem must lie with unmotivated students, incompetent teachers or unresponsive bureaucrats. Yet to find out just where the problem and its source(s) lie, it must often interrupt common sense and the self-understanding that goes along with it.

Interrupting Common Sense Logic

Common sense is the shared understanding that peoples have of everyday situations, the default logic appropriated to support it, and the judgments that issue from it. Often common sense is articulated in brief exchanges that virtually everyone accepts as true, and that at the same time reinforces the conditions required to sustain it as true. One example would be girls who were discouraged from becoming doctors, until the feminist movement began to challenge certain stereotypes.

Very often this was done with the best interest of the student in mind and with an eye to "reality" as defined by the existing situation. Women were not doctors. Few applied and few medical schools accepted them. Some girls who might have wished to be medical doctors bowed to reality and altered their expectations to fit it. The common sense understanding here was that women could not enter medicine and that few girls would want to do so anyway.

Today, when there is about an equal number of women and men graduating from medical school in the United States, the lie has been given to that common sense understanding. To change the earlier situation the critical pragmatist would not have social science build on existing common sense but would need to critically deconstruct it, showing how the mutually supporting standpoints result in perpetuating an existing but taken for granted inequality. Consider the following example that would have been common up until a couple of decades ago:

GIRL: I want to be a doctor, what courses do I need to take?

MIDDLE SCHOOL TEACHER: There are good careers in nursing or occupational therapy. I would not advise medicine.

GIRL TO PARENTS: Ms Jones says I should be a nurse rather than a doctor

PARENT: That is a good idea

GIRL: Ok, I wonder what I have to do to become a nurse.

The decision of the girl to change career goal would have been practical one, given a reality constructed through existing common sense, and the fact that medical colleges were reluctant to admit women and few women practiced medicine. However, given the fact that medicine was, for all practical purposes, closed to talented women existing common sense was also a violation of a basic principle of democracy, i.e., equal opportunity. Given too that certain medical conditions are experienced exclusively or more commonly by women, and that male doctors and researchers were often insensitive to them, existing common sense also had the real consequence of limiting understanding on female health issues.

Nevertheless there was a very clear logic that supported the existing situation. The logic was predicated on a strong division of labor where women were supposed to marry and raise children and men were supposed to work outside the home and have careers.

Medical schools hence felt that an expensive medical education for women would be a poor long-term social investment. And women who looked at medical schools found that indeed, almost all the students were men. So what was the use of applying? And if one was not going to apply why take all those chemistry and math courses, etc.

Given these expectations a certain reinforcing logic developed with the result that few women applied to medical school and very, very few were accepted. From the standpoint of any key stakeholder in the process this result was not only sensible, in the way in which common sense is sensible, it was challenged very infrequently and mostly in private. It made sense because of a series of interlocking syllogisms, where, whether accurate or not, one could have the best interest of girls in mind and still support the existing situation. Yet because the situation is self reinforcing, because it violates the ideal of equal opportunity, because it risks poorer health care for women, and because the doctor/nurse relationship mirrors the dominance of men over women, there was good reason to interrupt this reinforcing logic and explore the openings for change.

Intervention involved both understanding the different common sense logics and some of the more subtle ways in which they mutually reinforced each other. Suppose, for example, the intervention on behalf of women was to be led by a male doctor. Here the very relation of dominance that the reform was intended to challenge would be reinforced. Hence, critical pragmatism must not only be aware of the goodness of a reform and the common sense logic that may retard it, it also must be aware of the process used to implement it and to determine its direction. In many cases this means that sympathetic members of a dominant group must step to the side, providing needed service but not leadership, as the reform is developing.

The Pragmatic Temperament

In reconnecting science and values it is useful to think of pragmatism not as a set of fixed principles, but as a certain kind of temperament. This pragmatic temperament calibrates the scope of rational discourse and appraisal to include values and, in contrast to positivism, seeks to connect science to common sense as it works to refine each of them. To do this, the pragmatic temperament is skeptical of the positivist claim that values are *simply* individual preferences and instead it understands differences about values as an invitation to a conversation. This invitation holds out the possibility that values can be rationally considered and objectively appraised (LW 13). To say that a value claim is objective means that it meets the following conditions as suggested by Elizabeth Anderson:

- There is a sincere acknowledgement of possibility of error and possibility of changing minds, including one's own.
- Authority to give reasons is granted to the different claimants.
- Claims by the same party do not contradict one another, and when they do it calls for critical self-reflection. Each party is willing to apply critical reasoning to their own proposals as well as to those of others.
- There is good faith effort to seek a common point of agreement from which justification can proceed.
- There is openness to the introduction of novel considerations as reasons (Anderson 1993).

Conclusion

A value claim does more than simply express an opinion or a subjective desire, as the positivists believe. It directs attention: "Look at the sunset!" It makes a promise: "There is something worth seeing." It affirms a hypothetical basis for agreement, and it proposes approaches for living together even in midst of disagreement. The pragmatic approach to value emphasizes conversation and a mutual effort to convert by reason—not by force or violence. Given its understanding of values, pragmatism views research as both value infused and value concerned. The role of the researcher is to enrich the experience of the researched. Critical pragmatism adds the requirement of critical self-reflection and the engagement of others in jointly defining the problem and closing the gap between the researcher and the researched. The pragmatic temperament when applied to education would bring local understanding in conversation with expert knowledge allowing that the latter serves as an instrument to enrich the experience of the former.

Acknowledgments

My appreciation to the Spencer Foundation for supporting this project, to Fudan University for inviting me to lecture on this topic, to Denis Phillips for his comments on positivism and to Eric Bredo for his very comprehensive and insightful critique of an earlier draft.

7

The Conflict Between Intelligence and Community in Dewey's Educational Philosophy

For those who would allow prescriptive utterances to be candidates for philosophical statements, there remains the question of the criteria by which such utterances are to be judged. Some would insist that it is unfair to judge them on the basis of their ability to find implementation in practice. This point of view, like Plato's defense of his *Republic*, argues that an ideal, as an ideal, must not be judged by whether someone has seen fit to implement it, but rather on the consistency of its own logic. The argument has its share of validity. Mankind has probably been worse off because of the successful implementation of some ideas and better off because of the failure of others. Nevertheless the failure of a theory to find embodiment in fact, ought to be a clue that the theory has not taken all of the contingencies into account and even though such a failure can only tell us *that* something is wrong, it may also initiate an investigation which will eventually reveal *what* is wrong.

Those philosophers, Dewey among them, who have accepted the historical criterion as a factor in the validation of a theory, have implicitly placed their own theories under that same criterion. We begin then with history as the partial judge of philosophy and we begin also with the observation that the program Dewey laid down in *School and Society*, *The Child and the Curriculum* and *Democracy and Education* have yet to take effect on a wide scale in American education. It would of course be possible to turn our criticism in the other direction marking for scorn those who did not see the promise which the limited application of his ideas did raise and therefore, those who did not choose to apply them.

We prefer, however, to discover why these ideas did not speak to such people in the first place, and why men of practice, men confronted with the demands of expediency and reared to a consciousness which Dewey was trying to change, have not been able to take his suggestions seriously. Our examination, therefore, is to turn not on the practitioners, but on the suggestions.

Two concepts central to Dewey's educational philosophy are the concept of intelligence and the concept of community. He believed that the method of intelligence ought to be applied to the problems of community, but it is exactly this application which we find missing in American education. Where we find intelligence, we rarely find community and where we do happen to find community, we do not find intelligence. The discrepancy arises from the fact that while Dewey has been quite clear about what he believes education should be, the reasons for this belief have not been sufficient to convince those who are not predisposed to agree with him.

The problem for Dewey arises from the fact that he is never completely clear about the place intelligence serves in valuation. The crucial question is whether he believes that all values are to be determined by the method of evaluation, which is the application of the method of intelligence to the problems of human values, or whether the method itself ultimately rests upon an assumed set of values which determine its proper direction and use. Although it is clear in Dewey's writing that he did wish intelligence to enrich community, it is not always clear why it should be used in this way. Because of this ambiguity, educators have been able to take whatever side of the equation expediency dictated and sometimes, of course, they have taken neither intelligence nor community.

One of the defining characteristics of community, for Dewey, is a concern for "common problem (a problem arises when an experience is disrupted)." Intelligence is hopefully an adjunct of this concern, but it is not necessarily implied by it. Thus the method of intelligence can, to some degree, exist independently of such concern. If it is agreed that the method can be used to solve "common problems," then there ought to be some way to identify problems which are common, but here Dewey's clarity fails him. There are at least two possible ways in which this term may be understood. It might mean that there has been a mutual recognition by two or more persons that the experience of one of them has been disrupted. Or, it could mean that the experience of two or more persons has been disrupted and that there is a common factor which is identifiable as the cause of that disruption. Whether we take the first or the second meaning, we shall see in neither any necessary warrant for a mutual concern.

Suppose, as an example of the first meaning, that an old man, too sick to work and too poor to feed himself, seeks help from a neighbor and is told, "*You* have a problem." There has been a mutual recognition that a problem exists, but it would seem, at least in this example, that mutual recognition must be distinguished from mutual concern. Suppose again that the old man dies and that his former neighbor continues to live a prosperous and happy life, seemingly unaffected by the event. If this situation were to be judged strictly in terms of methodology, it might be supposed that after a serious investigation, the neighbor decided quite properly not to recognize the problem as common and hence not to enter into a special relationship with the old man. Perhaps he made a detailed assessment of his immediate enjoyments, of their conditions and their consequences (as Dewey would have him do), surveyed the effects of his own dispositions upon one another and decided that the continuation of this man's misery in no way affected his own reassessed values. Hence, it would seem that even Dewey would have to agree that there was no need for this man to enter into a social relationship with the other. Now, if it is objected, as Dewey might, that all human relationships are social ones, it is likely that the objection would be met with the qualified agreement that while this is certainly true, the kind of social relationship that had been established, made it in no way mandatory or beneficial to change the nature of that relationship by extending help.

Dewey probably believed, and rightly so, that if he could show that value statements could be verified, then it would follow that there were such things as common problems. Dewey's *Theory of Valuation* is an attempt to show just that. To him, value expressions are not, as Stevenson would have it, just subjective expressions of feelings or attitudes, but are signs that have to do with "the behavioral relation of one person to another . . . they say something and are of the nature of propositions."[1] He takes the case of a person calling "fire" or "help" as an example of someone trying to influence the behavior of others and he writes that when this cry is analyzed, it means: "(i) that there exists a situation that will have obnoxious consequences (ii) that the person uttering the expression is unable to cope with the situation; and (iii) that an improved situation is anticipated in case the assistance of others is obtained."[2] He then writes that: "There are thus involved (i) aversion to an existing situation and attraction toward a prospective possible situation and (ii) a specifiable arid testable relationship between the latter as an end and certain activities as a means for accomplishing it."[3]

Before we accept Dewey's analysis here, it is important for us to understand just what is testable in this situation and what is not. Dewey moves from the assumption that we can test the means necessary to end the existing situation, to the further assumption that we can also test whether this situation ought to be mutually undesirable. This movement cannot be justified. Heretics at the stake must have called to their persecutors for help. The indifference that these cries met resulted only from the feeling that what was a problem to one person was the solution to a problem for another. Again, there is no need to suppose that the consequences of this indifference had not been appraised and accepted. Dewey's analysis of verification here rests upon the assumption of the existence of common problems, unfortunately it does not prove that assumption.

It is precisely the notion that methodology can tell us not only how to solve problems, but also which problems are common and which are not that leads to a confusion concerning the source of values. The reliance on methodology arose because of Dewey's desire to avoid first the position which reduces values to subjective feelings and attitudes and second the position which holds values to be completely objective having an existence independently of being valued. Dewey believed that these two extremes could be reconciled by a closer inspection of the process of valuations. He noted that ends arise and take on value only when a particular activity has been blocked, but when an activity is moving along smoothly, we do not stop to appraise it. Hence the desirable can only arise out of a reappraisal of the desired. It is still not clear, however, whether Dewey believed that the function of valuation is merely to reinstate an activity, the direction of which has been blocked, or whether there are for him some kinds of activities which are potentially more desirable than others. If the latter is the case, then it is again not clear whether these activities might be desirable independently of being desired. On the one hand, Dewey believed that valuation does arise out of an unsettled situation where activity and satisfaction have been blocked and ends when the activity has been reinstated. On the other hand, he does demand that many situations which are unsettled or unsatisfactory for one person must in some way be accepted as problematic by and for another. This, for him, is the condition of community.

The Conflict Between Intelligence and Community | 125

This latter demand constitutes the major difficulty for Dewey's ethical theory because it cannot be supported by his notion of the desirable. Why should a person who believes that he has nothing to gain choose to recognize the problem of another as his own and why should he believe that the solution to such a problem is desirable for him? Does Dewey wish to say that the absence of mutual recognition is, itself, a problem? But for whom? Is indifference (the absence of desire) undesirable? The issue can be seen more clearly by looking at Dewey's views on the origin of desire. He writes in *The Theory of Valuation* that: "Desires arise only when 'there is something the matter,' when there is some 'trouble' in an existing situation. When analyzed, this 'something the matter' is found to spring from the fact that there is something lacking, wanting, in the existing situation as it stands, an absence which produces conflict in the elements that do exist. When things are going completely smooth, desires do not arise."[4] It is important to emphasize the fact that when Dewey says that desires arise only when there is something lacking in the existing situation, he is not speaking of any metaphysical privation, but rather of a specific situation in which activity has been disrupted by an extraneous event. When such a disruption does occur, then an end is projected which attempts to re-establish and redirect activity.

Let us return for a moment to the case of the sick and hungry man in order to see how the foregoing analysis would apply and whether we might now be able to find here a *common* problem. Certainly we can say that the normal activity of the hungry man has been disrupted and that he seeks help in order to reinstate that activity. If his neighbor had been reading a book just before his doorbell rang, it might be said that his activity has also been disrupted as he rises to greet the unfortunate fellow. In a sense then, it could be said that the problem of one has become the problem of the other. However, there is a certain ambiguity in this last statement. The problems are not exactly the same. Even though there is a common, identifiable factor, namely the poor man's need, this factor does not occur to both men in the same way. For the hungry man, his need is an uncompromisable factor in his problem; it is his problem. There may be a number of ways to satisfy his need, but the solution to his problem rests solely upon that satisfaction. Now for his neighbor, the need is the occasion for his problem but it is not necessarily the essential factor in its solution. He might indeed choose to accept the man's problem as his own and exert a great energy in its solution, but then again, he might not. It is entirely possible that after weighing the energy involved in helping the man, against that involved in shutting the door, he might decide to ignore the appeal and return to his book. Only in the first instance can we say that the problem has resulted in a mutual concern. In the second, neither the disruption of experience nor the mutual recognition of a common factor has resulted in that concern.

There is another distasteful possibility. Dewey does admit that an activity is sometimes disrupted without a definite desire being formed. "When someone finds that his foot has been stepped on, he is likely to react with a push to get rid of the offending element. He does not stop to form a definite desire and set up an end to be reached."[5] It is certainly not beyond the realm of possibility that a man could react to another man's request for help in the same way and with the same degree of awareness as he might, had the man just stepped on his foot. Of course it might be said that there is a problem with insensitivity, but since this is a problem which does not necessarily invoke a desire, it is questionable whether sensitivity can, for this person, be said to be desirable.

The ambiguity is itself the result of two conflicting desires held by Dewey. On the one hand he wants man to be responsible to man, but on the other he wants a man's values to be connected with a man's desires. Yet there is no reason why responsibility to other men must result from a careful reassessment of desires. Dewey fails to bring his desire for responsibility together with his method for determining the object of responsibility. His problem is complicated by the fact that the use of his method always issues out of the activity of an individual's experience and that it is the immediate enjoyments of this experience that must be coordinated if they are to qualify as values. It is not clear, however, why one person should be obliged to recognize other persons as anything more than mere means to the attainment of his own refined values.

It is more than obvious that Dewey did not desire that his method be interpreted in a narrow way. He did not see it as merely a means to already pre-established ends, but rather as a way to re-evaluate old ends and to create new ones. Yet even if we do accept this interpretation, the question remains whether the method, as Dewey sees it, might not rest upon certain value assumptions which are themselves unquestioned and absolute. What evidence could intelligence possibly yield which would lead Dewey to give up democracy and community as values?

The issue is whether or not all values are possible subjects for examination by the method of valuation, or whether the application of this method (at least by Dewey) is limited, defined and directed by certain unexamined desires. Although Dewey's answer is again not as clear as it might be, it is evident that if he wanted intelligence to rest upon a foundation of democracy, community and shared experience. He also wanted his method to be able to demonstrate that these were values which were intelligent. In order to support this latter point, much of his social philosophy was designed to show that scientific knowledge of evolution, of man and of society presents democracy and community as values to rational man.

One of Dewey's most influential arguments for social responsibility appeared in his book, *Individualism Old and New*, partially as a response to the depression. Here Dewey argues against the kind of individualism which measures worth by profit, and for a society based upon shared experience and joint participation in the making of goals. He argues that new conditions have made the old individualism obsolete:

> Certain changes do not go backwards. Those who have enjoyed high wages and a higher standard of consumption will not be content to return to a lower level. A new condition has been created with which we shall have to reckon constantly in the future. Depressions and slumps will come, but they can never be treated in the casual and fatalistic way in which they have been accepted in the past. They will appear abnormal instead of normal, and society, including the industrial captains, will have to assume a responsibility from which it and they were previously exempt.[6]

Even though the depression itself was a testimony to the soundness of Dewey's statement, there is still a certain degree of vagueness beclouding the idea of social responsibility. For while it is true that an industrialist (to use Dewey's example) would be foolish if he did not take the activity of others into account in planning his own, it is not at all clear why he must, or should encourage the participation of others in his own planning. Yet such participation is the condition which Dewey sets as essential for the realization of community. Certainly the industrialist might agree that there are times when his own self-interest can best be accomplished by allowing a large degree of participation, but then there are other times when it cannot.

For most people, Dewey's example is persuasive. Depressions are bad things and more careful planning (and control) should be taken to avoid them. Yet his example might not be convincing to all. A few people have been able to use depressions to increase their own well-being. Planning and foresight have often been employed for purely selfish ends and for those who have employed them successfully the question is whether there is any good reason why they should not continue to do so. This difficulty can only be resolved if we are willing to make a distinction between that which the capitalist desires and that which can be called a value. In order to do this we must return to Dewey's treatment of the relation between the two.

Dewey's major arguments in *The Theory of Valuation* are directed against the idea that value expressions are merely ejaculatory, that is, that they are merely expressions of feelings or desires. It is directed against the view that the objects of these statements are not capable of empirical investigation. Thus, Dewey rejects the *complete* identification of the desired with the desirable. For him, there is a distinction between these two and the distinction is made in the following way.

> Every person in the degree in which he is capable of learning from experience draws a distinction between what is desired and what is desirable, whenever he engages in formation and choice of competing desires and interests. . . . The contrast referred to is simply that between the object of a desire as it first presents itself (because of the existing mechanism of impulses and habits) and the object of desire which emerges as a revision of the first-appearing impulse, after the latter is critically judged in reference to the conditions which will decide the actual result.[7]

While Dewey is not willing to accept the idea that every desire is desirable, he does seem to suggest that everything which is desirable is desired; i.e., "the contrast referred to is simply that between the object of a desire as it first presents itself . . . and the object of desire which emerges as a revision of the first-appearing impulse, after the latter is critically judged." Whether the kind of dependence that Dewey establishes between the desirable and the desired can deal adequately with all value issues remains doubtful for it would seem that there are some things which are desirable but are not desired.

Dewey's difficulty is partially the result of an inadequate treatment of activity and especially of activity as it involves a lack. For him, lack is used to suggest a disruption of activity and to describe part of a process through which thought is initiated and activity reinstated. Dewey's error lies in the fact that he has confused two things which ought not to have been confused and it is this confusion which makes it very difficult for him to bring together his concept of value with his concept of social responsibility. He has confused the conscious awareness of a lack with the existence of a lack. It is probably correct to say that one usually does become aware of a lack when an on-going activity has been disrupted. It may also be correct to say that at that moment, thought is initiated and ends projected so that activity may be resumed. But lack and activity are not incompatible concepts. Bad men are bad not because they fail to act but because of the *way* they act, not because they do not experience lacks but because they do not perceive the lacks which are important, or at least they are not perceived as lacks. Dewey always uses the word "lack" to describe the disruption of a specific activity by a specific event in a specific situation, and it is precisely this usage which reduces the strength of his own social recommendations. There is, however, another way in which we can look at the concept of lack and it must be said that Dewey does begin to do so (at least implicitly) in his treatment of the ends-means relationship. Although this treatment only hints at a new way to look at this concept it nevertheless, does hint.

Since Dewey believes that ends are chosen in order to resume and redirect activity, he also believes that any meaningful evaluation of possible objects of enjoyment, or of projected ends must also include an evaluation of the means needed to achieve those ends. The life we live is lived with both means and ends; to sacrifice one blindly in order to achieve the other is to sacrifice part of that life. It is, therefore, a mistake to make a strict separation between means and ends for means are suffered and enjoyed as well as used and ends, once achieved, serve as means through which other ends are attained. Such separations do occur when means are looked at as necessary evils in the achievement of a given end:

> Means that do not become constituent elements of the very ends or consequences they produce form what are called "necessary evils," their necessity being relative to the existing state of knowledge and art. They are comparable to scaffoldings that had to be later torn down, but which were necessary in erection of buildings until elevators were introduced. The latter remained for use in the buildings erected and were employed

as means of transporting materials that in turn became an integral part of the building.[8]

Yet the meaning of Dewey's insistence that ends and means hold together is not always the same. Sometimes, as in the above passage, it seems to be a prescription which says that when the end is realized, the means are actually present in it. At other times it seems merely to suggest that an evaluation of the end must include an evaluation of the means and that therefore the acceptance of the end must include the acceptance of the means. Contained in the latter interpretation is the notion that choosing an end necessarily involves the choosing of means to go with that end.[9]

It must be understood that these two statements *are not* necessarily the same. To determine an end by a consideration of the means needed to realize it is not to say that the means remain when the end is realized. Even to include in the evaluation of an end the evaluation of the means is not to say that those means will be included in the realized end. When an end is achieved, the means, as valuable as they might have been (both as means and on their own account), are often left behind. There are of course some examples which can be cited in which the means do become part of the end and do in fact determine the nature of that end. The example Dewey sometimes uses of the bricks and the house does illustrate the point, but the significance of that point is lost; brick houses are brick houses, wooden chairs are wooden chairs, steel bridges are steel bridges. Certainly we might call the matter which goes into the makeup of a thing a means which is included in the end, but these are never the only means involved. There are always some means which are included in the end and some which are not.

There is one other factor which Dewey might well admit but which is important for further discussion. There is nothing inherently valuable about the unity of ends and means as such. There is, however, something valuable when both are used to serve an important function well. A wooden bridge is not to be valued when a steel one is needed.

The preceding discussion leads us to ask whether there is any end which carries its means with it as an inevitable part of its makeup. If we consider a human being in his totality, then there is a sense in which it can be said that he does carry the means of his making with him into every situation. There is perhaps nothing very controversial about this idea and it is in fact one which Dewey himself proposes in his treatment of the notion of character: "If an act were connected with other acts merely in the way in which the flame of a match is connected with an explosion of gunpowder, there would be action but not conduct. But our actions not only lead up to other actions which follow as their efforts, but they also leave an enduring impress on the one who performs them, strengthening and weakening permanent tendencies to act."[10] Since there is no way in which we can call back an act performed or decide beforehand that this act will have nothing to do with the character of this self, since every act leaves its traces in the self, strengthening some tendencies, weakening others, the nature of the self is determined by these acts. In a very real sense, the self is what it does, and then what is done to it. Here there is no question about whether we should or should not be responsible for our acts. IF we are irresponsible, we suffer the consequences of that irresponsibility. IF with every act we shut our eyes and pray to the goddess of luck, there will come a time when the goddess will not answer our prayers and there will also come a way of doing things, a way which is incompetent, which forces us to suffer the undesirable consequences of our own acts, yet a way which is difficult to alter.

When we examine Dewey's notion of character, however, it would seem that the necessary unity between ends and means holds only insofar as we are involved with a single self. When it comes to relations with other people, these conditions are somewhat different and the unity seems less than necessary. For while we might have to suffer the consequences of what we do (including what we do to other people), it is not apparent that we must suffer the consequences of how well other people live. Or, if we do suffer these consequences, it is not apparent that an event which produces undesirable consequences for them will necessarily produce undesirable consequences for us. It would seem then that concerning our own acts and our own existence there is no choice about the relationship of means to ends; the relation is both binding and necessary. Yet it would seem, also, that when we are acting upon an object, either a thing or a person, then there need be no necessary unity between ends and means. There is no compelling reason why, in Dewey's treatment of this relationship, we ought not treat these as *mere* means to our own ends. Even if we did come across a situation in which the force behind someone else's ends compelled a re-evaluation of our own ends, there is again no reason why we should accept the conflicting ends as anything more than obstacles which necessitate an evaluation.

There would seem to be a real difference in accepting the ends of others as legitimate value claims to be considered with our own in the same impartial light (as Dewey often says we should) and the view that sees these ends as obstacles which simply force a modification of our own ends. If one man, intent upon murdering another, should decide upon reflection merely to harass him for the rest of his life, it could be said that he has altered his original end in light of possible consequences. The claims of others have probably influenced his own judgment, but they have influenced it not as the impartial considerations, but as real factors in a real situation which can produce *for him* undesirable consequences. It is just not clear in Dewey's treatment of this matter why such claims should be taken in any other way.

The difficulty can be resolved only if we recognize that the concept of lack must apply to more than a specific event in a specific situation. It can be resolved only if we understand that while it is possible for a lack to halt activity, as Dewey believes, it is also possible for activity to continue in the midst of a lack. For a lack can apply as much to the nature of activity as it can to activity itself, and when Dewey speaks of "democracy," of "sharing" and of "community," he must be speaking of the nature of activity. There has been much lacking (Dewey tells us) in *laissez faire* societies, but there has been ample activity. Lack can apply to a rather pervasive "attribute" of a human being, or better, to an absence of such an attribute. It can be the reason why certain problems are never recognized and certain goals, e.g., social responsibility, never desired. Lacks can exist without desires; a man can live his life without appreciating beauty, without having any meaningful relationships with other men, and without participating in a community of men. He can live his life without these things and without desiring them. To say that something is lacking in this situation is to say that if he could come to experience these things, he would come to desire them. Sometimes, however, conditions are present which hinder some people from even considering these as values.

Suppose, for example, that a self-enclosed community of men lived in an environment which rendered them continually sluggish and run-down. Suppose again, that their bodily temperatures were constantly a half degree above what we consider normal, and suppose too that because of their isolation, they had never experienced any other conditions. Now it is obvious that their state of health would limit their activity in certain ways. We would find them in their living rooms or studies, not at all anxious to venture outside. Stuffed noses would preclude them from experiencing any of the fragrances normally enjoyed and every draft would be a hazard. Yet these men would have developed a value system, would experience conflicts in that system, would evaluate ends in light of means and would make decisions that would reinstate activity and lead to a certain degree of satisfaction. Not having experienced a better state of health, it is likely that they would accept their general condition as the norm and would then find their satisfaction within the limits imposed by that condition. Suppose, too, that one day a visitor came to them from another culture and told them that the fragrance of a certain flower was desirable; being intelligent, though stunted creatures, they not only attempt and fail to smell the flower, but also, upon noticing his robust stature, they begin an extensive examination of their environmental and physical situation. The stranger has been the occasion for a re-examination of their values, but this does not mean that the fragrance was not desirable before this re-examination took place. That the fragrance is desirable does not mean that it is desired, it only means that it would be possible, under certain other conditions, to experience the flower in such a way that its fragrance would be desired. Had the stranger never come, had there never been an awakening, both the flower and the conditions required to experience it would have been desirable. The smelling of the flower is the occasion for its recognition as desirable, but Dewey has confused the desirable with that occasion.

Whenever we say of an object that it is an object of enjoyment, we take for granted an environment which supports that enjoyment, as well as the effects of that environment upon the being who is enjoying. If an object is only a possible object of enjoyment, but a human being cannot enjoy it then certainly there is a need to investigate both the environment and its effects. However, the object is no less desirable because it is not desired and the lack which exists here is not the specific lack of a confined situation; it is a pervasive quality of this being who is experiencing.

There has been a good deal of concern over positions which insist upon a more rigorous separation of the desirable from the desired. Yet if we investigate this concern it will be seen that it results not from this basic assumption but from two accompanying ones. These two assumptions have been, first that there are some people who lack very little and second that these people can impose successfully their values on others. Now neither one of these assumptions need to be made and even if we grant the first, there is a good deal of evidence to suggest that we should not grant the second. We can at least make the distinction between the imposition and the acceptance of an authority on the one hand, and of a value on the other. The fact that some people, reared under one authoritarian system, are able to find a home under another equally authoritarian yet opposing system would suggest that the imposition of values is often less than successful.

As much as Dewey would have preferred to escape metaphysical concepts and thereby maintain a completely biological model of man and values, his affirmation of community must rest upon those concepts. Although intelligence "properly directed" does aid community, it does not justify it. Dewey is not simply attempting to provide a criterion for "properly directed," as Kant provided a criterion for a moral act; he is also trying to argue that intelligence is the best guarantee of its own direction and that its direction will be towards greater community. Intelligence alone, however, guarantees nothing except a keen assessment of the consequences of an act; it does not guarantee that the assessment will be made towards any particular goal or for any particular association of human beings and if such a direction is desired, then it requires a leap beyond biology into metaphysics.

Only if one is willing to treat the concept of lack as a pervasive quality can he argue successfully for a community of differences. Of course the value of society is to be found in the way it trains men to solve problems, but it is also to be found in the kind of problems which it can help men to recognize. We can take Dewey's notion of community seriously because we believe that men can complement and educate one another. When man comes into contact with other men with other values he is able to discover what he is, what he is not and what he can be.

Dewey, himself, offers a faint suggestion of a metaphysical concept of lack in an essay entitled "The Inclusive Philosophic Idea." In this essay he sets down the basis for understanding any object arguing that a thing has no existence apart from its qualities and that its qualities are developed only in association with other things with other qualities. He writes that "the qualities of things associated are displayed only in association, since in interaction alone are potentialities released and actualized."[11] And then, "the more complex is an association the more fully are potentials realized for observation."[12]

Although there are some difficulties in extending an observational concept to the normative realm of human relations, it nevertheless seems clear that Dewey has implicitly extended it in this way. If like other beings in the universe, man too develops himself through a variety of relationships, then it may be said that from the point of view of a person who has yet to develop a particular association, there is a lack, but it is one that may partially be filled. When we carry the argument a bit further, we see that the concept of lack supports the widest possible degree of individual difference. For as we restrict the activity of someone else, we also restrict the kinds of associations that we can have with him and this in turn constricts our own individuality. When activity must be restricted, as it sometimes must, our own self-interest, enlightened by the recognition of a pervasive lack, would demand that the same principles be used in restricting both the activity of ourselves and the activity of others. We may feel justified in restricting an act if it is evident that the act will severely limit the capacity to associate and if it is plain that the restriction itself does not limit this capacity more than the act. It is here that we find the rationale for the impartiality that is essential to community.

If there is the fear that a view which insists upon looking upon lack as a pervasive quality in human beings must be equated with one that sees man as a naturally sinful, naturally guilt-ridden creature, the fear is unjustified. Whether man does, in fact, feel guilty is not the issue here. The important question is the consequences of that guilt and here Dewey's treatment of man and his individuality provides a most adequate framework in which to answer that question. For if man becomes what he is through association, he must express what he is in order to associate. The effect of guilt is to hinder this expression. It results either in an overwillingness to be what others want him to be or in an adamant defense of what he is. In either case association is destroyed, in the first by absorption and in the second by polarization.

Dewey's genius is not to be found in the delineation of a method which scientists had used long before Dewey had described it. Nor is it to be found in his arguments for the extension of that method to the problems of society and values; he may have helped to justify the social sciences, but he did not create them. Rather it lies in the way that he articulated his belief that the method could be used to enrich community and in his vision that it might very well be used otherwise. Education is the institutional guarantee for the proper application of the method, but the guarantee holds only insofar as schooling is an exercise in community.

For the schools, the extended meaning of the concept "lack" means that the teacher has the *responsibility* to develop out of the classroom a community where differences are to be encouraged and varying abilities and skills developed and grounded. Moreover, she has this responsibility not only as the representative of society, which may or may not grant it, but as the representative of the child.

8

Critical Pragmatism and the Appropriation of Ethnography by Philosophy of Education

Critical Pragmatism and Local Understanding

Critical Pragmatists take seriously Dewey's concern (to paraphrase) that philosophers should address the problems of people, not just the problems of philosophy, and that philosophers need to appreciate the "force of empirical work in philosophy" (Dewey 1925). Traditional pragmatism tells us that thinking begins when experience is interrupted and a problematic situation recognized (Dewey 1910). Critical pragmatism takes the process one step back, holding that sometimes experience that *should be* perceived as unsatisfactory is not recognized as problematic. This is most common where power is unequal, and where dominant interests control information and communication.

Just how significant this difference between traditional and critical pragmatism is depends on how one interprets "problematic situation." If the problem is seen to be located in the consciousness of the experiencer, then the difference is significant. If, however, it is seen to be located within the situation itself, regardless of the conscious disposition of the experiencer, then the difference is in fact small.[1] While traditional pragmatists did focus on the effect unequal power had on the formation of common sense, it is, nevertheless, an issue that should be welcomed by traditional pragmatists.

Ethnography as a Tool for Philosophy

Ethnography provides powerful tools with which to understand the problems of people, as experienced in everyday life. Yet relatively few philosophers engage ethnographic research and even fewer incorporate its methods into their own work. This is somewhat odd given that philosophy began in Athens as a street discipline, and because proto-ethnography was an element of the Socratic method. Indeed, the ethnographer is motivated by the same concern as the philosopher—to locate the source of dysfunction, whether behavioral or cognitive. For the philosopher of education the ethnographer's question: "What is going on here?" is a prelude to questions: "what should be going on here?" "What productive alternatives might be now blocked from consideration?" "How can they be removed?"

Local understanding, drawn from "common sense," is often partial, serving to block from consideration potentially productive alternative narratives. This is especially the case when common sense has been formed under conditions of unequal power, or when initiated in response to seriously incomplete knowledge or to changing or unclear conditions. Ethnographic methods can be useful for critical pragmatism in cases where local understanding has become problematic, perhaps as a result of intercultural static, or changing conditions.

Critical pragmatism highlights situations in which power relations influence the formation and internalization of common sense serving to conceal alternative ways of understanding. It is thus on the lookout for systematic silences or distortions in communication (Habermas 1971) and works to bring these to consciousness and to resolve them. It differs from traditional pragmatism only in emphasizing that failure to perceive or define a problem is problematic in itself. This emphasis may be seen as a development drawn from Dewey's transactional understanding of the organism-environment (including the social environment) interaction, where each acts upon and is changed by the other (Biesta and Burbules 2003, 11). Yet there are many situations where the interests of one part of the social environment dominate and serve to define the terms of "common sense." In these cases the important question, as Freire recognized, is how to bring the problem to the forefront without reinforcing the relation of dominator to dominated in the relation of researcher to subject. Such reinforcement happens when the researchers impose their own definitions of the problem onto the subjects (Freire 1968; Feinberg 2012).

Critical pragmatism supplements traditional pragmatism's conception of power by recognizing that more than coercive force or violence may be the cause of power inequality (Wolfe 2012), and by highlighting those situations of inequality where local understandings are systematically silenced or communicative distortions go unrecognized. In such situations the distinctive task of critical pragmatism is to bring competing norms to the surface, to show how they impede experience and to encourage the formation of new ways to direct and enrich experience. Critical pragmatism seeks the source, often historical, of systematic silences or dysfunctional behavior in order to open up and evaluate avenues for progressive and emancipatory change.

Recent ethnographies have also taken a critical approach, highlighting situations where certain voices have been silenced or distorted (Behar and Gordon 1995). In addition to providing discursive opportunities for dominated groups, as the critical ethnographer does, critical pragmatism also uses these opportunities to help promote the opening up and evaluation of new channels for experience to flow. The aim is to reduce domination and enhance agency.

For the critical pragmatist, good educational research arises out of human needs and serves to improve human flourishing. One of the tests of good research for the critical pragmatist is whether it takes into account a wide range of values and whether it ultimately serves both to improve the situations of people and to provide them with intellectual tools for reflecting on their own immediate aims and interests. This entails the following starting points for the critical pragmatist:

1. Recognize that local understanding may be incomplete but not inherently defective. Incomplete understanding means that some important problems may go unacknowledged, and some productive resolutions suppressed.
2. View conflicting value claims as an invitation to a conversation and the beginning of an inquiry.
3. Recognize that expert knowledge can enhance inquiry by placing particular responses into more general frameworks. But that it can also be misused to reproduce relations of domination.
4. Avoid reproducing relations of domination by promoting reflection and criticism on these general frameworks by the subject.

5. Explore discursive and other tools that can be used by subjects to interrupt unproductive behavior, and explore new alternative approaches.

6. Provide an educational experience that transfers the means for continuing growth from researcher to the subject, either as an individual or a collective.

7. The inquiry process should leave those affected in a better condition to handle their own future difficulties. (Feinberg 2012).

Ethnography and the Question of Norms

Both ethnographers and philosophers are interested in norms, but in different ways. The ethnographer sees behavior that may be defined as dysfunctional by the larger society and seeks to understand why someone could rationally choose to behave in that way. The ethnographer is most interested in revealing implicit norms governing such behavior. In these situations the educational ethnographer's problem is to make sense of behavior that, according to standard norms, may seem limiting or self-defeating. This differs from the task of critical pragmatism because its aim is to reveal different modes of understanding not necessarily to guide change. The assumption that sense can be made of seemingly dysfunctional behavior implies that such behavior is functional, however limited it may be from an outsider's perspective. The ethnographer's task is to find out just what that function is. However, for the educational philosopher the answer to this question is not the end of an inquiry but rather the beginning of one.

For the ethnographer the question is just what kind of view of the world would make this behavior sensible. For the educational philosopher influenced by critical pragmatism the test of a good educational ethnography is whether it can be used to improve education. For the philosopher the ethnographer's question implies that there may be other views of the world that are potentially more useful or just. While it is often useful for ethnographers to bracket their own values, for the philosopher of education these brackets are an important component of philosophical work. It brings back into focus the educational point.

Take for example Ray McDermott's classic study of a reading group where Rosa, the poorest reader in the lowest reading group, always raises her hand just a beat after the teacher has called on the next student to read. While Rosa never gets called upon to read, as McDermott points out, two more immediate aims are satisfied. The teacher has succeeded in producing a smoothly running group and Rosa has succeeded in avoiding embarrassment. Of course from an educator's point of view the long-term consequence is disastrous, as McDermott's ironic title *achieving school failure*, indicates and Rosa's reading never improves (McDermott 1997). For Rosa the group is no longer a *reading* group and the point of the activity has been lost. For the critical pragmatist this lost value is what gives power to the ethnographic analysis. Problems are solved but they are the wrong problems. Certainly we do not want Rosa to be embarrassed, but we also want her to learn how to read. The philosopher's job then is to bring this aim—teaching Rosa to read—back into focus and to examine possible reasons for not attending to it.

When ethnographic methods are applied to education the ethnographer's educational values are part of the subtext, but they are bracketed. McDermott studies reading groups because, among other things, he understands the role reading plays in shaping opportunities for human flourishing, and because he wants students like Rosa to flourish. Paul Willis studies working class students because he must understand, in a way that his "lads" may not, that they are "having a laugh," all the way to a life of vulnerability and dependency, and he would like to see students like the lads to gain more agency over their futures (Willis 1978). Granted it would be possible for someone to read, say, McDermott, as a guide to how not to embarrass a poor reader and keep things going, but this would just miss an important point of a *reading* group.

For the critical pragmatist values are often in conflict with others, and part of the philosopher's job is to bring these conflicts to the surface so that they might be addressed. Rosa may not be learning to read because the teacher avoids recognizing and calling on her. But the teacher may avoid calling on her because she is under pressure to increase the performance of the majority of her students and because she does not have the resources to do that and to teach Rosa how to read at the same time. In other words she may be aware of conflicting values and have chosen to act on one rather than the other. To engage ethnography in a philosophical way would involve addressing this choice. This is not to deny the other, perhaps even more obvious, values that this research serves. McDermott's body of work actually encourages a wider definition of intelligent behavior than many classrooms allow. Rosa is, after all, setting aims and achieving them. Yet here too there is an unstated normative issue. Should schools operate on a broader understanding of intelligence, and, if so, what should constitute such an understanding?

Beyond the Post Modern Critique

The rhetorical questions often asked by post-modern theorists, "Whose meaning?" "Which history?" "Whose interest?" (Apple 1982) make problematic the assumption of the legitimacy of "ordinary usage." Post modernism, in its varied forms—feminism, critical race theory, post colonialism, whiteness studies, queer theory, etc.—complicates the task of philosophy by revealing different meaning systems and by questioning the idea of a single legitimate moral register. By a moral register I mean the extent to which a practice is marked positive or negative along with the intensity of that marking. For the postmodern scholar, shared meaning becomes "shared meaning," as it is *constructed* under conditions of unequal power, and the legitimacy of such unequal power is in question (Freire 1968; Foucault 1979; Bourdieu and Passeron 1977; MacKinnon 1989). Yet not all shared meaning is suspect and critical pragmatism seeks to understand what meanings are constrained and what steps might be taken renew and enrich them (Dewey 1988).

Both critical pragmatism and traditional pragmatism are concerned about understanding breakdowns in experience that impair opportunities for individuals to lead enriched, reasonable autonomous and collaborative lives. Yet for the critical pragmatist the concern about breakdowns in experience is not sufficient. There are times when experience is constrained but does not actually break down. In these cases unequal power, ingrained habits and customs, unimagined possibilities may all play a role in limiting the kind of experience people can have, even if the present experience seems to be flowing reasonably well. This is, for example, the case with Rosa. Neither the teacher nor Rosa expressed dissatisfaction. It is to some extent the case with Paulo Freire's work where much of his genius lies in making the peasants aware of repressed dissatisfaction while helping to ignite new visions for progressive change.

Critical Pragmatism and Judgment

The mark of a good ethnography is respect for the way in which the subject defines and responds to a problem. The assumption of rational functionality is the foundation of ethnographic inquiry and marks the goal of the ethnographic quest. "Find out what this behavior is functional for!" might serve as the ethnographer's mantra. Ethnography seeks an exploration of the *subjects' understanding* of the conditions under which their definition of a situation is constructed and it is guided by the assumption that the subjects' own definitions are in some way reasonable as a response to certain assumed conditions. The ethnographer's task is to then find out in what way it is meaningful. The question "what is going on here" is answered in terms of the way the behavior functions to fit a perceived environmental demand—even if a narrow one. Still there is a tacit but often sound judgment on the part of many educational ethnographers that what is functional for a certain narrow environmental circumstance is not functional for the larger environment that impacts it. A task of philosophy is to make this judgment explicit and to explore its reasons.

One way in which critical pragmatism complements ethnography is by revealing, interrogating and refining the ethnographer's normative assumptions as they are imbedded in the narrative. The philosophical work involves exploring counter narrative and their possible justifications. Consider the questions the critical pragmatist might ask of McDermott's study: Is the teacher aware of the tacit bargain she has made with Rosa? How might she explain it? For example has the size of her class increased in a way that she must decide where to allocate her scarce time? Have new standardized reading test and accountability requirements forced her to maximize the progress of the majority of students, even at the sacrifice of a minority? If, however, she is not aware of her neglect of Rosa, then the question is: what accounts for this lack of awareness? Behind these questions are philosophical concerns about educational equity and justice and what counts as fairness in the distribution of teaching capital.

Critical Pragmatism: A Spotlight on Local Creativity

In these post-modern times few of us live in a single "cultural" community but rather navigate across a number of different competing systems of meaning and value. With the help of local actors critical pragmatism can use ethnographic methods to identify conflicting normative imperatives, analyze roadblocks to fruitful communication and coordination, ascertain their source and explore opportunities for repair. As mentioned at the beginning of this essay, local actors often provide innovative solutions to local problems. In these cases critical pragmatism can aid education in a more general way by spotlighting and thematizing the local creative innovations to conflicting value.

Consider the following episode retold by the Principal of a Catholic parochial grade school. She reports to me that "A boy raised his hand (in my class). The book must have said something about divorce, divorce is wrong, marriage is forever. But he said, 'but they say you're excommunicated.'"

The Principal understood that the boy was calling for more than a simple factual answer such as: "Yes, divorce and remarriage is a mortal sin." Rather she understands that there is a deeper meaning to the question and she explains:

> I knew his parents were divorced. So you have to explain it in a way that doesn't hurt the child.
>
> I said, "You have to understand where the Church is coming from. If you are going to get married, if you are going to bring children into the world, they would like it to be for life."
>
> When I was a kid there was less divorce. Now there is more, so I went into explaining the Church's teachings. "They don't want people getting divorced and they don't agree with it because they want what is best for the family."
>
> Divorce now is quite in and you have to just say it so that you are not offending anyone and so that you are not just saying that the Church is saying that divorce is ok. So it is a very fine line, but I feel that in that kid's life, his parents are divorced and if I am going to stand up and pontificate and say, "Yes they are excommunicated, or they are going to go to hell," or whatever, it's totally not helpful to that child.
>
> So I have to say something that is still the Church's teaching but maybe give it a historical twist and try to take care of the kid. A lot of us feel that way. (Feinberg 2006)

In this episode the Principal is engaged in identifying conflicting norms and in addressing the damage that they could do in this local situation. By doing so she is liberating the child from a destructive dualism that has arisen as a result of the implication of the passage in the text—love your parents or reject your religion! She is doing the work of the critical pragmatist by identifying the normative quandary—the problematic situation: i.e., the Church has a certain position on divorce—marriage is sacred and divorce is a sin in the eyes of the Church. And it also has a certain power over the child. But the child's parents are divorced. Then she spells out the moral ambiguity in her own position. As a representative of the Church, the Principal is obliged to represent its position on divorce. She cannot just pick and choose, as she likes. However she is also aware of the vulnerability of her student and of the fact that this child may take away the message that his divorced parents are living in sin; that people who live in sin are impure, and their children tainted. Hence the conclusion the Principal wants to protect the child from is that his parents are impure and their impurity marks him as well and thus separates him from his classmates. The Principal is concerned about this unstated line of reasoning and worries about the psychological price the child will pay, in terms of shame and self-exclusion, if as a representative of the Church, she endorses its view that divorced people are morally stained, and allows the student to apply its implications to his parents.

With all this in mind she tells the child: "You have to understand where the Church is coming from," "*they* would *like* it (marriage) to be for life."

General Analysis

Here the Principal has done a good deal of the normative work. What remains for the critical pragmatist is to explore her response in a more general way. The Principal resolves her dilemma by shifting the Church's discourse from a religious, judgmental frame to a historical, explanatory one. She justifies this by asserting as *her* cardinal principle, "[don't] hurt the child." "Hurt" means do not exclude the child unnecessarily from the classroom community or force him to make a choice between loving his parents and loving the Church.

Still, she fulfills her obligation to the Church by explaining to the child its doctrine but she does so in a way that distances her own commitment from those formal doctrines, although she does so without criticizing them. She begins to refer to the Church as a "they" rather than a "we." She tells the child: "You have to understand where the Church is coming from," and then she alters the discourse on sin to a discourse on preferences—"they would *like* it to be for life." And the "*we*" of the Church is turned into a "*they*," distancing the judgment of the Church from that of the Principal.

Nevertheless, the hold of the Church on moral behavior is not completely abandoned. Rather she tells the child that the Church wants "what is best for the family" and the question: whether the Church actually does know what is best for his parents is an issue that she leaves alone allowing the student to leave the question open. Possibly, the Church might know better than the family itself what is best for it, but then again, possibly not. In switching the tone from moral to explanatory and in distancing teacher, parents and child from the official judgment of the Church, the Principal has done a good deal of repair work. Critical pragmatism can then draw on this work in a general way to display to others one emancipatory option.

The Contribution of Critical Pragmatism

It is in the code switching—from normative to descriptive, from the explicit to the implicit-that a lot of the creative work is accomplished and the gap between the child's situation and the doctrine of the Church is addressed. This code switching then creates space between Church doctrines and what is acceptable for the child to believe. The Principal has fulfilled her obligation as a teacher to inform the child of Church doctrine, but in her tonal shift, she has gone a long way in reducing its sting. She has respected the right of the child to shape his own conscience in light of information about the Church's teachings.

The critical pragmatist as a moral philosopher and researcher is attentive to the normative dimensions of this situation and is in a position to hear the moral register of the conversation.[2] One of the advantages of the ethnographic mode is that it allows philosophers to pick up on tonal shifts, which may be more difficult to perceive in a standard argument format. In the case of this Principal, picking up on the tonal shift in the ethnographic work allows the critical pragmatist to understand how Church dogma may be communicated in a non-dogmatic way in situations where parental respect is at stake. This leads to an important distinction between the message and its mode of delivery. Dogma may be delivered in non-dogmatic, relatively open ways while anti-dogmatic messages may be delivered dogmatically. The critical pragmatism should not assume that liberal values are confined only to liberalism; nor should it be assumed that liberalism is always liberal. When ethnography is appropriated by critical pragmatism liberalism becomes reflective and contradiction between message and tone can be recognized and addressed.

Conclusion: A New Role for Philosophers of Education

Ethnography can aid critical pragmatism where meaning systems clash, and become frozen. Critical pragmatism can aid ethnography in situations in which common sense is shaped by unequal and dysfunctional power relations and where consideration of productive alternatives is blocked. In these situations it can serve to locate the deeper assumptions that disable the consideration of alternative possibilities. For the philosopher of education the ethnographer's question: "What is going on here?" is a prelude to the questions: "what should be going on here?" "What productive alternatives might be now blocked from consideration?" "How can they be removed?" Philosophers of education can use ethnographic methods to locate the deeper assumptions that disable the consideration of alternative possibilities. Ethnography is a useful tool for addressing tensions between liberal values of autonomy, critical thinking and respect, and the values of local communities, some of which may not embrace liberalism. It holds promise for helping educators find the threads upon which new understandings may arise, and new forms of flourishing undertaken.

A Final Note

Given the precarious situation of both philosophy of education and educational ethnography there could be a fruitful role for this kind of work in improving classroom practice and in providing philosophy with a renewed role in teacher education. In the not too distant past philosophy of education was largely involved in exploring in a very general way the "ultimate" aims of education. This has been termed the "ism" school of philosophy of education.

The problems with this approach are notorious. It was often vague and removed from practice. Another, more recent approach, analytic philosophy of education, encouraged some interesting technical work, but its application to particular issues was also often remote. At this moment there is a very healthy diversity of approaches in the field but there are also real pressures from the outside to conform to the testing regime. I believe that it is well to resist this pressure in so far as it distorts the educational process. Yet I also think that there would be considerable benefit to the practice and institution of education, as well as to the field of philosophy of education, if there were a concerted effort—perhaps between philosophers and ethnographers, perhaps by engaging philosophers in field work—to begin to build up case studies that could illustrate ways in which teachers recognize (or fail to recognize) tensions in their own aims and to then use these cases to analyze alternative approaches to address them. Given recording and video equipment and the prospect of sharing material across institutions this could be a significant contribution of philosophy of education and an illustration of how critical pragmatism can enrich the educational practice.

9

Fixing the Schools

The Ideological Turn

Introduction

The recent reports on educational reform, with their renewed emphasis on the academic side of the high school experience, have been favorably received. The many reports, documents and books that have been delivered to the public in recent years decry the loss of purpose and intellectual vitality that the high school is depicted as once possessing. While there are important variations on the theme, most call for a return to a core curriculum that is comprised of traditional subject matter in science, mathematics, English and social studies. In addition, many ask that students become familiar with the use of the computer—that they become computer literate.

While a new emphasis on the intellectual side of secondary schools would certainly be a welcome change, with a few exceptions, the reports presented to the public are inappropriate guides for such a renaissance. Many are creatures of an ideological climate in which inquiry and dissent have been quieted and vocationalism, sometimes packaged as academic courses, is rampant. There are, of course, exceptions. Some of the documents represent serious attempts to understand the many problems that the schools face and to suggest viable ways to address them. Yet together the reports feed a questionable image of an educational system which has fallen away from a once golden age which, as the closing years of the century approach, we are called upon to recapture. For many, the prophet of this educational paradise lost was James Conant whose wise counsel, we are told, was cast aside by the anarchy that has become known as the 1960s and '70s.

My own recollection of the period when Conant wrote is different. I recall it as a time of intense racial discrimination when even the most elementary formal rights were denied to black people, when sexual discrimination was unconsciously accepted as a part of the natural order of things and when the call for equal opportunity beckoned white men only. I recall it as a time when racist, sexist and militaristic images filled the pages of school textbooks unchallenged while the equivalent of today's "moral majority" readied themselves to protest the reading of *Catcher in the Rye*. All of this was not Conant's doing, of course, but neither was it Conant's seeing. To remember Conant is certainly to recall one who has become recognized as a remarkable educational statesman, but it is also to recall the key architect of the military-industrial-educational establishment, the person who sold education to the government as our answer to Sputnik.

Given the present ideological climate, Conant is an appropriate symbol. His no-nonsense approach to education vocationalized the liberal arts—scientists for the military and linguists for the state department. Yet, those who are advocating a core curriculum, as most of the reformers are doing, might recall the dual system that Conant proposed—academic disciplines for the talented few in the suburbs and behavioral control and vocational training for most of the youngsters in the slums.

If the gold-plated age is somewhat tarnished and the veneer worn, there is yet little doubt about what it represents. It speaks to a time when, *The Blackboard Jungle* notwithstanding, students were obedient, test scores were high, authority was respected, standards were clear, and the work ethic was in place.

To understand these newest educational proposals, they must be viewed within the context of the ideological climate of the present time. Some of the reports, and here *A Nation at Risk* must stand out, contribute directly to an ascending ideology of statism and control. If discipline and order are not found in the school, they will not be found in the workplace, and production, consumption and national power will suffer. Other documents, and here John Goodlad's *A Place Called School* is the most impressive, provide an instructive yet incomplete account of schooling which remains to be filled in by the outcome of a larger ideological struggle.[1]

My own view will obviously color this analysis. It is that schools are indeed in a critical situation, but not quite for the same reasons that have been given by many of the reports. I believe that schools should help students develop the intellectual equipment and the cultural perspective needed to reflect upon the value of the various choices and commitments that they are to make in the self-forming process of shaping a life. The schools are in a crisis because they are failing to meet this goal. To some extent this purpose provides the school with a negative mandate, one which is shared by parents and others charged with bringing up the young. It is to help a youngster avoid making an irreversible mistake, one that would be so damaging as to preclude or sharply curtail future choices. However, it provides a positive mandate as well: to help youngsters develop the modes of thinking and critical perspectives which will enable them to make wise choices, and to participate critically in the activities of a political community.

It is this latter mandate which brings the schools into contact with general education and the liberal arts: not the liberal arts as a set of prescribed materials selected by Mortimer Adler for some reason known only to himself and Aristotle, but the liberal arts as they provide ways for reflecting on the life we are living and shaping. Indeed, there is nothing contradictory between a liberal and a vocational education insofar as the vocational work provides a way for a student to try on different modes of being. There is only something wrong when the vocational work is taken up to preclude reflection and to reinforce an already limited field.

Thus, when I speak of liberal education I have in mind a series of reflective activities in which youngsters use some available intellectual tools to reflect upon the shape that their life is taking. If science were taught as I would expect it to be, it would be to learn how our environment sustains and influences the kinds of beings that we are, and the humanities would be taught to show how, through the development of culture, human beings come to interpret the nature of that being. When the National Commission, or The National Science Board, or the members of the Twentieth Century Fund Task Force write about the need for more science, math and English, they do not have in mind the same things that I do. Rather, like Conant, they see these as weapons in a struggle for national survival, a belief which I do not wish to share. Even Adler, with all his it's-good-for-its-own-sake-so-let's-rub-their-nose-in-it argument, adds as an amen (in the second volume) that it's good for national defense, too!

The fact is that there has been a lot of nonsense packaged under the heading of this or that national commission, and this or that foundation report. Educational reports, especially those written by national commissions and educational foundations, are often about the business of creating social myths, and perhaps, as long as we understand this, we should not be too critical when we find that they have done their job well. There is art to the mythmakers' work and such art should be understood.

The Ideological Turn

While there is much conflict among the reports over important issues, together they reflect an ideological shift that is occurring in many fields. In medicine, for example, the shift is represented by the slow abandonment of the quest for national health insurance, the rising acceptance of a multitiered system, the increase in "for-profit" health schemes, and a cap on payment for Medicaid patients.[2] In civil rights and criminal justice the shift is reflected in the softening of affirmative action requirements and the weakening of interpretations of due process. One common way to view this shift is as a move from concerns about equality to concerns about efficiency, but I do not think that this description is completely accurate. For example, the reduced commitment to affirmative action has taken place within the context of a high unemployment rate. Unless one accepts a narrow, technical definition of efficiency, it is difficult to view as very efficient a society where more than seven percent of its population is forced to be unproductive. Moreover, the demand for efficiency in social service areas has been initiated as a response to an ever-increasing national debt which has developed as military expenditures have gone unchecked. In other words, inefficiency in national defense has sparked a concern for greater efficiency in social services and education. The ideological shift represents not a move from equality to efficiency but an attempt to reaffirm the legitimate basis of institutional authority and to quiet the various challenges that have arisen during the past fifteen years. This requires that the weight of the moral consensus be redistributed and that the voice of the institutional critics be muted.

In its attempt to reshape the moral consensus, education is actually following the lead of popular culture. In many of the most popular films of the late sixties and early seventies, such as *The Graduate*, authenticity and personal integrity were expressed as the supreme values standing in opposition to the established incentive and value systems. At the same time, the free school movement was at its height and many saw in this movement a way in which students, too, could experience the same authenticity and integrity. Since the public schools were viewed as the antipathy of authenticity, they formed the background against which these values could be expressed and became to some the symbols of conformity and inauthenticity. By the middle of the 1970s, the American dream again became fashionable and the establishment stood as a barrier not to personal authenticity, but to individual fame and fortune. The free school movement had passed; the reaction to public education was taking place in church-affiliated schools and if there was a problem with the establishment, it was that it was not conformist enough. By the early 1980s, even the military, which had been out of favor during the Vietnam War, had a popular renaissance. The training sergeant in the film *An Officer and a Gentlemen* could bark at his recruits that killing women and children was one of the highest forms of patriotism. With Ronald Reagan calling the action in Southeast Asia a noble war, the audience could not help but read Vietnam into the script. On the campus, the CIA again began recruiting while ROTC regained the respectability it had lost.

The weight of the moral consensus was affected by other events as well. High unemployment and the rising rate of inflation provided the incentive for people to scramble for available jobs and university students, faculty and administrators strained to keep track of a constantly shifting market. The consensus was also affected by the Soviet action in Afghanistan: it was an action which demonstrated that any superpower can have its Vietnam, licensing people to again use the behavior of "the evil empire" to the east as the measuring rod for our own morality.

The effect, of course, was to render the institutional criticisms and the values that generated them irrelevant—at least in the minds of many people. After all, what is the problem with a little inequality in the face of all of these dangers. It may be true, as the more radical critics have claimed, that the schools reproduce the relations of production, and perhaps the relations of production are a bit unequal, if not unjust. If the alternative is to turn over our industrial production to the Japanese, then we must continue to endure these inequities.

This is the climate in which the present reports on education have been issued. It is an atmosphere of threat and siege, a climate where a military-industrial giant is obsessed with the possibility of its own impotence. It is precisely the kind of climate where national chauvinism is likely to pass for educational wisdom.

It is the report by the National Commission on Excellence in Education, with all its talk of unilateral educational disarmament and its hyperbole about the rising tide of mediocrity, that best fits and reinforces this climate. It is not, however, the only one. The report by the National Science Board published shortly before *A Nation at Risk* anticipates its argument for school reform by linking it to the maintenance of economic strength and military security,[3] while *Making the Grade*, the report issued by the Twentieth Century Fund shortly after the publication of the National Commission on Excellence in Education, begins by endorsing the commission's concern.[4] There are, as we shall see, different voices, other reports which do not play upon or consciously reinforce the aggressive national agenda which has emerged with such force in recent years. While few of these voices challenge directly the ideological direction established by *A Nation at Risk*, some say reasonable things about the quality of classroom life. Yet the present climate has surely circumscribed the educational debate and sharply curtailed some important understandings.

The Creation of an Educational Ideology

It is *The Paideia Proposal*, not *A Nation at Risk*, which carries the subtitle, "An Educational Manifesto." Yet, if a manifesto is judged by its propaganda value and its effectiveness as a mobilizer, the subtitle should have been awarded to the report by the members of the National Commission. While Adler is certainly able to present his ideas in clear and simple terms, he does not have the same talent for the alarmist rhetoric that characterized the Commission's argument. And while some of his arguments are certainly simplified, there are, especially in the third volume, some words about educational procedure and some examples of classroom practice which should be taken seriously. That he idealizes American democracy as he does, and slips into arguments that link education to national defense, helps to locate him ideologically. However, his attempt is to provide an educational treatise and his work should be evaluated according to its success in doing so.

The same cannot be said for the report of the National Commission on Excellence in Education. The schools are a tool of national power and because they are floundering, the nation is at risk. As a manifesto, it has done its job—alerting us to the fact that a problem exists in our nation's schools. This, however, is all that can be said. Instead of carefully characterizing the nature of that problem, it has offered a series of rhetorical slogans which lead not just to oversimplification, but to misrepresentation.

According to the authors of this report, if the United States wishes to maintain its industrial and military superiority, it must bring a halt to what it sees as the erosion of educational standards. The Commission expresses optimism that this will be done because, as it patronizingly puts it, our citizens know that "education is one of the chief engines of a society's material well-being. . . . Citizens also know in their bones that the safety of the United States depends principally on the wit, skill and spirit of a self-confident people, today and tomorrow."[5]

While *A Nation at Risk* is only one of a number of reports that link industrial and military power to education, it is clearly the one that has received the most attention.[6] The fact is there are many good reasons for improving our schools. However, the relationship between good schools and a strong military or an efficient, productive economy is much more complex than any of the reports acknowledge. Nevertheless, it does not take a sophisticated economist to see some of the flaws in the argument. For example, a number of the reports decry the decline in student test scores and the poor performance of students in the United States when compared to those from some other nations. Yet, while students in the United States do not perform as well as those in France and England on a number of measured areas of achievement, there is no evidence to indicate that these lower scores have resulted in a comparably weaker military. Indeed, there is sufficient evidence to indicate that during the period when test scores have declined, the military has grown stronger.

The success that Japanese firms have had in penetrating the American market and the growing imbalance of trade between the two nations have been important factors in preparing the atmosphere for the reception of the reports. Indeed, *A Nation at Risk* identifies Japan as a major and troublesome source of industrial competition, which it is. In many respects Japan is performing for American education in the 1980's the same function that the Soviet Union performed in the 1950's. It is providing the dark incentive for restructuring the educational system. The reason for this is related to the large number of Toyotas and Hondas that are to be seen on the nation's roads and the equally impressive numbers of Sony televisions that are watched in American homes. The fact that Japanese students score quite high on standardized achievement tests while American students do not has not been lost on those who wished to find a reason for the decline in American industry that was evident a few years ago. The reasoning was simple and elegant, even if flawed. If Japanese children do well on standardized tests and if Japanese workers make more desirable cars than American workers, then if American youngsters would do better on standardized tests, American workers would make better cars. While the logic may be wanting, the formula actually seems to work. American students have begun to do better on standardized tests and the automobile industry is now making record profits. Only a skeptic might point to the "voluntary" restrictions that Japan placed on exported automobiles to account for the revitalization of the United States' car industry, or to the benefits that have resulted to American industrialists by the taming of the work force.

There are, of course, many reasons besides schooling and test scores that could be provided for the recent growth of selected Japanese industries. The fact that Japan invests less than one percent of its GNP on defense means that, in contrast to the United States, a much larger proportion of its budget can be invested in industrial research. It also means that many more of its scientists and engineers are involved in consumer research rather than military research. Indeed, the link between a strong military and a weakened consumer industry may be much stronger than the link between a weak educational system and either a weakened military or a weakened industry. If test scores made the difference, then, of course, the industrial threat from Israel should at least equal that of Japan. Given the enfeebled state of Israel's economy, however, any suggestion to that effect would be properly taken as an absurdity.

While the scores of Japanese students are indeed high, a closer look at the Japanese educational system suggests that it cannot be used to support many of the proposals put forward by some of the recent reports. For example, the reports are almost unanimous in calling for the development of some kind of merit pay system for teachers with rather steep differences in rewards. However, the formula for increasing salaries in Japan is, with minor exceptions, essentially based on seniority. Moreover, whereas teachers in the United States must usually undergo a trial period before receiving tenure, Japanese teachers are given tenure when they begin teaching. Many teachers in Japan would object to the recent reform proposals on the ground that they are too individualistic and would disrupt the cooperative activities of the schools.

I suspect that what is attractive about Japan to the American reformers is that it appears to be such a well-ordered society with a highly developed meritocracy. If one is willing to put aside Japan's discriminatory treatment of the Korean and Barakumin minorities, as well as the severe restrictions customarily placed on women, this appraisal is largely correct. However, in emphasizing the high achievement of Japanese students, little is made of those features of the Japanese system that are evidence of a commitment to equality or to the communal features of Japanese education. For example, the Japanese have a strong system of compensatory allocation which helps significantly to equalize the expenses that poor and wealthy districts provide for education. Moreover, there is some indication that this has an effect on measured achievement since Japan reports a comparably small mean variation on tests. The measures that Japan has taken to advance the goal of equality were overlooked by the American educational reformers.

When the reports were published, and as more and more educators began to cite with alarm the differences in the scores of American and Japanese youngsters, I began to wonder about the way in which the Japanese view their own educational system. I was fortunate to be invited to give some lectures in Japan and this provided the opportunity to talk to and interview a number of Japanese teachers, researchers and educational officials.[7] While I found considerable pride in the recent attention given to their schools, there were conflicting interpretations among the Japanese about the meaning of the high test scores. A considerable debate is taking place about whether these scores truly represent a high-quality educational system. While there are many teachers who feel that the tests do help to motivate students, there are others who believe that they actually hurt the educational process. For example, in an interview with several teachers from one of the few prefectures where a science test is not required for placement into a high school, this concern was voiced with special eloquence by the head science teacher. He feared that if the students had to worry about passing the test he would no longer be able to teach them how to be scientific. When I pressed him for an explanation he responded with an example. He noted that now he can take his junior high school students down to the pond, collect a sample of water and spend a considerable amount of time helping them analyze all of the living organisms that can be found in it. However, if an examination in science were to be required, he would no longer be able to do that. He would have to teach them how to pass their test.

This teacher's opinion was echoed to some degree in an interview with Mr. Hisao Saito, the Deputy Director General of the Secretariat for the Provisional Council on Educational Reform.[8] He cited the intensity of competition fostered by the examination system as the most serious problem of Japanese education. When I asked whether he would be concerned if the reforms proposed by the Council resulted in a decline in test scores, his response was that "we don't care about the results of achievement." His point was not that the Commission is unconcerned about the level of achievement of Japanese children but rather that the present examination system and the intense competition that results are likely constraining certain forms of achievement. Of special concern are those forms having to do with creativity.

These concerns are not unrealistic. There is little doubt that the examinations drive the educational system. Students are required to take a test to determine the high school that they will attend and they are later required to take a test to determine whether they will be accepted to the university. In both instances, the mechanisms for selection place severe penalties on failure. For example, students apply for admission not only to the university, but to the high school as well and they are allowed to apply to only one public high school. While all public high schools in a prefecture administer the same examination, each sets its own standards for a passing score. Since the test for all public high schools is given on the same day and since students can only apply to one high school, failure means either that they must go to a private, more costly and probably less prestigious, high school or else, as is the case with very few students, they must seek employment.[9] Moreover, there is a very strict, informal system of high school ranking (from the most to the least prestigious) and this gives each student a very clear understanding of his or her academic level. The high cost of failure requires that, before selecting the school they will apply to, Junior High School students must have a clear understanding of their chances for being admitted. The fact that most students do attend a public high school means that this requirement is usually met. Fujita explains one of the mechanisms that is used:

> Many junior and senior high schools arrange for their senior students to take several facsimile examinations by testing

companies (usually six to twelve times a year). After every facsimile examination, students are informed of their test scores in each subject as well as the total, and the relative standings among the students who took the same combination of subjects and among those who plan to apply for the same high school or university. In addition to these facsimile examinations, students are given . . . mid-term and final examinations every trimester. Thus, as OECD examiners reported on Japanese education in 1971, "Students . . . become more interested in examination techniques than in real learning and maturation."[10]

Thus, instead of taking the level of performance on tests as a sign of educational health, there are many in Japan who view it as part of a rather serious educational problem, a problem that is fed by the large number of industries that have developed as a result of the examination system. Publication enterprises regularly detail the success that students from different schools have had in being accepted to the various universities. The success of a particular high school helps to determine its position in the informal ranking system. In addition, a large number of students attend privately owned cram schools, called Jukus, which are conducted after school hours and function to prepare students for the examination. The more elite cram schools require that students pass an entrance examination to be admitted and I have been told that there are some which require that the child's mother remain home and not work outside of the house. In addition to the work at the regular school and the time in a Juku, many students are also tutored at home.[11]

Many Japanese are critical of this system, but it is unlikely that Japan will follow in Korea's footsteps and ban tutoring altogether.[12] However, many critics feel that unless key corporations and government bureaus stop hiring people on the basis of the university attended, the system will continue in one form or another. Whether one is a critic or a fan of the examination system, few Japanese (even those who believe that schools do a good job) are likely to agree that the scores on the tests are an indication of the high quality of the schools. There are too many other factors involved to attribute scores to the work of the schools alone.

Finally, it is somewhat misleading to compare the performance of Japanese and American high school students because the systems work in different ways. For the Japanese student the high school is a time of intense pressure and rigorous study. While this is also the case for some students in the United States, many do not begin to take schooling seriously until they enter a college or university. In Japan, however, the university is known to be a reasonably relaxing period in a student's career. The important thing is to get in. My own impression is that the graduate programs in Japan are generally underdeveloped which probably helps to account for the asymmetry in the flow of the graduate students between the two countries. Even if we were to accept the view that the test scores tell us something about the efficiency of the Japanese and American high schools, we must also realize that they do not tell us much about the productivity of the system as a whole. At a very minimum, we would need to know something about the scores at the point at which the representative student exited from the system. Yet this kind of measure would give to the tests more credit than they deserve. As Hidaka, a noted Japanese critic, observes: "If students graduating from my university were to take the . . . University Entrance Examination without prior preparation, their average scores would be far lower than those of candidates sitting for the exam. Indeed, I even doubt whether the teaching staff at national and other public universities would do as well as candidates if they were to take the same exam. This alone indicates the absurdity of the National Standard Entrance Examination."[13]

The Assault on Equality

While *A Nation at Risk* speaks of an act of unilateral educational disarmament, it neglects to identify a reason for this act. The report issued by the Twentieth Century Fund Task Force, *Making the Grade*, is more explicit. It believes that it is the emphasis on equality that has led to a decline in quality.[14] While the report does not propose that efforts on behalf of educational equality be discontinued, its recommendations, including one that would curtail the scope of bilingual programs, give the strong impression that equality and diversity have gone too far.

A few years ago, the authors of any proposal that linked programs undertaken on behalf of minority populations with a decline in educational quality would have felt compelled to offer some evidence to support their claim. It is indicative of the present climate that this report provides no such evidence. Rather, the observation feeds into a popularly held belief that the educational and financial costs of recent programs enacted for the benefit of minority populations have been too high. Having provided fuel for this belief, the recommendation that the commitment to equality be continued appears to be little more than a begrudging concession to convention.

The ideological slant of this report becomes apparent when one looks at the two different parts of the document. The first part is the actual report of the Task Force. While it is clearly the most prominent feature of the report, it takes up only the first twenty-two pages of the document. The second part is a much longer background research paper written by Paul Peterson which follows the part written by the Task Force. This paper was used by the Task Force members in writing their report and, as one would expect, there are recognizable similarities between the two. Yet the tone, balance and rhetoric is different. For example, whereas the Task Force endorses the view of the National Commission that there is a serious crisis in education and speaks of avoiding the "threatened disaster," the author of the background paper writes that "the crisis in education is greatly exaggerated."[15] And, whereas Peterson agrees fully with the Task Force that there must be a renewed federal commitment to educational quality, he observes, but the Task Force does not, that "it cannot be said that nationwide school integration has been put forward with undue haste. According to one account the degree of segregation in public schools was greater in 1980 than in 1970."[16] In contrast to Peterson's cautious words about the slow pace of integration, the Task Force lists the goal of dissolving racial divisiveness as one of the items placed under the general subheading "Excessive Burdens." Under the same heading the task force also mentions maintaining ethnic distinctiveness, thus suggesting that the two goals are incompatible and that schools cannot be expected to meet them both. There is no argument provided that integration must take place at the expense of cultural integrity, but the Task Force later builds upon this insinuated conflict in its suggestion that funds for bilingual programs be diverted. Peterson again provides a more balanced view: in reviewing the rather mixed evaluations that have been given regarding the academic effectiveness of bilingual programs, Peterson notes the studies that show their effectiveness in reducing the dropout rate significantly and concludes, "Even if bilingual education programs do nothing more than increase the number of Spanish-speaking school staff members, that may be sufficient reason for many Hispanics to support these programs."[17] Finally, whereas the report lays much of the blame for the perceived decline in standards on teacher unions, Peterson identifies the fall in teacher salaries as one of the problems that has afflicted education in recent years.[18] The Task Force does not mention this as a factor which has motivated teachers to join unions. Rather, it decries the spread of the trade union mentality in education. While the shift in tone from the background paper to the report is not radical, it is sufficient to tilt the substance of the report away from recent concerns to use education to empower minority groups. In so many words, the report lets us know that it is in the attempt to meet the demands of Latinos, blacks and other groups that the federal government has let its commitment to quality slip.

The assault on equality is subtle. Equality of opportunity is accepted by all of the reports as a proper goal of schooling which, of course, it must be if a proposal is to attain any credibility. Rather, the assault is on particular interpretations of equality which in *Making the Grade* is evidenced by the begrudging acknowledgment given to affirmative action programs. The Task Force notes that "even affirmative action programs registered some success, although most were hampered by excessive federal manipulation."[19] The nature of this manipulation is not stated, but the comment fits well with the declining commitment to such programs that we have witnessed on the federal level in recent years.

While traditional formulations of equality of opportunity are not challenged by the report, there is an indirect challenge made to developing interpretations of this principle. Two related interpretations are important in understanding the force of this report. However, because they are only implied by the document they require some explicit explanation.

The first is a view of equality that argued the appropriateness of judging inequality on a group as well as an individual basis. The implication of this argument is that some kind of quota system may be appropriate in applying affirmative action guidelines. The appropriateness of this interpretation is implicitly rejected by the report in its oblique reference to the federal manipulation of affirmative action. Since the word "quota" is left for the reader to insert into the text, the report provides no argument against the use of quota nor does it provide any discussion about the way in which quotas have actually been used by the federal government. There is not even a discussion about the extent of their use. Nevertheless, the intended message is clear. The use has been excessive.

The second interpretation of equality that is implicitly rejected is signaled by the attack on bilingual programs. This interpretation involves the right of different minority groups to help determine their own educational agenda. Again, the report does not spell out the reason for its objection to bilingual programs but its excessive anxiety about the effects of bilingual programs seems to reflect a much deeper anxiety about the power of minority groups to conceive of and affect changes in the schools.

Of course, the two interpretations of equality are related. If students who cannot read, write or speak English cannot be taught in their native language, then all of their other skills will suffer. By not allowing intergroup inequality to count as *prima facie* evidence of unjust discrimination, then we will have little choice but to explain the performance deficiencies that will likely arise as signs of inferior ability or as the result of a cultural deficiency fostered by the home. Here, the dissenting comment in the report by Task Force member Carlos Hortas is an instructive footnote to the committee's recommendation. In it Professor Hortas shows that the committee was informed of the underlying social purpose of bilingual programs and of their actual practices. While it is fortunate that the Task Force preserved individual dissent in footnotes to its document, there is no evidence that Hortas' comments were incorporated into the report. He writes: "No bilingual program in the United States promotes another language as *a substitute for English*. In fact, intensive English instruction is a part of every bilingual program. Bilingual programs attempt to show that English is not, in and of itself, a superior or richer language than the student's native language. There is a greater social benefit in promoting and encouraging linguistic diversity than in calling for specious uniformity."[20] The italics are in the original and refer to a comment made in the main document characterizing bilingual education as a substitute for English teaching and warning against a multiplicity of specific language programs in each community. It is precisely the linguistic diversity that Hortas would encourage that the larger committee fears.

All of this is not to deny that there is a real concern among the authors of the various reports about the ability of the schools to produce higher-level scientists and engineers. However, the actual growth in jobs in these areas will be relatively small when compared to the growth in jobs at the lower levels of the economy, and the problems of structural unemployment have not been solved although the tolerance for higher levels may be increasing.[21] The concern about bilingual education and affirmative action, together with the nervous lobbying for the recognition of English as the national language, are expressions of a general anxiety about the empowerment of minority groups.[22] In other words, they represent a curtailment of what the Trilateral Commission has referred to as the excesses of democracy that developed in the 1960s and 70s.

Education for a Unified Culture

Some nostalgics believe that there was once a time when people in the United States shared a common culture; a time when masses and elite were bound together by a common belief in the Bible and when elites were clearly recognizable and legitimated by their ability to read the classical texts in the original Latin or Greek. I don't know when or whether this time existed, but there are some who believe it can be recaptured, even if in a different form. My own belief is that any common heritage will have to be found in the struggles by which different peoples confront existing institutions and in the changes that result, both to the people and the institutions, in the course of this struggle.

The Paideia Proposal, written by Mortimer Adler on behalf of the Paideia Group, is an attempt to assert the idea of a unified culture built not on the Bible but on a curriculum that reflects a unified cultural experience.[23] Adler believes that there are a series of objectives and courses which should be prescribed for all primary and secondary school children, and he further believes that students should be allowed to take only these courses. (*The Paideia Proposal* actually comprises the first of three volumes. While it is the most publicized of the three, the third volume, *The Paideia Program*, with specific essays on pedagogy by members of the Paideia Group, is actually the most useful.[24])

Adler argues that all elective courses should be eliminated from the school curriculum and that vocational and specialized subjects should be undertaken only after a student graduates from high school. He believes that each student should undergo the same general program, one which reflects the basic goals of a liberal education. The subject matter that he proposes fits into three groups: language, literature and the fine arts is the first; mathematics and natural science is the second; geography and social studies is the third.[25] These are selected presumably because they relate most directly to the three goals of education which Adler identifies—individual growth, citizenship, and a vague category that he calls the development of "the basic skills that are common to all work in a society such as ours."[26]

Adler has presented similar proposals in the past, but the present climate is especially receptive and his work is receiving considerable publicity. The proposal is endorsed by a group of twenty-two leading educators who call themselves the Paideia Group.[27] There have been reports of individual schools establishing a curriculum along the lines suggested in the proposal. Adler's work has also been strongly criticized by a number of professional educators, often on the grounds that it does not take into account individual differences.[28] The actual substance of Adler's proposal does not, in fact, warrant the severe criticism that it has received, nor does it deserve the enthusiastic support that a number of admirers have granted it.

The *Proposal* itself contains very few useful guidelines for directing the educational process. It gives the appearance of specificity but not the substance. For example, there is the appearance of a rational argument for the elimination of vocational training but there is nothing which tells us what is to count as vocational training. We have no way of knowing whether a course that used the automobile to teach certain principles of physics would count as a science course or as a course in automobile mechanics. We do not know whether it would make a difference if students worked on a real car or if they only look at pictures of an engine to illustrate the principles. We are told that students are to be spared specialized courses. However, we do not know whether a course in black history from 1800 to 1950 would be seen as too specialized. Or, if so, whether a course in American history from 1800 to 1950 would be seen in the same way. The fact is that Adler provides no answers to questions like these because he confuses the label of a course with its substance. The difficult questions are not whether history or literature should be taught; it is whose history or whose literature. It is amazing that after the curriculum debates that have been raging for the past twenty years, Adler thinks that he can pluck a label out of the air and thereby provide the substance of a curriculum.

Adler's document has political significance, providing, as it does, rhetorical support for the belief that American society rests on a unified set of cultural themes which are known by some and can be taught by others. Adler does not offer a pedagogy; he creates a mood whereby education rides calmly over the political fracas secure in the understanding that it rests on an expertly sanctioned body of knowledge. The intensity of the debate over Adler's work is interesting only because there is nothing offensive in the substance of Adler's proposal.[29]

The Alternatives

One of the striking features about the documents discussed so far is that they are not based on any observations of actual schools, but rather draw their conclusions either from an analysis of statistical data about school performance or, as is the case with Adler, from some timeless ideals that have been pasted onto the present situation. This analysis is in sharp contrast to other evaluations which rely in varying degrees on direct classroom observation to fill in the details that *a priori* and survey methods must inevitably overlook. Three works in this genre include an impressively detailed study of the American school by John Goodlad,[30] a composite impression of the American high school drawn by Theodore Sizer,[31] and a report written for the Carnegie Foundation for the Achievement of Teaching by Ernest Boyer,[32] which like Goodlad's uses both survey and observational techniques.

There are a number of common features to these three works. First, all of them view schools in a much less alarmist fashion than does *A Nation at Risk* or *Making the Grade*. Second, all argue that the upgrading of the teaching profession requires not just the development of some form of career ladder for teachers, but also more autonomy for the local school. Third, while all advocate some form of a core curriculum, they each have an interest in improving more than the academic side of school life. All three authors believe that the school has an important responsibility for developing a sense of community among its students. Even though all are in favor of a core curriculum, their recommendations are sensitive to the pedagogical problem of relating the curriculum to the interests of the student. In contrast to the earlier documents, there is a diminished emphasis on declining test scores and a warning that we should not assume that the decline in such scores necessarily indicates a decline in educational quality. In addition, there is a strong concern about the vast differences in quality and opportunities that are presented by different high schools.

However, many of the specific issues that occupied the public's attention in recent years are missing from these accounts. There is no discussion of busing, for example, and one does not find in the index to either Goodlad's or Boyer's book (Sizer did not include an index) a reference to either sexism or racism. Goodlad explains this shift in emphasis by noting that while the struggle for equal access to education is not over, we have entered a new era in that struggle, one in which greater attention will be paid to what and how students learn in school.[33] While I would agree with the observation, I would want to emphasize that social class, racial and sexual differences in access to high quality education remains a major educational problem.

The analysis presented in these three books benefits when contrasted to *A Nation at Risk*. They are less doctrinaire than the report of the National Commission and they have a more balanced view of the problems and purposes of schooling. There is even some gentle sparring with a few points made by the National Commission. For example, Boyer, without naming his opponent, chides some reformers for neglecting the well-being of the individual in their concern for the national interest.[34] He also places considerably less emphasis on the school's role in developing scientists and engineers and considerably more on the need that future citizens will have to understand the social impact of science and technology.

There are, of course, differences among the reports and one could take exception to any of a series of recommendations. One could argue with Sizer for deemphasizing foreign language and physical education. We could quibble with Boyer about his suggestion that voluntary community service be made a compulsory part of the curriculum. And many people would take strong exception to Goodlad's proposal that tracking be eliminated. Yet, all of these proposals arise from a fuller understanding and a more sensitive treatment of schooling than those that we looked at earlier, and in doing so they provide balance to the recent string of pedagogical proposals. However, the situation is more complex when it comes to assessing the ideological place of these documents.

The Gentle Turn

If the documents under discussion place less emphasis on the relationship between education and national defense than, say, *A Nation at Risk*, they also reflect a tilt away from a more radical mode of educational analysis—one which sought to understand the mechanisms whereby schools help to reproduce an unequal social order. The tilt is gentle because the authors maintain much of the sensitivity to injustice and discrimination that inspired the more radical criticisms of schooling. For example, Theodore Sizer in his book, *Horace's Compromise*, notes that after visits to a number of schools serving different social classes,

"It got so that I could say with some justification to school principals, 'Tell me about the incomes of your students' families and I'll describe to you your school.'"[35] Nevertheless, while the sensitivity remains, the tilt is serving to blunt the kind of political and social analysis which the radical critique would use to explain why these inequalities persist.

The point of that critique is that a society which has large scale inequalities built into its basic economic structure will also have a mechanism to reproduce that inequality across generations. For a variety of reasons, it is argued that the schools have often served this function in modern industrial capitalist societies. Moreover, some of the problems found in schools may arise out of a need on the part of students or parents to resist the forces of reproduction. To the extent that this analysis is accurate, it means that educational reforms are likely to be implemented in such a way as to reflect in the classroom the unequal relations that exist outside of the schools. Thus, for example, we are likely to find that certain kinds of curriculum reform, say those that emphasize strict behavior discipline, rule-following and lower order memorization, will more often find their way into schools with children from the lower socioeconomic class while reforms that emphasize creativity or higher order conceptual skills will be more likely incorporated into schools with children from higher socioeconomic groups.

The analysis clearly needs refinement. Inequalities may persist above and beyond those that are required by the economic system; periods of rapid economic expansion may facilitate new instruction modes that are not simply reflective of existing economic relationships, and structural inequality may not require intergenerational inequality. Moreover, it has been too easy for critics to take this kind of analysis as a pessimistic appraisal, one suggesting that no efforts at school reform can ever be successful even on an individual level. (Were this the intended implication of the critical analyses, they would be as silly as the suggestion that the quality of training makes no difference in developing a professional pianist.) It is more appropriate to view such criticism as an attempt to understand the many factors, both inside and outside the school, which must be taken into account if successful, large scale change is to be achieved. A full understanding of classroom inequalities requires an analysis of school-society relations. It is one thing to show that inequalities exist. It is quite another to show why they continue to exist in the way that they do.

Of all the reform proposals only Goodlad's acknowledges that a critical literature on this subject exists, but even Goodlad is unable to engage this literature or to incorporate its insights into his analysis and recommendations. He observes that the division of high school programs into a vocational and academic track supports a two-class system and blocks opportunities for minority students.[36] He reports, without substantive criticism, on research which suggests that the benefits distributed by schools must, short of radical social change, reflect the benefits distributed by the larger economic and social order.[37] He concludes that the children in his survey had "quite different opportunities to gain access to knowledge during their years of schooling."[38] However, instead of pursuing the question as to the extent to which school inequality is a function of work inequalities, the argument is deflected into a discussion of the great difficulty that schools have in modifying the advantages and disadvantages provided by the home[39] and leads to a suggestion that tracking be eliminated and a core curriculum instituted.

The suggestions themselves are worth considering on their own account and Goodlad is certainly right to point out that "Accepting the need for society to have more typists, better automobile drivers and a steady supply of health workers does not necessarily justify . . . the development of programs in stenographic skills, driver training, and practical nursing in the nation's secondary schools."[40] While it is correct, the observation does not address the main point raised by the critical tradition: the reproduction of the relations of production depends much less upon the specific course label than upon the patterns of behavior that are encouraged and rewarded in the classroom. Even the elimination of tracking, a proposal which should be given much more serious attention than it is likely to receive, is, by itself, unlikely to overcome the differences that are reflected on a large scale in unequal economic relations. Goodlad deflects the discussion of economic inequality by viewing the home as the major source of advantages and disadvantages, thereby suggesting that the school can have only a modest effect on changing these inequalities.[41] By deflecting the analysis in this way and looking at the reproductive process only in terms of the family, he misses an important opportunity to understand the ecology of schooling. In other words, the advantages and disadvantages passed on by the family must, themselves, be understood in a context of work and schooling. To isolate the analysis of schooling and of the family from an analysis of the character of work is to fail to understand the important economic function that schools serve.

The difficulty is not with Goodlad's proposals. Indeed, many of his organizational and curriculum suggestions are constructive and, given the right setting, could improve the educational situation in many schools. Rather, the problem is with the limitations of the analytic tools that he uses to understand the direction of school reform. Schools are, among other things, reproductive mechanisms and it is important to understand the nature of the product that they are reproducing.

The difficulties that this limitation presents are more apparent with Boyer's treatment of schools than with Goodlad's. Boyer, along with Goodlad and Sizer, has been an articulate spokesperson for improving the working conditions of teachers. Among his recommendations is a proposal that would significantly improve the salaries of the teaching profession.[42] Unlike Goodlad, however, Boyer does not even acknowledge the significance of a critical educational tradition and this oversight contributes to recommendations which are likely to reduce, rather than enhance, the independence of the public school.

Boyer makes a number of recommendations to improve the condition of the teaching profession. In addition to recommending a substantial increase in salaries, his proposals include such things as sabbaticals, time off for study, and exchange programs.

The problem arises when the cost of implementing these and other proposals is considered. If schools are having difficulty meeting their present budget, they will certainly have trouble supporting Boyer's plan. Although Boyer does not provide any detailed suggestions about how his proposals will be financed, he clearly has the problem of funding in mind and makes a few suggestions which are intended to relieve the financial burden. The most significant of these is a proposal to increase the involvement of business and industrial support through direct grants to individual schools. To illustrate his idea he singles out for special commendation the "Adopt a School Program," which has arisen in some communities. In this program, a partnership is formed between a local industry and a school. Boyer mentions, as especially noteworthy, the good works in certain communities of energy utilities, oil companies, chemical manufacturers, and candy companies.

This proposal raises some serious issues. For example, it does not address the real structural problem with school finance and the implications of the fact that school revenue is one of the few areas where citizens have a direct say over their level of taxation. Since citizens have little opportunity to vote on other taxes such as those used for defense or highways, the school tax remains the one area where frustration can be voiced. This arrangement is one of the reasons it is so difficult in many areas to increase the education budget. Boyer's proposal does nothing to address this problem and leaves the fate of the school to the good will of the businesses in the community. Since public schools have not developed an independent intellectual tradition, this arrangement would increase the influence of special interest groups and would make the reproduction process more direct.

There is a related problem with Boyer's suggestion. All of the reports decry the lack of academic rigor in the schools but only a few decry the lack of intellectual debate as well. Goodlad is sensitive to the flat intellectual tone of many schools and Sizer captures the intellectual deficiency best in one of the anecdotes that he uses to indicate the flavor of a school. In a casual conversation with a senior boy, Sizer raises the question of registration for the draft. "Did it come up in school when registration was first required by the federal government? No. Did any of the guys decide not to register? No, but some of them may have forgotten to. Did any of the teachers raise the issue, perhaps in social studies classes? No. . . . We don't talk about things like that."[43]

There is no indication that this particular school was in partnership with a business enterprise or that it had been adopted by some corporation seeking to improve its image by doing good works. This is probably a reasonably typical situation. High schools are not generally intellectually active institutions and that is unfortunate. However, some high schools do have intellectually active teachers and these people already have enough hurdles to jump. For the teacher who might want to develop a unit on the effects of sugar on health or on the problems of hazardous waste or industrial accidents, Boyer's proposal would require special care not to offend the school's industrial sponsor. While it is unfortunate that a tradition of free and open inquiry has not flourished in public education, a company school is not quite the remedy that is needed.

Conclusion

Reform documents are not all equal. A *Nation at Risk* is a slim manuscript, but page for page it is clearly the most influential of the recent proposals. It has set the tone for the discussion about education and, because the character of that tone is harsh and one-sided, I have an appreciation for those authors who moderate their criticism of schooling, avoiding the unfortunate national chauvinism that marks the Commission's report. While I object to Boyer's failure to see the entanglements that he is endorsing for the schools, I agree with many of his suggestions for rejuvenating the teaching profession. While I can criticize Sizer for not probing the causes of the inequalities that he identifies, I can appreciate the sensitivities that his observations display. And while I do not believe that Goodlad goes far enough in analyzing the effects that the nature of work has on the nature of education, I can appreciate the fact that, in the present climate, he has gone as far as he has. Indeed, given the present political climate, I am doubtful whether one could go much further in critically analyzing the schools than Sizer and Goodlad have done without being dismissed as an irresponsible critic. Nevertheless, it is important to recognize when a compromise has been struck between influence and insight.

While there has been a lot of nonsense packaged under the heading of this or that national commission or this or that foundation report, the fact still remains that there are problems with the young that schools have not been able to address. The high illiteracy rate mentioned by a number of the reports is clearly one of them. However, the resolution of this problem will need an effort that goes far beyond the traditional practices of schools and will require far more understanding of cultural and linguistic diversity than even present bilingual programs have provided.

There is another problem too that is important to mention, but which has been neglected by all of the reports. It is the inability of the school, either through lack of will or lack of awareness, to provide students with the understanding that they need in order to critically reflect upon the political and cultural values that are being thrust upon them.

For example, a decision to enter military service ought to be taken very seriously after a searching understanding of the causes that one might be asked to kill or to die for. At this state in our history any youngster thinking of making such a commitment ought to know a great deal about our continuing relationship with Central America and the various techniques, from overt invasion, to covert economic sabotage, that we have used to overthrow indigenous, popular regimes. There should be an awareness of various interpretations of this relationship, both those which are available in the conservative and liberal presses and those which are not. These would range from interpretations which, like the Reagan administration, view our action as a struggle for freedom over slavery, to interpretations that see the government acting to protect the economic interests of a relatively few American corporations. While it would be important to allow youngsters to decide which of the various interpretations is most appropriate, critical reflection would require that they be informed of various possibilities and that they be encouraged to think through the implications of each of them for their own personal choice. It is, of course, difficult to say whether such an informed group would result in a stronger or a weaker military, but it would clearly contribute to a more adequately educated youth population.

At the present time the situation is not encouraging. Many youngsters, unable to find a decent job and inadequately prepared by their high school education to interpret this situation, have found that the military recruiting office presents an attractive alternative to unemployment. Some seem quite pleased to have the opportunity to defend their country's honor hoping only that we do it right this time—in Nicaragua. They want to help their president make them say "uncle."

This situation is fed by a culture machine which most schools have been both unwilling and unable to challenge. This summer, *Rambo* has been playing to packed audiences and, I am told, has often received standing ovations. I have been wondering whether educators could counter the impact of this cultural product by commissioning a film about a small, courageous group of Palestinians who, with great daring, offer their lives in a clandestine attack on the United States in order to release Sirhan Sirhan from prison. If the project mirrored Rambo, however, it would be too obnoxious to be educational. Yet the idea highlights the enormously difficult job that schools would have if they were to undertake the development of critical reflection in a serious way.

My own concern about educational reform is whether a sufficient intellectual and moral tradition can be established within the public, secondary schools to interrupt the reproduction process and whether the public schools could provide the intellectual climate that would enable young people to critically reflect upon the situation that they have been thrust into. The issue is not whether we should do our best to establish an academic climate in the high school. The question is whether we can do so in an intellectually honest and a politically open context.

Part III

Public School:
A Democratic Vision

10

The Public Responsibility of Public Education

The practices of state supported compulsory schools, what I, hesitatingly, will call (reflecting US usage) public education, has been challenged as exclusionary by groups of various religious and political persuasions in both the USA and Great Britain. In the USA fundamentalist religious groups arguing for fairness in the curriculum have asked that certain secular views be balanced by the presentation of religious alternatives. The most publicized issue has been the teaching of evolution and the request by certain fundamentalist parents that creationist views of the universe also should be taught as viable and alternative explanations.

While fundamentalist concerns about the teaching of evolutionary theory in the schools have been present for many years, present objections are different from past ones. In 1925, for example, the Scopes trial convicted a teacher for violating the law of the State of Tennessee by teaching evolutionary theory. In more recent situations, no challenge to the teaching of evolution has been offered. Rather the plaintiffs have asked that the teaching of evolution be balanced by the presentation of creationist accounts of the universe as another viable alternative.

While fundamentalist religious groups object to the schools' failure to acknowledge the viability of their interpretation of the universe, other marginalized groups object to the schools' failure to adequately represent their experience. Gay and Lesbian groups as well as feminists, along with ethnic and racial minorities, are concerned with an inadequate representation of their experience by the schools. Given these many different pressures on the schools, the question arises as to whether state supported schools can have any role in the development of a unified public.

The response to these pressures in the USA has been quite interesting. One argument sees the state as simply a mechanism for distributing educational resources, one which should have a very limited say about how those resources should be used. These people argue that the fundamental responsibility for educating children belongs to the parents and that parents should decide where their children attend school and what they should be taught. Another argument emphasizes the economic benefits of schooling and proposes a curriculum that would improve a student's ability to support himself and to contribute to the nation's economic well-being. Those who advocate this view want to narrow the offerings of the school, eliminating the so-called frill subjects; they want to increase the number of required subjects and they want to make the schools across the country increasingly similar to one another in terms of curriculum content. Those who emphasize the economic benefits of schools often do not see any conflict between their view and the one that advocates the widest possible choice for parents. This is because they assume that all parents and all cultures want their children to succeed economically, and because of this assumption they believe that a narrow, uniform, standardized curriculum is actually consistent with the widest amount of parent discretion. In other words, they advocate providing parents with more choice while reducing the variety of alternatives from which parents might choose. A third response insists that there in fact is a common culture and that children enter it by learning to identify its symbolic manifestations. This is the approach of E.D. Hirsch, Jr., who has developed a dictionary of cultural literacy which contains the thousands of items he believes students must be able to recall to be culturally literate as Americans.

The question I want to ask is whether there is still a possibility for a view of a public that is wider than those implied by the three responses that I have sketched above and, if so, whether this wider view has any implications for the conduct of state supported public education. In other words, what I seek is a public that is more than simply a distributor and recipient of resources, more than simply an agent in a market and more than a cluster of individuals who happen to consume a common set of symbols. I want to argue that the concept of a public makes sense in more than just a utilitarian way and that among the most important functions of public education is its relationship to that public as both recipient of its support and an important condition of its growth.

The debate over the role of public education in the USA arises out of a set of important historical and political conditions. The shifting patterns of immigration, for example, mean that it is no longer possible to rely upon a common European experience as a source of a collective identity. Most of our newer immigrants are coming from Mexico, Latin America, Korea, Vietnam and India rather than England, Germany, Italy and France. In one state, California, the majority of students in public schools are from minority groups and it is expected that sometime in the not too distant future this will be the case for public schools in the nation as a whole. In addition to demographic changes there have been important changes in cultural norms, leaving little consensus about roles, norms and expectations. Moreover, a large number of our problems require the collective action of groups that extend well beyond either the local community or the nation state, leaving unanswered questions about the boundaries of the public.

There is a concern in the USA that these changes have resulted in a fractured national identity. Some still believe that because public education should be responsible for developing the habits, loyalties and dispositions required for political membership, it is the role of public schools to mend the fracture and restore the identity. Yet in a society like the USA, and perhaps also like the UK, where little consensus exists about the proper direction of the nation, there is not sufficient agreement about the character of such an identity. We simply do not agree about the kind of public we want to have and without such agreement it is very difficult to determine the direction that education should take.

Some believe that the problem is exacerbated by the shift away from a European based population and hence by a change in the nature of the collective memory. For example a recent national survey of college students showed that a sizable minority could not, as the survey asked, identify the year that Columbus set foot on the Western Hemisphere, and many traditional educators used the survey to point out the deficits of American education. Yet one of the little noticed features of the survey was the way in which this question had undergone a subtle change. Instead of asking as it used to be done, "When did Columbus discover America?" it is now asked "When did he set foot on the Western Hemisphere?" Of course the reason for the change is that for many groups—namely native Americans—Columbus did not discover America and the wording is a belated acknowledgement that these groups were already there when Columbus arrived. The example is interesting in another respect as well for it requires some qualification of the "lost public" thesis. It points out that there have always been groups outside of the dominant consensus and that the supposed unity that once existed existed because alternative voices were effectively silenced.[1] Yet, of course, if Columbus did not actually discover America, then who cares when he set foot on it. Perhaps those with European ancestors, but that is fast becoming a minority.

Part of the problem is that for children from native US or Asian or black ancestry the character of their collective memories is different from that of the stereotypical white American from a European background. However, this is not the only problem. Indeed, in the eighteenth century the absence of a common collective memory and a shared conception of the public was one of the main reasons given for the need for public education. It was argued that without a public school system the country could not depend upon the shared values that modern nationhood required. The fact that most of the immigrants came from a Europe that was divided and in conflict was not a reason to abandon the public-forming role of state supported education. Indeed, it gave much of the force and power to those arguing for state controlled schools. Without a state controlled educational system, the conflicts of Europe would continue here. Thus it is not the simple fact of difference that is the cause of the loss of confidence in the public role of public education. Rather, the loss of confidence is the companion of the demise of the philosophical foundations of the public school movement, a foundation grounded in the Enlightenment.

The Enlightenment view was that there are such things as universal natural rights; that all people should aspire to recognize such rights; that all cultures can be judged from the point of view of such rights and that the function of an educated public is to hold people accountable to those rights. It was always possible to criticize public education for failing to live up to the Enlightenment creed or to view public educators as hypocrites for using schools to serve corporate interests. Yet these revelations alone would not have been enough to bring into doubt the proper function of public education unless there was doubt about the very conception of rights that purportedly supported the public school project. True, the public schools could be criticized for not living up to their purported obligation, but such criticism could well be taken as a demand for more and better public education. The self-confidence of public education came from the clear understanding that Western—and specifically US—society was the principal bearer of the ideals of the Enlightenment and that the public school was the site where these ideas were to be nourished.

I do not mean to discount other motives for the development of state supported schools, nor do I want to suggest that the development of a public concerned to advance the values of the Enlightenment was the most prominent concern. Clearly, many wanted to further public education to prepare the work force needed by industrial capitalism and to develop the dispositions and loyalties that an expanding industry and military required. Yet except for the deepest cynics it was the belief in the Enlightenment ideals that allowed these other projects to be advanced with limited guilt or despair. However, if we rephrase these projects in modern—or better, postmodern—terms, we can see how the crisis of confidence in public education has been accompanied by a shift in the evaluation of the Enlightenment project. In post-modern terms the foundation of public education was purchased by totalizing the white male, middle class, Eurocentered (US) experience. And the cost of continuing this ideal is the marginalization of feminine, homosexual, Asian, African, Latin American experience.

The above sets the problem. If the idea of a public is to be justified it must be able to address this criticism. Such a justification is required for an acceptance of public education as preparation for participation in that public. Alasdair MacIntyre sketched the problem in its starkest terms by denying that the possibility of an educated public any longer exists. By denying the possibility of an educated public MacIntyre implicitly denies the possibility of any intelligent, wider public that is capable of rationally considering the merit of different collective alternatives.

MacIntyre believes that the quality of independent thought that a member of an educated public requires is no longer present in modern society except in very specialized contexts.[2] As he puts it:

> Thinking has become the occupational responsibility of those who discharge certain social roles: the professional scientist, for example. But those topics thinking about which is of general social concern, thought about goods and the good, about the relationship of justice to effectiveness or the place of aesthetic goods in human life, about the tragic, the comic and the farcical not only in literature, but also in politics and

> economics, either are handed over to certain disciplined, but limited because professionalized, specialists or are dealt with in forums in which the constraints of disciplined exchange are almost always lacking.[3]

He concludes that "the educated public has been replaced by a set of specialized publics" (ibid., 25).

MacIntyre's narrative is set in the first half of the eighteenth century in Scotland where he proposes that a truly educated public came into existence. However, the public which came into existence in eighteenth century Scotland was also a public that was destined to end as the consequences of population and economic growth withered away the common standards that bound the public together.

MacIntyre uses this situation to elaborate the conditions that he believes essential for the development of an educated public. First there must be a tolerably large number of people who are educated into the habit of rational debate; they must understand the significance of different issues for their "shared social experience" and they must recognize each other as constituting a public.[4] They are thus contrasted with a group of specialists and with a passive public who provide an audience for the debate. Secondly there must be shared assent to the standards by which arguments are to be judged and third there must be a "large degree of shared background beliefs."[5]

For MacIntyre the demise of the educated public in Scotland represents the situation of modernity. "We possess in our culture too many different and incompatible modes of justification. We do not even have enough agreement to be able to arrive at a common mind about what it is we should be quarrelling about."[6] He believes that we do not have a conception of the good that can be agreed upon by the many competing groups in modern society and hence we lack the foundation for the development of such a public.

MacIntyre overstates the case in a number of ways which I will consider shortly. It needs to be pointed out here, however, that he has not established a case for the *impossibility* of a public in modern times. Rather his article simply describes a situation where a public does not happen to exist. I will not question the accuracy of that description but it is important to note that to conclude that the existence of a public is impossible in our times requires two additional steps. It requires an argument that social life has become so complex that it is no longer possible for a person with a reasonable education to sufficiently grasp its complexities. And it requires that it must remain complex. Hence we are fated to hand over deliberation about the most important matters to experts who themselves are limited by their disciplinary training. MacIntyre does not argue for either of these points although it is clear that he is assuming both of them.

MacIntyre does not actually voice the argument about the complexity of modern life, perhaps leaning on a frustration that many of us feel. Instead he is content to point out the inconsistent roles of modern education—both to prepare students to take up a particular occupational role and to think for themselves about matters of wider import. Yet these are only incompatible if we accept the idea that social affairs have grown so complex that they cannot be evaluated from the point of view of a particular role. However, if we do not believe that modern society is inexorably complex, or if we believe that we do have the capacity to reflect on the moral implications of our own role, then we need not be inclined towards MacIntyre's conclusion. MacIntyre himself appears to be somewhat underwhelmed by the strength of his own argument for in another essay on patriotism he seems to assume that certain characteristics of a public are still possible.

The lost public thesis, illustrated by MacIntyre's argument, can be addressed in one of two ways. One can recreate the unity between the conception of the good and the public by grasping one or another side of the two poles. First, one may, as MacIntyre does in his essay on patriotism, grab hold of a particular community and make it comparable to the public. Or, second, one can grasp a particular conception of the good and insist that such a conception is foundational for the development of a public.

In his essay on patriotism[7] MacIntyre argues against the view that the content of moral judgment is independent of the source of moral learning. MacIntyre challenges the view that "where and from whom I learn the principles and precepts of morality are and must be irrelevant both to the question of what the content of morality is and to that of the nature of my commitment to it."[8] He argues that "It is an essential characteristic of the morality which each of us acquires that it is learned from, in and through the way of life of some particular community." Moreover, there will be important differences in the way in which one community or another responds to particular situations[9] and with the institutional arrangements entailed by moral rules.[10] And thus "what I learn as a guide to my actions and as a standard for evaluating them is never morality as such, but always the highly specific morality of some highly specific social order."[11] It is only within communities that individuals become capable of morality and only within communities that they are constituted as moral agents.[12] Patriotism is defensible because of the intricate connection between morality and the way of life of a particular community.[13]

MacIntyre intends his discussion to be more than simply another description of the way in which moral socialization takes place. It is a discussion about the nature of morality and its particularistic roots. Yet the argument is peculiar, for in arguing that morality is always tied to the institutions and way of life of a particular community, MacIntyre appeals to a transcendent moral argument which requires the conclusion that morality is always particularistic. Or, to put my point somewhat differently, if MacIntyre's presentation is to be taken as an argument about morality and not just a general description of individual socialization, it requires that the argument itself be placed in a moral frame. Yet this frame is not that of any particular community. It is rather one that transcends particular communities in order to make the case that morality is always grounded in the individual community. Thus the "grasp a community" argument fails because it presupposes an appeal to a common good.

While MacIntyre tries to resolve the lost public thesis by grasping on to the particular community pole, John Haldane in his defense of religious education attempts to resolve the problem by grasping a particular conception of the good. This approach seeks to constitute a public by asserting the formative significance of a certain conception of the good. In the USA, for example, Allan Bloom's best seller, *The Closing of The American Mind: How Higher Education has Failed Democracy and Impoverished the Souls of Today's Students*, grasps the Enlightenment tradition as its conception of the good and uses it to argue against the splintering effects of an alien, relativistic, post-modern philosophy imported from Germany. Haldane[14] uses a similar strategy but instead of the Enlightenment he argues from the formative significance of Christianity and then uses this to argue that (barring parental objection) the devotional teaching of the Christian religion and its ethical implications should be an important part of the school curriculum.

What is questionable is Haldane's causal claim that modern morality stems from Christianity and the conclusion drawn from it that because Christianity was foundational, we should teach children its devotional doctrines. The argument sounds somewhat equivalent to suggesting that because American football had its roots in British rugby, American football players should practice playing rugby. What Haldane is really saying is that the British public should be formed around the ethical teachings of Christianity, because they were once formed around those teachings. Yet the idea that this should be done just because it has been done in the past is precisely what is at issue. In other words, Haldane has resolved the problem of the lost public by grasping a particular conception of the good.

If we think about particular issues like the question of abortion or whether the state should support schools that separate boys and girls, there are many factors that need to be considered and it is not clear to me that the doctrines of Christianity—assuming some unified set of doctrines—have special priority. Indeed, one can even question Haldane's causal claim that modern morality stems from Christianity in any linear way. It could be argued that only with the breakdown of the hegemony of Christianity did modern attitudes towards morality emerge. Here I do think that MacIntyre is correct: the problem of the public in modern society arises from its heterogeneity. The very fact that religious education—let alone Christian education—is now a subject of debate and contention is a sign of the kind of problem in which we are involved. However, that the abandonment of uniformity in religions is a factor in modern concerns about the public does not mean that the problems with which we are involved will be solved by a renewed emphasis on religious belief. It would, I suppose, be possible to develop a reasonable religious—perhaps Christian—curriculum. However, were it to truly represent the pluralism that exists in the larger society, it would be quite a different Christian education than the kinds of devotional studies most religious people have known. In other words, if a conception of the good were to be grasped that is adequate to the problem it would, in fact, have to grasp conceptions of a good.

To recognize the plurality of belief systems is not, as MacIntyre seems to believe, to deny the possibility of a public. A public does not require that all share the same belief system. Rather, it implies a certain amount of plurality and a willingness to grapple with questions of right and wrong within the context of others with different beliefs. The error in MacIntyre's view of a public is the mistaken idea that publics can exist only where general beliefs and legitimation structures are widely shared and where the only questions that need to be resolved are issues of application. One problem with this view is that the distinction between general principles and their application is not clear cut.

For example, in the abortion debates it could be said that both sides share the same general principle about the value of human life but that they differ about some of the factors that are involved in the application of that principle such as whether control over one's own body has priority over the value of human life. Yet control over one's own body is also a general principle that is likely shared by both sides and the issue at hand is which principle has priority. MacIntyre could argue that while agreement about general principles is not sufficient for the existence of a public, agreement about general principles together with agreement about institutional legitimacy is sufficient. In other words, since institutions determine the application of general principles, a public can be constituted through mutual agreement about both principles and institutions. Yet whereas agreement over general principles cannot provide MacIntyre with the public he seeks, agreement about both general principles and the institutions that apply such principles are too strong, leaving no room for the deliberation and debate that characterize conceptions of a public. Conceptions of the public need to leave room for deliberation and debate about matters that are not clear cut and these must even include deliberation and debate about which institutions are appropriate for deciding particular issues that are of common concern. At the very end of MacIntyre's book, *Whose Justice? Which Rationality?*, he acknowledges the issue and suggests a solution to it, proposing that the rational person is always grounded in a tradition while engaging "both in the ongoing arguments within that tradition and in the argumentative debates and conflicts of that tradition of enquiry with one or more of its rivals."[15] This is in fact a much more satisfactory position. However, it is not easily reconciled with the earlier part of the book and its emphasis on the incommensurability of traditions. Moreover, the conditions that MacIntyre establishes for judging the merits of two or more traditions would require that one first achieve native-like competence within each of the conflicting traditions. Hence, whereas in the earlier part of the book he appears to make translation and evaluation between traditions theoretically impossible, in the later part he makes it practically unlikely, at least for most people.

One difficulty with MacIntyre's conception of a public is the failure to consider non-cognitive factors such as the willingness to continue the discussion even in the context of fundamental differences about what should be done, or the ability to explore an issue from the point of view of a wider community. This second condition is complex because it includes the perspectives both of groups with which we have emotional attachments and of groups whose action affects the groups to which we are attached. However, these complexities simply indicate that the conception of a public needs to be open textured and fluid, allowing for shifting boundaries and commitments. It does not deny the possibility of the development of a public. Rather it enables us to look for a plurality of publics that both address specific problems and issues and relate to each other in a variety of ways.

Modern societies have their paradigm cases of working publics. For example, a jury has an obligation to render a judgment from the point of view of the law and in doing so its members have a responsibility to reflect upon factors such as racial or ethnic bias that may inhibit a reasonably impartial judgment. Other instances of publics can be found in small town meetings and community groups, in various consumer advocacy groups working to control costs or assure quality by establishing an open dialogue about standards and controls. Of course, all of these different kinds of publics can fall short and fail to meet appropriate standards. Juries do not always judge from the point of view of the law and jury members may frequently fail to reflect upon the influence of racial or ethnic bias in their decision. That they sometimes do fail to meet appropriate standards does not mean, as MacIntyre suggests, that it is impossible to do so. Rather it suggests the need for a more refined selection process or better training for jury members.

The question of whether or not the development of a public is possible is an especially important one for education. MacIntyre provides an unfortunate rationale for educational resignation on the grounds that intelligent public discourse is no longer possible and that schools cannot provide students with the means for joining public discourse. The alternative view is that there are many sites and locations where publics could be created but where they may not presently exist or where they exist in a truncated form. For example workers who labor on a common task but have little opportunity to discuss job conditions or the social value of their product constitute a potential public. However, if their discourse does not extend to these normative concerns, or if they cannot participate with other groups in addressing these concerns, they do not constitute a functioning public. Yet it clearly would be possible for schools to provide the means and to encourage the dispositions that are needed to prepare students for public discourse of this kind. There is nothing mysterious about the process which includes developing symbolic skills, learning to assess cause-and-effect relationships, understanding the tradition of rights that enables citizen groups to groups address issues of common concern and proving a nurturing, reasonable and democratic environment to voice such concerns.

Of course, the concept of a public requires more than local, transitory groups enabled to discourse and take action about particular issues. It also requires a commitment to actions and practices undertaken to sustain the free flow of ideas about the general well-being. In order for this larger multiple public to come into being it must be aware of itself as an entity through the awareness of its members both as individuals and as local publics. The development of this collective self-consciousness and self-understanding is constituted through debates by the public about the nature of the public. Under this conception the role of public education is to help create and recreate a public by giving voice to an otherwise inarticulate, uninformed mass.

There are, of course, complicating factors such as the ones I raised at the beginning of this essay. They are, however, factors which can be addressed by being mindful of the public role of education. For example, educators are rightly troubled by questions about how to treat creationist theory in the classroom. However, the difficulty comes not from concern about whether evolutionary or creationist theory is more adequate scientifically. If creationism is true it is not because of its scientific adequacy but because it accords with some group's revealed truth. It is precisely because such truth is revealed that it is not a public truth. Evolution is about evidential claims and therefore is public. Rather, educators are bothered with this issue because it represents a case in which there is an apparent clash between the revealed truth of the local publics and the teachings of the larger, collective public.

While these issues are not easily resolved, the responsibility of creating a public out of diverse voices requires that local interests, cultures, symbols and issues be heard within the context of a larger discussion. From the local point of view it would not be sufficient to provide a list of local cultures or events to be honored for a day or a week. Local voices bring local interests and standards from which to reflect on other standpoints. However, it is also not sufficient to simply include the local, as fundamentalist Christians advocating Creationism would propose, as a way to achieve balance among different points of view. If it is included then it must become a possible object of criticism from other standpoints and using other standards. The price of entry into the debate of the multiple public is that local ideals and values are subjected to critical evaluation from other standpoints. To enter the public-forming process involves risks as well as benefits and some may find the risks too great.

From the point of view of the teacher there are professional judgments that need to be made about the appropriateness of a certain course of study or subject matter for a particular group of students. Here issues of individual development, of emotional and intellectual growth, enter the picture. A student may not yet be ready to enter into a deeply critical discussion of her own cultural roots and, upon considering the requirements of future intellectual and emotional growth, a teacher may decide that it is inappropriate to probe such matters at a certain time. There are, after all, both emotional and intellectual requirements to cultural critique—both of the local and national. Nevertheless, while cultural pride has an important emotional role to play, the formation of a public ultimately requires cultural interpretation and critique. It is only as these elements are included in the curriculum that state supported schools can be said, without hesitation, to take on a public educative role.

Local communities may, of course, have serious reservations about the spiritual price they must pay for public education. Some may believe that to subject certain matters of faith to public debate is implicitly to place reason above faith and hence to surrender to secular forces before the battle has been joined.[16]

There are two responses that are relevant to this objection. The first applies to groups such as the Creationists in the USA who ask for equal time to present their arguments. In this case the very act of making the request for equal time implicitly carries with it the willingness to allow the limitations as well as the strength of one's views to be examined. To ask for equal time is hence to allow reason to question faith and to allow for the possibility that faith may be changed in light of reason.

The second response concerns groups that do not even want to go this far. These groups may view reason as always subordinate to faith or they may believe, as MacIntyre suggests, that the character of reason is itself molded by faith and tradition. We may respect the integrity of such groups for a number of different kinds of reasons. For example, we may believe that it is important for society to maintain a plurality of traditions and believing this we may feel it is important to allow a challenge to our faith in a universal rational principle. Or we may think that barring obvious harm to others it is best to maintain the right of parents to determine the most appropriate education for their children. However, while these are good reasons for not interfering with certain forms of traditional education, they are not good reasons for thinking of these as forms of public education. Whether public financial support for such schools should be provided will depend on considerations other than their contribution to the public forming process.

11

The Idea of a Public Education

Introduction:
The Public Role of Public Education

In everyday language, whether a school is described as "public" or not is determined by the way it is funded and by who is allowed to attend it (Callan 2004). Ideally however, a *public* school should also be defined and evaluated by its unique goal—to renew a public by providing the young with the skills, dispositions, and perspectives required to engage with others about their shared interests and common fate. Yet just what does it mean to renew a public and to engage one another? How is this engagement to take place, and what might it mean in a highly specialized class conscious, gendered, and racialized society to have shared interests or a common fate? Is there even such a thing as a public or is it simply a shorthand way to indicate a lot of individual people, each with their own interests and ideas who may happen to intersect and come together in a temporary way and on some issues? And, if the *public* is only a collective term for a lot of individuals, then can there really be anything unique about an education that is called "public"? And what does "engagement" mean? War is an "engagement" as much as a calm living room conversation. These questions motivate the debate over education today, and uncertainty about the answers fuels the desire to "privatize" education. The first task of this chapter then is to get some purchase on the idea of a public and to see how it can be applied to education.

A Brief History of the Idea of the Public

The idea of a public can be traced back to the Greek "Agora" where citizens would come to exchange both goods and ideas and where matters of state might be deliberated. Exchange is the central idea here, but the exchange is not only between a single seller and a single buyer, the image that dominates classical capitalism, for example. Rather, the image here is of a horizontal exchange among equals, doing many things at once, and where political discussion was a part of an everyday life. Selling and purchasing took place in the Agora, but so did playing, teaching and learning, arguing, philosophizing, and so on. And even though the citizenry comprised only a segment of the population, excluding women and slaves, the fact that the exchange was horizontal and brought many activities into the open meant that much identity work was being done as goods were exchanged. Athenians learned to be Athenians in the context of growing up in and participating in the Agora (of course, those who were not citizens also learned how to behave appropriately in a public place that was not exactly their own; Jaeger, 1939/1967, 140). It was here that the stories of Homer, of the past wars, and of the present threats were passed on, and it was here as well that children first learned of the Greek Gods and their quarrelsome and capricious nature.

Deliberation was certainly a part of this cacophony of activity; the Agora gave rise to the idea of an interest beyond that of the individual. Jaeger (1939/1967) describes the development of this interest as Solon (the ancient statesman and legislator) "warns his fellow-citizens against wearing themselves out in the blind and furious conflict of interest" (140). Self-interest, class warfare, and civil strife are the evils that tear a city apart (Jaeger, 1939/1967, 141), and Solon understood the need for an impartial body of law that would govern life and to which all citizens would have an allegiance. This idea of allegiance to an impartial body of law also provided a proposed public identity, an ideal, to shape an Athenian citizen, however imperfectly this may have been accomplished. This ideal is best expressed in Plato's (1986) *Apology* (3–26) and *Crito* (27–43) where Socrates appeals to the impartiality of reason to refute the charge of treason levied against him and then accepts his sentence as the will, however mistaken, of the city that has raised him. Public ascent to the governing laws of society as a sphere above partisan private interests was an important factor in the subsequent philosophical conversations that took place in Greece. For if there was something to the idea that the polis had a public foundation that was more than mere force in the service of the most powerful, then that foundation had itself to be public and available to all citizens (Plato 1945/1964). For a Greek philosopher such as Plato, that foundation was a commitment to rational deliberation.

For Plato, and Aristotle, it was the ability to understand and engage in the reasoning process that made one fit to rule, and this was not available to everyone. Reason and democracy were not coupled. Rather, democracy was the product of desire and was practiced by a collection of individuals. Reason was the process of reflection, a process through which a public was created. Reason, then, was public in a very limited sense. It was not available for all to comprehend, but for the few who were sufficiently insightful *to* comprehend, it could lead to an appropriate public life. The conclusions of reason were public when they were developed in the context of responses to all alternatives and addressed all reasonable counterarguments.

For Aristotle to appreciate the public nature of reason, one must first locate it properly. Whereas Plato sought a politics that would be as rational and as precise as mathematics, Aristotle understood that the standard of reason must be different in ethics (1953/1956) and politics (1948/1957) than in mathematics. Ethics like politics is not the precise kind of science as is mathematics, and to get it right one needs to recognize this difference. Aristotle understood in a way that Plato seemed not to that there is a human element involved in public deliberation about politics and ethics. Human interest is mixed with human reason. However, that element has the same basic interest as Solon had established: to dissolve potentially destructive conflicts and enable the right sort of people—those not burdened by private concerns and interests—to come together in a dispassionate way to deliberate about the most preferred course of action. Given that the majority of the people in Athens were women or slaves or both, this still meant that the role of deliberator was an exclusive one, one reserved only for the free males who were citizens.

Nevertheless, Aristotle rejected Plato's view that the role of education was to create political unity, by promoting the acceptance of a hierarchy of virtues with justice at the top. Instead, he saw the significance of diversity within harmony. He wrote, "It is true that unity is to some extent necessary . . . but total unity is not. There is a point at which a polis by advancing unity will cease to be a polis: There is another point, short of that, at which it may still remain a polis, but will none the less come nearer to losing its essence, and will thus be a worse polis. It is as if you were to turn harmony into mere unison, or to reduce a theme to a single beat" (Aristotle 1948/1957, 51). For Aristotle, a public school, one under the control of the legislator, although not open to everyone, was the instrument for preparing students for a public role.[1] In contrast to casual contemporary usage, for Aristotle (1948/1957) a school was public because (a) it promoted public virtues, and especially reason; (b) it prepared students for life in a public; and (c) it was controlled by a public body. A public education provided students with the disinterested dispositions and deliberative skills to engage in rational discussions about the overall well-being of the polis.

Two ingredients dominated the Greek idea of a public education. First was the development of what Aristotle called the rational faculty, and second was a shared identity in the construction of a public good. Hence the importance of friendship among equals for Aristotle's legislators, a friendship that they began to develop through the mediation of public education. Some centuries later, indeed at an unlikely historical moment, the Roman Cicero challenged Aristotle's doctrine of the exclusiveness of reason arguing that all men are equal in terms of their possession of reason (Sabine 1958, 164) and that "the state and its law is the common property of its people" (166), allowing that the people as a whole are a collective body with "a self-governing organization which has necessarily the power to preserve itself" (166).

The Eclipse of the Public as a Moral Reality

Two features of Aristotle's idea of a public need to be highlighted. The first is that as a deliberative body seeking to advance a common good, the public has a reality that is more than the sum of the individuals who compose it. The second is that a public refers to a process of rational deliberation about a common fate. The Reformation and, more important, certain interpretations of early capitalism served to eclipse both of these. Although Aristotle held that a public has a moral status and a reality in its own right, both of these movements stressed the exclusive reality of the individual, one as the agent of conscience and goodness, the other as the agent of desires and freedom. For both, individual authenticity was elevated over rational and collaborative deliberation as an ideal (Taylor 1992).

Moreover, Aristotle's idea of a public concerned a shared identity—membership in a polis—as well as a shared fate. Only citizens could be members of this public, not only because only citizens were capable of reasoning but also because only citizens were conscious of a shared identity, and only they were able to put private interest aside in deliberating about a course of collective action. The idea of the subordination of private interests to some larger public interest was eclipsed as the evolution of laissez-faire capitalism placed all desire on a common plain where the market would determine their worth (Satz 2010).

A critical difference between Aristotle's (and Cicero's) notion of the public and liberalism's idea of self-government involves the place of desire, and reflection. For the liberal, desire is the motive for action. For Aristotle, desire was not the motive for action but the cause for and the initiator of reflection. As an individual, I of course have desires, and in the private sphere it is quite natural, according to Aristotle, to act on them. However, for Aristotle, the public sphere serves as a check on individual desires and evokes mutual reflection and a concern to harmonize the desires of different individuals and to harness them in a communal effort to define and achieve a common good.

For Aristotle, what and how I desire in private may well influence my capacity to reflect on these desires in public. Hence the need for an education that stresses restraint and friendship "as the pursuit of a common social life" (Aristotle 1948/1957, 139). The aim of a good society is to shape desire in ways that enable a social good to emerge. Aristotle thus warns that "the masses become revolutionary when the distribution of property is unequal" (1948/1957, 79). Certainly not himself a revolutionary, he quickly adds that educated men become revolutionary when "the distribution of office is equal" (79). The point, however, is that for Aristotle, the reflection and control of individual desire is a condition and an aim of public life.

This is not so for the laissez-faire liberal. Indeed, outside of the initial moment when a political society is formed, the conception of a public, as a deliberative body seeking a common good, is eclipsed. In its place is a strong notion of majority rule, tempered by the idea of minority rights. There are exceptions to this picture. In America, Jefferson's plan for the formation of the University of Virginia is an important historical attempt to reintroduce some of the deliberative function of an

Agora into American education. Here engagement and deliberation were incorporated even into his architectural scheme for university housing (T. Jefferson, personal correspondence to L. W. Tazewell, January 5, 1805).

Rousseau's idea of the General Will is the most influential exception (Rousseau, 1762/1957). Although there are many contradictions in Rousseau's account of what this Will is, he tries to maintain the remnant of a deliberative body where individual desires are filtered through a stronger concern for the common good. As Delaney (2005) points out, "Rousseau argues that there is an important distinction to be made between the General Will and the collection of individual wills: 'There is often a great deal of difference between the will of all and the General Will. The latter looks only to the common interest; the former considers private interest and is only a sum of private wills. But take away from these same wills the pluses and minuses that cancel each other out, and the remaining sum of the differences is the General Will.'" Delaney (2005) points out that Rousseau can be understood in an almost Rawlsian (Rawls) sense—namely, that if the citizens were ignorant of the subgroups to which they belong, they would inevitably make decisions that would be to the advantage of the society as a whole, and thus be in accordance with the General Will.

Although scholars debate whether Rousseau ever did envisage a true deliberative process, what is significant is that the distinction he makes between the General Will and the will of all, the one seeking the common good and the other adding up the sum of private wills, is the distinction between Aristotle and classical liberalism. The liberalism of Hobbes, Locke, and Adam Smith renders the very idea of a common good invisible, and rendering it invisible renders it out of existence. Rousseau wants to again make it visible, and by making it visible—that is, by making it a goal of personal deliberation—he hopes to bring it back into existence.

As mentioned earlier, the idea of a common good when made the object of deliberation is the idea that Aristotle was seeking in his notion of a public. Yet once Locke entered the picture, expressing the right of the governed to pass judgment on those who govern them, and to do so in terms of their own personal, unreflective desires, the public could no longer be the same. Rousseau likely understood this, but because his General Will straddles both a deliberative and an absolute conception of the good, he never quite came to grips with it. What he did manage to do, however, was to make visible again the possibility of a public, and by making that idea visible in an age when democracy was on the rise, he set the stage for the political and the educational debates that were to soon follow in the works of Kant, Hegel, and Marx and, across the sea, in those of Jefferson and later Dewey.

Dewey and the Public

Of course, for modern American educators Dewey is the key figure, and some believe that by emphasizing the process of inquiry he actually resolved the issue between a system that promotes the will of all and one that advances the idea of a true public, where private interest is put aside for the sake of discovering and advancing a common good. But arguably one of the interesting features of Dewey's *educational* philosophy is that in his major educational works, he failed to examine the idea of *educating* a *public*, leaving the impression that a public is reducible to its individual members. Indeed, his definition of a public as all of those people affected by the indirect consequences of a direct exchange lends itself to such an impression (Dewey 1927/1988, 15–16). This might be seen as simply an oversight since Dewey opposed rugged individualism of the kind associated with classical laissez-faire capitalism. Yet it is more accurate to see in it the continuing influence of laissez-faire liberalism even on one of its most articulate opponents.

Recall that for the classical laissez-faire liberal, the ontology of the individual meant that only two forms of associations could be acknowledged as legitimate: associations of interests—which included markets and governments—and associations of sentiments—which included families, tribes, and nations. Although Dewey questioned this ontology, his educational philosophy is still influenced by it in the sense that associations of interests and associations of sentiment were both paramount in describing his educational ideal. His ideal school was an association of sentiment, or what he called a community, where true inquiry took place and resulted in cooperative activity. His idea of an education where children would ever expand their associations (Dewey 1916/1944, 83) was a vision of individual growth through expanded interests and inquiry. Yet given this vision, what then can we say about a public? Is such public growth possible, or is growth only restricted to individuals in associations of interest? Or is there some other way in which the idea of a public can be conceived, one that is better adapted to modern conditions?

Dewey believed that scientific inquiry would replace Aristotle's notion of reason as the engine of cooperative action, but this belief seems to assume a common standpoint or at least a shared end in view and for some seems overly optimistic. The question then is if this standpoint cannot be assumed, is a public still possible or must we then fall back on the idea that *a public* is simply a term used to describe individual desires in the aggregate? If it is the latter, then is the idea of a public education any more than an excuse for a state monopoly over education to be used to manipulate the masses? In what follows, I argue that the idea of a public education, properly construed, is an important vehicle for civic education in a democracy.

A Modern Conception of a Public: Pessimism or Manipulation

Alasdair MacIntyre is one of the few contemporary philosophers who share Aristotle's vision of an *educated* public. MacIntyre holds that a public consists of similarly educated people in close relationship with one another and who share similar ideas and have a mutual concern to advance the common good. Although MacIntyre shares Aristotle's idea of a public, he is pessimistic about the possibility of the formation of a true public in modern times. His pessimism rests on his observations that population increases make small face-to-face encounters of like-minded, public-spirited educated elites unlikely; that economic growth has obscured the significance of contemplation and deliberation; and that the influence of the educated class has diminished whereas the importance of the laboring and owning classes has increased. He also observes that the dissolution of the educated classes into the professional groups with their own separate interests and perspectives has disrupted the idea of reason as a unifying force (MacIntyre 1987, 1988). Although pessimistic about the possibility of a modern public MacIntyre is true to Aristotle's idea of a public—a shared identity and agreement about the foundations of rational justification. It is simply that he also believes that postmodern society makes the achievement of these ends impossible. One of the conditions that MacIntyre neglected to include is the rise of mass media and its capacity to manipulate public opinion. Hence, MacIntyre's view, although pessimistic, is also somewhat benign. A public was no longer possible, but whether that made matters better or worse was unsettled.

However, half a century before MacIntyre wrote, Walter Lippmann (1955) expressed grave concern about the way in which public opinion was mobilized to address critical events such as war. Here the problem was not the impossibility of a public formation but the way it had to be overheated for the sake of mobilization. As he explained referring to World War II, "It seemed impossible to wage the war energetically except by inciting the people to paroxysms of hatred and to utopian dreams. So they were told that the Four Freedoms would be established everywhere, once the incurably bad Germans and the incurably bad Japanese had been forced to surrender unconditionally" (Lippmann 1955, 23). Lippmann's (1955) answer is a return to what he calls a public philosophy, which involves the recognition of "precepts, which restrict and restrain private interests and desire" (114). And he makes it clear that "the public philosophy is addressed to the government of our appetites and passions by the reason of a second civilized and therefore acquired nature. Therefore the public philosophy cannot be popular. For its aims to resist and to regulate those very opinions and desires which are most popular" (162). For the "common man," [sic] reason and transparency may not always be the best means to transmit this philosophy, and Lippmann (1955) allows metaphor, myth, or religious dogma to take the place of reason where necessary. Thus Lippmann replaces MacIntyre's pessimism with a form of manipulative realism, which seems antithetical to democracy but which he feels is needed to protect it. He fails to address the question as to whether what he proposes to protect would, given his means of protection, be truly a "democracy."

MacIntyre and Lippmann fail to address adequately two considerations. The first is that in modern democracies, there is a strong expectation that citizens must be involved. Such involvement is not only a nice political ideal. It is quite essential for meeting the critical problems of our day. From simple recycling programs to the development of alternative forms of energy to combat pollution and global warming, citizen participation is critical, and adequate participation in a noncommand society requires high levels of public understanding. Granted, sloganeering and mobilization may also be effective. However, in a democracy these must be redeemable by sound evidence and reasonable arguments. The second consideration is that the *knowledge* that public opinion is being manipulated weakens the likelihood of public compliance. Since transparency is critical for democracy, this view creates a paradox. Either be transparent and paralyze joint action, or appear to be transparent while manipulating undemocratically public opinion. Hence, both MacIntyre's pessimism and Lippmann's manipulative realism are not just commentary, they also have the effect of weakening the possibility of public democratic will formation. Of course, Lippmann could respond that truly effective manipulation would be invisible, but this response is not only cynical; in an age of instantaneous Internet communication, it is academic and not very fruitful.

Deliberative Democracy: A Contemporary Alternative

Most recently MacIntyre's pessimism and Lippmann's manipulative realism have been challenged by the idea of deliberative democracy and the attempt to refine it (Gutmann 1987; Gutmann and Thompson 1996; Habermas 1971). Here the public sphere becomes an arena for the engagement of differences, and the public becomes a body of strangers so engaged. Dewey (1927/1988) provides the impetus for this movement, and in doing so he begins implicitly to acknowledge the public as more than either a community of interests or sentiments and implicitly would seem to allow that a public as a body can be educated. He writes: "Majority rule, is as foolish as its critics charge it with being. But it is never merely majority rule. . . . The means by which a majority comes to be a majority is the important thing: antecedent debates, the modification of views to meet the opinions of minorities. . . . The essential need, in other words, is the improvement of the methods and conditions of debate, discussion and persuasion" (207). Dewey's (1927/1988) quote with its emphasis on the antecedents of majority rule, including the concern for the opinions of minorities, can be read as a response to Lippmann's paternalistic notion of a public philosophy. Here there is an answer to MacIntyre's pessimism, but the answer is not paternalism. Rather it is the improvement of the conditions for deliberation. As Bohman (1996) puts it, "the deliberative process forces citizens to justify their decisions and opinions by appealing to common interests or by arguing in terms of reasons that 'all could accept' in public debate" (5). Maintaining and improving the conditions for deliberation and debate is an intergenerational task and has implications for the reconstruction of the idea of a public education.

Recently, philosophers such as Jurgen Habermas in Germany, John Rawls in the United States, and others have added to Dewey's concern to improve the "methods and conditions of debate, discussion and persuasion." Habermas's (1971) notion of an ideal speech community provides an idea standard, which can be called into play to evaluate apparent consensus about meaning and action and is critical to his notion of a public sphere. Nancy Fraser (1997) describes it as follows:

> The idea of a "public sphere" . . . is the space in which citizens deliberate about their common affairs, hence an institutional arena of discursive interaction. This arena is different from the state; it is a site for the production and circulation of discourse that can in principle be critical of the state. The public sphere in Habermas's sense is also distinct from the official-economy; it is not an arena of market relations but rather one of discourse relations, a theater for debating and deliberating rather than for buying and selling. (70)

Habermas believes that these evaluative principles are implicitly assumed by all communicative acts and hence can be called on to advance will formation in the public arena. Habermas's ideal speech community reflects Aristotle's notion of deliberation. John Rawls (1993) adds to this with his proposal that public deliberation be governed by what he calls the Burden of Judgment where we work to provide an account of public disagreement that "does not impugn the reasonableness of those who disagree" (55). Habermas has been criticized for ignoring differences of gender, race, and culture (Fraser 1997, 73), and Rawls for neglecting the way dominance privileges voice. Yet in their defense it could be said that the very idea of dominance and of racial and gender privilege as problematic adds substance to their more abstract formulations (nevertheless, concrete attempts to address this lack can be seen in the works of both educators and political theorists; Freire 1968; Gilligan 1982; Mansbridge 1980). Although Habermas and Rawls work to clarify the meaning of public reason, they both minimize the importance of a shared identity that both Lippmann and MacIntyre found so problematic and that the invention of public education in the United States and Europe was meant to address (B. Anderson 1983; Feinberg 1998; Mann 1957; National Education Association of the United States and Commission on the Reorganization of Secondary Education 1918). This oversight spells out the task of a theory of public education appropriate for today when pluralism and deep disagreement are acknowledged but the reproduction of a public in terms of identity formation and an education for reasonable deliberation are primary goals.

Yet Aristotle's model of like-minded, similarly educated equals joined together by friendship and reason is too demanding for contemporary times. If taken without modification, it leads to either MacIntyre's pessimism or Lippmann's manipulation. And if taken in parts, reason is separated from identity. Modern life is just too complex and modern democracy just too inclusive to expect that a single rational foundation will be acceptable to all. If public reasoning is handicapped by plurality and plurality retards a common identity, then the idea of a true public school as an education that prepares students for a life in a public requires a reconstructed idea of public education with reformulated notions of identity and reason.

This reconstruction will need to take into account two constraints that Aristotle did not feel compelled to address. One is the migration of rationality from citizen to expert that MacIntyre describes, and the other is the growing plurality and the loss of a public philosophy that concerns Lippmann. It will also need to address the position of liberalism that the *public* is simply a term for the aggregate of individuals who compose it and does not, as Aristotle thought, have a reality that transcends the sum of individual desires. In the following, I address these concerns through a reexamination of the contemporary restoration of classical liberalism and its argument for school choice. The object of this reexamination is to revive a notion of a public that is more than the aggregate of the desires of the individuals who comprise it at any given moment.

From Neighborhood Effects to Public Values: The Pitfalls of Choice

In this section, I will examine the major justification for substituting private, parental choice for a larger public good and show why this justification is inadequate. I will do this by reconsidering the idea of a public value, showing that it cannot be reduced to an aggregate of private desires, and then by distinguishing a number of different kinds of values from one another. These will include what economists call neighborhood benefits (Friedman 1955), which are the goods that one person accrues as a result of advantages that are given directly to another. These are closely related to what I will call shared private values. Both of these are to be distinguished from what I will call common values, which I define here as the shared understandings that generate existing private values preferences. Finally, I distinguish these from public values, which I define as common values regulated by discourse.

The concerns of MacIntyre and Lippmann are relevant in helping see the difficulty in moving from common to public values, but these difficulties do not refute the counterclaim to liberalism that the public has an independent status that includes but is not reducible to the aggregate of individuals that compose it. With this argument in place, I then reconsider the role of education in the construction of a public and show the different levels at which this work can be accomplished. Finally, I address the question of whether a school that reproduces a public needs to be state controlled and supported. Thus, by bringing the idea of a public back into view, I hope to sharpen the mission of a truly public school. I begin with the idea of neighborhood effects.

"Neighborhood effects" is a concept developed by classically minded economists to justify the compulsory transfer of funds from one person to another although claiming that such transfer need not diminish individual freedom or promote government intervention. The concept has been used in education to justify the use of tax funds to support the idea of vouchers that parents can then use to send their child to a school of their choice, whether private, public, or religious. The transfer of your funds for the education of my child is justified in this view, because, at least up to a certain point, the education of my child benefits you. In other words, when my child learns to read the entire community is better off in a number of ways and so it is not an infringement on individual rights to tax members of the community for the education of other people's children. Given the premises of market capitalism, this then allows for a legitimate transfer of funds from one party to the next and, according to this view, does not violate the basic tenet of classical capitalism, the freedom to determine how to spend your own money. The "neighborhood" then is shorthand for all the individuals who benefit indirectly from another child's education. A neighborhood benefit indicates a value that is shared by many, but it is shared by each of them individually.

Over time, however, according to these economists, the benefits of education begin to accrue less to neighborhood and more to the individual just as education becomes less general and more vocational. As this occurs the obligation of the community to support education is reduced, whereas the obligation of the individuals to support their own education increases. However, the basic point is to both justify maximum individual freedom through choice and then explain why it can be legitimate to tax one person to support the educational choice of another. The argument actually fails on a number of accounts; however, the most significant failure is the way in which it distorts the idea of a public.

It is important to distinguish the idea of neighborhood benefits as used by contemporary economists with the idea of public goods as developed by Aristotle. Neighborhood benefits accrue to individuals as aggregates. Public goods accrue to individuals but only to the extent that they identify with their polis. An example of a neighborhood benefit might be the shade that your neighbors get when *you* decide to plant a tree in your yard. An example of a public good would be a decision of the members of a neighborhood to plant trees for the sake of shade. In the latter, there is a communicative relation between the members of the neighborhood that results in recognition that more shade is needed and in the decision to plant more trees in order to provide it. In the former, no such communicative relationship need exist. Hence, with the idea of neighborhood effects people benefit from the shade even if they have no other relation to one another. In other words, they all benefit, but they do so separately.

The result of the idea of the neighborhood effect as the dominant rationale for tax-supported schools and for parental choice is to make invisible the idea of a public as involving membership in a community and to reduce the idea of a public to that of individuals each acting and benefiting separately. Given this reduction, it is a very easy step to disparage the idea of a public school as not aiming to reproduce a public but rather to substitute government aims for parental ones. Hence the rhetorical shift whereby public schools become "government" schools and where state-supported compulsory education becomes a questionable "state monopoly" on education. The result is not only the justification of tax dollars to private and for-profit schools but, much more important, the dismissal of any but the most minimal and superficially measurable guidelines as appropriate for appraising the worth of education. Yet as we will see a "public" benefit, which, the argument for choice neglects, is not the same as benefits to all its individual members, and freedom is not the same as choice.

Choice Is Not the Same as Freedom

There are conditions when the introduction of choice policies actually serves to distort preferences. Consider the following example: All of the parents on K Street prefer to send their children to the neighborhood school. They prefer this because the neighborhood school, although not the best academically, is pretty good, and because they want their children's school friends to be their neighborhood friends. There are actually many benefits to this, including the reinforcement of norms when neighbors know each other through knowing each other's children. However, once choice is introduced, all parents realize that their desire for the overlap of school friends and neighborhood friends is no longer possible. Hence, each parent lists as his or her first choice the best academic school in the town. Some parents are successful; others are turned down. Some do get the school in the neighborhood, but it is no longer the *neighborhood* school. It is only located in the neighborhood. It is not of the neighborhood. The result is that no parents get their preferred school because the preferred school would be a neighborhood school with all neighborhood children. And although some parents do get their second choice, the best academic school, most do not. In this case, the introduction of choice results in denying parents their preferences and in making them worse off than they would have been without choice.

Think then of the potential relationships that might have developed between neighbor and neighbor through the mutual care for their children as having had a potential reality, aborted though it was. The group then would not be reducible to all of its members, because although all the members remain the same, their relationship to one another would be different. In one setting they are essentially isolated from each other, whereas in the other they are, through their children and the school, in communicative relation with one another. Here the group develops a kind of ontological status or a reality that although including the desires of its members is not reducible to those members, because it creates possibilities for new and more reflective desires to be formed. Choice has not added freedom to the group because the desire formed under choice—to attend the best academic school—is not the same as a preference that is shaped through shared communication and reflection. Missing is a mode of communication among individual parents that is essential in the formation of shared values. Without such communication in selecting the best academic school for their child, all of the parents can be said to now hold the same values, and in this sense they are shared, but they are shared serially, by each individual, one at a time.

Although public values are to be distinguished from neighborhood effects, interpreted as shared values held individually, they also have to be distinguished from common values, or the acknowledged but often implicit background conditions that generate shared judgments and emotional responses. To see how common values function, consider the following example from Ian McEwan's novel *On Chesil Beach* (2007), a story of opportunity lost. The time is 1962, just before the sexual revolution begins. The scene is the first night of marriage. The characters are the husband, anxious to consummate the marriage, and his musically talented and fragile wife who loves him deeply but dreads the conjugal act. Their inevitable breakup is due to her offering to love him as his wife but to allow him the sexual freedom to satisfy his desires with other women whenever he feels the need. The offer repels him; he takes it as a sign of impurity, and the brief marriage ends in a quick divorce, a divorce that as the sexual revolution advances, he comes to deeply regret.

On Chesil Beach illustrates what I mean by common values. They are the assumed understandings and norms that frame or set the emotional register through which the scene is played out. Here, the common values that bind a husband sexually to his wife also disallow a wife to give her husband *permission* to have sex with other women. There is an unbreakable bond between love, sex, and marriage that is sanctified by the community, where faithfulness is defined through the sexual bond. This background understanding frames the husband's response, whereas the wife is willing to challenge it. And because the bond is interpreted through communal norms, neither partner has the license to redefine it, even for the sake of the marriage itself. Some years later, after the sexual revolution gained traction and the background values were challenged and when, given mutual consent, the tie between faithfulness and the sexual bond could be loosened for special circumstances, the husband in the story now sees how his prior response had been socially constructed through the common values of the time. Of course, by then it is too late for him.

This background understanding that shapes the emotional responses of a given time and place is what I am terming *common values*. Pippin

(2010), in describing Nietzsche's view of the soul, sums up nicely what I am getting at by the idea. He writes of Nietzsche: "The soul is merely the name for a collective historical achievement, a mode of self understanding of one sort or another, what we have made ourselves into at one point or another in the service of some ideal or other" (3). *On Chesil Beach* illustrates Nietzsche's point beautifully and in doing so also illustrates what I mean by a common value and the way it differs from neighborhood effects as shared individual values held individually.

I want now to argue that a key function of a public is to reflect on common values in a way that makes them public values. And I want to argue that a critical role of a public school is to provide students with the background understanding and the skills required to do this together, as members of an emerging public. There are many advantages, and a few disadvantages, in having such schools state supported, but I will address that topic after a closer look at the meaning of a public.

Aristotle: Too High a Standard, Too Short a Time

Aristotle's understanding of a public as a group of similarly educated like-minded people, friends, committed to a single common good, and able to deliberate without the cloud of self-interest, clearly, is too narrow for contemporary times and to adopt it leads to either the pessimism of MacIntyre or the manipulative realism of Lippmann. There are areas where this ideal must break down. Although the Athenians may have engaged in public deliberation about war and peace, their generals did not engage in public deliberation about strategy. Public deliberation has limits, especially where goals have already been set and the concern is about the technical means to achieve them. It is in the latter discussion where experts have their most significant place, although they also have important roles to play in informing a public about the feasibility of goals as well.

MacIntyre's pessimism is grounded in a misunderstanding of this division of labor between goal setting and strategy. Yet one of the first parameters of public formation is to distinguish between accountability to a public, which all elected officials and their appointed aids must be, and public deliberation, which involves a general population in setting and reflectively assenting to norms set through a deliberative process. Without these amendments, Aristotle's model becomes a template for cynicism or despair conditioned by both increased plurality and an idealized and impossible conception of rationality. With them we can come to see both plurality and discordant conceptions of rationality as constraints on a public deliberative process. And when we do this, we will also have a clearer idea of the unique task of a public school.

Reconception of a Public

Given these constraints, one way to think of a public is not, as Aristotle did, as a group of friends committed to a common good but as a group of strangers tied together by consciousness of a common fate (Williams 2003) and in direct or indirect communication with one another about the viability of commonly held value. The following is an expanded definition. A public is an authoritative body of (mostly) strangers

- with separate affiliations and identities,
- connected by common concerns,
- who care about the interests and opinions of others,
- who communicate a willingness to seek common principles and seek shared strategies to work out differences, and
- who have direct or indirect authority to shape a common future.

Membership in a public overlaps with political citizenship, but it is not the same. Citizens possess rights to define and pursue the good life, to exercise freedom, and to enjoy liberty. Members of a public, by influencing social and institutional arrangements, work to secure the conditions of everyone's freedom (E. Anderson 1999, 329). This membership in a public entails communicative engagement about mutual benefits and hence may address the limits of liberty. Publics are not agents and thus do not *act* as a body. Rather, governments when appropriately controlled are the agents of the public. Governments act; publics, by setting a tone and developing norms of evaluation, influence and evaluate government action.

The dominant image of a public as a deliberative body, something like a small town meeting, is inappropriate for today's world. A town meeting may be one forum for a public formation, but it is not the only one, and the image is inappropriate for most instances of public formation because it is too immediate and too concrete. It suggests a single gathering in one place at a specific time to deliberate over a specific issue. Yet members of a public communicate with each other in many different ways and over extended space and time.

Standing in Line as an Example of Public Communication

Take the act of voting, for example. Many political scientists and economists point out the futility of voting. For any single person it is inefficient, rarely does a single vote determine an election. In some cases, for example, when members of the same family intend to vote for completely different candidates, a lot of time could be saved if they just agreed to stay home and to not vote at all. The same principle of efficiency applies when you know that your candidate is going to win (or to lose) by a landslide. Yet many people, in seeming defiance to the principle of efficiency do continue to vote. Are they simply irrational, or is there more to their decision than meets the eye?

It is certainly irrational if the act of voting is seen as doing only one thing—casting an officially recorded preference. Yet another way to think about the act of voting is not as just doing one thing but as doing two things at the same time. The first is stating a preference, but the second is legitimizing a system of setting preferences by standing in line. Now to those who vote under conditions of certain defeat or victory, this second thing—the standing in line to vote may well be the more important of the two. Voting is an act of a citizen. It is the exercise of the right to state an official preference. Standing in line to vote is something else. It is a visible signal by a member of a public that voting is an important civic responsibility that serves to legitimize a democratic system itself. Standing in line is not stating a preference. It is an act of mutual communication of members of a public, each of them strangers to one another, about the importance of maintaining institutional legitimacy. And in this communication, the legitimacy of the system is maintained. This is why some people worry when voting turnout is low or when young people do not vote. It is also why terrorists will often try to attack the voting process itself. If people are afraid to communicate legitimacy to one another, then legitimacy itself dissolves.

The Concepts of Racism and Sexism as Examples of Public Norm Setting

Members of a public are engaged in mutual communication reinforcing common values, for example, voting. However, they are also engaged in a reflection on the appropriateness of common values and their consistency with one another. This reflection may take place over extended periods of time and in various ways, and through different venues, providing common values with their public status. It is here in the engagement of collective reflection on common values that the creative normative work of a public is performed and where the public actually creates and endorses new norms, moral inventions if you will, to address new facts and new situations. The evolution of the concepts of racism and sexual harassment are examples of this intergenerational public work.

The idea of sexual harassment is relatively new and likely was formulated officially and in legal terms in the 1970s. Yet for the idea to be articulated in legal terms, much work needed to be done. Harassment suggests more than just bothering another person. It involves getting in the way of their performing an accepted and legitimate role. It is not harassment when someone stops a person from robbing a bank, but it is harassment when one is unable to perform a legitimately assigned task. Before the idea of sexual harassment could take shape, the notion that the sexual division of labor had to be rejected as natural.

For the idea of sexual harassment to take shape, the prevailing idea that the proper place of women was in the home and that their singular purpose was to raise children and care for their husbands had to be challenged. Until the idea of a natural sexual division of labor and the common values associated with it were openly questioned, women who sought to have careers outside the home were viewed as misplaced, overly ambitious intruders on the man's domain. The exceptions were wifelike and mother-like roles such as nursing or school teaching or roles that placed women in a subordinate position to men. These roles were acceptable because they were seen as akin to a woman's "natural" work. Without this challenge, the "male" behavior that dominated the work place—sexual jokes, girly calendars, the glass ceiling, and so on—were the accepted common values of the time.

The idea of harassment applied to women required that this idea of a "natural" sexual division of labor be discredited in both individual and collective consciousness and that a new normative template be substituted for it. As the idea of sexual harassment developed, then items such as nude posters or demeaning jokes in the workplace become more than just a personal matter congruent with the common values of the time. They become social, political, and sometimes legal matters.

The concept of racism provides a similar evolutionary trajectory. The word *racism* did not appear in any major English language dictionary before its inclusion in a 1933 edition of *Webster's* where the term *racism* was placed in its "New Words" section and was perhaps the first official acknowledgment of the term (Neilson and Knott 1933/1950). It was defined then as now in terms of the *belief* in racial superiority, but race did not mean quite the same thing then as it does now. The historian George Fredrickson (2002) tracks the first scholarly use of the term *racism* to the 1920s where it "was first applied to ideologies making invidious distinctions among divisions of the 'white' or Caucasian race, and especially to show that Aryan or Nordics were superior to other people normally considered 'white'" (156). The inclusion in *Webster's* coincided with Hitler's rise to power but did not seem to have any specific application to the treatment of Black people.

Encyclopedias reveal a similar history. The 1910 *Encyclopedia Britannica* defines race as a "tribe, breed, or group of plants, animals, or persons descended from a common ancestor" (*Encyclopedia Britannica* 1910–1911, 774). Beyond a short paragraph, there is nothing further mentioned. The 1936, 1947, and 1957 versions have expanded sections on race but no explicit category for racism. This continues until 1968 and 1974, when more detail on the various attributes of race is added. Ethnicity is equated with race (the article speaks of "East European" races) in the 1968 edition, though no direct entries on either racism or racialism is noted. Racialism is dealt with within the text on race but does not garner a separate entry until the 1974 edition and then in the context of a discussion of historical occurrences, such as the Civil Rights era. As the discussion shifts over the years, history replaces biology as the relevant conceptual framework, and before "racism" becomes an official entry, there is an expanded discussion on the conflicts of African

Americans. By the 1986 and then the 1998 editions, "racism" is an entry of two-page length, with more detail. Of course, these changes did not just take place through scholarly instruments but rather these instruments reflect and then reinforce movements that occur on the street and in the courts, which are then reflected in school texts.

The emergence of the concepts of both sexual harassment and racism as reflections on and challenges to existing common values adds an important intergenerational dimension to the idea of a public and gives public will formation perspective and distance that more traditional notions tend to bypass. In both cases, as aggrieved individuals begin to develop their own collective voice, a value commonly accepted by the dominant groups—that Whites are of greater worth than Blacks, or men are more able than women—is set apart from other dominant common values and reflected on, sometimes as a response to protest or other social events, sometimes as a result of litigation, sometimes in repulsion over systematic and obvious injustices. Hence, public values emerge out of the critique of specific common values and form the premises for a new and *renewed* rationality, and a unique role for public education to transmit and refine those values also emerges.

Identity and a Common Fate

The first question of public education is not who shall control it, parent or state, or even how it should be financed (Gutmann 1987). The primary question about public education is how to initiate students into this ongoing intergenerational conversation where they understand that this conversation is about them. It involves creating bonds of trust where new citizens understand that others are able to engage in reasonable discourses, where each accepts the burden of justification, and where students learn to reject servility both intellectually and emotionally, for themselves and for others (Callan 1997, 152–57). It also entails the extension of Aristotle's idea of friendship beyond those whom we know or with whom we share close relationships. Danielle Allen (2006) explains this goal in her concept of political friendship, which she defines as "not an emotion, but a practice, a set of hard-won, complicated habits that are used to bridge trouble, difficulty, and differences of personal experience and aspiration" (xxi). Political friendship extracts its qualities from personal friendship allowing that we all enjoy a life that although not common or identical is nevertheless shared in terms of events, climate, environment, and the likes and begins with the awareness of the fact that "we are always awash in each other's lives" (Allan 2006, xxii).

In returning to the question of public education, it is useful for us to consider the preconditions of political friendship such as the habit of recognizing, publicly acknowledging, and rejecting servility or promoting habits of deliberation that accept the burden of judgment. These are subtle skills and require exceptional pedagogy to teach. For example, recognizing servility involves sensitivity to the behavior of the quiet and "good" student and teaching a student not to be servile may require delicate navigation with parental or cultural norms. For educators, it also involves teaching less articulate or shy students to develop the skills needed to give expression to their own ideas and values within a public forum (Mansbridge, 1980). Still, the development of political friendship must often be done at a considerable distance and thus will not have the emotional ties associated with personal friendship. In its place must be a kind of complicated trust. "Trust," because it provides others with the benefit of the doubt about their intentions. "Complicated," because it has reservation about the capacity of others to act on my behalf, and because it allows that interests, both my own and others, can change as communication increases.

Public understanding does not only mean that individuals must comprehend their common problems and the alternative solutions to them. It also means that each person must have reasonably secure knowledge that every other person understands a problem and is willing to comply with the accepted solutions. And, to cement this understanding, all persons must also know that other people have the same level of secure understanding about their (the first party's) understanding and willingness. For example, it is not sufficient that everyone just understands that there is a concern about global warming, or even that they be able to appraise the evidence for it. In addition, they need to know that others are aware of the problem and that they too are inclined to comply with the policies to address it. Otherwise one person's compliance will be seen as futile and everyone has good reason to become a free rider on everyone else. Thus, that person must have secure knowledge that Persons 2, 3, 4, and others have the same knowledge as she or he and that given this knowledge their compliance is secure. "The same understanding" means not only knowing the objective conditions and evidence but also an awareness of the intersubjective conditions that lead to compliance. To secure compliance, Person 1 must know that Persons 2, 3, 4, and others have a similar understanding of Person 1 and then of each other.

In a democracy, this kind of knowledge—both vertical and horizontal—stabilizes commitment and avoids the free rider problem that economists are so fond of citing where one person takes advantage of the goodwill of others. In reality, of course, there will always be free riders. The goals of an education that is public in the strict sense of the term is to encourage students to act *as if* everyone had the requisite knowledge and was willing to comply, with the understanding that their act has communicative value and serves then as a model to encourage compliance. This requires a pedagogical strategy and a curriculum where students are provided respect and where they learn to air their different views while respecting the views of others. Political friendship also requires sensitivity to the interests and standpoint of strangers and it is where students learn to listen to and address the concerns of others.

Review

The Agora provided an informal space where people developed shared understandings and common interests. Aristotle began to formalize this identity in his discussion of the education appropriate to membership in a public, which he largely identified with the education of rulers and legislators. The interests that developed were then both vertical—the good of the polis—and horizontal—the enjoyment and respect provided to one's peers. This horizontal factor was critical. For even the best ideas required sacrifice, and friendship provided the trust that others would not take advantage of your willingness to sacrifice for a larger good. This reconstruction of the Agora is helpful in allowing us to see two sides to truly public education. The first is an engagement in an intergenerational conversation about the public good, and the second is a concern to provide others with a voice in that conversation. The first reflects Aristotle's vertical concern—the good of the whole. The second reflects his horizontal concern—the respect due to all engaged in the conversation. Today there is a planetary dimension to both of these concerns. Identity has extended from the polis to the globe. Whereas once a shared fate was bounded by the walls of a city-state, today it can extend to the concerns of a planetary community and where there is in addition to more local fates, there is also a global one, dependent on the care of the planet.

Setting an Agenda for Public Education

The goal of public education is to renew a public by providing the young with the skills, dispositions, and perspectives required to engage with strangers about their shared interests and common fate and to contribute to shaping it. This goal is consistent with conventional education and the development of a reasonable level of proficiency in traditional subject areas, and it certainly does not preclude the importance of education for the development of useful and demanding skills. Indeed, this is a condition of education in general, whether public or not. The idea of a *public* education simply adds another dimension to this, and it is as much concerned with matters of pedagogy and method as it is with subject matter.

Since that conversation between strangers extends across generational lines and involves the development of the capacity to reflect on and address common values, sometimes to renew them, sometimes to change them, a public education requires students to understand and develop their own agency. It also requires that they gain perspective on their own commitments and emotional responses. Distance and perspective are gained in the academic curriculum by developing the habit of reflecting on one's own production, whether it be a work of art, a piece of writing, an argument, a math proof, or a craft production, and to see it through the eyes of others. This is one reason why open discussion and critical peer evaluation are important components of public education, and why subject matter proficiency alone (Hirsch 1987), although necessary, is not sufficient. Perspective and distance is also gained through the nonformal aspects of school life in terms of the inclusiveness of the student body and the teachers and the way in which interaction among different cultural, religious, racial, and social class groups is encouraged. In schools where students from different background can intermingle, stereotypes can be directly addressed and uncritically accepted assumptions can be reconsidered.

Must a Public School Be a Government School and Must a Government School Be a Public School

The present debate about public education involves school choice, and I now want to return to that topic. For the most part, the idea of choice as it is advanced today by neoconservatives is not consistent with the idea of a public education. This is because it encourages parents to select schools along class or racial lines or because of some other group similarity. This need not be the case (Brighouse 2000), but often lacking is the face-to-face-encounter with children from different groups that is essential to a public formation. In many cases, these schools diminish the idea of a public.

Nevertheless, given the homogeneity of neighborhood schools (Reich 2008) and the present tendency of people to live in neighborhoods where their neighbors share their outlook, it is not clear that government-supported neighborhood schools are always a lot more public in the sense that I have described it here. Moreover, there are sometimes acceptable academic reasons for educating together students who share important similarities. Age and maturity level is one obvious case. Special needs and maintaining cultural coherence in certain cases of vulnerability are sometimes others (Feinberg 1998; Kymlicka 1995). Given these and other exceptions, we can still make very broad distinctions.

For example, a public school is distinguished from a private school whose specific task might be to reproduce a certain class or to provide students with the outlook of that class. And it is also to be distinguished from many religious schools whose distinct mission is to reproduce a congregation loyal to a specific set of devotional beliefs. This does not mean that religious and private schools cannot serve important public ends; they often do. Yet if they were to also be thought of as public schools, the uniformity they seek would need to be addressed and they would need to be publicly accountable. I have addressed this elsewhere and so will not go into it here (Feinberg 2008). However, here it is important to distinguish schools that serve a public good from schools that reproduce a public, where students are taught to engage with strangers about a common fate.

What needs to be emphasized is just how much this understanding differs from the current usage. The present understanding of a public education is framed in economic terms with the emphasis on support. Given this understanding, then the civic ideal of a public school, as the site where a public is reproduced, is replaced by an economic function. Schools function to produce marketable skills. Given this shift, then of course it makes sense to enable parents to choose the schools that they want for their own children, and as long as it meets minimum state standards it may sometimes make sense for them to receive state support, given the broad requirement for equality of opportunity. Yet my argument has been that in losing sight of the public role of public education, we lose the process of public formation altogether and that this is a very high price to pay.

Acknowledgments

My appreciation to the Fellows and staff of the Spencer Foundation for their comments on the presentation I gave on this topic when I was a Faculty Fellow in 2007–2008. My appreciation also to Eamonn Callan for his helpful comments on an earlier draft and to Sara Shrader for her careful reading of the chapter.

This research was supported in part by the Spencer Foundation.

12

Culture and the Common School

Introduction

In this essay I want to join with Richard Pring in examining the role of the common school, and specifically I want to address the question: given the flattening out of the cultural hierarchy that was the vestige of colonialism and nation-building, is there anything that might be uniquely common about the common school in this postmodern age? By "uniquely common" I do not mean those subjects that all schools might teach, such as reading or arithmetic. Nor do I mean just subjects that might serve a larger public purpose, but that might be taught in either publicly supported or privately supported schools. Rather I mean subjects that speak to the shaping of a child's identity as a member of a common community in the way that the common school was intended to do when its commission was to develop and maintain a single national or colonial identity and loyalty. Thus I want to argue that there is a kind of connectivity that common schools should foster even as the nation-building and colonial past is rejected, and that this connectivity is what is common about the common schools. I also believe, but will not argue the case here, that the kind of commonality that I am arguing for requires a certain degree of ethnic, religious and class heterogeneity, and also that it requires high levels of public funding and public incentives. However, this paper is restricted to arguing that even as the nation-building and colonial projects are rejected, the common school still has a future and can play a unique and important role in a post-colonial world.

The Ranking of Cultures

The question whether the common school has a future is relevant in the post-colonial context because of the radically different historical times in which it developed. The common school was invented to move people from a rural and agricultural economy to urban and industrial ones, while constructing a national culture out of local, linguistic, immigrant or colonial populations. Here the idea of culture brought with it a ranking system where groups were measured by their presumed capacity to model dominant cultural forms. In the United States immigrant cultures were evaluated in terms of their closeness to or distance from the Anglo ideal. Western and Northern European culture ranked high, requiring little assimilative work. Southern and Eastern European culture ranked low, requiring a good deal. The capacity of non-Europeans, such as Asians, or Native Americans to assimilate was compromised by their cultural deficiencies, while Negroes [sic] were viewed as essentially incapable of true assimilation. The common school then had the task of assimilating those who could be assimilated and of socializing (at least as much as possible) those who could not. Those who could be assimilated would learn to internalize the norms, values and standards of the dominant culture. Those whose capacities were culturally compromised would at least learn to appreciate their superior status while those who were incapable of assimilation would be socialized to follow the rules laid down by their superiors.

The educational abuses of this conception of culture are now commonly acknowledged. Native American and Australian Aboriginal children were torn from their families to linger in some middle ground—deprived of their own culture yet not quite cultured enough—rejecting one, rejected by the other, residing in a space of deprivation and alienation, and "Negroes" were refused any but the most menial schooling. In addition, the natural resources of whole continents were exploited and the exploitation justified as serving the needs of a superior culture while all the time memories were destroyed and linguistic traditions fractured.

A Flattened Cultural Horizon

Things seem different today. Colonialism, at least in its political form although not yet in its economic one, is in retreat, and postmodern sensitivities have encouraged us to abandon the view that cultures can be ranked from the highest to the lowest. In its place stands an understanding of culture that Geertz (2000, 42–67) aptly labels and defends as anti-anti-relativism, and that Bourdieu, in less diplomatic terms, would call anti-symbolic violence (Bourdieu and Passeron 1977, 1–68). This new understanding is the foundation for the postmodern celebration of irony where dispassion and distance are validated, where passion and commitment are outdated, possibly dangerous, and where the deconstruction of narratives is the intellectually safe course to take.

While the history of the common school is somewhat different in England, continental Europe and the United States all shared a common understanding of its role in advancing culture and nation and of reflecting standards by which the civilizing capacities of different groups of people could be judged. It is a carry-over from this conception that we still use the same word to indicate both membership in a certain form of life and to indicate as well those few of us with exquisite taste. To be filled with culture is to be filled with the right kind of Culture. Those who attend fine art museums and classical music concerts are Culture-full. They have taken the best that civilization has to offer and made it their own. The so-called "savage" was one devoid of any culture at all. Under the colonial regime, education was a value-filling enterprise and Culture provided the ultimate test of the worth of any individual and any educational program. Education was thus seen as the process of taking the children of savages as well as those of the insufficiently cultured and providing them with as much Culture as their biology or psychology would allow.

The Problem of What to Teach when Culture Becomes "Culture"

Today, this conception of cultural hierarchy has been flattened out. One sign of this flattening is the popularity of scholarship where Culture is placed between quotation marks or some rhetorical equivalent, to indicate its function as an object of description for social science and its demotion as a sign indicating exquisite taste, discipline and "good breeding"—just the right combination of nature and nurture—to a now suspect instrument of legitimation and class domination. This theme of "Culture" as power and domination informs educational theorists who see resistance as the major pedagogical task (Willis 1978), or who describe the schooling of children from one cultural group into the forms of another as symbolic violence (Bourdieu and Passeron 1977).

This rejection of the claims of "Culture" as indicating good breeding and viewing it instead as a cloak for the legitimation of power and domination raises an important issue for philosophy of education: in the light of this flattening where a Culture of value is reduced to a culture of domination, what are we to teach and how can this teaching be justified? One popular response is to give up on the task of assimilation because it is seen as no more than the imposition of one cultural group on another, and instead to involve education in multiple socializing projects where students are taught the rules of the game of the dominant economic group and provided with the skills needed to play it, but where deep values and beliefs are left alone to be nurtured by family, religion and cultural communities. Here the image is not of a hierarchy of cultural values in which education involves learning to appreciate the values of the highest cultural group, but rather of a horizontal structure of cultures in which each is separate from the other, and the educational task is to ensure that the more powerful do not impose their values and norms on the other.

In each of these schemes the school has an important cultural policing function to perform, but it is vastly different in the one than in the other. In the first the policing involves purifying the curriculum to see that it represents only the "best" that "civilization" has to offer. Teachers are screened for any trace of an undesirable local accent, while textual representations are always of some cultural or national ideal. In the second, the policing is concerned with detecting instances of cultural imposition and hegemony where teachers and texts are screened for their inclusiveness.

Yet the idea of inclusiveness that informs this policing is easily seen as one of cultural separation and reification where all norms, especially dominant ones, are *simply* artefacts of one cultural group or another, where each (and especially oppressed ones) has a right to reproduce its own meanings without interference by the school, and where the school has an obligation to respect any and all cultural meanings. Given that the utilitarian aspects of culture can be taught by almost any culturally separate school, the very idea of a common school system comes into question since the flattening out of culture challenges the idea that there is anything common for the common school to teach and that any attempt to do so can only be understood as exerting symbolic violence on children from outside some dominant cultural norm. This flattening of the normative aspects of culture, while effective in challenging outdated hierarchies, presents problems for any ideal of education as a culturally independent normative activity, leaving the discourse about the aims of education to the descriptions of social scientists or to rich but largely suggestive narratives of critical theorists.

Some members of the latter group have even suggested abandoning the concept of culture because they fear it serves to open up the practices of the powerless to the powerful, or, even more disturbing, it allows the powerful to represent the powerless (Abu-Lughod 1991, 149–52) and thereby to increase their vulnerability. While this "remedy" seems to me to be linguistically dogmatic, it nevertheless suggests a level of instability with the concept of culture that can be used to refine and address the educational dilemma that I have described.

As a replacement for the concept of culture, some cultural theorists have introduce the idea of "positionality," an idea designed to capture the power inequality entailed in the relationship between the observer and the observed or the researcher and her subject, and implicitly to coax cultural scholars to give voice to the oppressed, to undercut the assumption of cultural coherence and to emphasize contradictions and misrecognitions (148), as well as the fact that the researcher herself always approaches the study of culture from a particular social position. The advantage of this move is that it serves to remind scholars and educators of their own privileged positions within a university and to provide an opening for those not so privileged to be heard on their own terms (140).

However, there is the danger that in its attempt to allow fluidity into the study of culture, "positionality" is itself reified in the process as if each of us had but one and only one position from which we observe and interpret. Hence the categories of male/female, oppressed/oppressor, white/non-white, colonized/colonizer become as fixed as the hierarchy of cultures it was designed to overthrow. There is the added danger, especially for ethnographic researchers, that as they focus on the experience of one marginalized group, that group is allowed to interpret the experiences of other marginalized groups. Witness, for example the depiction of women, teachers and Pakistan immigrants in Willis's classic study of working class students (see, for example, Dolby et al. 2004).

For educators there is the added problem of subsuming the educational discourse within the new postmodern, normatively flattened understanding of the idea of culture. Unlike some forms of social science where participation is subordinate to observation and observation is subordinate to description, in education, observation is subordinate to participation, participation is subordinate to intervention, and intervention is for the sake of the *growth* and *development* of the other. In other words, the descriptive categories of the social sciences take on a prescriptive role when it comes to the activity of educating. Educational theory must always supplement description with prescription for the sake of intervention and growth. (Even a decision to let the child move ahead on her own without active intervention is a prescription guided by an idea of growth if it is to be seen as an *educational* decision.) Thus, any concept of culture that merely flattens out the normative dimension of educating is deficient as an educational theory.[1] While educational scholars may view such flattening as a healthy antidote to the normative pretensions of a dominant group, they need also to understand its limitations as a conception of culture-for-educational-purpose.

Culture-for-Educational-Purpose

Hence the conception of culture (as well as positionality) needs reworking as culture-for-educational-purpose. In doing this reworking two dangers need to be avoided. The first is the danger of re-establishing a strict hierarchy of cultural value, much in the way that Samuel Huntington does in his book, *Who Are We?* (2004), where he holds up the Anglo-Protestant, upper-class male as the model American. The second is the danger of so completely flattening out the worth of different human practices that all forms of intervention are viewed only as expressions of class hegemony or where an act as seemingly innocent as a field trip to a fine arts museum is taken as but another example of symbolic violence. Certainly educators must appropriate the discourse of culture and positionality, but they can only do so after reworking the basic categories so that they move from the passive to the active voice. The educational concern was summed up well by Edward Said (1978) in his critique of Orientalism and its practice of fixing differences between people so as to render them unbridgeable.[2]

All of this presents a major dilemma for the common school. For if the idea of a cultural hierarchy is suspect, and if the road map to growth is not to be found in adopting the ways of the dominant culture, but if the flattening out of cultures makes the notion of growth problematic, then what is the basis for educational intervention and for the prescriptive activity that education is?

The dilemma requires that we interrogate the colonialist conception of culture further, a concept that developed as a result of the separation and apparent isolation of western countries from their new subject. This separation created the idea of distinctness as a reality and culture as an ontological category that described, signified and ranked difference. We have now questioned the politically incorrect conception of cultural ranking, but we have maintained the idea of culture as an ontological category describing a reality that exists apart from the people that express it and that bind some together absolutely and separate them from others. This view of separateness is taken as a corollary of the rejection of the ranking of different cultural forms. Cultures cannot be ranked for the same reasons that any series of different kinds of things, apples, oranges and string beans, cannot be ranked against one another (except possibly on another dimension—say, nutritional value).

Given this view of the distinctness of cultural forms, an even more radical view seems to follow—that communication cannot take place across cultures, and if this were really the case, the task of the common school would be virtually impossible. While not everyone who accepts the view that cultures are distinct and cannot be ranked would accept this implication, the reason for its rejection requires a deep critique of the idea of culture as an ontological category depicting separate and uniquely distinct entities. Culture-for-education-purpose suggests that the mistake is the assumption that culture has an ontological status that subsumes individuals. It raises questions about a basic image underlying this view: that is, while a person existing within one cultural formation can adopt as a tool the practices of another, she cannot truly exist as a member of both. She belongs to one while visiting the other. The ideas of symbolic violence and cultural penetration are both expressions of this image of the ontological status of culture and of the need to protect cultural formations. Yet underlying these images is a very conservative understanding of culture.

While today expressions of concerns about symbolic violence and cultural penetration are concerns expressed by and for members of vulnerable groups, the conception of culture is a hang-over—turned upside down—from the colonial period where separation, physical, psychological and spiritual was critical to the purity of the dominant group and where at any moment its members could fall into the heart of darkness, seduced by temptations of women, wine and song. Today, the ethno-centered chauvinism of the colonialist conception of culture has been shed, at least by the dominant theories in cultural anthropology and cultural studies, but in the popular mind, and perhaps in the corners of many disciplines, the *thingness* of culture remains. Meaning and significance are said to separate members of one cultural group from those of another. Separation is seen by some as a good thing, one necessary to protect cultures, as if they were some kind of precious material that contact with others would dilute.

Of course cultural intermingling cannot be denied as a factual matter and just as many seek separation, many others applaud this intermingling. To take care of the slack on a descriptive level, a new concept—"hybridity"—has been developed to indicate those at the margins of two cultural groups who come together to form a third and new culture. Yet this concept actually reinforces the *thingness* of the idea of culture. Granted it allows for some leakage, but it still suggests the affirmation of two or more pure cultural forms, out of which some third emerges. While people differ in what they think about separation and intermingling, this discourse reinforces a certain problematic conception of culture as things, as distinct objects.

Now I want to suggest that this thingness is inappropriate for educators and for the idea of culture-for-educational-purpose and it is time not only to break ranks with the colonialist past, but also with part of the postmodern present that continues to be informed by it. It is time for educators to strike out on their own, and to reshape the conception of culture as an educational concept by admitting that a central task of the educator is to facilitate the growth of meaning in children and the capacity for critical, reflective evaluation and by allowing that much of this can only happen if we enable children to move beyond what we loosely label "their culture." In other words we need a conception of culture that can acknowledge that the function of education is one of development and growth into agency, where agency involves the capacity to form one's own values, informed by, but not limited to, certain ideas drawn from a particular collective formation that we loosely term "a culture." To address this task is to also begin to address the question of what can be distinctly common about the common school in this post colonial age.

The philosopher Jonathan Glover suggests a response to this question when he writes:

Just as a Species may flourish in a particular ecological niche, so the development of individual personality may depend on the support of a group. Like climbing plants searching for something to hook on to, we look for such support, as with the random allocation of the psychological experiments, the group has no shared basis. But as climbing plants flourish where there is support, so our sense of ourselves flourishes in groups with enough in common to take on a life of their own. This dependence on the shared understanding of a group is brought out by differences of language. When you speak a foreign language poorly, you have to say simpler things than you would like to; in doing so, you present a simplified version of yourself. (This does not only apply to talking about another language. It can also hold in another country where they speak a version of your own language. Turns of phrases, humor, and tone of voice are part of a "language": which may be different. One way of drawing the boundaries of a culture is to take the region where such signals are understood). (Glover 1991, 197–98)

It should be added to Glover's remarks that, since there is never a one-to-one mapping of the signals of one person with those of another and since there is never a complete absence of common points, what we call *a* culture is never complete nor is it ever incomplete.

The language that we use is an important component in this liberation of the concept of culture from its roots in colonialism. We speak about "his culture" or "her parent's culture" as if culture were a thing that we possess. Or we say that such and such is an infringement of her "cultural rights" as if culture were some kind of fortress that serves to protect us from an alien force. Or, we say things like "sexual equality is not recognized in that culture" (as if culture were a space in which certain otherwise reasonable norms were legitimately relaxed). These ways of speaking about culture suggest that it is either personal property, or it is a bounded entity that protects and constrains individuals who share it. Culture, rather than individuals, is treated as having agency while the individual is defined completely by membership. In this understanding individuals exist only as members of singular and unique cultural formations. Here *culture* is the object of value serving to insulate otherwise vulnerable individuals from outside and foreign influences. The implication is that when educators impose another culture on children, they mislead children like the Pied Piper through false promises about the wonders of the larger society. The important concern behind this criticism is that children will grow up neither belonging to the world of their parents nor fully capable of navigating the larger social order.

Now there is something obviously correct about this picture when we recall Native American children forcefully removed from their parents; Aboriginal children brought up as white in Australia; fractured relationships between child, parent and community. The lesson is clear: children are harmed when their parents and their parents' communities are not respected. Yet the important lesson should not be that culture defines us without remainder, or that we are of such pure and vulnerable material that we will crumble just by contact with the cultural other. The right lesson involves understanding the important role children's initial encounter with meaning plays in their development. It is not that their identity is exhausted through this encounter.

The wrong lesson leads to the wrong educational conclusion, that parents, as the carriers of culture, always know what is best for children, that they are the only legitimate agent of educational authority, and that their "culture" (as if they were members of one and only one culture) contains everything that the child needs for growth and development. While few educators act on all of these assumptions all of the time, and while still many make the opposite mistake of dismissing the parent's culture, they give rise to a kind of bad feeling, when it is pointed out that a certain teaching is inconsistent with the practices or beliefs of a parent's culture. Yet this bad feeling arises out of a constricted notion if interaction based on the colonial image where connections are assumed to always be hierarchical and never horizontal—always from "upper" to "lower," "dominating" to "dominated," "oppressor" to "oppressed"—and not across actors at the same level but within different "cultural" formations.

That this bad feeling is sometimes not educationally productive can be seen if we turn away from cultural to religious concerns. In the United States, for example, science teachers are allowed, indeed often required, to teach about Darwin's theory of evolution, but they are often expected to do so without criticizing intelligent design theory or creationism. And, fearful of reprisals, doubting their own legitimacy as cultural authorities, many teachers simply skirt the topic of evolution, allowing parents and ministers to serve as the final authority of scientific beliefs.

This bad feeling is expressed also by those legal and political theorists who argue that parents should have exclusive control over their children's education and that the state should provide the resources to achieve it. It is also expressed in Court decisions in the United States such as the Yoder case (*Wisconsin v. Yoder*, 406 U.S. 205 (1972)) where the Court allowed Amish parents to excuse their children from an extended education because it might alienate them from their religion and their culture. Now, there may be justifiable reasons for some of these practices, but unless we get the reasons right, we are likely to see the exceptions as the rule, rather than what they are, at best, excusable exceptions. In order to get the answer right educators need a more serviceable conception of culture, one that allows us to take into account what we know about growth and development as it occurs in an age of increasing engagement across local and global boundaries.

Culture as Culturing

As a way to develop this more serviceable conception of culture-for-educational-purpose, I begin with a simplified example that is intended to suggest a more fluid conception of culture, culture as process rather than thing—culture as *culturing*. I explore the concept of culture from an educator's standpoint, a standpoint where intentional intervention for the sake of growth comes with the role and where part of this intervention involves social continuity through the reproduction of symbolic forms and significations and another part involves social discontinuity through the introduction of new symbolic forms and significations. The first of these is summed up by the ideal of communal participation; the second, by the ideal of autonomy.

The concept of culturing must thus aim for a middle ground somewhere between the smug self-certainty of the colonial conceptions of cultural hierarchy and the paralyzing self-doubt of the postmodern normatively flattened conceptions of cultural difference. Without this conceptual work there is no good argument against a utilitarian conception of schools where scores on standardized tests or parental preferences are the only standards of educational quality.

I want to begin with a personal example, one that I consider an instance of cultural creation at its simplest level. A few years ago my wife, a friend and I took a car trip from the South of France to Barcelona. After securing our hotel room we found a small local delicatessen and, quite hungry, we stood in line to order food. I saw people in the booths eating some kind of fish and decided I wanted fish as well. When I got to the counter I realized that I had long forgotten the Spanish word for fish, along with most of the other words that my three or four years of high school and college Spanish had supposedly taught me, and whatever I did utter might have been French or German, or gobbledygook, but it was not Spanish, or, at least it baked no fish for me.

As I tried to communicate with the person behind the counter, the line was growing longer and longer, and I eventually stepped aside to let others order. When the line diminished again, I returned, somewhat hungrier and somewhat more desperate. Attempting again with a few more possible utterances, I was about to give up, when I had a brilliant thought. I looked the clerk squarely in the eye and mimicked a swimmer's crawl stroke. I could see the metaphorical light-bulb go off in his head, and, almost dancing, he cried out, "Ah, feesh!"

I see this example as a moment of cultural creation in the sense that a common meaning was established. Feigning the crawl stroke while standing in line in a delicatessen meant that I was hungry and wanted to satisfy that hunger with a serving of fish. This was a moment of cultural creation, of culturing, because meaning was produced, enabling coordinated action to take place. Granted, the meaning was quite thin, after all I really wanted baked fish and I got deep fried, but nevertheless it was a moment in which a shared meaning was established and a connection made. And, of course many other but related meanings were already in place for both of us. We shared an understanding of the function of a delicatessen and how customers and counter people generally interacted. He could assume I was there because I was hungry, wanted to eat and was willing to pay for my food and I could assume that he was there to provide the food and collect the money. Teachers and students of course may have more complex tasks since meaning must be established on a thicker basis and, where there are larger differences between the meanings in the home and the meaning in the school, less can be taken for granted.

What we call a "culture," such as *black* culture or *Jewish* culture or *Korean* culture, involves all of those elements of meaning—in each of these cases, quite thick—that a group of people share, that they take for granted in acts of communication or appreciation and that they transfer, either through informal or formal education, to new generations. These include not only words strung together in sentences, but art work, music and religious practices, which join people together around shared meanings *and* sentiments. And they include what we call traditions or those practices that have developed deep historical meanings that when activated make visible an imagined connection to one another and to past and future generations. The Passover tradition is a story about people who lived long ago told to each new generation in the process of the construction and reconstruction of a Jewish identity.

This way of thinking about culture is useful for avoiding the unproductive question of whether we can translate from one culture to another, and assuming that a negative answer means that we cannot render judgments across the so-called "cultural boundaries." Translation is always possible, and translation is always partial. It is always partial because we never know all of the links to which a single utterance leads. My "fish" conjured up the long car ride to get to Barcelona, a wish that I had stayed awake in Spanish class, a frustration that a clerk in a Barcelona delicatessen could not figure out what I was trying to say. *The clerk's* "feesh" might have conjured up "another long day and another linguistically inept American!" But people, not cultures, translate and they do so with greater or lesser success as gestures, words and signs allow. When connections are made we are culturing.

Sometimes coordination will require only a thin connection, like the gesture of swimming, to start to build up a thicker one. In my adventure at the delicatessen, I was able to take for granted the fact that the clerk was familiar with swimming and he could recognize a crawl stroke when he saw one. Thin as it was, it was a connection—a moment of cultural creation. When the connections are thick, your interlocutor and you can finish each other's sentences because you share history and experiences, but even there static sometimes arises when, for example, one party, to the embarrassment of the other, says more than he should because he does not get what is at stake here, at this moment, in this situation. Clearly, the example is rather benign, but it allows us to think of culture in a more dynamic, open way and thus to begin to understand what might be at stake when we are concerned about what some call acts of cultural penetration or symbolic violence.

Yet before getting too far ahead of myself, I want to add another dimension to this picture, one of appraisal, or significance. In the example of cultural formation, evaluation was taking place. I would have preferred baked to fried, but frankly, I was happy to take what I could get at the moment. The clerk, frustrated by my inadequate attempt at Spanish, might have preferred me not to hold up his line any longer. For purposes of politeness, good business sense or political correctness, or just plain expediency we obviously did not even try to communicate these evaluations to each other, but it is likely they were there. Imagine what would have happened if I wanted lobster and ordered it in a kosher restaurant. No matter how otherwise thick the meaning that we shared (say we spoke the same language, etc.), this would have set us apart.

The question then is not just one of translation—we always translate and we always fail in translating all there is to understand. Concern over cultural imposition may be less about translation and more about evaluation, or about the factors that make it difficult to enter into another person's evaluative shoes. Since one of the features attributed to culture is the role it plays in centering people, providing a focal point for evaluation (an uncle of mine used to ask, "Is it good for the Jews?"), it is natural to think of culture as the foundation for evaluation. And then, if we think wrongly, that meaning cannot be translated across cultures, and then we are likely to think, incorrectly, that evaluation also cannot travel.

While there are tragic moments when different groups may surely differ about the value of an event—what is good for the Jews is tragic for the Palestinians—there is nothing about evaluation as such that would not allow people to come to agreements from different standpoints about many things. So to illustrate the limits and opportunities to bridge different evaluations, let's take another road story and instead of highlighting culture let's allow for a dense set of shared meanings and highlight class, or the way in which different evaluations arise from different material conditions.

Some time before our trip to Barcelona, my wife and I were travelling with an old graduate school friend who had just recently been divorced. In college we had been quite close, sharing the same religious, economic and educational backgrounds and coming from the same community. We enjoyed many of the same things and, as students, had done many of them together. In common sense terms, we belonged to the "same" cultural group. However, many years had passed since we had last seen each other. For my wife and myself this trip was a celebration of sorts, of a new position for my wife. For our friend it was a more painful journey, one where she hoped to heal some wounds and recover from a difficult divorce.

After a couple of days travelling together my wife and I noticed that at lunch and dinner time our friend would excuse herself and return to her hotel room, meeting up with us at some later time. At first we thought she was just tired until we realized that she was very concerned about the cost of many things whereas before she had been more extravagant than we were. We finally realized that from our standpoint good restaurants were affordable but from hers they were too expensive. This explained why she often insisted on stopping off at a local bakery and grocer where she would buy bread and cheese to take to her hotel room. We began to realize that her divorce had placed her in a very different financial position from ours and while our prospects had risen, hers had fallen. In other words, we could take for granted certain material comforts and support that she could not.

On the phenomenological level, this difference is what "economic class" means—economic class is all of those material supports that are available or absent that one can depend on in living a life of a certain kind. As Marx noted long ago, economic class position influences evaluation and it creates or constrains certain opportunities. In my example our different material situations led to different evaluations about what to count as an appropriate restaurant.

Now on a large scale, and in different circumstances, envy or contempt along with other emotions create static when attempting to bridge the evaluative gap caused by class difference. Yet here there was, as far as we could tell, no such emotion, and still bridging the gap was certainly not easy. To be located in a certain economic class is to be embedded in a set of material conditions that allow certain possibilities to be considered or rejected as real enactments. My wife and I could decide between the comparatively high price bistro or the equally up-scale cafe a block from it. And, until we realized that this choice was not comfortably available to our friend, we took this range of possibilities for granted, even though a few months earlier, when my wife was not working, we ourselves would have been more cautious.

When we did realize our friend's financial concerns, economic class location created problems of communication even though our educations were very similar. Nevertheless a kind of awkwardness set in that had never existed before. We knew that to insist that the meal be our treat would have been seen as paternalistic. We feared that if we were to suggest that *she* name the restaurant, she would then know that we knew more about her situation than she might have wished to reveal. To go ahead and continue to eat in up-scale restaurants would have been uncaringly callous.

Granted this micro level example has many limitations. We not only shared a history with our friend, that history included a similar background and a shared education. My wife and I were highly motivated to understand what was going on and to do what we could to resolve it. And it helped that we could recall when we were in a similar situation in Norway, running out of money. We could recall skipping meals, eating all the meals we did take in university cafeterias, watching with envy as shoppers in the market-place would think nothing of buying expensive pastries or exotic meats. These memories helped ease the awkwardness of the moment and allowed us to discuss the situation with our friend. This option is often more complex in a school situation where power relations determine how a situation will be defined. Whatever its limitations, however, the example suggests the material, communicative and emotional gaps opened up by class position and some of the possible areas available for reconstruction.

To function within a thick network of meanings (what we commonly call a culture) and within a thick set of material conditions that we take for granted (what we call economic class) provides high levels of understanding and predictability. To operate across what we commonly call culture and class increases possibilities for misunderstanding and unpredictability, but contrary to some theorists, misunderstanding and unpredictability are not destiny. Recall how Hurricane Katrina showed us in the most dramatic way possible, the effects of class location can become visible to everyone. Even President Bush, who initially seemed more concerned about his friend Senator Trent Lott's house, and losing his own youthful playground, eventually had to acknowledge the face and the fate of poverty. Yet first expressions are important indicators of what class and culture have allowed us to take for granted, and the example is a powerful corrective for those who believe that all that is required to foster mutual understanding is to bring children from different backgrounds together in a *common* school. Because each child stands in a different position with different assumptions, commonality is not given. It is a task to be achieved when the significance of background factors are accounted for in the task of shaping and extending meaning—of culturing.

The conceptions of culture and class that I have presented have the advantage of avoiding reification, and rejecting the simplistic relativism of those who claim that translation or evaluation across culture or class is impossible. Culture is not a thing. It is neither a property that we own, as in the phrase "my culture," nor is it a fortress that protects us from harm by sealing us off from alien influences. It is simply a network of meanings, meanings that enable coordinated action and appreciation, thick in some places, thin in others, connected more or less to shared personal or historical experiences.

As nodes thicken and are sustained across generations, some people come to think of themselves as a "we" and shape their identity through their participation in a multiple set of nodal configurations. Those who do not share this identity from the inside—and strictly speaking no-one completely shares the identity of another from the inside (it is always a matter of more or less)—can access features of it circuitously, indirectly and partially through other strands of meaning. When the distance is great, we are like a stroke victim whose brain is working to make new pathways in order to express and to comprehend. In short, we are never completely cut off from the other, but then again neither are we fully part of the other. Those who share a certain nodal position for one set of meanings will not share others to the same extent. For example, years ago when computers were first introduced to the faculty at my former those who were part of the Macintosh culture could take for granted a lot of operational procedures that those who were members of the DOS culture could not. But then these Macintosh people might have shared very little beyond that. Similarly, two people sharing the "same" religious nexus and who will respond in the same way to their standardized religious symbols may not share the same racialized or gendered space.

Historically one of the roles of nation states, what Benedict Anderson (1992) calls "imagined communities," has been to fix meaning and evaluation, what is called loyalty, across classes and to bridge cultural differences at the points where networks of meaning thin out. In the past the common school served to stabilize a national identity by fixing meanings and significances through formalized systems of instruction that standardized language, and constructed a more or less shared canon of myths and stories. In other words, the common school served to shape the intersubjective meanings and significances required for coordinated action on a national scale, and in this creation of meaning and signification, new opportunities for shared experiences and thickened meanings above lines of culture and class differences were often created. While this process was rarely smooth, it contributed to a sense of the nation as some kind of imagined family where each of us, no matter how strong our personal grievance, believed that we owed something to other members that we did not owe to the outsider.

To some extent this imagined community still informs much of what we do and constitutes much of who we are. Some of the time we think of ourselves as members of a national community sharing a common history and a common destiny. Sometimes this is a good thing as when we come together to help victims of a natural disaster and sometimes it is more troubling as when we commit aggression on another nation, but whether good or bad, the nation too gets reified as if it were a thing that we own, as when we speak of "my nation," or as something that owns us as when we speak of "my obligation to my country."

In conservative theory, these three elements, culture, position and nation, are ideally neatly nested within one another where the nation is bound together by the shared norms of culture and where each position functions in a mutually supportive way to serve the larger national community. And where this community then serves God. When things get "out of order," tempers flare and sometimes purges occur.

In more radical theory, there is considerable tension between these different points with national identity hiding the exploitative qualities of social position. In the former, nation lends its reality to position and culture. In the latter, nation serves as a fiction to conceal the reality of a cultural identity based on position and inequality. The proper educational program for the first is patriotism; for the second, resistance.

The process of globalization allows us to see the fluid nature of these meaning systems. The process whereby excess loyalty is directed toward the nation state is breaking down. The basic insight that globalization theory begins with is that absolute national sovereignty is an idea whose time has come and whose time is swiftly passing away. It is to be no more. If globalization is hard on national identity, it may be even harder on cultural identities as witnessed by the way people who have moved to other places reshape their informal relations over a few generations—witness the large number of marriages across religious or ethnic boundaries. And, finally, whatever position is salient in one context need not be so in another. There and then a doctor, here and now a medical technician; there and then a professor, here and now a parking attendant; there and then a proud land-owner, here and now a construction worker. For the conservative who wishes to reinstate the idea of nationhood and national identity, these changes are disturbing because they disrupt the ideal of the all for one, one for all, single culture, unified religion, sense of national identity. But the changes should also give warning to the radical theorists who, seeking agency in cultural or positional identity, assume that any individual is totally defined by the role he or she may play in the drama of a human life.

The Task of the Common School

To liberate meaning from the limitations of traditional conceptions of culture, position and nation should enable educators to avoid some of the reductionist tendencies of popular notions of culture, class or nation. In other words, when we are thinking of the education of children, and the shaping of their identity, it is important that we do not treat them just as an instance of cultural, class, gendered, or national formations. While it is important that children understand the ways in which these forms work, there is an irreducible element to the self that must be attended to, an element that is unique and that needs recognition. The philosopher Jonathan Glover again captures this when he writes: "Out of all the people in the world, this particular one happens to be me. This (to me) important fact is visible only from my perspective. An objective description can indicate that each person, including Jonathan Glover, has a particular viewpoint from which they see the world. But it cannot mention something that I care about: That I am Jonathan Glover, and so that perspective is of particular interest to me" (Glover 1991, 65).

It is this irreducible element, this one time only, unique member of the human species, that educators cannot allow to be subsumed under culture or class, race or gender or nation alone. Certainly there are times when protecting the thick nexus of meaning into which a child is born is the most important thing to do for the child. As Glover puts it we do depend on the shared understanding of a group and in most cases children are done a great disservice if they are taught to discredit that understanding and those whose lives are constructed through it. Yet, to repeat his metaphor of growth I mentioned in the previous chapter, just as the growth of a plant depends on seeking out the air and light on which all of the plants in a certain ecological niche depends, so the growth of a child depends on participating in a larger global context as both a planetary animal, dependent on and responsible for the conditions of life on earth, and on being recognized by others as an irreducible, unique member of that planetary species known as the human race. The unique role for the common school then is no longer one of laying a national identity over local ones and creating a single imagined community. It must now serve to open up paths of communications across different local communities and across distinct national ones. Without this task, the common role of the "common" school is merely a utilitarian one where all children must learn certain skills in order to live and work in their society as it is. But common skills do not a common school make. They can be taught in any school with a minimum level of accountability to a central authority. A *common* school has the task of opening up avenues of communications across different communities by teaching students how to engage in the enterprise of thickening meaning where co-coordinated action can serve growth by generating new interests and visions.

In some way this idea is not too different from that of Dewey, who saw education as both a process of initiation and of growth where growth entailed new interests and extended associations. However, Dewey was still operating in the context in which the dominance of one cultural group was assumed and with a common insensitivity to the richness of the cultural heritage of others. I think that even for Dewey who had for his time a very generous sense of assimilation, and certainly for most of his contemporaries, who had a less generous one, thickening meaning was a task that local minorities had to do as they interacted with dominant social norms. It was not a task that children of the white Anglo majority were expected to perform. In this sense Dewey was as much a part of the nation-building process as was W. T. Harris, the Hegelian educator who served as the premier North American philosopher of education prior to Dewey (see Feinberg 1974). Dewey's advance over Harris was that he understood that much of this engagement needed to be undertaken with respect for the traditions of minority communities.

Culturing is not just a matter of pure understanding or of interpretive empathy, but rather is a precondition of the increasing connectivity and coordination needed to communicate across local and global communities. Nevertheless, in teaching children to expand their imaginative capacity, we are also teaching them to enter into the framework and meanings of others and to consider their point of view in choosing how to act, both individually and collectively.[3]

13

Uncommon Identities
Hard Cases

Introduction

In this essay I address two questions: When should a public school be obliged to recognize group differences? And how should it do so? The complexity involved in addressing the issue of difference can be illustrated by two different court cases. In the first, decided by the United States Supreme Court in *Wisconsin v. Yoder* (1972),[1] the Court allowed a group of Amish parents to remove their children from the public schools after the eighth grade. The parents had argued that schooling beyond the eighth grade was disruptive to their communal life, and the Court agreed on grounds having to do with the uniqueness, isolation, and peaceful nature of the Amish community. The dissenting justice argued that the decision disadvantaged individual Amish children and denied them opportunities that were due every American.

In the second case, *Mozert v. Hawkins County Board of Education* (1983),[2] a group of parents requested that their children be allowed to absent themselves from a classroom because they believed that the required text presented sinful material that threatened their children's religious identity. This case was decided by a federal court against the parents on the ground that exposure to another way of life did not constitute a direct challenge to the parent's religious beliefs.

These decisions are both compatible with the values of liberalism, even though they seem inconsistent with each other. On one hand, parents have a right to form and enter communities, to live without interference from state officials, and to pass on their values and beliefs to their children. On the other, schools have an obligation to promote children's right to freedom of association, personal growth, and equal opportunity. This obligation requires teachers to provide students with the information and insights that will enable them to reflect on the values and beliefs of different communities and to accept or reject these values for themselves.

Both cases tested the extent to which the school must go in facilitating each of these rights and addressing the question of which should have priority when they conflict. The *Yoder* decision suggests that there are instances in which the school must refrain from its normal obligation of promoting individual growth in order to facilitate the right of a community to reproduce itself. The *Mozert* decision suggests that there are times when the school must not honor the preferences of the parent in order to facilitate the child's intellectual growth and development.

Although the courts needed to sort out the specific factors that enabled them to rule as they did, the cases are similar in one critical respect. The plaintiffs did not ask the school to do anything to advance their communal identity. They simply asked it to refrain from doing something that they believed threatened to disrupt it. Moreover, in both cases, the court felt that to permit such restraint under existing conditions would predictably lead children to accept the belief system of their parents and to do so without the benefit of exposure to alternative views.

As complicated as these cases are, the fact that the parents were not asking schools to do very much that was different from what they would normally do limits the considerations that the courts needed to address.[3] Parents were asking that schools take a passive and neutral role regarding identity and that they do nothing that would provide children with material that would lead them to question their parents' commitments. The problem arises because "neutrality" in these cases cuts children off from certain opportunities and narrows their understanding of the larger society. It also arises because the effect of neutrality in these instances in all likelihood is to *propel* the students without due consideration into the one secure belief system that is available to them—their parents'. The courts' differing responses in the two cases illustrate that the nature of the particular group and its relation to the larger society are important considerations in determining how to apply liberal principles of noninterference and equal opportunity.

In both cases the same principles were at stake. The parents were appealing to the classical liberal ideal of noninterference and arguing that they should have the primary say over their children's beliefs and education. The state was assuming that the basic authority of the school to teach civic virtues, to provide for intellectual growth and, especially in *Yoder*, to encourage equal opportunity limited the parents' rights. Neither set of parents was asking that public resources be used to support their communal identity. True, the *Mozert* parents were asking that alternative material be made available that would not violate certain religious concerns, but they were not asking that this material explicitly support those beliefs.

These cases and the understandable controversy surrounding them continue to influence the way the issue is framed. It is generally assumed that schools should have no role in promoting the agenda of a specific group and that they are allowed only a passive part in subgroup identity formation. Although the courts and liberal politicians and educators have gone in one direction on this issue, arguing in ways that allow only *individual* benefits to be considered, many advocates of multicultural education have moved in the opposite direction and have assumed that any claim to cultural status should automatically entitle the *group* to special educational recognition and support.

Advocates of multicultural education hold that the school has a responsibility to recognize group differences and to encourage children with certain racial, ethnic, or sexual characteristics to express their distinctiveness from the mainstream by supporting a primary affinity to people who are most like themselves.[4] Yet this view assumes that children are already identified with a culture and that they are identified with a single one, and it also assumes that all cultures are equal in terms of their claims on educational resources. Both of these assumptions are problematic. Although most of this chapter addresses the question of cultural claims on educational resources, I want to briefly turn to the question of identity and to the claim that schools should support children's affinity to those most like themselves.

Multiple Identities

Identity is the attribute we give to an entity that has the capacity to organize experience and to be experienced and to experience oneself as a coherent whole. Human beings have identities. We *experience* ourselves as ongoing, organized, and organizing centers of experience-as selves. We remember our past, anticipate our future, and connect both to our present. Moreover, we also have *identities as*—we experience ourselves related to some, but not all, other human beings. We believe that these people share our memories, present interpretations, and aspirations. The question whether they really do share these things is important, but more important is the shared perception that these are held in common. For one does not check each and every memory when affirming one's affinity with another. Rather, the perception of common memories, interpretations, and aspirations is sufficient to create a bond with people, some of whom may be distant and physically unconnected to one another. Yet this *identity is* open and fluid, and there is no a priori reason why we should accept our connection to only one group.

From an abstract point of view identity is fluid. There is no single racial, class, or gender identity, and there are many examples with regard to race and class, and even sex, in which individuals change categories. Some "African Americans" found that they could "pass" for "white," and within a few generations their children saw themselves as, and were seen as, white. People change their social class and then their children experience life through the framework of the new rather than the old class. The same is true of religion. Gender is experienced in so many different ways that the traditional idea that there are only two sexes is now controversial. Alternative sexual orientations and preferences, cross-dressing, sex-change operations, and so on all suggest that sexual identity is somewhat fluid.

People may move from one to another category as individuals; the categories themselves may allow for a great deal of gradation, which then blurs the sharpness of the distinctions between them; and some categories are important for a while and then they fade, to be replaced by others. For example, whether one was a first son was, but is no more, a major category of social and economic distinction in the West, and it is still so in many Asian countries.

Identity labels do not indicate any fixed and stable position. There is no one way to be "female" or to be "male," and there are many ways in which conventional males exhibit female behavior and in which conventional females exhibit male behavior. And the same is true of class. Moreover, the entire concept of race as a biological given is highly suspect, and to establish an identity on the basis of a fictive biological category can be a mistake of large educational and social proportions.

If race means anything, it is a cultural and historical category, but cultures are notoriously fluid; they signal evolving cores of meaning, and the whole concept of cultural identity only makes sense in relation to other cultural identities. Hence, for example, when I am abroad I am American, when I visit my friend's church I am Jewish, when I take the bus through the black neighborhood, I am white, and when I need a bathroom, I am a male. Identity, it may be argued, is much like the bubbles in champagne: It comes into play at different moments and then fades. Only identities do not fade forever. They remain inactive until circumstances stir them again, and it is the very specific play of all our identities—together with our internal experience of the interaction of our self with others—that gives each of us our specific character.

This is not to say that identity is completely free-floating. After all, when I am in Europe I am a U.S. American, and I am never a Korean or a Mexican. Moreover, others respond to physical characteristics, posture, complexion, dialect, and so on as if we were one kind of person and not another. And if that response is consistent with a social, cultural, or biological heritage, it will often reinforce that affiliation. Traits cluster together in ways that produce certain expectations that when disappointed provoke sharp reactions of surprise or shock. These reactions bring into relief the belief that these traits belong together and provide an occasion either for anger and rejection or for reflection about what to count as identity.[5]

The complexity of identity suggests that the idea that schools should support children's affinity to those most like themselves is a more difficult injunction than it appears, because it involves strategic decisions about who a child is most like. This is not to argue with the basic point of the injunction—that children should care about their identity and that they should be aware of the way it is shaped though culture. It is simply to note that there is nothing automatic about this process. Decisions are made all along the line about what cultural entity a child belongs to and whether it is appropriate for the schools to support an identification with that particular entity. These decisions are never clear-cut but are based on different factors.

When an attribute becomes a formative feature of identity, a number of things happen. The attribute is taken to signal something larger than itself. It becomes a sign for more complex historical, social, and political formations. To take on an identity means to take on those larger formations as well. It is not sufficient, for example, to have a dark skin in order to receive recognition as an African American. One must also be seen as, and see oneself as, a part of a certain historical formation.

Who Cares about Cultural Identity?

Different people care about cultural identity for different reasons. Mature members of a culture care about an identity precisely because to be a mature member of a culture means to have been shaped by it, to participate in it with ease and to enjoy doing so, to understand that such enjoyment is dependent on other people enjoying it, and to accept a commitment to reproduce that capacity in new members. Those outside of the cultural formation may also care about it, but in a different way. They may enjoy the culture as observers of its practices; they may delight in being in the midst of a diversity of cultural expressions; or they may feel that their own culture is more secure because the principle that enables recognition of the importance of this culture also enables recognition of the importance of their own.

Yet those outside a given cultural formation may also be indifferent or even hostile to another cultural grouping, feeling that its fate is no concern of theirs. From the point of view of this indifference, there is still a minimal liberal principle in play. All people have a right to their own self-defined cultural formations as an extension of the right to freedom of association. They would not necessarily have a right to use the resources of public education to reproduce that formation.

The Argument against Multicultural Education: A Reconsideration

Critics who are concerned about the social effects of structuring public education around specific identities are uneasy about using schools to heighten children's awareness of the importance of certain attributes—skin color, sex, ethnic background, parental income—that they happen to share with some but not all other citizens. They object to schools' contributing to a heightened sense of differences, differences that are constructed within the context of public political formations, and they are concerned that active recognition of the "child's group," instead of broadening the child's awareness of different forms of the good, narrows it.

Some object that since public schools are supported with resources to which everyone must contribute, it is illegitimate to use these resources to encourage children to think of themselves in narrow and particularistic terms. Others are concerned that if public schools teach children to differentiate themselves from one another on the basis of cultural difference, they will not identify themselves with the nation as a whole and will not develop the wider scope of sympathy that national unity and collective welfare require. The fear is that more assertive forms of cultural expression will lead to a rejection of the common identity and that a child who is educated in a narrow cultural framework will not develop sufficient sympathy toward members of other cultural groups.

There is an additional concern that, were the schools to advance the multicultural platform, there would be an endless splintering of identities. Hence, if today blackness is a category for special treatment, tomorrow it may be Cuban blackness versus Haitian blackness, and so on. Or if today schoolgirls are encouraged to assert their identity as women, tomorrow working-class schoolgirls may be encouraged to reform their identity in opposition to middle-class ones.

In addition to these concerns there is the perceived danger of over-defining the individual child and fixing her identity too early. After all, people are not just one thing. True, they may be *identified as* a this, but they are also *identified as* a that and another that and another. The fear is that if public schools recognize children in terms of a single identity group they will do them an educational disservice because they will ignore other potential identities. (This is perhaps one reason for the sometimes scorned remark made by some teachers that they do not see black children, Asian children, or Hispanic children. They see only children.) The concern is that active recognition fixes a child's identity to a given group on the basis of otherwise relatively inconsequential attributes such as skin color, gender, or parental background, and it rejects the idea that a school should attempt to set a child's destiny simply because the child shares with others a certain attribute.

This is an important criticism. Children do not have a choice about possessing certain attributes, and as the critic rightly understands, attributes alone do not identities make. Whether one is born a with a vagina or a penis, dark-skinned or light, to rich parents or poor is not a matter of choice for the child. Children come to school with a certain color skin, from a certain ethnic or class background, and with certain sexual characteristics. What is a matter of choice is the significance that is granted to this attribute and whether schools and society at large decide to view it as a source of affiliation and a center for identity formation. No one attribute, including the beliefs and practices of one's parents, automatically carries with it an identity, but children can be treated in a way that encourages or discourages them to form their identity around certain features that they share with specific others.

What some critics of multiculturalism fear is that identity recognition forecloses certain options that should be the child's alone to foreclose. In other words, the critic of multiculturalism fears that when the school takes a certain attribute and uses it to advance a certain targeted identity, it is presupposing the child's affiliation and in doing so it is seriously miseducating the child. The fear is that this is miseducative because one of the key goals of education is to develop the child's capacity to eventually choose her own affiliation.

Yet the schools cannot keep all options open, and it is not as if children do not come to school with certain directions, patterns, and identifications already marked.

Two Forms of Recognition

All children deserve respect as persons, and this involves respect for those features of the self that relate them to others, including religion, sex, parental beliefs and practices, and race. This basic respect is a form of collective recognition, for it acknowledges more than just the individual child and his or her intellectual or social potential. It also acknowledges that the child is already identified with certain groups. This kind of recognition is minimal. It requires teachers and others to allow children to express their differences as long as they respect the rights of others to do the same. It does not require that teachers encourage students to express their differences, nor does it require the teacher to do anything to raise a child's awareness of her or his own group identity. Minimal recognition is generally uncontroversial. There are exceptions, however.

Consider, for example, when children wear cultural items that are offensive to children from other groups or when certain symbols or items of clothing may be taken as challenges to legitimate educational authority.

If the intent of wearing a certain symbol is to intimidate members of other cultural groups, say a KKK pin, in a context in which it is reasonable to expect that they will be intimidated and thus inhibited from expressing their own cultural forms, then passive acceptance is something different than minimal recognition and is educationally irresponsible.

Minimum recognition is something that should be granted to all students. It is a part of the liberal ideal of respecting each individual and is an important component of teaching children about different conceptions of the good. There are, however, as I will show, cases in which more than minimal recognition is required and in which the school has a responsibility to take an active role in advancing a child's identity and sense of belonging to a certain group.

What a person becomes, how she experiences her connections to others, is related to the categories in terms of which she is seen by others. She is not just an abstract person with abstract rights but stands as a certain kind of self. This certain kind of self is a part of her *identity as*. This *identity as* is dependent on many factors, including both how the self is recognized by others and the categories of recognition that are available in a given society. For example, a first son is accorded public recognition in Japan, but not in the United States. Or, if you are the seventh son of a seventh son born to an Irish family you may find that people have unusual expectations of you.[6]

Minimal recognition involves respecting a person as an individual without necessarily calling attention to any special feature of identity. It also requires showing respect within the constraints that are appropriate for a person who occupies a certain role or who has an identity as a member of a certain kind of group. Hence, for example, in cultures where there are strong markers between men and women, between people of different occupations, or between first sons and every other sibling, minimum recognition entails showing respect within the constraints and forms appropriate to those distinctions.

In liberal societies, minimal recognition in the classroom requires that a teacher understand children's cultural background and the way it influences their responses to certain situations. Here minimal recognition might entail fitting one's teaching into the style of the cultural group with which one is working, dressing as they expect a teacher to dress, and allowing their meanings to be reflected in discipline and classroom management. If the group does not value competition, for instance, the teacher might decide not to use it as a way to encourage achievement.

Minimal recognition often requires a passive stance on the part of the teacher. Children may be allowed to bring in items that are important to their own identity as members of this or that group. And, if a student felt bad because classmates looked down on her because of cultural or racial affiliation, the teacher may become more active in promoting the self-esteem of the child. This could entail encouraging her to bring in cultural items that speak to the accomplishments of the group. Recognition here is still minimal, however. It is provided in order to aid the child's performance or comfort in the classroom, and it may or may not have any importance for the culture itself.

A second kind of recognition, robust recognition, is different. It requires the teacher to take active steps to engage the child in a way that will strengthen her affiliation to a given cultural group. In other words, robust recognition requires the teacher to steer the child toward a certain kind of membership and help her develop an *identity as a person of this kind*. It requires, for example, not just that children be *allowed* to bring cultural symbols into the classroom but that they be *encouraged* to do so (assuming that the group wishes to display their cultural heritage). Robust recognition also involves directly teaching children outside the targeted group to understand and appreciate cultural practices that are specific to the culture of the marginalized student.

For example, questions have been raised about whether ebonics, a form of speech used by many African Americans, should have a role in the instruction of African American children. Although the debate over ebonics is usually about what is required to effectively teach black children—and whether ebonics is a true language—it should also be a debate about the requirement for robust recognition. Given the view that many linguists hold that ebonics is a coherent nonstandard English dialect, the argument from robust recognition would allow that it is a critical component for encouraging group identification. In addition, if the group has been stigmatized in part because of a devaluing of the dialect itself, then additional steps may be needed to inform those outside of the group of the way the dialect works, the distinctions it allows, the grammatical structure it exhibits, the meanings it can convey, and the history of its development. They need not be taught ebonics, but they may need to be taught about ebonics.

It should be added that there is nothing in the example used above that would deny the importance of teaching standard English to African American students. The argument for doing this is obvious from an economic standpoint as well as from a literary and cultural one. Children have a right to all of the linguistic forms available, and anything that prevents them from participating in the activities of the larger society is suspect. To provide robust recognition through ebonics is different, of course, from what we do when we teach a foreign language such as French or Japanese. But there is an important similarity. We do not ask children to choose between French and standard English. We ask them to enter into another way of speaking and thinking.

When the distinction between minimal and robust recognition is applied to different groups, it can help us to sort out some different claims. For example, children of voluntary immigrants certainly have every right to minimum recognition, but their case for robust recognition is usually weak. If people have chosen to leave a country to seek a better life elsewhere, there is often an implicit waiving of their right to have the group identity maintained through public resources.

There are exceptions to this waiver, but for most people claims to cultural resources are most effectively advanced on the basis of individual rights to free association or educational rights to cultural resources in order to serve individual educational needs. It is on this basis, for example, that bilingual education is reasonably justified for many groups. It is necessary as a bridge into American society. Nevertheless, there is a reasonable expectation that public resources will be used to make such children somewhat less like those in their original country and somewhat more like those in their adoptive one. Minimum recognition is certainly due them, although even here, as with groups that may command robust recognition, certain cultural practices that are viewed, say, as sexist or as abusive to children may be legitimately discouraged by the schools.

On the Question of Robust Recognition: The Example of Deaf Education

There are some who believe that more than minimal recognition is due, especially to endangered cultural groups. They hold that because modern society actually threatens their solidarity, schools have obligations to provide them with robust recognition and to provide the teaching required for the culture to continue. As we have seen, there is something to this claim, and the more potentially new members are dissuaded from participating in a culture, the less appealing the culture is likely to become.

This may create a downward spiral: the failure of new members to participate in the group makes the group less attractive for new members to participate in. Moreover, it is probably true that modernity contributes to this condition by providing alluring opportunities outside of the traditional cultural formation. The question is whether these two factors alone are sufficient to oblige the school to extend robust recognition to a group. There is a controversy raging among deaf educators today that can be used to test this claim, and it illustrates that the implications of an educational policy that focuses on individual "need" can differ from those of one that focuses on "cultural integrity."[7]

Deafness has been treated alongside blindness as a disability and, as with other "disabilities," the recent tendency in education has been to mainstream deaf children into regular classrooms. The idea has been to provide these children with what is called "the least restrictive environment." Thus, rather than place these and other children who are perceived to have some kind of learning problem in special settings of their own, they are provided with the extra aid that they need to function in a regular classroom. Hence blind children might be provided with Braille textbooks or with readers, and physically disabled children might have an aide who would help them to walk or go to the bathroom. And deaf children might be assigned someone who would sign for them and would aid them in other ways to access the world of oral English. This includes the use of sign language that mimics English, as opposed to American Sign Language (ASL), which is distinct in terms of word order and other linguistic traits and which is viewed as a product of deaf people themselves.

Those who accept the deficit view of deafness believe that the goal of education should be as high a level of integration with hearing children as is possible and that education for the deaf should enable them to take advantage of the opportunities provided by the larger society to all people. Deaf children are to be taught that, with the exception of the absence of hearing, they are just like other children.

This approach to deaf education is viewed by certain advocates of the deaf as both misguided and extremely harmful. The critic objects that the goal of deaf deficit education—the label they give to the present form of deaf education—is to assure that deaf children can function in a hearing world even though they claim that functioning is destined to be at a very low level for most.

A considerably different understanding of deafness and of language is found in the cultural view of deafness, which the critic of the deficit view advocates. According to this view deaf people constitute a unique culture, and because it is unique it has its own language. Hence, signing that mimics English is an inadequate substitute for the signing that arises as the product of that culture and as such constitutes its own language. Deafness is not, according to this view, a deficit to be overcome, and signing is not just one among many modes of representing English. Deafness is no more a deficit than is Frenchness. It is a way of being and of connecting to others who share the same way. To try to "change people" so that they are better able to communicate with hearing people is likely to cut them off from those with whom they already share an identity and with whom they have the greatest possibility of developing a rich cultural life.

In this argument the objection that was raised earlier—that educating a child into a specific identity presupposes a choice that should be made as a result of education, not prior to it—is answered bluntly. By being born deaf the child is already connected to a system of meaning and meaning making! If the schools fail to recognize this, they are not enhancing the child's ability to choose. Rather they are cutting the child off from the meanings that allow choice to take place.

The educational goal that is attached to the cultural view of deafness includes maintaining solidarity with the deaf community. Thus, for example, the teaching of lip reading is largely frowned on, not just because it is said to be ineffective by these critics but also because it is a signal of cultural ambiguity that creates identity problems for the individual child. Integrative education is rejected in favor of separate schools in which children are taught ASL. Advocates for ASL hold that "it is a language in every sense of the word, relying on visual, rather than auditory, encoding and decoding. ASL has a complex, rule-governed phonology, syntax, and morphology."[8] Thus, according to this view, the proper way to look at deafness is not as a deficit but as a culture, and given its status as a culture, it is believed that there is no way to evaluate it from the outside:

To evaluate the world of the deaf community, extrapolation from the hearing world is of no use at all. Is it better to be deaf or is it better to be hearing? . . . Of course, the answer makes no sense except in relation to a "cultural frame." To know what it is to be a member of the deaf community is to imagine how you would think, feel, and react if you had grown up deaf, if manual language had been your main means of communication, if your eyes were the portals of your mind, if most of your friends were deaf, if you had learned that there were children who couldn't sign only after you had known dozens who could, if the people you admired were deaf, if you had struggled daily for as long as you can remember with the ignorance and uncommunicativeness of hearing people, if . . . if, in a word, you *were* deaf.[9]

The advocates of this view are reluctant to allow any project—including surgical implants to aid hearing—that would weaken the deaf child's identification with other members of the deaf culture. Lane writes:

> The decision to surgically implant a young deaf child is ethically unsound for a reason yet more fundamental than the several I have given. There is now abundant scientific evidence that, as the deaf community has long contended, it constitutes a linguistic and cultural minority. I expect most Americans would agree that our society should not seek the scientific tools or use them, if available, to change a child biologically so he or she will belong to the majority—even if we believe that this biological engineering might reduce the burdens the child will bear as a member of a minority. Even if we could take the children destined to be members of the African-American, or Hispanic-American, or Native American, or Deaf American communities and convert them with bio-power into white, Caucasian, hearing males—even if we could, we should not. We should likewise refuse cochlear implants for young deaf children even if the device were perfect.[10]

Lane makes the case for separate schools for the deaf on the same grounds: minority cultural status provides a special entitlement.

Why Cultural Uniqueness Fails as an Argument for Robust Recognition

My concern in this section is not whether there should be separate schools for the deaf. There are technical issues that will need to be addressed by deaf people and those who educate them before this question can be answered definitively. Assuming that these are resolved in a certain way, much of the argument presented above is compelling in terms of the needs of deaf children. Lane goes beyond the needs of individual deaf children, however, and offers an argument *for* the robust recognition of deaf culture. That is, he seems to think that our educational programs are obliged to preserve deaf culture even if the technology were available to enable all children to hear. In invoking minority status as an argument for cultural entitlement, Lane is supporting his case by implying that it is wrong to interfere with the reproduction of a cultural group by altering a child's orientation even if such interference (1) is inconsistent with the parent's desires, (2) will do no physical harm to the child and (3) is not objected to by the child.

Consider, however, a slightly different situation than the one described in the quotation. Suppose there was a way to determine whether a fetus would be born deaf and also that there was a pill that the mother could take prior to birth that would allow the child to hear by raising the level of a certain hormone. Assume too that the pill has no undesirable side effects for either the child or the mother. Given these assumptions it would be hard to say that there is something wrong with taking the pill. Yet, if it is not wrong for the mother to take the pill, why is it wrong on the day the child is born to have the child be given a droplet of medicine or a surgically implanted device that would have the same effect? To do so, of course, would be to perform a biological intervention, and it would change the child's cultural destiny. Yet is this so different from the change to a child's cultural destiny effected when a family immigrates to a country where the children will learn to speak a different language? Indeed, if anything, it seems less intrusive because by being enabled to hear, an otherwise deaf child of hearing parents is being brought closer to her family's culture. Immigration, on the other hand, often leads to alienation from the parents and their culture.

Given the availability of an alternative, I am hard pressed to think of a good reason why a woman should be forbidden to take the medicine. True, as mentioned before, every person who leaves a community makes it harder for those who remain. Over time, if enough people leave, the incentives for maintaining the language and the customs diminish, and given this diminution even fewer people may choose to remain in the community. When this happens it is a cause for much sadness on the part of everyone because the loss of a culture is the loss of a unique mode of human expression. Nevertheless, the prospect of loss is not sufficient to force new people to enter the culture, to prevent older members who wish to leave it to do so, or to constrain the right of parents who are in a position to select a culture for their children.

There is something misleading about the linkage between African, Hispanic, and Native American cultures on one side and deaf culture on the other. One need not reject the idea that deafness constitutes a culture or that there has been a history of deaf oppression that resembles that of other groups—a point that Lane goes a long way to make and makes rather passionately. The problem is that in the case of deaf children with hearing parents—which is the group being addressed—there is often no intergenerational carrier of this oppression.

That by some accident of birth I am born deaf to hearing parents does not mean that the history of oppression by hearing people toward deaf people incurs a special obligation to me. It only means that there is an obligation not to oppress *me* now. Yet it may be as oppressive to force a deaf person, especially were the technology available to allow her to hear, to participate in deaf culture as it would be to require that she have nothing to do with that culture. The fact that there is a deaf culture will not solve this dilemma, and, given a choice between effective hearing technology and education into deaf culture, hearing parents of otherwise deaf children would have strong reason to bring children up within their own hearing culture.

The obligation to people who are presently deaf is not owed because some unrelated deaf person was discriminated against a hundred years ago. It is owed simply because society has an obligation not to discriminate now. If mainstreaming deaf children is discrimination, then that is reason enough to end the practice. This has little to do with an obligation that the larger society has to cultural preservation, however. It has to do with the obligation society has toward individuals who happen to share a certain characteristic. What we owe is owed to the children themselves. It is not owed to their families or to members of a group who share that characteristic.

Indeed, to suggest otherwise in this case is to allow that we use children without good reason for the advancement of a culture's good, not for their own good. (I use the indefinite article rather than the possessive to indicate that the choice in my example is not to support *their* culture, but rather to determine *which* culture will become theirs.) One can accept the idea that deaf people constitute a culture but still question whether this fact *alone*, regardless of the potential for hearing or the wishes of the parents, should direct children who are born unable to hear, but who yet might be enabled to hear, toward that culture. And, one can still raise this question without rejecting the potential value of separate schools under present conditions.

The more general mistake is to believe that any successful argument that establishes a collective group as a culture is sufficient to establish conditions for special educational consideration. Yet to take cultural integrity alone as sufficient for robust recognition would require that virtually all cultural groups receive such recognition—even those whose practices mutually exclude the recognition of the other. Cultural integrity is often a necessary condition for robust recognition, but it is never sufficient.

What We Owe to Endangered Cultures

There are reasons that can be used to support the claim that robust recognition is owed to members of a group whose culture is in danger of passing out of existence. Although this claim is valid with some endangered cultures, it is not so with all.

One difficulty is that it is also often difficult to know what it means for a cultural group to "pass out of existence." We can understand, for example, that the Shakers passed out of existence because they simply could no longer reproduce themselves. When it comes, for example, to Polish-American-Jewish culture, however, it would be hard to say whether it is passing out of existence or whether it is being amalgamated into wider streams of Jewish-American culture, say, Eastern European Jewish culture and whether today most American Jews of Polish origin had any real interest in sustaining it.

There are a lot of reasons why one might want to try to preserve an endangered culture, but only a few of them entail an *obligation* on the part of the public to do so. Certainly, for example, a commitment to diversity is one of these, but diversity alone is not sufficient to tell us which cultures to preserve. An argument for robust cultural recognition as a public obligation needs a stronger basis than preservation of cultural integrity.

There are two ways in which this basis may be strengthened. The more common is as a side effect of aiding individual children who *because of denigration of their culture* are considered at risk. Here the argument is that without robust cultural recognition, the child will suffer certain serious deprivations or the child will be denied certain opportunities that it is generally reasonable to think that all children should have. Here the active engagement that is associated with robust recognition is acceptable, but only to advance the position of the individual child. This differs from minimal recognition. Here denigration of the culture is the cause of the child's being at risk. In minimal recognition the cause is irrelevant. What is important is that cultural recognition will aid the achievement of the child.

The other argument relates to the issue of cultural endangerment, but it is also concerned about the source and the conditions of such endangerment. I believe that if a case is to be made for deaf education along cultural lines, it will be made successfully only in terms of the first of these arguments. Some other cultural groups better represent the second.

To say that robust recognition for deaf children is better argued on the ground of individual need or of opportunity denied is not to suggest that culture is irrelevant to the success of these arguments. Indeed, the fact that the conclusion to a successful argument should lead to robust cultural recognition suggests that culture does matter. What is important in these cases, however, is that it matters that it makes a difference to the life of the individual child. As Lane writes:

> How does the deaf child's sense of self develop in a hearing family? He observes that commonly one adult will approach another and move his mouth rapidly for a long time, and the other responds likewise, or perhaps engages abruptly and inexplicably in some activity. If there are hearing children in the home, they will behave in the same way among themselves, and they will perform this seemingly dumb show with adults. "I noticed people watching each other's faces," a deaf educator has written, recalling her childhood, "but I saw only a blur of lip-shapes, mouths opening and closing, stretching and puckering into lines and circles. Why were mouths so interesting? Mouths bored me." "Lip-shapes" are rarely directed at the deaf child, and when they are, they are indecipherable; his own mouthings go unnoticed. Sometimes the family seems able to presage events: they open the front door just when people are waiting there; they arrive from another part of the house just when the child has hurt himself and cried. These may be

some of the first inklings that *something is wrong*. If the child is the object of excessive oral drills, which are painful and frustrating, the concept emerges: *Something is wrong with me*.[11]

What makes the argument so forceful is not any obligation that might be owed directly to deaf culture but rather that without an engagement with deaf culture the child will have a stunted life. She will not be able to enjoy the richness of meaning that deaf culture could otherwise provide. If the author is right and neither existing technology nor the understanding of the hearing community is adequate for meaningful cultural integration, then surely the child should be brought up in a way that will enable her to communicate with people who have a meaning system that she can access and enjoy. If the argument for teaching children who cannot hear through the ways of deaf culture is successful, it will be because there is an equivalence between what nonhearing children need and how they are to think of themselves in terms of language, artistic modes of expression, and a community of affiliation. True, this is a more generalized conception of need than the one commonly employed. A hard-of-hearing child may simply need a hearing aid to enable her to access the prevailing cultural forms. Other children may need eyeglasses. In the present case, what is needed is a way to access and create meaning. The success of this argument will have to do with issues that are addressed to the benefit of the child. Beyond this it is hard to see that anything is owed to deaf culture as such. Yet this is not true in all cases in which claims are made on behalf of cultural groups.

What Are Group Rights and Why Are They Problematic?

Will Kymlicka notes that group rights consist of three factors. First, the members of the group have certain claims that they can rightfully press against the larger society, and they do so as members of the group. Second, the group has authority to control the behavior of individual members. Third, the larger society can treat individual members in terms of their membership in groups.[12] Those who support liberal democratic education are rightfully suspicious of educational claims based on group benefits and group rights on the grounds that individuals need to be free to associate with each other on their own terms and that notions of group rights would interfere with such association.

Indeed, much of the history of group rights is an overly restrictive one. It includes occupational classifications handed out and enforced according to religious affiliation, marriage restrictions based on race, and educational opportunities restricted according to family position and limited to males. Hence there are reasons to be concerned about an educational system that is constructed on the basis of group difference, however well intended the argument for it may be.

Nevertheless, I have already presented one case—*Yoder*—which appears to be an exception to the rules, and I have suggested some tentative reasons why this exception may be justified. True, this decision is a little off-center of our concern because it does not advance the use of public educational funds to support the reproduction of a particular cultural identity. Instead it supports the nonuse of educational funds to *allow* unabated the continuation of cultural identity. It judges cultural reproduction on a par with equal opportunity.

In other words, the court ruled that Amish culture and the solidarity of the Amish community were of sufficient value to overrule normal expectations that schools should advance individual opportunity. Granted, both *Mozert* and *Yoder* were argued within the constitutional guarantee of religious freedom, but the overall argument had to do with the place of the group in the larger society. For the Amish, the group's relative isolation was an important consideration in the decision, whereas in the *Mozert* case, the fact that the group otherwise participated in the activities of the larger society was a consideration against their claim.

These rulings suggest that although there is a good reason for placing a heavy burden of justification on group rights, the appropriateness of lifting some of this burden needs to be determined with attention to social and historical contexts that will differ from group to group. It is with this difference in mind that I want to take a look at the way in which need, group standing, and historical injustice may create special categories of educational obligations. These categories differ from most cases of educational entitlement in that they identify certain kinds of people for special treatment. They also differ from each other in terms of their recognition of a group, as opposed to an individual, right.

Need, Standing, and Historical Injustice and the Creation of Special Educational Obligations

NEED

Within the context of a liberal, individualistic society such as the United States, special entitlement arising out of economic need is consistent with the commitment to the ideal of equality of opportunity. It fits with the belief that no one should be held back simply because of the economic position of her parents or because of other artificial roadblocks. Hence the argument that a talented, motivated child should not be held back because her parents cannot afford to provide the kind of education appropriate for a person of her ability is acceptable to many in terms of their general understanding of fairness and merit. This understanding, which forms the basis of programs such as Head Start, is reinforced in many ways and is imbedded, for example, in the folklore of the country as one of the reasons people come to America.

The category of need is not, however, a category of group entitlement and does not usually call for robust recognition. People are placed in the same category for administrative purposes. From the point of view of the administrators of the system they are related only in terms of what they have not—educational resources. Their entitlement is not granted because their need is accompanied by a strong class consciousness that bonds them to others with a similar need. Nor is the entitlement provided because anyone might believe that they should be so bonded. Rather, for these purposes each has his or her own separate history, meanings, projects, interests, and so on. This administrative category is, of course, available for those who do share an identity, racial, class, or otherwise, and the participation of cultural minorities in programs such as Head Start or Upward Bound indicates that people otherwise identified with one another do use them. Nevertheless, in these cases it is not ethnicity, gender, or nationality that forms the basis of the recognition. It is economic position and the chance that without aid certain deep-seated liberal principles of fairness will be violated.

The acknowledgment of need is perfectly consistent with liberal individualism. It focuses attention on the individual child while allowing that certain categories of individuals may require extra aid. There is, however, another step in this progression from individual to group entitlements that, also consistent with liberalism, focuses attention not on individuals as such but rather on individuals as members of certain identity groups. This progression can be seen in the notion of standing.

Standing

Economic position is only one of a number of factors that could limit a child's ability to develop and express her talents and ability. The reduced level of opportunity for women is a clear instance of the way in which cultural factors can reduce opportunities as much as economic ones. Women have been raised in the same families as their brothers but have been systematically placed in positions with less public status and authority. This suggests that economic disadvantage is not the only roadblock to achievement. Cultural bias and reduced educational and economic opportunities reinforce each other to produce a lowered standing. And what may begin as a cultural or an educational difference results in an economic difference that in turn reinforces the ways in which women (and other classifications of people) are treated both culturally and educationally. The problem is not simply one of individual merit denied. It involves the fact that certain attributes, here related to sex, have been elevated to the status of a group identity, and that identity has been assigned a lower standing which in turn affects each individual who shares that identity. It is not exactly need that is denied but something like the stature and status that would otherwise be due had women been truly considered equal to men.

In order to address the issue of standing it is important to focus attention on those who share certain "innate" characteristics, such as sexual attributes and skin color, and who, because of this characteristic, have been assigned a lower status.[13] In this case, robust recognition is a significant factor in addressing lower standing. Unlike need, with respect to which the group classification is addressed, if at all, as an accidental feature of the problem, here the classification is acknowledged to be its primary cause. Yet because the problem of standing is still viewed as a problem of individuals *of a certain type*, this recognition is often indirect, seeking to improve opportunities and role models for this type of *individual*.

Because reduced standing negatively affects not only opportunities that are otherwise made available by institutions but also the way in which individuals come to think about themselves, as well as the aspirations they hold, and because standing defines "ordinary" institutional practice, a systematic and extraordinary effort is needed to effect the desired change. Robust recognition does this, but only by providing opportunities for individuals that will enable other members of the groups (as well as those outside of such groups) to see themselves in a different light and to develop higher aspirations and skills. In other words, here robust recognition works to allow individuals to see themselves as members of a group. It does not, however, work to increase the solidarity of the group itself, although this may be an unintended consequence.

Although recognition here still works to address the concerns of individuals, it is different from the need-based approach. The need-based approach functions to eliminate the one characteristic that is shared by all of those who are selected—poverty. An approach that deals with lowered standing requires students to be addressed in terms of attributes that will persist even after a change in educational and economic status has occurred. Because low standing is reflected both externally—in reduced opportunities—and internally—in rechanneled and lowered motivation—and because these reinforce one another, it is important that they be changed at the same time.

Lowered standing, however, does not call forth a group right but rather a group-*based* entitlement. The latter results when some people have been wrongly denied the treatment that should be afforded to individual, rights-bearing citizens because of a characteristic that they all share and when steps are initiated to correct this problem. The characteristic may be blue eyes, black skin, short stature, or the physical apparatus needed to bear children. The people who have this characteristic may or may not share a lot of other things, and they may or may not care about each other's welfare or think of themselves as sharing an identity. All of this is irrelevant to the claim that they all have.

This entitlement is not a group right because it does not advance the coherence or the status of one group *over* another—although it may use an existing sense of identification in terms of role models to enhance its effect; nor does it seek to provide recognition to members of one group *over* those of another. It does not *confer* special group status. Rather, it uses group membership to identify and correct past acts of discrimination, acts that have resulted in inadequate educational, economic, and social positioning. It allows special attention be provided to those who share the attributes that bring forth this entitlement. It does not, however, require that they renew their ties to one another on the basis of those attributes.

Historical Injustice

When the issue involves African or Native Americans there is an additional factor to be considered, and this factor establishes race and culture as categories for educational recognition. In these cases, the task is not only to correct inequality of opportunity or, as with white women, to increase standing. It is also to pay a debt that is owed as a result of unprecedented violation of human rights and liberties.

This debt arises not only because of systematic violations of the rights to life and liberty of individuals. It also arises because of historical violations of the cultural foundations through which meaning is constructed. In these cases the recognition of identity involves more than simply the fact that need and identity overlap. It involves an independent component that would remain even if the material well-being and the standing of the group matched those of other individuals.

To see this point, consider the various ways in which individuals from different cultural background might be represented on certain holidays. For example, when Columbus is recognized positively, what is being remembered is the (European) discovery of America—not the exploitation of the native population. The fact that Columbus was Italian is incidental. Although Italian Americans may feel a special connection to the event, their identity as Italians is not an essential part of the public recognition. If Columbus had been Austrian or Irish the public meaning would be the same. There are other public symbols—the Statue of Liberty is the most famous—that serve to recognize the pluralistic character of the country as such. In this case what is being recognized is a general ideal rather than any particular manifestation of it.

Martin Luther King Day is different from both of the above. Its importance as a national holiday cannot be separated from the historical experience of a specific group of people. Martin Luther King Day represents the ideal of freedom as embodied in the civil rights movement and the people from all races who worked for that ideal. And, through that movement, it represents the long-standing struggles of the African American people for freedom and dignity. The very meaning of this symbol is constituted in the people who are recognized through it. It is not, as with the Statue of Liberty, the quest for liberty of all ethnic groups that is being celebrated. It is the struggle for freedom of a particular group with a very specific history that is being celebrated by all. At the same time Martin Luther King Day, as the symbol of hope and liberation of this group, is the most important representation of the possibility of national redemption. The holiday expresses the journey through slavery of black Americans while it holds out hope for the unity of a nation of black and white alike.

Native and African American people have special claims that their struggle, their suffering, and their achievements be recognized.[14] The institution of slavery and the assault against the American Indian not only violated individual lives, they violated essential elements of collective and individual development.[15] These violations and those that followed from them are accountable for many of the problems confronting these communities today.

The forceful rupture of a culture has real consequences for living people, both in terms of truncated expectations and opportunities denied and overlooked, and in terms of a general social attitude of accepting as part of the natural state of affairs lower levels of material well-being. Recognition of these crimes requires that the experience of these people not just be subsumed under that of minority groups in general nor used as an illustration of the success of pluralist policies and liberal ideals. The historical record speaks of an experience that is different in kind and of an initial violation in which pluralism and the right to maintain one's own culture on one's own terms using one's own resources was not even a recognized alternative.

What is now at stake is not just the child's affiliation and identity as an *American* Indian or an African *American* but the nature of that identity in the American context. The story that African and Native Americans are peoples whose lives and histories make up a significant part of the American experience (along with those of other minority groups) is not sufficient and does not reflect the truth of their experience. They are separate chapters in the American story, and they offer compelling and competing narratives to the dominant account. Here robust recognition involves shining the spotlight on these separate chapters, enabling those inside to hear them acknowledged by those outside and enabling those outside to hear them told by those inside.

14

Affirmative Action and Beyond

A Case for a Backward-Looking Gender- and Race-Based Policy

Recent political changes in this country have in part been a response to a changing sense of moral obligation and a belief that the liberal agenda has moved beyond what many people can accept as a fair and just distribution of educational and occupational opportunities.* One of the most prominent targets of this change has been the policy of affirmative action, a policy that was enacted to aid members of specific groups to advance both in school and at work.

The Problem: Race-Based or Need-Based Affirmative Action

A number of people sympathetic to traditional affirmative action practices have been willing to compromise with its critics by shifting from a race- and gender-based policy (RGAA) to a need-based (NBAA) one. There

---

*This essay was written before recent the Supreme Court decisions weakening race and gender based affirmative action. It is slightly edited to eliminate passages that are obviously dated. It is included in this collection both for historical significance and to bolster the elements of RGAA-based affirmative action that still remain. It is also included because many of the arguments are now useful in evaluating proposals for reparations that have been made since this article appeared.

is obviously political pressure for such compromise, especially in light of the assault on RGAA-based affirmative action but the pressure is derived from a sense that the moral foundations for the present practice are shaky and that a morally more adequate policy is available—need-based affirmative action (NBAA). NBAA affirmative action policies would no longer target minorities and women exclusively, but would instead extend the benefits of affirmative action to all talented poor people, including white males.[1] As a result, affirmative action would become class- rather than race- or gender-sensitive.

Besides its anticipated political appeal, the moral attractiveness of this policy is that it fits many people's initial idea of fairness—that individuals should be given equal opportunity to advance independently of the deficits or benefits provided by their parents and without consideration to accidental characteristics, like race and gender. Yet moral ideas can be more complex than they initially seem and given the strong moral and political appeal that the NBAA substitute carries, it is important to examine some of the considerations that support the present alternative before deciding that need alone will serve all of the morally legitimate functions of the present system. Hence in this article I reexamine what I take to be the moral foundations of the present practice and argue that an RGAA approach to affirmative action is not only morally defensible, but serves certain important ends that an NBAA substitute could not serve.

In making this argument I am not rejecting the idea that need has a role to play in determining the distribution of educational and occupational benefits. I am only arguing that need alone does not address the moral foundation of the RGAA-based policy. Moreover, the argument presented here should not be taken to suggest that the present policy does all that is morally required. Indeed, at the end of the article, I show that at least one of the most powerful reasons for a race-sensitive policy can be only partially addressed through affirmative action and that addressing this reason fully would require that affirmative action be folded into a more broadly based approach to the problem of inequity.

Affirmative action is a practice that profoundly affects education at all levels. It helps determine the racial and gender composition of faculties and it has an influence on the mixture of students in specific schools and on what these students are taught. It is an important factor in the determination of successful candidates to colleges and professional schools and it has a role to play in the cultural climate of work as a harassment-free.

What Affirmative Action Is

Affirmative action began with Title VII of the Civil Rights Act of 1964, which prohibited discrimination on the basis of race and sex and which was later augmented by a number of executive orders that regulated federal contracts and set goals and timetables for hiring minorities. University admissions was not an immediate target of affirmative action, but it too has become one through litigation and through administrative interpretation of existing laws. Given the importance of colleges and universities in supplying and renewing the nation's managerial and professional labor force, the extension of affirmation action enforcement to universities is perfectly reasonable. The actual exercise of affirmative action policy in the university can include many different features, from the relatively uncontroversial concern to seek out women and minority candidates to apply for positions, to more controversial programs that seek to select or hire women or people of color as a way to increase their numbers within the student body and the faculty. This sometimes has been accomplished through establishing separate performance standards for women and minority applicants, such as when the military academies allow women to do certain exercise routines differently from men or when a law school granted admission to some African-American applicants even though their scores are lower than some unsuccessful white applicants.

The purpose of affirmative action is to reduce discrimination and increase the number of minorities and women in the relevant positions. While there is obviously some overlap between economic status and group membership, the spotlight of affirmative action has not been aimed at the poor as such but at women and members of certain minority groups, some of whom are also poor. The reasons for this are complicated and constitute much of the subject matter of this article. However, the general idea is that past and present discrimination has been systematically exercised against members of these groups and has thus resulted in the underdevelopment and inadequate utilization of talent. Many also believe that this discrimination is a violation of the constitutional right to equal protection. Advocates of the present practices believe that people from these groups historically have been denied opportunities to develop their talent and to be admitted and hired on the basis of a fair competition. Thus race- and gender-based affirmative action is justified because it seeks to correct this distortion and to end the effects of past and continuing discrimination.

The RGAA-based affirmative action cut across economic groups holding that the effects of past acts of discrimination linger in the present for members of specific groups and that members of these targeted groups, no matter their present economic or social standing, continue to be denied reasonable benefits and social standing. Past discrimination has, under this interpretation, handicapped all members of the targeted groups—even some who may be relatively well off economically. Affirmative action seeks to remove impediments caused by such discrimination and to enable members of these groups to advance as they might have done otherwise.

The Role of the Principle of Equality of Opportunity

The ultimate purpose of affirmative action is to reestablish the elements of fair competition that are embedded in the ideal of equality of opportunity. Because historical discrimination and its lingering effects apply only to members of some groups and not to others, the application of the principle of equality of opportunity is usually circumscribed by affirmative action to members of these groups.[2] Those outside the targeted groups may appeal to equal opportunity to justify individual claims to advancement and have successfully sued to counter individual acts of discrimination that blatantly favor individual women or minority members over a more qualified white man. Nevertheless, the focus of the policy remains women, blacks, and members of groups that have suffered systematic acts of historical discrimination. It is in this sense that the policy of affirmative action differs from most policies that are concerned to advance the ideal of equality of opportunity and that have focused attention on the impediments to advancement that arise because of economic need alone.

Because affirmative action is intended to correct for systematic discrimination against members of certain historically disadvantaged groups, it has not been, except in a limited sense, an NBAA policy. For example, the spotlight of affirmative action might well shine on a college that eliminates women's gymnastics even though all team members come from professional and upper-middle-class homes. In contrast, it might allow a college to eliminate men's baseball even though all the members of the team come from a white lower-working-class background.

Need does come into play in an indirect way given that the groups that have been the focus of affirmative action contain many of society's most economically vulnerable individuals. Yet when affirmative action is applied to them it is not just because they are economically vulnerable, but because of the effects of historical and systematic acts of discrimination. While there is a larger principle of equality of opportunity that lies behind the practice of affirmative action, it is the fact that this principle has been systematically violated for members of certain groups that motivates the narrow focus. It is in this sense that the present application of affirmative action is race- and gender-based rather than NBAA.

An NBAA policy would shift the focus of attention away from group membership and would instead illuminate individuals and their economic situation. Advocates of this change see it as forward-looking and as rewarding talented members of any group who are motivated to succeed. An NBAA policy is not only seen as consistent with many people's idea of fairness; it is also viewed as consistent with their idea of democracy, because it serves to advance talented individuals regardless of the background or beliefs of their parents. Advocates argue that the present policy encourages a sense of victimization and entitlement.

Amplification of the Arguments against Present Race- and Gender-Based Policy

The arguments against race-based affirmative action are not new and most have been voiced in one way or another since the policy was formulated in the 1960s and 70s. However, in the last few years they have gained considerable ground politically as the economic stakes have been raised. The continuing erosion of the middle-class failure to significantly reduce and stabilize the reduction of percentage of people living in poverty[3] has created a more difficult climate for implementing affirmative action policy. Fewer people can assume that if they fail to get one decent job they will get the next one that comes along. Consider, for example, that temporary jobs account for 20 percent of all new positions, and that many of these jobs are in the professional areas—such as law, stock trading, and accounting—areas that have been frequent targets of affirmative action.[4]

The fact that many of the most profound causes of middle-class insecurity are beyond the control of any single person leads to a close scrutiny of more proximate factors, such as affirmative action hiring. The increasingly globalized economy makes many once locally rooted firms accountable to a management thousands of miles away, often in a different country. This distance reduces the level of local responsibility and sense of corporate citizenship.

The easy flow of capital from one area of the globe to another means that American labor competes at a disadvantage with global capital. Many jobs that were once secure because of an advantage gained by manufacturers who located close to their main markets now disappear almost overnight because modern means of transportation and communication have diminished the advantage. Yet the effects of globalization are not easily seen or controlled. The beneficiaries of affirmative action policy make for much easier targets than do international conglomerates creating a climate in which arguments against affirmative action are amplified, echoing off the walls created by changing global economics and resulting middle-class anxiety.

Conservative and Liberal Varieties of NBAA Affirmative Action

The NBAA alternative to current affirmative action practices would change the focus of the program from one that seeks to open opportunities for women and members of certain minority groups to one that seeks to advance talented and motivated people from any group who may be held back because they are poor. This change has received support from both liberals and conservatives.[5] Both object to certain aspects of the present system, such as granting preferences to children from professional families just because they happen to have a Hispanic surname while providing no such preferences to talented white children from poor families. Many liberals and conservatives alike see this as unfair and to the extent that choices of this kind are encouraged—as they are, for example, when Hispanic surnames are simply counted as meeting affirmative action standards—it appears as if affirmative action policy is advantaging advantage and disadvantaging disadvantage.

Insofar as economic conservatives—those whose identity is defined by commitment to free-market practices—can allow for government intervention, the NBAA approach is consistent with their basic ideology of promoting market efficiency. It allows the differences in educational attainment and income to remain while enabling ambitious and talented people from all groups to rise to the top. It also assures that deserving individuals are not passed over simply because they are not members of some preferred group. Liberals and conservatives differ, however, in terms of the extent to which they want to define economic need in ways that would protect some of the gains made by women and minorities.

Conservatives are generally not concerned about an unequal distribution of income, position, or status. The indifference is consistent with the general reluctance of the economic conservative to advance government regulation of private industry. It is thought that market factors alone are sufficient to correct for inadequate selection and that companies that overlook talented women or racial minorities will, in the long run, suffer competitive disadvantage and will lose out to companies that hire from the entire pool of talent regardless of race and gender. Government interference in the market is said to exact an important cost in terms of allowing inefficient companies to survive. Moreover, government intervention exacts a high administrative cost, which in the long run makes American business less efficient in the world marketplace.[6]

In the case of gender inequality, this indifference is also consistent with the cultural conservative's commitment to the ideal of the "traditional" two-parent family with the mother at home raising the children and the father working outside of the home to support them. Given these two commitments—the one to an ideal market, the other to an ideal family—inequalities are seen as acceptable differences within the market or as reasonable pressure to return to the norm of the traditional family.

The actual consequences of NBAA policies that do not attend in any way to the present racial distribution of positions would be especially severe on African Americans and would result in a significant decrease in the number admitted to colleges and universities. "The Scholastic Assessment Test, . . . despite its many imperfections, still provides a rough measure of academic preparation. In 1993 approximately 14 percent of the 1,044,465 high school seniors who took the test came from families having incomes below $20,000. Among the white students in this presumably disadvantaged group, the average score was 872 out of a possible 1,600 while Hispanic students averaged 725 and the black figure was 693."[7] The results of a change from a race-based policy to an NBAA policy would clearly be to redirect some of the resources presently being spent on African Americans to white males. Of course, given the larger percentages of poor people among the ranks of presently targeted groups, it is reasonable to expect that white males would still have a comparably smaller percentage of their numbers receiving benefits. Nevertheless, given the size of the group, it is certain that a significant portion of present benefits would be shifted away from those who presently are eligible to receive them. Moreover, the shift from a race-based to an NBAA policy would have a multiplying effect. It would not only reduce the number of African Americans admitted to competitive undergraduate colleges, but it would reduce even more the number of successful applicants to graduate and professional schools.[8]

One of the differences between the conservative and the liberal approaches to NBAA affirmative action is that the liberal does worry about its implications for racial distribution. Some liberals argue that any reasonably sensitive indicator of a student's level of disadvantage would yield a higher relative proportion of blacks. Kahlenberg, for example, advanced a complicated rating scheme that would advance college applicants partly on the basis of a score on a disability index that would include parental income, education, and occupation as well as the quality of the applicant's secondary education, neighborhood, and family structure.[9] The more disadvantaged an applicant is in these areas, the more points would be granted as a way to offset lower scores on admissions tests. Such a system is proposed as a way to offset unfair disadvantages. Kahlenberg argued that this scheme would probably not result in significantly fewer African Americans' being chosen for positions. The implication that we are supposed to draw is that under this scheme African Americans would not lose out in terms of numbers admitted, and that handicaps provided for disadvantages would actually result in a higher level of talent being represented in our nation's colleges and universities.

Whether this prediction would prove accurate is difficult to say. However, given the premise of the NBAA alternative, one must wonder why liberals would still be concerned with the effects of such a policy on blacks or any other group. If the problem is the underrepresentation of the *disadvantaged as such*, rather than the *black* or *female* disadvantaged, why worry about a particular group of disadvantaged people? It would seem that we really should be concerned only about whether talented and motivated but disadvantaged applicants are receiving a fair shot at admissions and not whether successful applicants are black, white, women, men, short, fat, thin, or tall. Given the basic premise of the argument—that the problem is the disadvantaged as such—the conservatives have the day. Even test bias is not to be judged on the basis of whether some racial groups score at the same proportions as the majority. If our concern is the disadvantaged as such, and if we believe that present college curriculum and grading policy are appropriate and impartial—issues the liberal proposals have not contested—then a test is biased only if it incorrectly predicts ultimate performance.

Kahlenberg and other liberals who seek class-based affirmative action appear to be hedging their bets—a shift from race to class will not, they argue, really disadvantage blacks.[10] But why would they hedge unless they thought that race presents—as I believe it does—a very special kind of disadvantage? Without such an assumption, the conservative critic could effectively point out that the liberal advocates of class-based affirmative action have decided beforehand which groups should be represented at the higher level and that, given this decision, they are simply trying to make it more acceptable to the white male population. Yet, the conservative might continue, if the aim is fairness and if we are truly open to the question regarding the cause of disadvantage, why worry beforehand about whether a certain racial distribution results? Liberals who see merit in switching from a race- to a class-based form of affirmative action have yet to address this question.

Some Differences between the Two Approaches to Affirmative Action

The NBAA alternative presupposes that the only legitimate function of affirmative action is to correct inequities in the marketplace that arise because some talented women and some talented men from many different racial and ethnic groups are not well positioned to take advantage of educational opportunities and to develop their talents. Those who advance an NBAA view believe that every legitimate goal that is presently served by the race- and gender-based approach also can be served by the NBAA approach—talented but poor and underachieving women and minority members will be identified and educated. However, they also believe that it will do more because it will also advance poor and talented white men. Yet this approach overstates the case in a number of important ways and misses some of the noneconomic factors that affirmative action, as it is presently practiced, is intended to meet. The situation of women provided a strong illustration of the limits of an affirmative action policy that is rooted solely in economic need.

Economics versus Culture

Although raised in the same families as their brothers, women had been systematically placed in positions with less status and authority. This suggests that economic disadvantage is not the only roadblock to achievement. The reduced level of opportunity for women has been grounded in cultural and educational factors as much as it is in economic factors. Indeed, these three elements reinforce each other in the sense that what may begin as a cultural or educational difference results in an economic difference that in turn reinforces the ways in which women are treated both culturally and educationally.

It is certainly quite possible for one to accept the view that the primary goal of affirmative action is to correct inefficiencies in the market that result from misplacement of talented people without accepting the belief that the only cause of undeveloped talent is an economic one. This has been one of the focal points of a race- and gender-based approach that is largely overlooked by the NBAA alternative.

Merit versus Standing

Another difference between the two approaches is that while both stress the importance of individual merit, the present practice seeks in addition to effect a cultural and psychological change that goes well beyond the benefits awarded to the successful individual applicants. Hence attention is focused on those who share certain "innate" characteristics—color or sex—and who, because of these characteristics, have been assigned reduced social standing. Because this reduced standing has negatively affected the aspirations of many and has frequently defined "normal" institutional practice, a systematic effort is needed to effect the desired change. Targeted assignment and selection is a way to educate the larger public about what *should* count as standing and to help all members of the stigmatized groups think differently about themselves. Unlike an NBAA approach, which functions to eliminate the one characteristic that is shared by all of those who are selected (poverty) and to separate those chosen from those not chosen, a race- and gender-based approach selects people on the basis of features that will persist even after a change in educational and economic status has occurred. It is believed that the change in status can serve as a reminder that such characteristics should not be taken as a sign of reduced ability or competence.

FORWARD- VERSUS BACKWARD-LOOKING PERSPECTIVES

Finally, those who argue for an NBAA policy of affirmative action do so from what they see as a forward-looking perspective. Their goal is to advance the idea of equal opportunity and to reduce inefficiencies in the economic system by assuring that talented applicants are not overlooked because of their economic situation. Certainly the RGAA-based affirmative action also advances forward-looking consequences since any policy that finds and cultivates talent will increase the chances that society as a whole will also benefit. However, RGAA-based policy largely limits its search for this talent to certain groups on the grounds that it has a special obligation to members of these groups as a result of past acts of discrimination. Thus whereas an NBAA program is driven primarily by a vision of the future economic benefits to the society, a race- and gender-based program is partly concerned with a debt that is owed to members of certain groups. Insofar as the effects are forward-looking they are so within a framework that brings specific groups into relief.

For example, to the advocates of a race- and gender-based approach, it will not do simply to toss a coin to determine the educational benefits of two equally talented, equally poor students when one belongs to a group with a long history of discrimination and the other is, say, a child of recent immigrants. Indeed, equal talent may be an unnecessarily high standard in many cases where affirmative action is called for. This is because sometimes affirmative action may involve a debt to a group of people whereas the selection of the most talented person among any and all applicants is best understood as a future investment for society at large. The moral force of this difference is well understood and is expressed, for example, when veterans are given certain preferences in exchange for a service rendered to their country.

Affirmative action in certain cases should ideally be thought of as a part of a special obligation owed to members of certain groups. In these cases, to the extent that it is an investment, it is so within the confines of specific aggrieved groups. Advocates of this ideal would agree that affirmative action should be forward-looking in the sense that wherever a choice is available society should seek to pay its debt in a way that will advance a relevant social interest. However, they would emphasize that society *should* seek to pay its debts. This means that to the extent that debt is involved, affirmative action must involve a group-specific policy. In these cases the aim of affirmative action should not be to maximize interests in general, but to serve the specific interests of members of the aggrieved group.

Thus there are three primary reasons for a race- and gender-based approach to affirmative action that an NBAA approach fails to meet. The first is to correct inefficiencies in the system resulting from unfair treatment. In this case the NBAA approach wrongly assumes that economic barriers should be given exclusive consideration.

The second reason for the present practice involves the educational and motivational benefits that may be served by advancing members of previously excluded groups into positions of authority and power. In this case the NBAA approach fails to address the issue of stigmatized groups.

The third reason involves the issue of a social debt and the presumption that society, in its treatment of certain people, has incurred unusual obligations. The NBAA approach fails here because it views affirmative action only in terms of a social investment. That the NBAA substitute does not address these reasons very well should be an important factor in weighing its merits and demerits. However, before deciding whether the present approach should be maintained, there are some specific objections to the race- and gender-based alternative that must be addressed.

Arguments for Shifting from Race- and Gender-Based Affirmative Action to Need-Based Affirmative Action

In addition to the belief that the RGAA-based affirmative action encourages a sense of victimization, there are additional arguments against existing practices and in favor of shifting the spotlight of affirmative action from racial and gender categories to economic ones. The first of these is that the focus on groups is inconsistent with the American tradition and leads to a misguided conception of group, as opposed to individual, rights. This, if carried to its logical conclusion, would ultimately serve to Balkanize the nation.

For example, Nathan Glazer argued that affirmative action violates the fundamental American consensus arrived at with the voting rights act of the 1960s that America is to be a union of "states and free individuals, not a nation of politically defined ethnic groups." He holds that affirmative action negates the principle that "all citizens would have equal rights [and that] no group would be considered subordinate to another."[11] Glazer's objection is based on the belief that affirmative action rests on a recognition of groups as rights-bearing entities and that this recognition endangers the principle of individual rights. The objection raises two issues that I will return to in a subsequent section but that are useful to mention here. One of these is whether affirmative action is correctly characterized when it is depicted as a group right. The second is whether group rights can ever be justified, and, if so, under what circumstances.

A second argument against affirmative action holds that those who are helped the most by affirmative action targets have been hurt the least by past discrimination. As Goldman puts it:

> Those with Ph.D.'s or other professional qualifications, who will benefit from the policy by being awarded jobs are not those members of the groups in question who have been appreciably harmed by such discrimination. . . . [Moreover] reverse discrimination . . . cannot constitute reasonable compensation for past injustices toward members of minority groups or women. This is because the numerical goals are specified in terms of groups as a whole, while they nevertheless function to benefit specific members of those groups. Further, the individuals benefited (for example, women just coming out of graduate school with Ph.D.'s) are generally those who have suffered least from prior discrimination.[12]

This is an argument with strong appeal to both the political Left and the political Right. The Left sometimes rejects affirmative action on the grounds that it can never resolve the real problem, which is the vast sea of poverty generated by a capitalist economic system. Hence, to the Left the problem is that the largest group of poor people never make it to the point where they might even be candidates for those positions that make affirmative action a relevant consideration. The Left has an important point and it is one that I will examine more closely when addressing the question of affirmative action as payment of a historical debt. And that provides a strong rationale for recent proposals for reparations. A strong case along these lines has more recently been made by Ta-Nehisi Coates in his "The Case for Reparations."[13] However, the all-or-nothing premise on which this evaluation of affirmative action is made is surely problematic.

The political Right finds the same argument attractive precisely because it supports its suspicion that affirmative action is unnecessary and serves to discriminate against white males in favor of often less-deserving women and blacks. Since a part of this argument has already been addressed in my treatment of economic and cultural barriers to advancement, I will not examine it in further detail. However it should be kept in mind that the argument that I am addressing in this article is not whether need should be a relevant consideration in the application of affirmative action principles. It seems to me obvious that need has a legitimate place in considerations of social positions. My concern is considerably narrower. It is whether NBAA affirmative action can serve as an adequate substitute for race- and gender-based policies, and in order to answer this question we must understand the multiple functions that can be used to justify the present policy.

A corollary to the above argument against affirmative action is that not only does affirmative action serve to advantage the least discriminated against members of the targeted groups, but it also serves to stigmatize all those women and minorities who are deserving and would have competed successfully anyway.[14] This is an argument so commonly heard and yet so obviously problematic that I will treat it briefly here instead of coupling it to the other objections that must be examined in considerable detail.

The problem with this argument is that it begs the question and assumes what it sets out to prove. That is, it is an effective argument only if it is assumed that most remnants of discrimination have been eliminated and that few, if any, *truly deserving* candidates are now admitted under affirmative action standards.

Granted, many women and members of minority groups might not need affirmative action in order to be successful even in the real world with its remnants of discrimination. Granted too that the practice of affirmative action does allow many people to wrongly claim that every successful women or black succeeded only because of affirmative action. However, if affirmative action is truly a justified policy—that is, if those who are aided by it really do deserve the advantage it provides—then the stigma placed on both the real beneficiaries of affirmative action and on their somewhat more talented "look-alikes" who have advanced without the benefit of affirmative action is wrong.

The issue should not be whether affirmative action is used to stigmatize people. It should be whether it does or does not help us to make good decisions regarding admission and hiring. If it does not do this, and at the same time confuses people about which women or which blacks are qualified, then there is a real problem with affirmative action itself. If, however, affirmative action does contribute to better decisions, then the stigma should be blamed not on affirmative action but on an overall misunderstanding that the public may have of its goals and effects. If this is the case, the solution is not to eliminate affirmative action, or to alter its focus, but to do a better job of educating people about the purpose of the practice.

The problem with those who argue against affirmative action from the standpoint of stigmatization is that they rarely address the nature of the standards that would tell whether affirmative action results in inferior appointments and hiring. My own sense is that affirmative action has widened the considerations used to determine successful applicants. For example, there is greater concern about the ability of managers and professionals to relate to a diverse work force and group of clients. In widening the standards there may be loosening of technical prerequisites in some instances, such as push-ups for women at West Point. However, it is just as likely that in forcing a wider net to be spread among white males as well as women and people of color, even technical standards have been raised in many instances. In cases where technical prerequisites may have been lowered in order to accommodate other factors, the merits of the trade-off must be examined in terms of job performance. However, it should not be assumed offhand that to widen the considerations relevant to selection is the same as failing to contribute to better decisions.[15]

There is another argument that is closely related to the one claiming that affirmative action advantages the least disadvantaged. This one holds that those who must pay the price of affirmative action are those who have benefited least from the discriminatory practices that affirmative action is intended to address, and that many of these people had little if any involvement in the initial acts of discrimination. I will look closely at this argument in a subsequent section.

Why Affirmative Action Is Not a Group Right

There are two ways to think about a group right. In the first and strict sense of the term, the concept of a right is employed to advance or protect the position of a people who share a certain identity and the right is granted or denied to people because of that identity. Here rights are afforded to the group as a group and exercised by its members as a function of their membership in that group. Because the right is granted to the group as such and held by individuals as long as they belong to that group, a group right often serves to increase the coherence of the group because it serves as a constant reminder to its members that their identity and their well-being are bound to their role as members of that group.[16]

A system of group rights places a strong burden on members within the group as well as on members outside to act in ways that recognize the group's integrity. Indeed, to leave the group may quite literally mean to lose one's identity, as is symbolized by the orthodox Jewish family who sits Shiva, a way of grieving for the dead, for the child who marries outside of the religion.

In a system of group rights, select privileges are given to individual members just because they belong to a certain group and others are denied for the same reason. While members exercise privileges, it is the group itself that holds the right to recognition. Individuals are recognized in terms of their status as members of the group. Hence, for example, individual Jews in the Middle Ages often had the right to lend money for interest until such time as they converted to Christianity, at which time they lost the right. They often did not have the right to hold public office while they were still Jews. However, this right might be gained by conversion to Christianity.

A strong notion of group rights—one that is backed by state power—can have a number of obnoxious features because the group is given the legal authority to control individual behavior in areas such as marriage, worship, dress, and work. In liberal societies, state power cannot legally support anything like this level of group rights, although individuals may not be forbidden from voluntarily joining groups that would seek to exercise such control over them.[17]

The contrast between this strong system of group rights and the modern system is captured by the debate in the French assembly over the status of Jews and whether they were to remain classified as Jews or were to be considered French citizens. Prior to the French Revolution, Jews had separate group status and were recognized, not as individuals or as citizens, but as Jews. When a vote on this issue was called in the national assembly in 1771, the argument for the disestablishment of the Jewish corporate existence was summed up by Clermont-Tonnerre: "One must refuse everything to the Jews as a nation, and give everything to the Jews as individuals. . . . It should be repugnant to have . . . a nation within a nation."[18] The vote to change the status of Jews was, of course consonant with the rise of individualism and the idea that each citizen was to count as one person rather than as one member. Hence Jews were no longer a member of a separate rights-bearing group, but existed as individual French citizens who might or might not choose to associate with other Jews.

No one, of course, believes that affirmative action approaches anything like the system of group rights described above. However, this is often the specter that forms the background of concerns about the Balkanizing effects of race- and gender-based policy. The confusion between the kind of group status described above and the kind that is implied by affirmative action is best captured by distinguishing between a group right and a group-*based* right. The latter results when some people are wrongly denied the treatment that should be afforded to individual, rights-bearing citizens because of a characteristic that they all share. The characteristic may be blue eyes, black skin, small bones, or the physical apparatus needed to bear children. The people who have this characteristic may or may not share a lot of other things and they may or may not care about each other's welfare or think of themselves as sharing an identity. All of this is irrelevant to the claim that they all have.

While it is true that affirmative action exists in part to advance equality of opportunity for members of certain groups, it is wrong to think of it in its present form as a group right in the first sense of the term. It does not seek to advance the coherence or the status of one group *over* another—although it may use an existing sense of identification in terms of role models to enhance its effect—nor does it seek to provide recognition to members of one group *over* another. It does not *give* special group status. Rather, it uses group membership to identify and correct past acts of discrimination against individuals, acts that have resulted in inadequate educational, economic, and social positioning and that has effect the future condition of subsequent generations.

Affirmative Action Confused with a Group Right: The Strategy of Simultaneity

Affirmative action is sometimes mistaken for a group right because of what may usefully be called a strategy of simultaneity. This is a strategy that is intended to increase, without quotas, the percentage of a group's representation in a given field by opening up educational and employment opportunities on the one side and by developing motivation on the other. The idea behind the strategy is that opportunities and motivation are mutually reinforcing, such that by increasing opportunities for members of a group their motivation will improve and that as motivation improves more opportunities will become available. It is a policy that is intended to advance individuals' chances for fair treatment given underrepresentation resulting from historical discrimination suffered because of shared characteristics such as sex or skin color.

Simultaneity indicates policies that seek to increase the number of targeted minorities both within and between different fields at approximately the same time. It aims to change the cultural practices and self-conceptions that encourage discrimination or enable it to continue. The fact that some affirmative action policies are intended to lift the status of members of a group simultaneously should not be mistaken for the promotion of a group right. Simultaneity is a strategic move that is intended to have the effect of breaking institutional deadlock where the action of isolated decision makers is unlikely to have the desired effect.

To see this point, consider the once long absence of African-American quarterbacks in the professional football leagues. It is hardly plausible that black players lacked the natural talent to play that position until a few years ago. It is more likely that the prejudice of players, coaches, and owners resulted in this exclusion. What is hard to understand is why the profit motive and the desire to win did not for so long override this prejudice at least among the poorer and least able teams.

One partial explanation has to do with institutional deadlock or what Carmichael and Hamilton call institutional racism.[19] One can imagine a situation in which at every level even a coach with the best of intentions would think that preparing a talented black child for quarterback would be a disservice because of the perception that the coaches at the next level would never put a black athlete in that position when there are white boys who can play it. This means, of course, that even a coach with the best of intentions at the next level of play (say high school) would have a double reason not to play a black at quarterback: first, because the coaches at the lower levels have not trained any talented black players for him to work with and second, because the coaches at the next level (say college) have never played a black at quarterback. And, of course, this situation undoubtedly has an effect on the inclinations of the athlete as well who "realistically" wants to be trained for a slot where he has a chance of playing. Finally, there is an added effect on fans, who, seeing no black quarterbacks in the professional leagues, have the perception reinforced that blacks are not suited for leadership positions. Thus a culture is created and maintained whereby, even if no one ever wished to discriminate, discriminatory practices are created and maintained.

Simultaneity is a strategic way to break such cycles. It is intended to affect the way in which members of targeted minorities think about their opportunities for a good life within established institutional structures and it is intended to change the way established institutions structure opportunities for minorities and women. For example, a few years ago an otherwise bright girl may well have decided not to pursue medical education if she was unable to associate womanhood with a medical career because she did not know of any female physicians. Similarly, even if the faculty wanted to increase the number of women in medicine, they would have had difficulty doing so if girls, seeing few women physicians, decided to pursue different courses of study. Simultaneity seeks to break this impasse by working on both ends at the same time. In this case it sought ways to admit more women applicants into medical schools and into prestigious internships while also encouraging more girls to pursue a course of study that would lead to medical school. The increase in the numbers of female medical students and physicians over the last decade and a half is an indication that affirmative action can play a significant role in addressing historically generated inequalities.

Simultaneity says that certain kinds of roadblocks are rooted deep in historical and cultural practices and that special attempts must be made to remove them. It is a way to break those instances of underrepresentation that are the result of systematic and enforced past discrimination that have resulted in present cultural formations that continue to discriminate and reinforce reduced social standing. The policy is best understood not as "reverse discrimination," as some critics have labeled it, but as a way to address historical and systematic acts of discrimination that have resulted in a collective level of competitive disadvantage or constrained motivation.

Group-Based Rights as Violation of Individual Rights of Others

One objection to the policy of simultaneity is that even granting that the policy does not function as a group right on the inside, it does so on the outside. In other words, although simultaneity does not necessarily serve to strengthen the coherence of targeted groups, it does serve to deny to those outside of the group certain benefits that are rightfully theirs as individuals. Hence, for example, the white male applicant to law school with good grades and strong test scores is turned down and a place is given to a black applicant with lower scores. This issue is addressed, with some success, by Ronald Dworkin in his consideration of the Bakke case. Dworkin sums up his argument:

> Affirmative action programs seem to encourage, for example, a popular misunderstanding which is that they assume that racial or ethnic groups are entitled to proportionate shares of opportunities, so that Italian or Polish ethnic minorities are, in theory, as entitled to their proportionate shares as blacks or Chicano or American Indians are entitled to the shares the present programs give them. That is a plain mistake: the programs are not based on the idea that those who are aided are entitled to aid, but only on the strategic hypothesis that helping them is now an effective way of attacking a national problem.[20]

For Dworkin, race is an acceptable factor to use in admission if doing so serves an important national goal and if the racial exclusion that results is not based, as it was with, for example, quotas *against* Jews and blacks, on the view that one race or group is inherently better than another.[21] He notes, for example, that potential legal skill, as reflected in scores on a law school admissions test, is obviously an important consideration in making selections to law school since it is generally better for a country to have available the services of more rather than fewer competent lawyers. However, skin color may also be relevant under certain circumstances, such as when there is an undersupply of adequately trained lawyers available to serve a given racial or ethnic group. For Dworkin, affirmative action rests on a perfectly reasonable guess that by admitting and training more black lawyers and doctors this problem of underrepresentation will be addressed.

What is important to notice about Dworkin's argument is that it directs extra resources to any group in which an undersupply of professional or other relevant talent or resources exists. The force of this argument is to show that test scores or other signs of ability do not, by themselves, entail a right to a position and it thus allows for flexible standards of admission and assignment. However, his argument needs refinement because it does not recognize the differential merits of the claims of equally needy groups.

The problem with Dworkin's argument is that it is indiscriminate with regard to what it counts as a national problem and therefore is not a strong justification for what he seeks to accomplish. Suppose that a new immigrant group is, along with African Americans, also underserved with regard to its professional talent in comparison to some national standard and suppose that special admissions could solve the problem. Given Dworkin's argument, members of this group would have the same claim on affirmative action resources as would members of underrepresented African-American communities. And this would be true even if they came to this country precisely because the quality of medical and legal services here is better than that available to them in their homeland.

Yet, even though there are very good humanitarian reasons for providing adequate medical care to members of new immigrant groups, the implication that they should have an equal claim with blacks to affirmative action is surely wrong from a moral standpoint. The moral force of affirmative action for African Americans is not just that they are less well served by professional talent than other Americans, although this is a condition that we should worry about. Rather, the moral force behind affirmative action for African Americans is based to a very large degree on the historical reasons that led to their being underserved.

Dworkin is both right and wrong when he says that "the programs are not based on the idea that those who are aided are entitled to aid, but only on the strategic hypothesis that helping them is now an effective way of attacking a national problem."[22] He is right in the sense that no one, even those students with the highest grades and scores, is entitled to become a doctor. One is entitled to a place in a medical school only if there is reason to believe that a publicly recognized need will be met. He is wrong if he also assumes that African Americans do not have a special claim on the health resources of this nation, a claim that includes but goes beyond need.

One final concern with Dworkin's article has to do with a possible implication regarding the way in which individual members of different racial groups are to be assigned places in the medical system. While Dworkin is probably correct that educating more black professionals will probably result in some improvement in the professional talent available to inner-city areas, affirmative action is certainly not the most efficient way to serve this goal. If the primary goal is to increase the professional talent available to black people, then professional schools should give priority to applicants who agree to spend a reasonable number of years serving black people. It is likely that such a policy would give an advantage to African-American applicants, but it would do so only if they had the desired motivation, not because they are black and not because that blackness has resulted in discrimination and reduced standing.[23] While there is every reason to be in favor of a policy that seeks to select people who will serve underrepresented areas, it would be racist to expect that only those admitted under affirmative action should be *obliged* to do so.

Affirmative Action as Addressing a Historical Debt

For some people the moral basis of affirmative action involves more than addressing patterns of systematic discrimination and reduced standing. For Native and African Americans it also involves historical acts of such egregious nature that special obligations have been created for the larger society. These obligations are often confused with the other reasons for affirmative action, but they are inadequately captured by the kinds of moral appeals that otherwise would be quite acceptable. For example, the frequently expressed concerns of liberal defenders of affirmative action to create a work force that reflects society at large is consistent with attempts to correct perceived distortions in the marketplace of talent but it does not signal the presence of a historical debt.

In the cases that I am addressing, the task is not only to correct distortions in equal opportunity and to enable otherwise silenced voices to be heard. It is also to pay a debt that is owed as a result of unprecedented violation of human rights and liberties. Were such a debt to be widely acknowledged, as I will argue it should be, it would be clear that the problem with affirmative action is not that it offers too much, but that by itself it offers too little. The conclusion is not to eliminate affirmative action, a move that would clearly reduce the percentage of college-educated people and professionals who come from these groups, but to augment it in ways that would address very basic concerns of health, safety, and general education. These considerations are also important in assessing proposals for reparations.

I am aware that to view affirmative action with regard to certain groups as a part of a historical debt goes against the tide of most respected thinking on the matter and is in need of justification. However, the fact that affirmative action is not concerned about the underrepresentation of all groups in all areas—for example, the proportion of Italian CEOs—suggests that there is a prima facie recognition that members of different groups are positioned differently with regard to claims for assistance. The problem is not with the implicit recognition of the underlying moral intuition—that a debt is involved. Rather, it is in describing the debt in a way that it is acceptable to both liberals and conservatives. Liberals wrongly believe that to acknowledge such a debt involves acceptance of a group right. Conservatives such as Justice Scalia rightly reject the idea that present-day whites are guilty of a *historical* transgression, but then wrongly conclude that because historical guilt is absent, so too is a debt.

The Controversy over the Debt

Justice Scalia, one of the strongest opponents of affirmative action, was also one of the few to view it correctly in terms of a debt owed to certain members of our society. His opposition arose because he believed that the advantages provided to individuals from targeted groups by affirmative action policies are most often wrought from members of other groups who have not participated in the initial injustice and who were often in almost as vulnerable a position as those who receive its benefits. Justice Scalia expressed this objection forcefully:

> My father came to this country when he was a teenager. Not only had he never profited from the sweat of any black man's brow, I don't think he had ever seen a black man. There are, of course, many white ethnic groups that came to this country in great numbers relatively late in its history—Italians, Jews, Poles—who not only took no part in, and derived no profit from, the major historical suppression of the currently acknowledged minority groups, but were, in fact, themselves the object of discrimination by the dominant Anglo-Saxon majority. To be sure, in relatively recent years some or all of these groups have been the beneficiaries of discrimination against blacks, or have themselves practiced discrimination,

> but to compare their racial debt . . . with that of those who plied the slave trade, and who maintained a formal caste system for many years thereafter, is to confuse a mountain with a molehill. Yet curiously enough, we find that in the system of restorative justice established by the Wisdoms and the Powells and the Whites, it is precisely these groups that do most of the restoring. It is they who, to a disproportionate degree, are the competitors with the urban blacks and Hispanics for jobs, housing, and education.[24]

Scalia is concerned whether anyone can be legitimately expected to pay the debt, but he quite openly suggests that, if anyone can be found who should pay it, there is indeed a debt to be paid. One of the questions he raises is why one might think that some groups that have been discriminated against are owed a debt whereas others, also discriminated against, are not owed one.

The most important fact about the debt that is appropriate for addressing through affirmative action is that it results from a forced, involuntary act that brings about serious and long-standing intergenerational disadvantages. Both sides of this are important. Many immigrant people suffered serious disadvantages when they came to this country in relation to individuals from other groups who were already here. However, these immigrants were not forced by anyone in this country to come *here*. They came because they believed that here they would be better off than they were in the home country. Clearly, many members of many groups were discriminated against once they arrived here, as Justice Scalia rightly points out, and it is still important from the point of view of fairness and equal opportunity that these discriminations, to the extent that they still exist, be removed. Nevertheless, they alone are not sufficient to warrant a policy of affirmative action and this is because of a second point.

The important point of comparison is not just that members of a group were discriminated against or even that in some individual cases the physical and emotional harm could have been initially equal between members of two different groups. Certainly the life of Boston Irish immigrants in the 19th century was a life of everyday degradation and humiliation. Indeed, the remnants of this discrimination remain in terms like "paddy wagon." Some modern-day descendants of European immigrants may well feel like Scalia that the fact that both European immigrants and African Americans suffered discrimination creates an equivalency that therefore invalidates the special claims of the latter. An equally relevant consideration in terms of whether a certain group deserves special consideration is whether the discrimination here resulted in members of a group being worse off than they would have otherwise been had they chosen to remain in their native country.

Scalia wrongly assumes that the proper point of comparison is the initial treatment between different groups and that an equivalency is established by virtue of the fact that both groups suffered an initial moment of discrimination (although it is hard to see how anything could be comparable to slavery in its physical and spiritual degradation). However, the point of comparison is incomplete.

For example, with the exception of African and Native Americans, the discrimination against Irish immigrants may have been unmatched in the last century. Yet one reason that affirmative action is not an appropriate policy for Irish Americans is not just because they have now reached parity with other groups. It is also because, in addition to their voluntary immigration, their situation was still comparatively better here than it was in Ireland where, in addition to crop failure, they had to cope with British occupation and brutality.[25] It is not only the level of material degradation that affects the judgment about how well or how poorly members of one group faired in comparison to members of another. It is also the conditions under which they arrived in this country to begin with. To arrive as an involuntary slave in shackles, possibly with one's family destroyed and almost certainly with one's family ties severed, is already a condition of extreme physical and spiritual degradation.

Regardless of to whom the debt is owed, Scalia believes that its costs are an unfair burden on the nondiscriminating immigrants, and because of this he believes that affirmative action itself is unfair. It forces payment from those who were not victimizers. The assumption that Scalia makes is that those who did not benefit directly from the initial act of discrimination are not obliged to compensate for it. Yet his conception of benefits is overly narrow, myopically focused on the individual, and confuses guilt and obligation. Certainly he is correct to suggest that his father should not be thought guilty because of slavery. However, this is not the same as saying that no obligation is owed.

Scalia's argument takes no account of the national capital that accrued as a result of the forced backbreaking labor of slaves, nor does he consider how such labor contributed to the eagerness of immigrants to come here. Certainly he and his father benefited from this labor and the question is whether, through this benefit, a debt is owed.[26]

Of course some people may have immigrated not because of anticipated material benefits—life for the settlers and immigrants was usually no picnic—but rather for the spiritual, social, or political freedom they felt awaited them in America. Yet this makes Scalia's argument even more difficult to accept. Suppose that instead of slavery being assigned to members of a specific racial group, it were assigned on a random basis to immigrants. Suppose that potential immigrants knew before leaving home they would be randomly assigned to positions in the new land and that some of them would be wrenched from their families, chained onto ocean ships where many would die, and arrive here as slaves. Suppose too that they knew that this number was not incidental but comprised about 15 percent of the overall American population and about 50 percent of the overall population in the southern states. Given this random assignment, it is hard to imagine that many European immigrants who chose voluntarily to come to America would still have taken the chance to do so—including Scalia's father.[27]

This is one reason why Scalia's argument does not have the moral force that he believes it has. To the extent that slave labor was needed to support the real—not some ideal—economy of the United States, we all benefit. All voluntary immigrants benefited—first because their ancestors' exemption (i.e., the fact that even if they came as indentured servants they could be assured that they would not wind up as permanent slaves) was undoubtedly a factor in their decision to come here in the first place and second because they never had to carry the lower standing that being a descendant of a slave entailed.

However, Scalia's argument is only incidentally about benefits. It is first and foremost about obligations. Do those who benefitted from an earlier act of discrimination, even if not the perpetrators of that discrimination, have an obligation to those who were its victims? The crucial issue is what if any obligation the children of immigrants have when they or their ancestors, who were once subject to discrimination, now stand as the beneficiaries of the forced subjugation of others. Scalia seems to believe that they have none. I believe that he is wrong.

Granted, under some conditions the person who benefits from an act of discrimination does not owe a debt to the person who is discriminated against. I have just been turned down for a house because, unbeknownst to me, the landlord is anti-Semitic. You then come along and rent a house that otherwise would not have been available. You do not know of the initial slur and had nothing to do with it. Clearly the landlord owes me some compensation if I can prove my case. However, your role is benign and you should not be the party providing me compensation. You are in a better position than you would have been had the discrimination not occurred, but this position does not make you liable.

However, the lack of an obligation to compensate in the above instance relates only to a legal context. To the extent that a landlord must pay for discrimination and to the extent that the market will bear it, the cost of that payment will be passed on to renters. There are benefits to those who exist as nonvictims and nonperpetrators within a climate of discrimination and there are certain costs involved to these same people when a price is paid by the perpetrator for past discrimination. Affirmative action is in part a way of estimating this cost and extracting compensation.

The moral obligation is considerably higher if you actually know about the initial discrimination and then act so as to take advantage of it. In such cases you are indeed liable for the benefits you receive at the expense of others. Moreover, you are liable even if you have also been the victim of discrimination or if your material condition is the same as or even worse than my material condition. This is obvious. One is not excused of armed robbery, say, because one is receiving food stamps.

Scalia is also wrong in his view that the discriminated-against offspring of an immigrant did not discriminate against the child of the slave. The color of trade unions and neighborhoods tells a very different story. True, there are many reasons why this discrimination was the expedient (perhaps even necessary from an individual standpoint) thing to do, but it was still discrimination.

Immigrants understood quite well that they were connected to a stream of opportunities that could be cashed in by future generations and that is precisely why many of them came to this country and endured the hardships involved in doing so.[28] They were also aware that blacks were not a part of this stream, and, sadly, many times they fought to keep it this way.

In contrast to the benefits the immigrant could anticipate, at least over some generations, slaves were denied not only the right to earn and to vote, but also the right to have their intentions receive public standing, even when those intentions involved the disposal of the wealth they created. Moreover, their descendants had to continue to struggle for these basic emblems of public standing.[29] To be the descendant of a slave is to be involved in a significantly reduced stream of intergenerational opportunities and benefits as well as a degradation of everyday life.[30] When contrasted with members of other groups who belong to the same generation, African Americans continue to experience the effects of reduced opportunities.[31]

There is something quite right about Scalia's concern that there is a problem when we attempt to address these injustices, but it is important to be clear about what the nature of that problem is. The problem is not that compensation is provided or that children of immigrants, even those who themselves have been victimized by discrimination, have an obligation to provide some of it. It is that the burden often falls unduly on the most disadvantaged of these groups, especially in the places where people of color have advanced,[32] and that the burden is not adequately shared. Scalia's concern is best illustrated by a hypothetical case in which, for example, say, 20,000 people benefit from a past injustice but only one white male blue-collar laborer is singled out to pay the cost.

Yet the situation is not quite as dire as Scalia seems to think and the courts have recognized this problem and have been reluctant to address past discrimination when the cost would fall unevenly on a single individual rather than on a more diverse and unspecified group. Thus, for example, the court has been more friendly to encouraging preferential hiring where many are denied and but one is chosen than it has been to accepting preferential firing where specific and identified individuals bear the cost of correcting generalized past discrimination.[33]

However, the fact remains, as Scalia correctly reminds us, that there is a certain cost to affirmative action policy to some individuals even if the specific individual who is bearing that cost is not known. If race were not a consideration there are indeed instances in which, on the basis of grades and test scores, some other student would have been admitted to medical school or some other applicant would have gotten the job even when we comfortably do not know who that might have been.

Yet race *is* a consideration partly because it has operated across generations to skew the present-day competition in a way that, without a vigorously enforced affirmative action policy, perpetuates a pattern of selection that has been directed against other individuals—in this case, African Americans—by historical and persistent patterns of discrimination. Thus without affirmative action it could be said that some present student would have been denied admission to medical school or some successful applicant would have failed to be admitted to college. And this would have been the case even though these students stand as victims of a long string of historical discrimination.

What Scalia's objection suggests in the case of African Americans is not that race-based preferences are unjust—there are always many factors that tip the balance toward one rather than another applicant and race is appropriate when attempting to correct the effects of past *racial* injustices. What Scalia's objection better points to is the need for the burden to be shared more widely.[34] It is not an argument, as he seems to think, for rejecting the idea of affirmative action altogether nor does it adequately support his insinuation that there is no burden at all because there is no one single person who actually owes the debt. To share this burden more widely might mean, for example, a policy aimed at rectifying the full cultural, social, and economic damage that has arisen following the American holocaust that was slavery and the slave trade.

To Whom the Debt Is Owed: A Return to the Question of Group Rights

Yet if Scalia is wrong about whether a debt is owed, there is still an issue regarding to whom the debt is owed. It is not immediately obvious that the debt for slavery is owed to the descendants of the slaves, since it was not they but their slave ancestors who were the target of the harm and who suffered the actual harm of slavery. Indeed, one avid defender of affirmative action rejects the idea that we owe present-day African Americans anything because of the harm that was done to their slave ancestors and he rejects this idea because he believes that it is a racist ground for offering the benefits of affirmative action.[35] His argument is worth considering because it will help us to clarify the nature of the debt owed.

Fiscus argues against a justification of affirmative action on compensatory grounds because "to hold that descendants of the millions of blacks harmed throughout our history are entitled to compensation for the long-past injury of their ancestors is to violate the first principle of compensatory justice—that recipients of compensation be the ones harmed."[36] He rejects, as racist, an alternative idea that all blacks are equivalent to members of one family and therefore deserving of compensation. This rejection is based on his belief that such a notion "equates, legally and morally, individual black men and women with their racial identity. It says that race is more important than anything else in determining worth and responsibility—indeed, in determining basic identity. It is, in a word, racist."[37] Similarly racist to him is the idea that the present "generation of whites should pay for the sins of earlier generations."[38]

Fiscus's alternative is to accept the assumption that talent is distributed equally among the races and, on the basis of this assumption, to view underrepresentation as a sign of injustice that must be corrected. The legal force of the argument then lies in the enforcement of the equal protection clause. "Distributive justice as a matter of equal protection requires that individuals be awarded the positions, advantages or benefits they would have been awarded under fair conditions."[39] Under this view, whenever there are proportionately more whites in a position than are represented in the larger society, we have a probable instance of discrimination even if whites lay claim to those positions "using putatively more objective measures of merit."[40]

Whatever we may think about the racial distribution of talent—and there is good reason to think as Fiscus does that African Americans are usually placed lower than whites of equal innate ability[41]—this argument has many weaknesses. First, it fits any group that does not have its proportional share of positions and certainly serves to water down any special claim that blacks might have. Second, even if one does assume an equality of talent, there are other nondiscriminatory factors that may play a role in the distribution of positions. Different individual interest is one of these, as is the cultural capital of the family in relation to positions within the larger society. A family of musicians is more likely to produce musicians, even given equal innate musical talent, than a family of nonmusicians. To ignore these factors or to believe that they require state action to "correct" is to impose a standard of uniformity on cultures that would be intolerable for all.

Moreover, since Fiscus rejects the idea that we should compensate for past injustices, it is hard to see, even if the present differences arose as the result of past discrimination, why present individuals should be expected to pay the price. He rejects this idea as racist when it comes to compensatory justice, but it is hard to see why he should think it any less racist when applied to distributory justice. Unless he believes that there is some unfair historical basis for the way talent is presently expressed in grades and test scores, then surely it is racist to deny a position to a white person on the basis of some abstract assumption regarding equality.

Consider that Fiscus's argument begins at the point at which two individuals—one black and one white—have decided to compete for a given position. Yet much of the problem of representation comes well before the decision to compete and arises at the level of interest, motivation, self-concept, and the like. The fact is that many individuals do not enter the competition because, for a variety of reasons, they have been persuaded to pursue other, less competitive avenues. (Think of the potential black quarterback described earlier.)

Any reasonable affirmative action policy would surely want to address the problem at the level of motivation and interest as well as at the level of native ability. Motivation and interest, however, connect to a history in which what any present-day student may want for himself or herself is connected to what that student's parents and grandparents were *allowed* to want for themselves. Yet if we are barred from looking backward to find the reason for compensation, as Fiscus's argument suggests, then the fact that the difference between my present interest in law and your lack of interest in the same subject can be accounted for by the fact that racism barred your grandfather from pursuing a career that mine was encouraged to respect should be irrelevant.[42]

The priority that Fiscus's argument gives to talent across groups is indiscriminate in terms of cause and therefore provides too broad a criterion for the application of affirmative action principles. One need not believe that there must be an exact correlation between the distribution of talent and the distribution of positions in order to believe that a distribution is unjust. There are, as Dworkin correctly points out, many legitimate reasons for choosing one applicant over another and some of these are not exclusively related to talent in the more obvious sense.[43]

This is important to recognize for a number of reasons. One of these is that it blunts the relevance of research that reinforces racist assumptions and institutions (research that Fiscus's argument ironically encourages) by claiming to prove that the racial variations in IQ scores are due to genetic factors. A second is that it casts doubt on the morally questionable assumption that professional education and status are rewards for being born with high intelligence regardless of what one does with that status. One does not need to assume equality of talent in order to judge a distribution of positions unjust. All one needs to assume is that for most positions more than enough people possess an *adequate* amount of talent to do the job at a high level of competence, and that moral reasons for selecting some segment of the adequately talented are being systematically ignored.

Finally, one need not be as concerned as Fiscus is about the reportedly racist assumption behind the idea that African Americans belong to a single group and that it is because of harm to past members of the group that they are owed compensation. To argue that someone is owed compensation because he or she possesses a certain trait in common with others—even membership in the same family—is not to claim that individuals are to be identified with that trait and only with that trait in each and every respect.

Suppose, for example, that I am told that I am one of but five living relatives of a recently deceased and very wealthy person and that each of the five, none of whom know each other, is entitled to a fifth of her estate. Given that none of us knew the other before this happy event, there is little reason to think that we have much in common or that we need to be treated the same in any respect other than that involving the liquidation of the estate. True, we belong to the same family, but that is probably a very incidental part of who we are, even though in this instance it is the sole determinant of what we are owed.

Without the reference point of slavery, it is hard to understand why we should pay more attention to the lingering causes of discrimination against blacks than the lingering causes of discrimination against immigrants. True, the lingering effects of discrimination against African Americans persist more intensely than discrimination against older immigrants, but it is not clear that this always holds with respect to discrimination against newer immigrants. Whatever the statistics of well-being between different groups may be, without the distinguishing experience of slavery, any difference is one of degree, not of kind.

Fiscus objects to rooting the consideration back to slavery because he believes that doing so is racist, and while he is wrong in this objection, it is important to see in what way he is wrong. Earlier I noted that the point of comparison for the immigrant is the difference between how life might have been there and how it actually is here. I then noted that for the present-day African American, the parallel question might be how his or her condition might have been without the institution of slavery in comparison with what it actually is. For most immigrants the right answer is probably that life here is better in some important ways than it would have been there. Yet a critic could make a similar case for the great-grandchildren of slaves.

The critic could note that for any particular present-day African American the right answer is not that his or her life would have been better without slavery. Rather, the right answer is that this particular life would not have been at all because of the simple biological fact that the genetic material and cultural experiences and historical events through which his or her identity is constituted would have been entirely different and that the person thought of as *this* individual simply would not have existed.[44]

Now this answer is problematic from a moral point of view only if one believes as I do that extra consideration is due to the descendant of the slave and that the slave's descendants have claims the child of the immigrant does not have. It is problematic because it complicates the base of comparison and, given the assumption that living is better than not being born, suggests that slavery provides no harm—in a strict sense of that term—to the present-day descendants of slaves. Discrimination causes harm now.

Given this response, the question remains why should we think, as I do, that given two children, we owe more to the child whose great-great-grandfather was enslaved than we do to the one whose great-great-grandfather worked in a sweatshop and that we do so even if the great-great-grandchildren are presently in a similar material condition. After all, while not all of the wealth created by the latter was stolen, as it was in the case of the slave, a lot of it was.

Up to now I have treated the comparison between the immigrant and the slave as unproblematic, leaving it to moral intuition alone to decide that something more is owed to those whose ancestors were forced to come here compared with those who had a choice. Now I want to press those intuitions by asking: Why should the matter of whether immigration was forced or voluntary matter to the grandchildren of the original sojourners? Indeed, if we say that the grandchild of one is better off here than he or she would have been if he or she had stayed in the original country, should we not say of the grandchild of the slave that he or she too is, at least, not worse off because of slavery than he or she would have been without it? My point is not that he or she is better off here than he or she would have been if the family had been permitted to stay in Africa. To say this is to assume that without slavery everything would have remained the same—except better. Yet, as noted above, without slavery everything would have been different, including those who are now alive. Hence, it could be argued that in both cases—that of the immigrant and that of the slave[45]—the original decision did not harm the descendants even though in one case the decision was a voluntary one and in the other it was made by others, first through kidnapping and second through enslavement. Granted, the descendant of the slave is probably less well off than the descendant of the immigrant, but so too are the descendants of newer immigrants less well off than descendants of older immigrants, as are possibly the descendants of some who remained in parts of Africa.

Certainly the fact that, say, the Polish American had an ancestor who chose to come to this country while the African American's ancestor was coerced into coming made a big difference to the ancestors themselves. However, why, one might ask, should it make a difference to their *descendants* if, in both cases, their descendants are better off than they would have been had the fate of their ancestors been different? True, the child of the Polish immigrant is better off than he or she would have been were it not for the institution of slavery, but then so too is the descendant of the slave. Or, to put it differently, why should we think—as I believe we should—that somehow discrimination against African Americans is different in kind—not just in duration or intensity—from discrimination against European immigrants?

A Debt Owed to the Slave

Fiscus is in fact quite right—we do not owe a debt to *present* individuals as compensation *because* of the harm done to their ancestors by slavery.[46] However, he is wrong to assume that no debt is owed to anyone. Rather, the debt is owed to the slave and, just as with a will, the debt to the slave is not canceled once the slave has died or once slavery has ended. Fiscus, of course, would object: If the debt is owed to the slave, what sense does it make to pay the descendants of the slave? If I steal money from you, I have not paid my debt by compensating your brother or your neighbor. Why then should it be thought that I have paid it if I compensate your great-grandchild, or nephew, or your neighbor's great-great nephew or grandchild?

There are two answers to this question. The first is that as with any debt where the line of beneficiaries is blurred, one does the best one can, and in this case it is obvious that compensating the descendants of slaves in general is the best one can do to compensate any particular slave. Yet this answer tells us why descendants of slaves deserve compensation. It does not, to return to a point made earlier, say why they deserve to be compensated in a way that the descendants of immigrant wage laborers do not. After all, it could be argued that while it is true that slaves had all the fruits of their labor confiscated by others, immigrant wage earners had a lot of their labor confiscated. Hence while they may not have labored for as long or had as much of their labor stolen as did the slave, nevertheless the same principle holds.

Why Compensation Is Owed the Descendant of Slaves and Not Descendants of Immigrant Wage Earners

A second answer to the question of why compensation is owed the descendant of the slave is that present-day descendants of slaves deserve compensation because the institution of slavery violated essential elements of collective and individual development[47] and that this institution and those that followed it must be seen as accountable for many of the problems confronting the African-American community today.

The situation with immigrants is very different. While immigrant labor was exploited, immigrants were still allowed the autonomy to form intentions and to act on them, including intentions to have families and the expectation that these families would remain intact. Moreover, immigrants' intentions were usually publicly acknowledged and the fruits of their labor that remained after death were disposed of as they were willed. True, where severe exploitation existed, immigrant wage earners were only allowed to pass on a relatively small amount of what they may have legitimately felt they had a right to pass on. Nevertheless, the right to have intentions recognized and to be acted on through publicly sanctioned practices and institutions formed a framework for cultural empowerment that was not available to slaves. What this means in simple terms is that immigrants, while denied one kind of opportunity, were positioned so that subsequent generations could take advantage of other kinds of opportunities that came along and that this was not the case for the children and the grandchildren of slaves. Unlike the slave, the laborer never lost *the right* to pass on material wealth; he or she just lost a lot of the material wealth that might have been passed on—or at least some did sometimes. Nevertheless, a primary motivation allowed the immigrant but not allowed the slave was the possibility for intergenerational advancement, and over time such advancement often did occur.

For the slave the situation was different. It was not first and foremost wealth that was stolen. Rather, the right to be considered the kind of being who could possess wealth was denied. There was, of course, a theft of material wealth—of the wealth created by sweat and blood. However, this was only a secondary loss since slaves were not allowed to be thought of as property owners. The first loss was the loss of public recognition as full human beings—a loss that involved the public denial of intentionality and of their right to have rights. (This loss is intensified because it occurs in the context of a society in which everyone else is supposed to be equal.) And this loss has cultural and intergenerational as well as individual significance, and continues to rupture social standing and well-being.

The loss is the rupture of a would-be string of meanings and intentions that, when reconstructed, extends from the initial victim to those individuals in the present generation who are otherwise the beneficiaries of would-be stolen labor.[48] The material wealth that was lost and the means for repayment is a stand-in, a token, for the spiritual theft that still cuts across generations. It is represented in a reduced status and in an attitude on the part of members of society, even many newer members, that material deprivation, as represented by lower levels of income, housing, education, and health, is a more natural, more acceptable, position for African Americans than it is for the rest of us. Affirmative action as it presently exists is, of course, an inadequate mechanism for correcting this loss. With the possible exception of reparations, its only advantage is that it is better than most other alternatives on the table.

It is not just, or even primarily, the liberal principle of equality of opportunity that was violated by slavery. It was the conservative and, even more, primary principle of the right to hold property and the right to pass it on to whomever one wants, a right that requires the social recognition of one's intentions. Yet the violation that was slavery goes deeper than the question of private property and its legitimacy. Women were also denied the right to own property in many instances, but they were not denied the right to allow their *male* offspring to own property. Moreover, had slavery occurred in a socialist society where all property was held in common by all citizens, the fact that slaves also were held in common would not mitigate the crime. That some people would be able to form and act on their intentions and to have their intentions publicly recognized and served while others would not be allowed to do so would constitute the same kind of cultural violation.[49] What was therefore violated was not just this or that individual's rights, although this certainly is part of the violation. Nor was the violation just a violation of a specific right or set of rights—property, free speech. It was the right to be considered a person and to establish the material requirements required for flourishing across generations that belonging to an accepted cultural group entails.

To see the violation in terms of a culture instead of just in terms of individuals does not necessarily imply that all present-day African Americans are somehow the same or that their identity is exhausted or even confined by their racial identity, as Fiscus believes it would. Nor does it imply that all are only and exclusively a part of one culture and that is African-American culture. Like everyone else, African Americans can belong to many different cultural groups and have many different beliefs. There is no essential paradigm to which all African Americans must conform. Yet it is not just as stand-ins for the object of the slaves' would-have-been-intentions that the claim for special consideration is made. The rupture of a culture has real consequences for people in terms of truncated expectations and opportunities both denied and overlooked and in terms of a general social attitude that accepts as part of the natural state of affairs lower levels of material well-being. Affirmative action—that is, race-based, backward-looking affirmative action—can be part of a strategy for repairing the rupture. It attempts to reconstruct the opportunities to which intentions and expectations must be attached. It is less than adequate because it involves relatively few positions assigned to relatively few individuals, and cannot serve as a substitute for the material benefits enjoyed by the rest of us as a result of a history that included the institution of slavery. Yet it surely should have a place in a policy of reconstruction.[50]

Conclusion: The Question of Need Reconsidered

Those who believe that the existing race- and gender-based affirmative action policy should be replaced by NBAA considerations assume that existing affirmative action policy violates the principles of fairness and equal opportunity by advancing people because of certain accidents of birth. The argument in this article has shown that there are strong reasons to question this interpretation of existing practice and to be skeptical of proposals to replace it with an NBAA program. However, to reject the idea that a blanket consideration of need can serve as a substitute for considerations of race and gender should not be taken as an argument that need is irrelevant and should have no place at all in considerations of merit. Need has a role to play, but it is not a solo one.[51]

Acknowledgments

The early stages of this research were funded in part by the Spencer Foundation. I am also greatly indebted to the Benton Center at the University of Chicago for providing the time for me to complete this work. I want to also express my appreciation to my colleagues at the University of Illinois, James Anderson, Nick Burbules, Pradeep Dillon, Belden Fields, Jefferson McMahan, Deborah Merit, Ralph Page, and William Trent, as well as to David Blacker of Illinois State University, Eric Bredo from the University of Virginia, and Phil Jackson of the University of Chicago for their comments on early versions of this paper. A special appreciation is due my assistant, Maria Seferian, for her help on the many versions of this paper. I want to also thank the faculty and students in the Department of Education at the University of Chicago and the University of Virginia for comments on earlier versions of this article.

15

Faith and the Pedagogical Limits of Critical Inquiry

Toward a Generous Reading of Religious Schools

Some features of life are so much a part of us that we take them for granted and have difficulty examining them in any careful and systematic way. The process of maturation involves extending those taken-for-granted features of life to encompass larger commitments and wider communities, which to varying degrees are incorporated into our evolving selves. The child becomes a parent, the student a teacher, and so on. Maturation also involves the capacity to distance some of these commitments and to examine them in light of other possibilities. As Martha Nussbaum explains, endorsing the Socratic task of education:

> The central task of education . . . is to confront the passivity of the pupil, challenging the mind to take charge of its own thought. All too often, people's choices and statements are not their own. Words come out of their mouths, and actions are performed by their bodies, but what those words and actions express may be the voice of tradition or convention, the voice of parent, of friends, of fashion. This is so because these people have never stopped to ask themselves what they really stand for, what they are willing to defend as themselves and their own. They are like instruments on which fashion and habit play their tunes, or like stage masks through which an actor's voice speaks.[1]

The idea of critical reflection that Nussbaum presents involves the development of the skills of rational argument, but it also involves a personal encounter with one's self—with one's "own" commitments and communities. Indeed the cool technician of syllogisms and truth tables may be quite disabled when it comes to the task of *self* reflection, appropriating these skills to ward off reflecting on the commitments but rather to win arguments.

Yet the Socratic ideal—that the unexamined life is not worth living—to which Nussbaum gives her own allegiance is unclear about just how much of a life need be open to critical examination. As Charles Peirce pointed out, we require a certain stability of belief in order to critically assess other beliefs that we hold.[2]

Faith and Reason

Religious belief is a problem for those committed to an unyielding view of critical reflection. Few deeply religious persons have done the kind of research that would speak scientifically to the rationality of their commitment to a single religious community. They have not surveyed the world's many religions, nor have they tested their beliefs against those of others, and they have not weighed the evidence in favor of God to the evidence against. Very few people take on religious commitments in this way, and those who do often choose to reject religion altogether. Indeed, it would take an extraordinary act of theological sophistication to address the biblical gaps and contradictions that young students are expected to overlook. In the beginning, there was the conundrum—where did Cain and Seth's wives come from? Was there a second Adam and Eve, a second Garden of Eden? And without these wives, who would have begotten those who begot us?

Yet the critical thinker is looking in the wrong place if he or she thinks to measure sacred texts in terms of the consistency of their logic or the surface credibility of their claims. It would be better to first understand the functions that religious doctrine serves before dismissing it as irrational, incoherent, or incredible, and, given these functions, to ask whether there might be a wider conception of rationality than the one commonly associated with critical thinking that can engage religious belief. In the absence of a more generous notion of inquiry, there is little about religion that could live up to these rational standards.

Take prayer as an example. When people pray, it sometimes looks as if they are petitioning God. Given the petitioner view of prayer, we should be able to discern the relative merit of different religions by comparing their effectiveness in producing certain results. Controlling for difficulty we could, say, have Mormons and Catholics pray for different sick people to get well and then see the frequency with which a healthy person gets well. Mormonism will be superior to Catholicism only if their prayers yield a better rate of recovery. Although many people do pray in the hopes of influencing God's will, this petitioner's understanding of prayer misses the point. Among other things prayer is a way of being with other people, of establishing connections while acknowledging our common vulnerability and dependency.

From the standpoint of the unyielding critical thinker, the greatest danger is premature commitment where children are forced to accept a belief long before they have the capacity to assess it. For the believer, however, the greater danger is that critical reflection will go too far, too soon. For teachers committed to fostering both religious commitment and critical thinking, their awareness of these twofold dangers creates considerable anguish, for they see limited grounds for compromise. They feel caught between an unyielding conception of rationality and an equally unyielding conception of faith. Most stay with faith, but a few brave teachers make attempts to reconcile the two.

Mr. S and the Nicene Creed: Limits of Critical Inquiry

One of the foundations of Catholicism is a doctrine called the Nicene Creed. The document strains logic because it seems to violate the rule that one cannot be both an X and a not X at the same time. The creed holds that mutually exclusive categories—human and divine—are not really mutually exclusive in the case of Jesus. It reads, in part,

> We believe in one Lord, Jesus Christ
> the only Son of God,
> eternally begotten of the Father,
> God from God, Light from Light,
> true God from true God,
> begotten, not made,
> of one Being with the Father.

> Through him all things were made.
> For us and for our salvation
> he came down from heaven:
> by the power of the Holy Spirit
> he became incarnate from the Virgin Mary,
> and was made man.
> For our sake he was crucified under Pontius Pilate;
> he suffered death and was buried.
> On the third day he rose again
> in accordance with the Scriptures;
> he ascended into heaven
> and is seated at the right hand of the Father.
> He will come again in glory to judge the living and the dead,
> and his kingdom will have no end.

Virtually every child who goes through a Catholic school is expected to be able to recite the creed, to accept it as true, and to use it to guide moral action. Yet historically the creed came to be accepted only after a strong challenge by an alien belief system, the Arian Creed, and only as a result of a decision at the Council of Nicaea in 325 CE to adopt the present creed and declare the alternative a heresy. In many ways the Arian Creed seems considerably easier to accept from a commonsense standpoint than the Nicene. The Arian Creed holds that Jesus was just a man—made, not begotten. Yes, a model of kindness and goodness, but not a god—"just a man." Most devout Catholic schoolteachers take on the Nicene Creed as second nature, and students are expected to know it by heart and recite it on appropriate occasions. Teachers who have reservations about many other features of the Church, such as its stand on birth control, homosexuality, and divorce, will often say, "But the core of Catholicism is that Jesus is both fully divine and fully human"—the basic principle laid out in the creed.

In my observations, only one teacher, Mr. S at Sisters of Struggle and Hope, encouraged high school students to question the creed in the classroom. He asked them to revisit in a nonpartisan way some of the historical criticisms of it. S wants his students to understand the creed historically. As he explains his somewhat unorthodox teaching method:

> Church history is just a series of arguments over the last two thousand years. And the way the church is now is just

because one side of the argument won. And so what I like to do is just try to get us back to that argument. And the kids are amazed that, for instance, when they say the creed every Sunday at church, they're taking a side of an argument that is long dead to them, but they're taking a side still. And what I do [is] I bring in the other side of the argument, and then we talk about it. I mean, the creed is about who is Jesus. And we talk about who is Jesus. Because the other side of the argument, the one that lost, the Arians, they had pretty much just as Christian a position as the Nicene fathers did. Nicaea said that Jesus is both God and man. And the Arians said, "That's a crazy thought," because, taking off, that matter and spirit cannot dwell within the same substance, that Jesus was man but Jesus was not God, not fully God. And what they were trying to do is preserve the holiness of God. And they saw the Nicene people as trying, sort of corrupting the nature of God.

I asked how the students responded.

S: Well I think, on the one hand I think they like it. They like being given the freedom to think for themselves about these matters of religion. Because religion here in this area is hugely ingrained, and I'm grateful that it is. And these are stories that they've been given. And now they're being able to think about it as young adults. I mean it's really treating them as young adults with growing intellects. However, the downside is that I also sort of ruin it for them.

INTERVIEWER: How so?

S: Well, I sort of take the mystery out of it. It's the first time that they're hearing that biblical literature as we have it was also committee documents at certain points. That somebody put the canon together. It's also the first time that they're hearing that the church is also sort of a committee that is sort of manmade. And so there's that, they get so frustrated, so very upset about it, because they sort of, well, it's just such a shock. I mean, it's like tearing them. I think it's part of the adolescent growth process that they want to be taken seriously as adults in their own right, but it's also a very scary thing. So there is that sort of frustration as, like, then they go all over, the pendulum shifts all the way over to the other side. Where they used to take the church so seriously before, and now they can't take it seriously at all. And I hope the pendulum then shifts back to the center.

Mr. S worries a good deal about the effect of his approach on the faith of his students. He believes that what he is doing is theologically sound although pedagogically dangerous, and he continues to try to strike a reasonable balance. He does not want the students to engage in the historical debates for debate's sake alone. Rather, he hopes that they will experience the respectful reflection that he believes, at its best, religion represents. He hopes the debate becomes more than just an intellectual exercise for his students and results in strengthening rather than alienating them from their religion, but the balance is not an easy one to maintain.

While he believes that his students appreciate his open approach, he fears that by taking the mystery out of faith, it may "ruin it for them."

S: We're reading the Bible, and they realize, many of them, most of them for the first time, that there are two creation stories. And it hurts them, and the classic question is why did they lie to me? And it's hard, at this age, to find that gray area and to explain to them that your priests and your parents and your religious formation teachers, they didn't lie to you. They told you the same truth that I'm telling you now, that God created the world. But now we believe you're of an age to read the text and think, okay, yes I know that God created the world. What does this text say that can further inform this? What do these texts, these two different texts, say?

I: So you fear that by opening up the historical argument, you'll puncture their faith?

S: Yeah. I mean, that has been said as much, that while, high school's a strange age. I think it was for me, and I can say it is. Because it's an age in which you want to grow up, in which you want to be treated as an adult with a mind and a body and a spirit all your own. But when you are given freedoms, it's a scary thing as well. And what I want to do in my classroom is give them freedom to think. But that's scary, too, because it sort of takes the mystery away from the Church, that if I present it as a series of arguments, they just look at it as manmade laws, manmade things, easily dismissible.

I: How do you respond to that?

S: What I tried to do in that class is always present it as "These are arguments about truths which we will never see, but truths which we believe on faith." And I try to make sure that they know that religious truth cannot be proven by any other means but by what we call faith.

There are, then, limits to how far he wants his students to go in the conclusions they draw from these historical arguments, and although rehearsing the historical narrative with them would seem to provide openings for alternative ways of understanding the religious mysteries, he does not want them to reject the religious "truth."

And I make sure that they are in agreement with me that we believe that there is some kind of mysterious creation of this world. And that mystery we're going to call God. And we're going to believe in and [have] faith that God created the world. That God gave humanity a special place in it, and that it was an act of beneficent love. And so with that, then we go to the text. But even that's not enough to support the discrepancy in the text.

In S's mind, his efforts to engage the students are not empty exercises in critical thinking. They are connected to his own understanding of the nature of the Christian tradition. He holds that the sacred includes not just the text but also the long line of interpreters engaging one another in a historical discussion that extends across generations, and he wants his students to experience and participate in this discussion. Thus, through reconstructing these debates, he seeks to create a bit of the sacred in his own classroom. He believes that as they become aware of these arguments and began to participate in them, in some way they are participating in the very divine legacy that is true Christianity.

At its best, S believes that reliving the arguments can bring his students in touch with their faith and help to personalize it:

> I did Aquinas, and I just took the five proofs, which I suppose is probably the most famous. And in the past years, it's actually worked. I think I got something of the Scholastic in the classroom. Because I started by asking the question "Where and in what ways have you actually felt God to be truly existent in your life?" And a lot of people said, "I was in nature. I was on a hike with my family." And from that discussion, then, it was pretty easy, then to talk about Aquinas. Because then, you have Aquinas, who is like the thirty people in the classroom, trying to prove in some way that God does in fact exist. So the argument from causality is not some kind of philosophical game we were playing in the classroom, but the argument from causality, then, is "Brenda, does this in fact summarize what you were feeling when you were in the woods that day, and you saw that tree, and you thought that surely there must have been a tree before this tree, and et cetera." And that's the only way that, I mean I guess it goes back to the debate about philosophy, you know. You can have a very technical philosophy, or you can have philosophy which serves the purpose of expressing the truth. And that, you know, that was for me, why, I think, philosophy is a good tool but not a wonderful end.

Pedagogically, however, the balance is not easy to maintain, as S recognizes. Ultimately it is the faith of religion and not the reason of philosophy that sustains belief, and argument can potentially alienate one from faith. Yet argument can also ultimately deepen it, as he tells me:

> God's will is always in a sense inscrutable, but God's will is a little less inscrutable when in community, and when this conversation is going on. So conversation and community bring to a little more self-evidence this mystery that we're all trying to figure out. So it will never be really figured out.

In a sense, the catechism and the Bible and all the texts are meant to be sort of fleeting. But the catechism, the Bible, and all these texts, the creeds are products of community, and the results of conversations that have been going on. So in having this conversation, I wonder if there's a way of just being honest and letting the truth come out a bit more. And I don't know how to put that to a sixteen-year-old.

There are somewhat different issues here, depending on whether it is Aquinas's proofs for the existence of God that one is addressing or whether it is the Nicene Creed. One may continue to believe in God even if convinced that the logic of Aquinas's arguments is flawed. Yet it is difficult to see how one could continue to believe in the divinity of Jesus if one found the Arian Creed to be sound.

The balance between rational argument and faith is a very difficult, perhaps impossible, balance to maintain at the level of the Nicene Creed. Hence it may well be that the student's resistance here, and the teacher's fear of the alienation that the questioning of the creed produces, arise because of the very critical role that adherence to this creed plays. It is likely that questioning, debate, and even discussion cannot go all the way down and must end at this place, with this creed. Mr. S is aware of this when he tells me, with some despair, "Attending to historical argument is just the method, but I think I've started to confuse the method with the actual goal."

Two Competing Conceptions of Rationality

Before looking more closely at Mr. S's concerns, I want to introduce two different and somewhat competing conceptions of rationality, which I will refer to as propositional and pragmatic.

Propositional rationality, as I am using the term here, is often associated with scientific inquiry. It insists that a rational true belief be consistent other true beliefs, that there be convincing evidence for such a belief, and that the belief correspond to a real external state of affairs as determined by publicly verifiable evidence. In contrast, pragmatic rationality holds that a belief is a guide for action, and this means that one must not only reflect upon existing commitments but also allow these existing commitments to be a factor in measuring the worth of any given reflective act. To return to Nussbaum for a moment and the Socratic task that she asks us to use as a model for education: in accepting his own fate—the death sentence dictated by the Athenian court—Socrates decided to reject the "rational" arguments of his friends, not because they were wrong but because to act on them would be to contradict his life's commitment as a citizen of Athens, a commitment developed from his dependence on Athens for his physical well-being and his moral development.

A commitment to pluralism is aided by a commitment at the educational level to pragmatic rationality where reasonable reflection connects to one's preformed and ongoing commitments. Given this commitment, Mr. S's concern is well justified, not because pragmatic rationality is superior to propositional rationality but because the rational thing to do now has something to do with who I am and what kinds of beliefs I have made as I have lived a life. And it does not mean, as perhaps he feared, that people committed to a certain set of religious beliefs must now refuse to hold those beliefs if impartial arguments cannot show definitively that they reflect the real state of affairs. Rather, to adopt pluralism as a desirable way of organizing society is to allow for an additional and more generous standard of rationality as a governor of the systems of educational and political life.

Pragmatic rationality allows that a belief is "warranted"[3] if it does not interfere with other beliefs that we hold and if those beliefs enable us to live productive, satisfying lives. Noninterference, as I am using the term, means that two beliefs may either cohere, and thus support one another, or function separately as long as they do not inhibit action. Pragmatic rationality allows that beliefs may live together in the same tent even if they are not entailed by one another or even if they do not support one another. There is here a live and let live attitude for many of our beliefs, and, indeed, people may hold contradictory beliefs. A parent believes in racial equality but also believes that children deserve an education free of racial tension. These beliefs may well exist side by side without tension as long as the person does not have to choose a school for her own child. If she does have to choose, then they will conflict if a choice *must* be made between a mixed, racially tense school in one neighborhood and a racially homogeneous but harmonious school in another.

If they do get in each other's way, then "inconsistency" becomes a problem leading to inconclusive action or paralysis. When this happens, then evidence and reasons are called for to resolve conflict between beliefs and to re-enable action. For example, if we believe that water boils at 100 degrees centigrade, but we heat it to that temperature and it does not boil, then we need to alter belief, perhaps by holding that the boiling point can change, depending on atmospheric pressure and whether you heat it while above or below sea level.[4] This view of rationality is somewhat elastic given that the inconsistent beliefs may, sometime in the future, handicap action; it can be prudent to conduct test runs on dormant beliefs to expunge the potential conflicts. Nevertheless, I could believe firmly that water boils at 100 degrees centigrade while also believing that the boiling point of fluids is related to atmospheric pressure, and I could hold these two beliefs simultaneously as long as they did not hamper my action. Critical reflection in this view need not just be a response to an immediate impasse, but it has a preventative function as well.

The contrast between these two modes of rationality is significant. The ideal for propositional rationality is purification. The procedure is to purge the mind of as many inconsistencies as possible and to hold on to only those beliefs that can be supported by sufficient evidence. The ideal for pragmatic rationality is reasonable peaceful coexistence of beliefs for the purpose of engagement, community, and action. Like two neighbors with different lifestyles, inconsistencies may live side by side quite peacefully as long as the noise level and messiness of one are inaudible, invisible, and harmless to the other, and as long as the other's compulsiveness to mow the lawn and trim the hedges does not involve trespassing on the neighbor's property line.

The conception of rationality that one adopts will determine how generous one will be in evaluating religious instruction because there is a core to most religions that extends beyond what those outside the religion will see as propositionally acceptable—a core that is, for the outsider, nonrational. Pluralism requires a conception of rationality that is generous, allowing many conceptions of the good and many systems of belief to gain support. However, it also requires a conception of rationality that is not permissive and that is able to maintain reasonable educational standards.

For the pragmatist, standards of evidence remain important, of course, but a school is judged not only in terms of the beliefs it transmits but also in terms of its developmental possibilities for children, where authenticity, autonomy, and critical reflection are valued as a part of the commitments that are fostered.

Critical Reflection in Religious and Nonreligious Traditions

For the most part children develop their initial conception of good from their parents and other significant adults, but liberalism requires that they not be *destined* to live out this conception and that they have opportunities to reflect upon and revise it. The skills involved in critical reflection, viewed as the capacity for reflecting upon, choosing, and revising one's conception of the good, are viewed as an essential component of autonomy. Without this capacity a child is fated to live a life chosen by other people and by chance alone.

With the increasing importance of schooling in the formation of opportunities and life plans, many educators view critical reflection as an essential aim of education in modern, liberal societies.[5] Schools that fail to help children develop these skills do not meet the standard of adequacy that liberal institutions require. However, when it comes to religious education, there are significant differences within liberal society regarding what to count as autonomy and critical reflection.

In one view the specter of indoctrination looms over the very idea of religious education. Religious "education" and religious indoctrination are one and the same, and faith must always trump reason.[6] Because faith can never be inspected by reason, any form of critical reflective inquiry on religious beliefs is subversive and will be discouraged. While the cloak of reason may be displayed in harmless ways, anything that threatens to expose the weakness of the faith will be filtered out of consideration.[7] Given this view, religious education protects the basic tenets of the faith from evaluation and blunts critical reflective thinking.

In another, more friendly view of religious education, it is argued that critical reflective thinking can only take place within the context of a well-developed tradition, and religious traditions provide solid foundations for reflective critical appraisal.[8] Without a religious foundation children will likely become the victims of the dominant cultural tendencies and will develop few filters to appraise the egocentric commercialism that bombards them every day in this most materialistic of cultures. From this point of view, all moral reflection presupposes a certain standpoint, and the role of religious education is to provide that standpoint. We do not just ask how to be good in general. We ask how to be a good parent, a dutiful employer, and a loyal friend.[9] Here religious education provides the material for addressing these questions as well as for reflecting on different alternatives. Indeed, whether we agree or disagree about a particular answer, religion allows us to keep in mind what is at stake in moral deliberation—the well-being and spiritual health of a community that extends beyond ourselves. In learning to be religious, we also learn to be reflective and to ask, "What would a good person of my conviction do? How can I be a good Hindu, Muslim, Christian, or Jew?"[10]

Analysis

Those who advance an idea of propositional rationality, and the sense that truth claims must be sensible (subject to falsification by evidence)[11] and consistent, would argue that Mr. S's problem is that he is unwilling to take reason far enough so as to encourage his students to submit to its conclusions wherever it may lead them. In seeing argument as the means to an already established goal, he is denying his students their autonomy as rational beings. And, even though there may be some merit to his understanding of religion as a historical dialogue, it is still a dialogue in which the students are expected to come out nodding in agreement to those who have presumably found the one right answer in the official dogma of the Church. Thus Mr. S, according to this view, is caught in a trap of his own making. He wants the students to think critically, but ultimately he wants to decide for them just what the right answer should be. He does not want to reject the Nicene Creed, just to think about it. And, when his exercise threatens to alienate them from their own religious beliefs, however irrational they may be, he loses his nerve and backs off.

I want to argue, against this critic, that Mr. S is right to be concerned and that the view of rationality presented by this imaginary critic is too narrow and constricting, failing to capture the rational character of the students' response to the assault on the Nicene Creed. And, because it fails to capture the way in which the response is rational, it fails to appreciate the dilemma that Mr. S is experiencing. In the cold logic of the critic, halfway to the truth is not enough, and Mr. S's loss of nerve is no justification for not moving all the way. Yet this view has its own absolutism and fails to understand the limits of its own conception of rationality.

Let me begin to defend Mr. S by suggesting that there are considerations that rest outside the "truths" of Catholicism that can help us to understand his hesitation. In other words, we need not be Catholics or religious believers to understand the strain that S feels. Putting aside the fact that S himself has a commitment to the beliefs expressed by the Nicene Creed and feels that it expresses a profound truth, his internal conflict is not between the rational and the irrational, but between two different conceptions of rationality—the propositional and the pragmatic.

From the outside (that is, for non-Christians), Mr. S's discomfort may be justified as pragmatically sound, arising from a fear of the danger that the propositional will replace the pragmatic and that his students, having accepted too constraining a view of truth, will lose an important guide to maturation, even if from the inside it is expressed in other terms—that they will fail to see the "truth" expressed through the Nicene Creed.

Narrowly speaking, a commitment to the "truth" of the Nicene Creed is not a commitment to either a rational or an irrational doctrine. By itself, the Nicene Creed is nonrational. It has to do with faith, commitment, and membership, and not the way in which premises follow conclusions. If it is taken as true in any propositional sense by believers, there is nothing that compels nonbelievers, by the power of the argument alone, to take it the same way. And the same holds in reverse.

Pragmatic rationality would take a lighter view of things. Human beings make investments, they build on capital that others have created, and they should not walk away from this investment lightly, even though walk away they might. Regarding religion, this investment begins at an early age, involves much work, and leads to an enfolding with and by others who have made the same investment and whose payoff depends partly on a shared participation in some of life's most significant experiences. While there may be times when it makes sense to move away from one's own religious commitment, to do so without due consideration of the special meaning a given tradition has in one's life would be pragmatically irrational. From the pragmatist's point of view, the mistake made by the advocates of propositional rationality is to focus exclusively on arguments and not to include in the calculation the work involved in the development of a religious identity and the benefits of the coparticipation that come from it.[12]

The Rationality of Religious Partiality

Prayer, faith, and devotion, not argument, are the foundation of religious communities. Both the words of the prayer and the comportment of those who are praying are expressions of human vulnerability, dependency, and humility. Whether we kneel, bow our heads, prostrate ourselves, or pyramid the fingers of both hands, we are signaling our weakness and frailty. But the way we pray, the words we say, the way we say them, the language in which we utter them, the posture we assume as the words are uttered, and the rules we abide by that tell us how old you can be before you utter them, and who is authorized to say them, are all signs of a person's membership in one particular religious community and not another. Once a person learns to pray, it seems like second nature; but it is also easy to forget the effort that goes into learning how to do so in the accepted and proper way and in thus constructing and reconstructing a religious community.

Learning to Pray

Prayer and the activities associated with it are complicated matters. One Jewish school that I studied hired a prayer master primarily to teach children the correct words and method of prayer. This is understandable, given that the children in the Moses Day School were expected to pray in Hebrew and that biblical Hebrew has its own peculiar features, quite distinct from Modern Hebrew, which is spoken on the streets of Israel. Indeed, when a Jewish child is bar or bat mitzvahed, depending on the portion of the Torah required for that week he or she may be reading for close to an hour.[13] While it is perhaps unusual, even for Jewish schools, to hire one specialist to teach the techniques of prayer, prayer frames the activity of religious schools.[14] It usually begins and ends the day, and frequently each class begins the period with a prayer.

In learning how to do prayer work, students are internalizing communal rhythmic patterns, postures, and practices, thereby establishing a bond with similar prayer workers across space and generations. And in this work, teacher and student reconstruct the community. Even when there is no specialized prayer master to supervise this activity and when a special language is not a requirement, considerable effort is spent on both the teacher and the students' part, and sometimes, as in the episode below, prayer work is an explicit instrument to connect children of different ages and races within a school.

Building a Faith Community

As we walk into the second grade classroom in the Catholic School, the teacher explains to the students that "the eighth graders are going to help you with prayer so that when they go to church, you will know what they are doing." Each second grader is paired with an eighth grader, and the eighth grade teachers explain that if they can get one prayer down today, that would be nice. The students start, and out of the general mumble I can discern phrases from different students. "All mighty God," one second grader says, "forgive me for I have sinned." Another says, "I confessed to almighty God I have sinned." An African American eighth grade girl is working with two white second graders, having them say hosannas. One boy says the prayer in front of the teacher with his eighth grade tutor standing proudly at his side. When the boy successfully completes the prayer, the teacher gives him a high-five.

The eighth grade teacher says to her students, "You might also teach them the symbols we use before prayer and what it means." And then, crossing herself, she says, "The Lord is on my mind, on my lips, and in my heart." A second grade girl says her prayer successfully with her eighth grade tutor by her side, and the eighth grade teacher applauds when she is finished. When the class is about over, the second grade teacher says, "Second graders, what do you say to the eighth graders?" And they respond, "Thank you." Walking away with the eighth graders down the hall, I hear an "I confess . . ." and "The Lord is on . . ." coming from the second grade classroom.

Learning to pray illustrates something important about becoming a Catholic, for both the second graders and the eighth graders. The second graders are learning the mechanics of the faith, how to join in and say their prayers. The eighth graders are learning what it is like to be a senior member of a community responsible for initiating new members into the mechanics of attachment. They express the frustration of adults who have had a hard time instructing the young. When the class is over, for example, one of the eighth graders complains to the teacher that "the kids don't listen to me," a complaint that caring parents and teachers make often. Here in this classroom, then, a group of children (eighth graders) have become, momentarily, a group of responsible adults, and individual second graders are on their way to becoming members of an embracing community.

From the standpoint of propositional rationality, the words said have no significance. From the point of view of pragmatic rationality, they allow us to see beneath the surface to the work involved in becoming a Catholic and the benefits that belonging to an embracing and enduring community provides. From the stumbling of the apprentice to the frustration of their tutors, there is no doubt that hard work is being done here. The pride that apprentice, tutor, and teacher take in the successful performance is an expression of the "we" that is forming and of the intergenerational project that is entailed by the notion of a faith community.

Reflection: Discomfort and Commitment

Reflection is an engagement that brings out familiar but taken-for-granted features of a situation, and thus it is always in some sense self-referential and partial. While I may reflect on the meaning of a passage in a book or a remark of a friend, the object of that reflection is a meaning that I once took for granted but that now appears problematic to me. The passage may seem inconsistent with the meaning I gave to the rest of the book, and I need to now see how it might fit. Do I need to change my understanding of the book, or might I have misread the passage? My friend's warm words seemed inconsistent with her cold stare. Have I done anything to annoy her? Might I have just misread her look?

Reflection has as its object *some* (not all) feature(s) of a self, and as such it is inherently tied to commitment. The root of the term is physical—a glance in a mirror. The noodle on my chin, the smudge on my nose are hidden until I see them reflected. But when I see the smudge, I am not seeing it from my exclusive vantage point. Rather, I see the face with the noodle peering back at me, as another would see it, and with some mild discomfort but not the full disgust that another might feel. I just feel a need to wipe my chin. Nevertheless, even though I do not have exactly the same feelings as my audience, I contain its gaze within my own. I see the noodle on the chin as they would view it—as out of place and in need of removal.

There are some experiences where we may be more content with an imaged audience rather than a real one and where reflection matters little. Since I expect never to sing in public, I perform only for my own pleasure. Yet part of that pleasure comes as I hear myself in a way that I would want an audience to hear me. Not in how they would, in fact, hear me—which is, in fact, the reason I do not plan to sing in public—but in the way I imagine they would hear me if only they could hear me the way I hear myself. For me, the performance and my "hearing" the performance as my imaginary audience would "hear" it provide the pleasure of the experience. I am pleased because I create my own audience and then hear my voice through my image of the way they should hear it. On good days, I am tempted to take a bow. On those rare moments when I actually do *hear* my voice crack, I am disappointed in myself because I understand just how much I have let down my (imagined) audience. At that moment, I can no longer keep the performance in my imagination, and I cannot fully control the way my projected audience hears the performance. A bit of reality has crept into the activity and intruded on my imaginary triumph. My letdown comes from having let down that audience, imaginary though it may be, that serves as the condition of my pleasure. In reality, I know little about public singing, and those few occasions when I have had enough courage to tape my own voice have been occasions to forget. Reflection, in this case, is difficult precisely because it allows me to hear as that audience would truly hear, not as I imagine that they might.

Reflection kills undisciplined imagination and can be risky and painful. It can lead to resignation and defeat. If it were a real audience standing out there, challenging the glory of my creation, I would never again attempt another serenade. It can also lead to paralysis, as when a person tries to second-guess herself all the time, as might have been the situation of Mr. S, when the very foundation of commitment is under inspection in a classroom.

Yet, as Mr. S is so courageously aware, reflection is also a necessary condition for development. Teachers, coaches, directors, and conductors serve as mirrors, refining the image we have of ourselves and reflecting back to us the way they experience our behavior. A youngster keeps swinging and missing the ball. The coach pushes him three inches closer to the plate, and his batting average improves. With a mere push, he now sees the invisible line that separated the end of his bat from the ball. The push opens his eyes to a new way of being in that space that defines the batter's box. Nevertheless the push is not without its discomfort, especially if it seems to come out of nowhere. It feels like an insult, almost an assault, and if done by, say, the catcher on an opposing team, it would be cause for protest.

There are two kinds of pain associated with critical reflection. The first is illustrated by the push and involves a shared understanding of success and failure and a clear-cut consensus about a performance. It is a momentary jolt that leads from failure to success. Another, more difficult example comes when there is no clear-cut consensus about the value of a given performance but where there is a possibility, unperceived by the performer, of a better performance. The youngster has a good batting average but tends to hit mischievous bloopers between second base and center field. In practice, the coach walks up to him, takes hold of the batter's legs, and gently pushes them into a wider stance. Singles turn into doubles, triples, and home runs.

Reflection often requires exaggeration and even distortion. The director deliberately exaggerates the actor's body language, showing her that she is unintentionally communicating fright, not fight. The conductor consciously embellishes the singsong phrasing of the choir, allowing them to hear how miserably banal they sound.

In another context any one of these acts could be taken as a cruel satire of an incompetent performance, but in the teaching context such mimicry should provoke a critical eye within the actor herself and, if successful, should initiate a change in her performance. Unlike perhaps the role of the director or the conductor, the role of the teacher or the coach is to limit the occasions on which they need to be called and to allow the student to internalize the standard required to evaluate and readjust her own performance. In the teaching act, then, reflection is paired with criticism, performance, and growing autonomy. In this context, critical reflection is an act that often requires another but that is also undertaken to achieve a greater level of autonomy and independence from the other.

Critical reflection is the opposite of both narcissistic admiration or self-loathing and the paralysis that comes with both of them. It is undertaken as a way to improve practice by making adjustments while keeping the standpoint of another in mind. The conductor listens to her symphony as the audience would hear it and adjusts the volume and tone accordingly. Yet just as autonomy requires that we free ourselves from the paralyzing effect of self-love, it also requires that we free ourselves from the gaze of the other and develop the standpoint of an independent person. In the final analysis the batter must determine exactly how wide a stance he should have, the actor just how best to express fight, and the conductor how to modulate the string section.

The aim, then, of critical reflection is not just to improve this or that performance but also to open new ways of seeing and engaging a world. Reflective teaching asks for a certain amount of empathy from a student—the student must see or hear as the teacher does—but it is empathy that reaches for a different standpoint in order to better see something about ourselves. When we look into a mirror, we are seeing ourselves in a way that, while not usually available to us, is nevertheless quite a common view from the standpoint of others. I might have trouble seeing the noodle on my beard, but you do not.

Self-reflection has to do with who we are and, within limits, the way in which we choose to engage with the world, allowing us to see who we are at this moment (a knock-kneed batter, a befuddled actor, a scratchy singer, or a careless eater) so that we may also see the potential that remains yet unrealized. The critical element is required not just to see this momentary self but also to understand the way it is situated in a nexus of openings and possibilities. And it takes place as a commentary on our ongoing commitments—to become a better batter, a more consistent actor, a pleasant singer, or a neater eater.

Extended Identities and Critical Reflection

Our identities extend beyond our own skin. Devotion to *our* religion, like loyalty to our nation or affirmation of our ethnicity, is an aspect of an extended identity and could, in some sense,[15] have been otherwise. As noted in the sections above, it takes work to become Lutheran, Jew, or Catholic. To take on a religious identity entails learning to perform certain practices, coming to understand their meaning, and learning to accept certain beliefs as one's own. Yet to engage in critical reflection entails distancing one's self from certain practices and meanings, entertaining doubt about certain beliefs, and being willing to consider evidence and arguments that might counter those beliefs.

Both those who are skeptical that religious education can foster critical reflective thinking and those who believe that it is a condition of such thinking are aware of this dichotomy. The difference is that the first one holds that the test of critical reflection is the capacity to distance oneself from one's own religious commitments, whereas the second assumes that there must be a reasonably fixed platform from which the light of critical reflection can be extended, and that religion must be that platform. Thus, the skeptic will fail to see any critical reflection short of a total examination of the premises of one's own faith community, while those who speak for the faith community will see such "reflection" as destructive nihilism on the route to annihilating the very standards that any meaningful criticism must employ.

The question of the relation between religious instruction and critical reflection is really two questions. First, what are the limits of critical reflection within religious education? And second, given these limits, what possibilities might religious education provide for critical reflection? The answers to these questions vary from one religious school to another, and resistance builds as the inquiry gets closer to what believers take to be the foundation of their faith. Given the work that goes into becoming a believer of a certain kind (a Lutheran, a Jew, a Muslim, or a Catholic), this is perfectly reasonable, and the critic who assumes that the only kind of critical inquiry acceptable is the one that pits my present beliefs against all comers is proposing, at least from the pragmatic point of view, a largely problematic standard. If I am searching for something new, finding my "investment" wanting, I still give the benefit of the doubt to the faith I was raised in. As a Catholic, I might look at Hinduism, Buddhism, Islam, and so on, but my pivotal point will most likely be the religion I know best, Catholicism. Are the rituals of Buddhism as rich as those of Catholicism? Are those of Islam? And is the moral guidance, first of Buddhism, then of Judaism, and then of Islam, as sound as that of Catholicism? When we are born into a religion (or an antireligion), we are born to a point of view, and that becomes our initial guide for making comparisons. The process is rational in the sense that it provides a familiar standpoint from which to make a comparison.

Critical reflection is considerably different from the kind of resistance that some recent educational theorists, following Paul Willis, seem to valorize.[16] Critical reflection may result in resistance, and resistance may result in critical reflection. However, resistance may be blind, and critical reflection may result in a greater rather than a reduced accommodation to the rules and regulations that authority lays down. Yet to encourage critical reflection, even if the object of such reflection is not as deepseated as the Nicene Creed is with Catholicism, is to court risks because the conclusions that any student may arrive at cannot be guaranteed.

Conclusion

I have argued that a pragmatic conception of rationality is appropriate to evaluate the partiality that people show to their own religious traditions and to the education that they receive in those traditions. Once this conception of reasonableness is acknowledged, a rational reconstruction of the religious core becomes possible in terms of the kind of investment people make in the co-construction of a religious identity. From the pragmatic point of siew, allowing this nonrational core the benefit of the doubt may be the right and rational thing to do, even though from a propositional point of view gaps in the logic may be apparent.

In providing a generous reading of different and even conflicting religious educational traditions, pragmatic rationality is consistent with the requirements of liberal pluralism. Yet a generous reading is not the same as a permissive reading or one that holds that liberal pluralism must value all religious education equally. Liberal pluralism also requires that schools promote the frame of mind and understandings needed to sustain and reproduce the basic principles of liberal pluralism. These include the basic requirements of all societies (reasonable security and safety), the basic requirement of liberalism (autonomy and intellectual growth), the basic requirement of pluralism (reasonable respect for difference), and the requirement of democracy (public accountability). Because these are the conditions for the reproduction of liberal pluralism, they must also be the conditions of any state-approved education. In the next chapters I examine these conditions.

16

On Public Support for Religious Schools

Introduction

The issue of public support for religious education, which I examine in this paper, is a part of a larger question about the authority of parents to influence the religious instruction of their children both within and beyond traditional public schools. It involves the question of the limitations, if any, that should be placed on this authority, and whether state refusal to support religious education of the parent's choice may be viewed as an illegitimate denial of parents' rights to guide their children's upbringing.

Public support of religious education can come in different forms, such as direct grants to religious schools for instructional purposes; vouchers which parents may use to support their children in religious as well as private schools; tax credits which will enable parents to deduct tuition to religious schools on their income tax; or changes within public education that would accommodate the religious beliefs of parents. Such changes range from proposals to bring back school-sponsored prayer, to posting some version of the Ten Commandments in the school, to including instruction in religious education in the public schools. In this paper I focus on the question of public support for separate religious schools and will leave the issue of religious instruction within the public schools for another time. The paper is not an attempt to decide once and for all whether public support for separate religious schools has merit, it is rather to orient the arguments for and against such support, and, by implication, to change the character of the debate.

Here I examine two arguments for public support for separate religious schools. The first is that parents who send their children to religious schools are penalized because not only must they pay tuition for their own children, but they must also pay taxes to support public schools. The second is that public schools have a monopoly on education, and this monopoly, and the lack of competition it entails, is the reason for the poor state of education.[1] Moreover,[2] some religious educators argue that this monopoly places fiscal stress on religious schools, forcing them into financial hardship. In order to break the monopoly, parents should be allowed, with the support of public funds, to send their children to any viable school, including religious schools.

From the point of view of some devout parents of limited means and their defenders, this situation presents an intolerable double bind. On the one hand they may be unable to afford the money for parochial school tuition or the time for home schooling while on the other hand they will have limited influence over the education of their children within the public schools. Many feel that this situation is unfair and wish to change it, either by advancing public funds for religious schools or by granting individual parents more authority over the content of their children's education within the public schools.

In this paper I explore the fairness of the present arrangement. I show that it is based on a consensus formed during the 1920s that established a strong conceptual separation between public and private spheres where, for the purposes of education, religion is relegated to the private sphere. I ask whether this conceptual separation is still viable. I explore different proposed reasons for altering this conception of the private-public divide when it comes to supporting religious schools, and show that there are reasons, both from the point of view of religion and from the point of view of the state, to be cautious about a radical change in the present configuration of support. One implication of this argument is that fairness is not a matter of public support for separate religious schools. Fairness depends on the quality of public education available for poor children.

Although I am critical of present justifications for extending public support to religious schools, I want to leave the question open whether, perhaps under somewhat different arrangements, say with more state supervision and greater public control, some religious schools might merit public funds. I do not know the answer to this question, but I believe it is an important question to consider. In the following, however, I show why the present arguments are seriously flawed and would likely do considerable damage to both public and religious education in this country.

The Prevailing Consensus

The foundation of the existing but shaky consensus was forged in the 1920s when the U.S. Supreme Court in *Pierce v. Society of Sisters*[3] overturned an Oregon law that required children to attend public school and prohibited attendance at full-time parochial schools. Although acceptance of the legitimacy of private and parochial schools has been a part of the prevailing consensus ever since *Pierce*, there has been considerable controversy about government support for parochial schools. For much of the 1800s and all of the last century the Court has interpreted the Establishment Clause of the Constitution as prohibiting direct support for instruction in religious or parochial schools. Thus while the courts have allowed children to attend parochial as well as private schools they have been reluctant to provide parents or schools with the enabling means to support instruction in those schools. In effect this has meant either that such schools have been available only to those who can afford to spend their own private wealth on their children's education or else that such schools have had to subsidize the education of poorer children through tuition waivers and scholarships. Parents who send their children to religious schools must also pay taxes in order to contribute to the running of public schools. In return religious schools receive a tax-exempt status that allows tuition costs to be reduced.

There are a number of reasons given for the present consensus. The exit provision can be defended as essential to the exercise of conscience in a free and effective manner. Freedom of conscience must, within the limits allowed by children's interest in their future autonomy, allow parents considerable latitude in the way they educate their children, and a right to remove their children from public, state-supported education and place them in religious schools is consistent with this freedom. *Pierce* allows for this exit and thus accommodates parents who find public school to be too great a burden on a child's religious heritage. However, it provides an incentive in the form of free "tuition" for parents to keep their children in the public school. Those who wish to make public funds available for education in religious schools believe this incentive is wrong.

The consensus also allows a benefit to the public schools. It provides them considerable freedom to pursue a secular curriculum without constant pressure from religious groups who, seeing no alternative to public education, would be more vigorous in pursuing their aims within the public schools.

ARGUMENT AGAINST THE CONSENSUS

Since *Pierce* there have been a few concessions made to children in religious schools, often related to arguments that can show an overriding benefit to the child.[4] While indirect support is an area of considerable litigation and confusion, these concessions have, until recently, stopped short of providing any support for instructional programs. However, recent legislation in the state of Florida, and a recent State Supreme Court decision in Wisconsin (*Jackson v. Benson*) upholding legislation that allowed parents in Milwaukee to receive state vouchers to cover expenses in private and religious schools, have begun to challenge the accommodation that *Pierce* initiated. In support of this erosion, it is argued that the fact that children will be supported to attend public, state schools, but not private or religious ones, inhibits the free exercise of conscience for those without the means to overcome the barrier tuition places in front of them. The response often involves an appeal to the Establishment Clause of the Constitution and to the phrase, reportedly first articulated by Roger Williams and later Jefferson, "the wall of separation" between church and state. The response is intended to indicate the will of the founders to bar public support of religious expression regardless of income level. Nevertheless, although few disputants challenge the Establishment Clause, there is considerable debate over how high the wall of separation need be.

Some of those wishing to lower the wall question whether the Establishment Clause is intended to bar support to any religiously sponsored activity or simply to practices of worship that constitute the core function of religion. In certain Court rulings some government aid has been allowed for certain nonreligious functions performed by religious orders. At various points the Court has allowed public support of busing to religious[5] schools and for purchasing nonreligious textbooks[6] while it has attempted to navigate a rather treacherous distinction between aid to children attending religious schools and aid to the schools themselves or the religious instruction therein.

The Challenge to the "Government Monopoly" over Education

The most vocal challenge to the prevailing consensus arises from those who want to break what they call the "government monopoly" over education and provide funding that would enable parents to send their children to religious schools.[7] This challenge is especially strong among advocates of vouchers, some of whom, in their desire to enhance parental choice—which they believe will raise both efficiency and quality standards[8]—would allow religious schools to constitute one of the options.[9] There is a less vocal challenge coming from the other direction that either would abolish most religious schools as we now know them,[10] or place much stronger restrictions on their operation.[11]

Legal scholars disagree about whether a recent willingness of the Court to support certain activities of religious orders is a change or whether it is really a return to a time before the Grant administration when opposition to public support for religious education began to gain ascendancy, partly as a reaction to Catholic schools by the Protestant mainstream.[12] Before this time it was more common for governments to lend support to religious, and especially to Protestant, oriented public schools. Some scholars[13] argue that the barrier between public and private schools was built largely in response to anti-Catholic sentiment that developed in the wake of the Know-Nothing party and fear of immigration. Thus according to this view the wall of separation has often been one of intolerance, and the more lenient tendencies of recent courts are really a return to a previous relationship between government and religious schools (although the earlier relationship disfavored Catholic schools while advancing Protestant practices). The effect of the argument is to lend credibility to a growing leniency on the part of state and federal courts regarding government aid to religious education.

The Appeal to the Market

Somewhat ironically,[14] these conceptual and historical arguments have been bolstered by the growing market ideology that classifies education as a consumer good best delivered through parents' choice of their children's schools.[15] Market critics of the present system view public schools as a government monopoly and object to the double burden—tuition and taxes—that parents who choose to send their children to private school have to pay.

These critics believe that many of the same financial benefits that are extended to what they call government schools should also be extended to private and religious ones and they are especially concerned that poorer parents who could not otherwise afford tuition be provided with vouchers to send their children to these schools. Some[16] also point out that some democratic countries (e.g., the Netherlands) do support religious schools, suggesting that there is no necessary inconsistency between a religious education and a commitment to democracy. The effect of the argument entails a loosening of the strong conceptual distinction between public and religious education that was implied in *Pierce*.

In addition to aid to religious education, the line between religious and state interest arises in other, related areas. For example, there is the question of how far and under what circumstance state educational interests can intrude on religious educational interests. The courts have had difficulty holding to a consistent line on these cases. In some rulings, such as the famous flag saluting cases,[17] or the arm band rulings[18] during the Vietnam war, the Supreme Court has required the state to back off, asserting either the liberty interests of the parents or the free speech interest of the students as reason for rejecting school-imposed rules and rituals. In other cases, such as *Mozert*[19] where parents wanted their children excused from certain classes because of their religious beliefs, lower courts have found that the larger community's interest in orderly schools is sufficient to override religious objections to school programs, and the ruling has been allowed to stand by the higher court.

Conflicting Conceptions of Public

There are four relevant principles at stake in the question of public support for religious schools and they are not always compatible. First, there is the Establishment Clause of the Constitution that has been interpreted as prohibiting state support for religious (read devotional) instruction. Second, there is the right that parents have to guide their children's education. (This interest is interpreted by critics of the prevailing consensus as entailing a right to enabling means.) Third, there is the free speech interest of the child. Fourth, there is the future liberty interest of the child, or the interest that the child has in his or her own future autonomy and in his or her capacity to choose.[20] While this is not an explicit constitutional principle, it would seem to be a necessary condition for the future exercise of any right.

Admittedly, the potential conflict between these principles is great and the lines are often enormously difficult to draw. For example, if a child does an oral report in a public school on "What Christ Means to Me," is she exerting her first amendment rights of free speech or, because a teacher required an oral report, is the school supporting a specific religious point of view? If schools prohibit such a report are they inhibiting free speech or upholding the separation between church and state? Do the same issues arise if the only Muslim student in a class writes an essay "What Islam Means to Me"? What if a teacher assigns an essay asking students to express and defend their deepest beliefs? Should she add "but not religious beliefs"?

The conception of "the public" contained in the *Pierce* ruling relegates religious education to the private sphere, assuming an inseparable divide between public and private. This divide allows private schools to do things that would likely be disallowed in public schools[21] (and has even been used to uphold the right of parents to send their children to schools that promote racial segregation).[22] However, this freedom comes at a price: the denial of public support for a function that is compelled by the state. Thus in *Pierce* the wall of separation allows private and religious schools a good deal of freedom in determining their individual programs, but does not provide them public means for carrying out a state-mandated function, while the public schools are provided tax dollars for exercising this function but are subject to the constraints of democratic and bureaucratic accountability.

Since *Pierce*, notions of both public and private have been constituted in terms of an exchange between freedom from government control and an (implicit) parental waiver of the *right* of one's child to government support for his or her education.[23] It is important to note that this distinction is not based on anything that public or religious schools do, but on how they are sponsored and to whom they are accountable. If a school were sponsored by and accountable to a religious organization but had exactly the same curriculum as the public schools and a student body and teaching staff that reflected the demographic characteristics of the community at large, it would still be placed on the private side of the wall.

This view of the public is considerably different from that implicit in either the market view of reform or in some nonmarket arguments for support of religious schools. The advocates of educational markets reject the strong conceptual separation between public and private because they largely reject the exchange between freedom and control. Government interest is seen as just a cover for the entrenched interests of teachers and administrators, and tax support for "government" schools alone is seen simply as one way to maintain them as the favored interest. The "so-called public school" is thus simply a name for channeling funds to support these interests over others. If there is a public, according to this view, it does not reside in one institution, but rather in the free decisions that individuals make regarding their different and distinct interests. The real public is the result of agents acting freely in a market in which their interests can be met. In this view private and public are interpenetrable and the government's proper role is to maintain the conditions for meaningful choice. The public is really just the sum of private choices plus whatever mechanisms are required to maintain them.

This conception of public should be distinguished from another emergent version where it arises from the play of different interests that work to balance themselves out creating a tolerable level of stability. Under this view religious expression needs to be allowed, not because of any particular commitment to a market ideology but because, like any other bottled-up expression, it can serve as a source for destabilizing the delicate balance of the political system.[24] Under this Madisonian version the public realm consists of the natural balance of different interests groups, and allowing religious expression is just a way to assure that different viewpoints have the means to be articulated. Given this view, religious schools should be allowed, but the conditions under which they might be supported by public funds would be governed by concerns of stability. If supporting religious schools were to improve political and social stability, then this would be taken as an argument for support. However, there is no intrinsic reason here to *support* religious groups and concerns about promoting irreconcilable factions have often served as an argument against support for religious education.

Problems with the Market View of Education

There are three arguments that are entailed in the market view I want to address. The first is that because public education constitutes a government monopoly on education, public education is inefficient. Because public schools are inefficient monopolies, they serve to disempower consumers and weaken education. Markets are the remedy that monopoly requires, and choice programs that include private and religious schools are the remedy that the monopoly over public education requires. The second argument is that poorer children are disadvantaged by this monopoly, and that this requires state subsidies to poorer parents to send their children to schools of their choice, including religious schools. The third argument is that the state should be neutral concerning the individual's choice between religion and nonreligion. When the state develops incentives that advance nonreligion it violates this neutrality. The remedy is to provide individuals with the means to choose without weighting the incentives on either the side of religion or nonreligion. These three arguments taken together constitute the most prominent case for public support for religious schools.

On the Question of a Government Monopoly over Education

At the foundation of this case is the belief that government schools constitute a monopoly over education and that providing parents with vouchers that could be used for religious schools as well as others introduces healthy competition into the system. Moreover, by allowing those vouchers to be cashed in by *parents*, the problem of support to religious education is overcome. The state then is not supporting religious schools per se, but rather the parents' right to choose.

The appeal of this argument is obvious. If accepted it would allow both the liberty interest of the parent and the interest in maintaining the Establishment Clause to be advanced. However, the argument rests on the view that the government (translate, public school teachers and administrators) represents one interest among many and that public schools as presently defined should not be provided any special advantage. This view is problematic on a number of counts.

First, while it is true that public schools enjoy a certain advantage over religious ones, namely, they do not need to charge tuition, religious schools enjoy a different kind of advantage. They can create an environment that is consistent with the parents' own belief system and can control children's experience in ways that are likely to lead to children's adoption of that system.

It is only because public education enjoys more patrons than do religious schools that the market advocate can credibly conclude that free tuition is a greater advantage than controlling a child's belief system. However, this conclusion is the result of hindsight. If the numbers worked the other way, then it would appear that the religious schools had the advantage, and that public schools were not monopolies at all. In such cases, since religious schools would be chosen because they support the very same beliefs espoused by the parent, a strong argument could be made that they curtail children's future ability to choose among different conceptions of good, thus violating their future liberty interests.[25]

To judge whether an enterprise holds a monopoly by how many customers it has rests on a problematic standard. One could just as soon argue that, given their great ideological advantage, religious schools have not lowered their prices sufficiently to challenge the competition in any serious way. If this view were accepted, then to allow support to religious schools would actually be to provide them with a market advantage. It would provide them with the benefit of free tuition, compatibility with parent's values, however broad or narrow, and maximum control over their student's belief system. If we stay with the market metaphor (and as we will see, it is a metaphor) it would be somewhat like subsidizing drivers who really wanted to drive a Lexus but otherwise would have settled for a Toyota.

Granted, whether this analogy is convincing depends a lot on whether anything significant is at stake in enabling parents to exercise maximum control over a child's experience. However, here market advocates concede a lot when they allow that vouchers should be given for *education*. The classical market does not work that way. In that market people are allowed to shop for the kind of commodity they *feel* they need; not for the kind of commodity that someone else *tells* them they need. Dollars are not earmarked for shoes only. If I want to walk around with holes in my shoes so that I can purchase expensive wine, the market allows me to do so.

Educational marketeers are not challenging compulsory education, they are only challenging its mode of delivery. Certainly, this is appropriate given the complexity of modern society and the likelihood that children could never lead successful lives without schooling. Yet by singling out schooling and making it a special market there is the recognition that there are important educational issues that are not the parents' alone to decide.

Friedman attempts to justify this constrained market by arguing that society has a stake in education because some level of education is required for social stability.[26] Whatever one may think of this argument, however, it is not clear how it justifies public funds to support the educational choices of individual parents. Nor is it clear that support for education into separate and exclusive systems of devotion would go far in advancing stability. What it does do, however, is reinforce the view that more is at stake in education than serving the interests that parents have in reproducing their own values.

An Inadequate Conception of Public

Once this recognition is granted, then the narrow conception of public emerging from market choices alone must be seen as insufficient. The idea of *public* now also includes those who hold that education should be marked off as a special and compulsory market segment, and this group is wider than those who happen to be consumers in that segment. This public will only be satisfied if religious schools can be accountable for those functions for which education was made compulsory. One of those factors will involve the renewal of a critical-minded public. This requires, both on the part of the existing and the emerging publics, an understanding of the social and political conditions a democratic society needs for its own renewal. And it requires citizens who are able to advance interests that extend beyond their local group. Once this conception of the public is understood, then the thin public advanced by the market view will be seen as inadequate, because it need not attend to this extended interest.

The private choices of parents alone acting on behalf of their individual child is not sufficient to satisfy the educational conditions that renewal requires. It is important, of course, that parents serve to advocate on their child's behalf, but parents are not responsible to the larger democratic constituency. This fact alone renders the very concept of a "government monopoly" misleading because it fails to address the character of accountability. Public schools are engaged in shaping and reshaping the citizen base of the nation.[27] They are responsible in a way that parents are not in passing on the basic outlooks, values, and skills required to function in a self-forming democratic community, and democracy requires that the agents of this reproduction ultimately be accountable to a representative citizen body.

Granted, many religious schools do a good job in developing these values[28] and some public schools do a less than adequate one. However, performance is only part of the issue. Accountability is the other part. To speak of a government monopoly over schools is like speaking of a government monopoly over Congress. It makes little sense as long as the accountability to the larger public is adequate. If it is not adequate, the solution is not just to hand funds to private parties to make our laws or to run our schools. It is to improve the level of accountability.

It is also significant in this country that different schools have different local flavors and that districts compete for teachers and administrators. Granted, there are unifying pressures across districts. However, many of these come from the private sector such as textbook manufacturers, or from business and federal government initiatives that would likely be (or, as with desegregation, gender and disability issues, arguably should be) felt in most religious schools. To speak of schools as a government monopoly also fails to acknowledge the relative autonomy that teachers have once they close their door and begin to teach.[29]

There are many political and sociological reasons to allow parents to opt out of the obligation to send children to a public school, the most important being the recognition of the right of conscience and the possibility of the tyranny of the majority over a minority. This right also allows that private groups may help to provide enabling means to do so, but it does not require other citizens to support an education that is inconsistent with their best understanding of the vocational, political, and intellectual requirements for future citizens, and that is not accountable to their elected officials.

Parents who send their children to free public schools may be taking advantage of an incentive, but they need not be seen as enjoying a privilege. Rather they are engaging in one of the critical responsibilities of a democracy, providing one's children with the intellectual resources to see beyond the horizons set by immediate family, community, and religious circumstances and to take on the attachments and concerns of the larger national community. Often a good education puts some parental values and many parental prejudices at risk. Religious schools may develop these attachments as well. However, they are not obliged to do so and hence need not be negatively evaluated when they fail to do so. Public schools should be evaluated in these terms.

True, one of the marks of tyranny is the attempt by the larger community to force those parents whose conscience leads them in other directions to send their children to a public school. Yet those who leave public schools should not think that they do so without cost to anyone else. Parents who send their children to religious schools take advantage of the lower tuition that a tax-exempt status allows. And, while some argue that the state should be able to aid nonreligious church activities, the argument is just as well turned around to argue that governments need not waive property taxes on nondevotional religious sites such as school buildings because to do so adds to the burden of other taxpayers. Viewed in this way the privilege is not to those who send their children to participate in the larger citizen-making community but rather to those who are given an extra tax incentive to take advantage of their right to exit the public schools and place their children in private or religious schools where they need not participate in the larger citizen-shaping consensus. The benefit is also to other believers who provide support for such schools at a discount due to tax advantages they receive. Thus their charitable dollar goes further because other citizens are willing to provide such a discount. The force of this argument is even greater in those cases in which parents are given tax breaks for avoiding the consensus-forming process and sending their children to private or religious schools.[30]

While a liberal society must make room for parents who, for reasons of conscience, do wish to remove their children from the citizen-making consensus of the public school, it must also try to assure that extraneous incentives do not overwhelm those parents otherwise inclined to send children to public schools. These incentives may be negative ones such as drugs and violence, or they may be the positive ones that arise when the resources of private schools and public tax policies combine to enable the opportunities private schools provide to far outstrip those available through public ones.

Proponents of vouchers to religious schools recently have made much of the fact that wealthier parents enjoy the right of exit within the system because they are able to move from a less to a more desirable school system. They thus believe that this is an argument for enabling poorer parents to have the same right and also to be able to exercise that right through both private and religious schools. However, the fact that wealthy parents can choose to move to another district is not an argument for enabling others to opt out of the citizen-making consensus formation. Rather it is either an argument for compensatory taxes to raise the quality of the less desirable districts or it is an argument for decoupling residence and school district.[31] These would have the same desirable effect, to reduce incentives that are not born of conscience for parents to remove their children from the citizen-making consensus of the public schools.

On the Question of a Citizen-Forming Public

Of course the above argument is irrelevant if either the market or the Madisonian views, taken in their extreme forms, are correct. Under the market view, the public does not enter into anything like a citizen-forming consensus. Rather, parents act as consumers and, out of the sum of their choices, new citizens emerge. Under the Madisonian alternative, narrowly construed, there are simply perspectives that need to be expressed, but there are no special insights or skills that are unique to citizenship, and thus there is no privileged perspective that needs to be stamped as that of a citizen. Given this equality of perspective, there is no reason to privilege one kind of school over another. Indeed, some will argue that it is dangerous to act as if there were such a perspective for it is precisely this assumption that lead to the anti-parochial school movement that had to be corrected by *Pierce*.

The problem with this view is that it is inconsistent with the very idea of democracy in which citizenship is actually an office, one that participates in the selection of leaders, and that requires the skills needed to evaluate those who govern. These skills are many, but at their foundation is a willingness to critically reflect on different kinds of authority, religious, intellectual, and governing, from a perspective that includes the good of the society at large. Part of this good includes the idea that other factions must also be allowed to flourish as well as one's own. This is a good that public education must be responsible for teaching. It is also a good that private and religious schools may *choose* to teach as well, but unlike public schools, the decision is theirs to make.

On Religious Schools and Citizenship Education

To suggest that there are outlooks, skills, and concepts that democracy does and must privilege is not to say that public schools, as they presently are constituted, are the only educational institutions that do so. Nor is it to say that such schools always do so successfully. It is simply to suggest that there is a system of accountability in place that, when working correctly, enables public inspection and evaluation of the process through which these skills and outlooks are developed. Certainly, these skills and outlooks are not the only important things that children learn in school. And indeed, some religious schools may do a better job in teaching solidarity and certain neglected virtues, such as selflessness; some religious schools may even do a better job than some public schools in teaching the virtues and skills of citizenship. It is simply to say that public schools must remain accountable to a body that is constituted as citizens rather than as congregations.

Conclusion: How High the Wall?

The question that needs to be asked about public support for religious schools is whether the wall of separation between church and state education needs to be as high as was implied by *Pierce*, or whether there are reasons to lower it. The answer depends on understanding that public education has a special function in American society in giving shape to a public consensus about the character of the future citizenry. Granted, the consensus is always fluid and never so precise that it can be summed up by a list of traits that we all agree on. Rather public schools provide the arena in which present citizens can carry on a discussion about the way in which a future citizenry should be shaped.

The arena may highlight different needs at one time or another as the shape of the consensus is altered. Nevertheless, the fact that public schools are available means that education is a matter that concerns us all. A metaphor like "government monopoly,"[32] a metaphor inappropriately taken from commerce and applied to education, takes charge of our thinking and the critical role of public education in maintaining democratic forms of life is rendered invisible. To better understand how education can serve democracy is to challenge metaphors that reduce democracy to consumer choice or interest-group politics. This understanding allows us to better orient ourselves with regard to the current dispute and to place the burden back where it belongs, on the actual performance of public schools with regard to democratic understandings and on the accountability of those religious schools that might wish public funding for maintaining democratic understandings. Once we have oriented ourselves we may decide that the wall must be maintained as it is, or that it is too high or too low, but we will do so keeping in mind the need to maintain a public consensus-forming process regarding the character of citizenship education.

There is, of course, a monopoly that matters educationally and that is the monopoly that a set of ideas has over a child's choices. Imagine that for one brief moment a preschool child is able to glimpse all of the values and beliefs that exist as reasonable alternatives to those of his or her parents and that she might be exposed to during her education. Then, imagine as soon as her parents select a school to match their values that vision disappears. However, just before it vanishes from view the child realizes that as soon as the choice is made all other possibilities will be erased from memory. From the point of view of the child if his or her parents choose a school aiming to reproduce their own values by limiting her exposure to others, then the school together with the child's parents holds a monopoly on the process that will shape that child's world view. Whether it be a public, a religious, or a private school, this is the kind of monopoly we should be concerned about.

Acknowledgments

Appreciation to King Alexander, Nick Burbules, Jason Odeshoo, Larry Parker, Alan Phillips, Tyll van Geel, and Maria Seferian for reading earlier versions of this work.

17

Reconciling Liberalism and Pluralism in Religious Education

There is an implicit tension between two important sets of democratic values, i.e., liberalism and pluralism. This tension is manifested in certain forms of religious education. Liberalism supports values such as autonomy, freedom of speech, and association. Pluralism is an aspect of freedom of association and is committed to enabling the flourishing of many different kinds of communities, religious, cultural, political, and so on. However, not all religious communities are committed to the values of liberalism. Some reject autonomy; others reject equality; and some reject both. For example, prior to The Second Vatican council many liberals were suspicious of Catholicism because they believed that it represented anti-democratic values, and given the views of Pius IX (1846–1878) the longest-reigning Pope in history and an avowed foe of democracy, liberals were justified in this belief. Of course this suspicion was often returned as The Church hierarchy rejected liberalism, associating it with moral relativism, and atheism.

My professional interest in religious education arose as part of my central concern with education and democracy. I believe that democracy has two educational requirements. First a respect for pluralism, and for the rights of parents to educate children into their own religion, and second a commitment to reproduce liberal values, and especially a capacity for and a respect of autonomy. These two requirements need not always be consistent with one another, and historically they often come into conflict. A problem arises, for example, when we begin to *force* parents to educate children for autonomy, but problems also arise if we assume that parents have absolute educational authority over their children—as if children were their property. This issue has come to a head in a number of legal cases and the courts have not always been clear or consistent in deciding them.

When I wrote *For Goodness Sake: Religious Schools and Education for Democratic Citizenry* (2006)[1] the country had been in the midst of a religious revival and many conservative commentators were calling for a renewal of religious education in the public schools, claiming that religion, and especially Christianity, was the foundation of American society. I was and am skeptical of this claim for a number of reasons. First, it neglects the Enlightenment and Deist heritage of the country; second, it marginalized other religions, including non-believers; and third, it should not matter in some deep sense whether the Founders were religious or not.

I did not feel any more comfortable when the claim was broadened to include the Judaic tradition as well as the Christian one, or even all "Abrahamic" religions. This expanded claim seemed wrong in different ways. First, the religious traditions are not the same. Second, there is often in such a claim the implicit assumption that Judaism is the stem of which Christianity is the flower, or Judaism was preparatory for Christianity. Third, it seemed almost as exclusionary as the first claim. And finally it seemed no less false than the first.

Nevertheless, at its base the claim involved an empirical question. Was there something different about a religious morality than a secular liberal morality? Or, to put it concretely: Is the teacher who responds to a bully with "How would you like it if I did that to you?" doing anything different than the teacher who asks, "what would Jesus (or Mohammed of God) think?" I spent five years trying to answer this question and in the process observed religious classrooms and interviewed religious teachers. The result was the book *For Goodness Sake*, and the answer was a qualified yes it can make a difference by providing students with a heightened awareness of their responsibility to an intergenerational community. Sometimes this is restricted to the members of their own religion, and to the norms it promulgates, but often the community is larger, as for example in the case of Catholic school teachers who taught lessons on the ways in which gay people are oppressed in American society.

The other important lesson is that it is a mistake to essentialize religion by freezing it in time. As a boy I used to walk past the headquarters of Father Feeney in Cambridge, Massachusetts on my way to work in my father's store. Feeney was a renowned anti-Semite. While he was eventually excommunicated, his views on Jews reflected those expressed in the Baltimore Catechism that taught the Jews were Christ killers. It also taught that Mohammed was a murderer and a thief and that Protestants were apostates who, unless they converted, would be denied entrance into heaven. However, religious institutions, like all other human products, respond to their environment and evolve. The last time I passed by it, Father Feeney's old headquarters in Cambridge was occupied by a coffee shop.

Subsequent to Vatican II the Church adopted a much more ecumenical stance, apologized for its past anti-Semitism, and rewrote its catechism expressing genuine respect for other religions. Indeed, the diversity among the Catholic schools that I studied was noticeable. There was a feminist teacher who taught the girls to be skeptical of the patriarchy of the Church and who viewed it as a usurpation of the Church's original mission. There was a Priest who encouraged the students to join a boycott to object to the employment and environmental policies of a multi-national company; there were surprises in other schools as well. For example, a Jewish school prominently displayed a picture of *Martin Luther* King in its entrance hall. There were also schools that were quite conventional. In some Catholic schools students were allowed to debate alternatives to abortion, but not abortion itself. In some Protestant ones creationism was taught as the true account of human development and evolution was depicted as false and students were taught that women were subordinate to men. In a conservative Jewish school almost everything was open to question, except for the policies of the Israeli government.

Many of these schools taught their children that their own tradition is in some important ways superior to others—according to a Lutheran teacher, Catholics thought they could bribe their way into heaven and Mormons and Moslems belonged to religious cults. According to a teacher in an Islamic school Christians were polytheists, and so on.

As a liberal I find this level of religious chauvinism difficult to accept. But as a pluralist, I find it quite necessary. Religious chauvinism is to be expected as the price that liberalism pays for pluralism. For me the test is less in the substance of the belief, or in the firmness with which it is held. The test is the respect accorded to the rights of other individuals with different convictions to believe what they will. I am less sanguine about schools that teach children to reject evolution, that teach that women are subordinate to men, or that fail to respect the rights of gay and lesbian students. In this case liberalism should properly extract a price from pluralism—respect for the individuality of the child.

Many religious teachers fully understand this and view their vocation in terms of human flourishing. Their task is to teach students how to be human within a certain community—to give and receive love; to experience gratitude, to be with others and to be open to beauty, to feel with others and to allow others to feel with them. As one of my teachers, Erazim Kohak, writing about pain and grief, put it in his beautiful book, *The Embers and the Stars*: "When humans no longer think themselves alone, masters of all they survey, when they discern the humility of their place in the vastness of God's creation, then that creation and its God can share the pain. For the Christian, the Cross symbolizes that reality; confronted with it, the human is not freed of grief, but he is no longer alone to bear it. It is taken up, shared."[2] Jews and Moslems and many non-believers have different ways of symbolizing that reality. It is a mistake to think that in its emphasis on individual rights liberalism negates this experience or renounces the humility that feeds it. Rather, in setting certain ground rules of respect it provides the condition for its fullest expressions.

18

Religious Education in Liberal Democratic Societies

The Question of Accountability and Autonomy

I. Introduction

In this essay I ask what level of accountability a liberal state should expect from sectarian education. I argue that educators in liberal societies are justified in tilting the playing field in favor of liberalism and that they can do this while respecting the rights of those who object to liberal educational practices. I suggest that the liberal policy maker has tools available for mitigating the tension between parents' right to direct their children's education in a non-liberal way and the state's educational obligation to its future citizens. I contend that a child's autonomous development within a tradition is but one consideration for the policy maker. Another is the education required in reproducing a liberal pluralist society across generations.[1]

I allow that autonomy is possible to develop within orthodox, even non-liberal traditions, although I remain unconvinced that this is necessarily an important goal of many orthodox non-liberal traditions. However, I believe that one mistake to avoid in considering this issue is the assumption that autonomy is an all or nothing affair, that we are either autonomous or we are not. Autonomy is in fact a relative matter; we critically choose parts of our lives while we leave many others unexamined and unchallenged. Moreover, the development of autonomy may require different things at different stages of childhood. At the early stages a loving parent who is supported by a close and caring community, whether liberal or not, may go a long way in developing a stable self, and thereby may well serve an important role in the child's development.[2] Later on, however, great degrees of autonomy may well require the intentional development of reflective critical skills.

Granting that individuals may develop some level of autonomy within orthodox traditions, even those in which broad critical thinking is discouraged,[3] there are additional considerations that the liberal educational policy maker must take into account. Educational practices in liberal democracies must also be evaluated by whether they are an appropriate and effective way to reproduce the intersubjective understandings and the institutional practices that are needed to sustain a liberal democratic society in which a plurality of different conceptions of the good will be allowed to flourish. Educators representing the interests of such a society must be concerned not only with the future autonomy of one child, but with producing the kind of social understanding in which future adults have developed the political skills required to maintain autonomy at acceptable levels for all.

There are a few points that need to be kept in mind as the background for this discussion. Most important is that the tension that I discussed above is not a tension between religious and public education per se. Many religious schools are concerned to develop autonomous individuals and to maintain the political structures through which autonomy is nurtured. When these schools fail to develop reasonably autonomous adults, they have, like non-religious liberal schools, failed on their own terms. Moreover, there are all too many public schools that have failed to promote autonomy in an adequate way or to nurture a concern for the kinds of political and cultural institutions through which autonomy may flourish.

Thus the discussion that follows about the different interests of citizens and congregates addresses idea types. It is intended to focus on different forms of accountability, and in some cases on the different interests they entail. In real life these interests often overlap, but not always. Some church schools do not see their mission as the preparation of democratic citizens, and they would not shy away from being called non-democratic. However, for public schools such a label, if it meant that they were failing to provide adequate education in democratic living, is a damning criticism. To be called a public school entails the idea that this is a place where one should learn the skills and attitudes required for living together in a democracy. A public school must aim to reproduce a public. This is not an idea that is entailed by the label "religious school," as such.

One additional preliminary point: liberal democratic countries differ in their treatment of religious education. Some, such as The Netherlands, use public funds to support devotional schools while others, such as the United States, draw a rather strict line between public and religious education, providing funds only for the former.[4] This situation both raises a critical question for all liberal societies and provides constraints for any policy framework that is to be adequate to all liberal democratic societies. The critical questions are: what constraints on religious education and what degree of support are compatible with the main tenets of liberal democracy, and under what conditions might support of different kinds be allowable? The constraint requires that the framework respect the different histories of each country while taking into account any relevant cultural and demographic factors. Once these are in place, the policy framework may be implemented differently in each country, but there should always be a bias toward education that promotes autonomy across generations and social groups. The rest of this essay is an elaboration of this point.

In Section II I discuss some of the potential lines of conflict between religious liberal education and public education. I do this by looking at two different educational roles, that of the citizen and that of the congregant. In Section III I examine, and find wanting, a number of arguments that have been advanced recently in support of public funding for religious schools. While Section III finds no single reason derived from liberal educational theory that is sufficiently compelling to require support of religious schools, it does not find that such support must be rejected. Rather it allows that there may well be local considerations that may tilt the decision for support one way or the other.

The proper conclusion up to this point in the argument is that citizens in liberal democracies are not illiberal if they choose to deny public support to religious schools, and that those who complain about a government monopoly when funds are denied to religious schools are wrong to suggest that such denial is illiberal. I do not argue in this section, however, that such support must be rejected or would necessarily be illiberal, and I do not think that it need be. I treat this question in Section IV where I look at a potentially more fundamental reason for denying such support—that it would be tyrannical to take tax funds from one believer in order to advance the beliefs of another. I show that this is a serious criticism, one that served as part of the motivation for the First Amendment to the United States Constitution. I argue, however, that this issue was not fully settled by the First Amendment and that a creative tension still exists. I allow that a democratic consensus could decide to support religious schools, but that this support should always be conditional. In Sections IV and V, I suggest, by way of example, some of the conditions that need to be satisfied. I argue that any support for religious schools must be predicated on the school advancing individual and social autonomy, and that this would require accountability to public as well as to religious bodies. In Section VI I briefly suggest what such an arrangement might entail for the traditional way in which we conceive of the public/private divide.

For citizens of the United States, there are First Amendment issues involved in these considerations, but because these are specific to one country I address them only briefly, and cannot pretend to speak to the many complex legal issues involved. I do point out one situation in which the religious clauses of the First Amendment—Congress shall make no law respecting an establishment of religion, or prohibiting the free exercise thereof—may well be in conflict with one another. Moreover, in this chapter I do not ask a more fundamental question—whether it is a good idea educationally to provide public support for religious schools. To address this question we would need to examine three additional issues—first, whether religious instruction adds significantly to moral education, as is often claimed; second, whether the various conceptions of the good that are represented by religions would not be better sustained without public support; third, whether support would improve or detract from the quality of non-sectarian public education. Thus, for example, if religion were to add some significant dimension to moral education that other forms of education could not provide, as some religious educators have claimed, then there would be positive reasons for providing support to religious schools. However the task of this chapter is not to address these issues. It is to consider whether, and the conditions under which, liberal states can allow public support for religious instruction without compromising their liberal ideals.

II. Congregants and Citizens

Congregants and the Character of Religious Schools

I define a congregant as a person who belongs to a congregation that collectively advances a set of religious beliefs, adheres to a set of religious practices, and expresses and furthers those beliefs and practices. One reason that congregants set up religious schools is to reproduce their practices, beliefs, or attitudes in subsequent generations.

Thus, one important purpose of many religious schools is to raise children into adults who will have the outlook, points of view, beliefs, and affiliations of one group of congregants rather than another. A religious school may, of course, do other things. It may teach young students to read and write; it may teach vocational skills; it may provide a safe haven to escape a public school thought to be dangerous; it may provide more discipline, or more kindness, than a student could find in a public school, etc. It may isolate children from the influence of peers that their parents disapprove of. Yet none of these functions require a religious school per se, although many congregants may choose to provide them for religious reasons. For many congregations, however, religious schools serve to pass on the beliefs and practices of the faith.[5] Many congregants support religious schools as a way to extend their religious mission, and for many this includes developing children who become religiously committed adults of a certain kind.

CITIZENS

A citizen is an officer in a democracy. Citizens have the obligation to reproduce the objective and subjective conditions of democracy. Citizens reproduce the objective conditions by paying taxes that are used to maintain social stability, support the general welfare, and provide the judicial, military, administrative, electoral, and educational institutions required to maintain the society. Citizenship education should aim to reproduce positive attitudes toward basic liberal democratic principles. Among these principles are: (1) equality—citizens are supposed to be judged on their merit and not on the basis of race, creed, sexual orientation, gender, etc.; (2) freedom—citizens have the right to act on the principles dictated by their own conscience; (3) mutual well-being—citizens have rights to conditions that will enable them to flourish.

Public schools need to be evaluated in part by how well they reproduce the subjective conditions required for the fulfillment of these principles and on how effectively they teach children to value these ideals and practices. They are to provide children with the skills and outlook that are the necessary conditions of individual and collective flourishing. Public schools are accountable, directly or indirectly, to a political body that is ultimately elected by the citizenry. When schools fail to perform these basic functions, then this body is expected to take note and to institute corrective measures.

III. Four Fallacies

In this section I test the claims in support of public funds for religious education by examining four arguments that are used by congregants to advance state support to religious schools, and I show the fallacies that they entail. In the following section I explore the basic principles that are at stake in this issue and expose more adequate considerations.

THE FALLACY OF THE MINIMUM

A number of countries that provide state support to religious schools also have a national curriculum, thus assuring that certain topics are covered by each school. This is the case, for example, in The Netherlands and, now, in Great Britain. Advocates of state support for religious education will sometimes claim that the national curriculum together with an adequate state testing policy is sufficient to meet the requirements of the citizenry that students learn the skills required by the society. Moreover, it is argued that since religious schools are providing the rest of us with a service by teaching reading, writing, etc., that the state should provide funds to support this education.

However, for many citizens it is not the just the minimum that is a problem for state supported religious schools. A minimum speaks to the issue of accreditation, *not* state support. The issue that is relevant for state support is not minimal. It is the meaning that is attached to and goes beyond the minimum that is of concern. A fundamentalist school, for example, may prefer not to teach about Darwinian evolution, but if there is a state standard that requires Darwin be taught, then it must do so. However, the national standard does not state the context in which instruction about Darwin is imbedded. While many religious schools may make a strong effort to meet the spirit as well as the letter of the law, fundamentalist schools often drill their students on the most effective creationists' response to scientific evolution, with the purpose of inoculating students from evidence supporting evolution.

The problem is not that students cannot answer questions about evolution correctly if they are asked to do so on a test. The problem is that they have been taught to assume that the answers that evolution gives to the question of species development are wrong and that those provided by creationism are right. The students are not scientifically illiterate, but they are scientifically misinformed.[6] The citizenry should be concerned that the school has taught as true and scientific a belief that scientific evidence and the scientific consensus *does not support*.[7]

THE FALLACY OF PUBLIC SCHOOL TYRANNY

Congregants argue that it is unjust to single out religious schools for exclusion because it is as unfair to favor non-religion as it is to favor religion, and when it comes to issues of belief, we are all congregants—creationist and "secular humanist" alike. Schools that teach certain doctrines of science as if they were the truth without providing the religious alternative, if supported exclusively by public funds, are being favored. This is the force of the charge that schools are the "Churches of Secular Humanism." However, this defense rests on confusion between the non-religious and the anti-religious.

The confusion allows some critics of the present arrangement to conclude that to force religious parents to pay taxes to support public schools is a form of tyranny. If the claim that schools teach the "religion" of secular humanism were accurate, then the schools, according to this argument, would be teaching the doctrines of one religion over those of others and, at least in the United States, would be in violation of the Establishment Clause. Nord, for example, uses such an argument to support his claim that public schools are hostile to religion and to conclude that, in order to mitigate this hostility, creationist "science" should be taught alongside of evolution.[8]

The charge of public school tyranny is inadequate in at least two counts. First, public schools are (or should be) accountable to all citizens, and their programs are (or should be) open to inspection, challenge, and debate through the political process. In the end a particular parent may well object to the conduct of the schools, but there are avenues for collective citizen change. Second, public schools do not teach the doctrines of Secular Humanism. They teach, or should teach, biology, chemistry, etc. Secular Humanists believe that these subjects leave little, if any room, for the supernatural. Others, however, believe the complexity and order revealed by such subjects are a sign of divine intervention.[9] The fact that public schools may be silent about such issues is neither an endorsement of a secular humanistic nor of a theistic understanding of nature. It is teaching students what scientists understand about the natural world and how they go about gaining such an understanding—through the methods of science.

To defend the public school against a blanket charge of tyranny should not be confused with the acts of individual teachers or administrators, which may in fact be inadequate, incompetent, unprofessional, or tyrannical. If a teacher belittles a child's belief, whether that belief be based in religion or not, it is a form of professional tyranny and should be seen as unprofessional. Yet public school teachers can also misuse their positions to advance a religious tradition, such as when Christian teachers join with Christian students to meet before school to pray around the flag post, signaling a commitment that non-Christians often find offensive and unwelcoming.

The blanket charge of public school tyranny, however, is not addressed to individual violations of professional responsibility. The charge is that public education as an institution serves to discourage or belittle religious belief. The only valid basis on which to judge this charge is in terms of policies that affect student rights within state supported schools, and which impact on their ability to express their beliefs, religious or otherwise. Students should be allowed, as the US Supreme Court has noted, to protest government policies[10] or to absent themselves for religious reasons from patriotic exercises.[11]

It may be debated whether or not these decisions are sufficient. Some may object to having any patriotic displays in schools, while others might believe that parents should have more authority to remove their children from classes that they find religiously offensive. Granted there have been Court decisions that some congregants object to because they believe that they create an environment that is hostile to religion. These include prohibiting a football team from praying together publicly before a game or not allowing a valedictorian to invoke Jesus as his personal savior. Those who oppose these decisions argue that they serve to silence religion and to create a hostile environment.[12] Yet these are decisions that other congregants agree with, and the practices are banned not out of hostility to religion as such, but because they are perceived as using a school platform to advance a particular set of religious beliefs.

The Fallacy of the Exclusive Stakeholder

In the United States the idea of vouchers to private and religious schools has been advanced on the grounds that public funds are being provided to support parental choice, not religious schools. Should the parents choose religious schools, then the support is only indirect and unintentional. One of the reasonable concerns about an argument that provides parents with the ultimate authority over their children's schooling is that it may marginalize the democratizing mission of publicly supported education. In other words, it leaves to parents the decision whether or not to advance the inter-subjective understandings and the institutional practices needed to sustain a liberal democratic society. Yet if public funds are to be used to support education, there is an implicit understanding that other citizens, and not just the child's parents, need to have a stake in that education. Moreover, these citizens do not have a stake in education in general, but in advancing specific kinds of education and in discouraging other kinds of education.

In a liberal society the public has a stake in advancing education in which students learn the basic norms of the society, including the norms that call for respecting people who differ from themselves. Parents with strong religious commitments may or may not share such an interest, and the basic principles of liberal society require that their own beliefs and attitudes must be respected. It does not, however, require that public support be provided to help them pass these beliefs and attitudes on to their children. This may be construed as an argument to support not just public schools, but also support for private schools, including religious ones, that advance democratic ideas.[13] If private and religious schools were willing to undergo serious monitoring along these lines and to be accountable for the reproduction of democratic practices, as public schools should be, then this implication might well be acceptable. However, as things now stand, there are practical as well as philosophical problems with the state monitoring religious institutions this closely.

Regardless of how the above implication might work out in practice, the need to respect illiberal parents does not entail the requirement that society aid them in transmitting, through publicly supported church education, their illiberal views to their children. Even the question of whether to allow self-supporting schools that promote illiberal values is not just a matter of freedom of conscience. It is also a question of the rights that children have to an education that extends beyond the views of the parents. And certainly whereas freedom of conscience applies to the development and expression of one's own beliefs, it does not apply, except indirectly, to the transmission of those beliefs to one's children in publicly supported institutions. Children have a right to grow up with a reasonable possibility that they will have opportunities to develop beliefs that are different from their parents,[14] and the liberal state does not compel students to attend school—private or public—in order to reproduce the views of their parents.

The question of support for private and religious schools is complicated by a number of factors. Among these is a preference on the part of most religious schools to hire teachers who belong to its faith. This means that public funds are expended on selected hiring practices.[15] This preference is perfectly understandable given the desire to maintain the specific denominational flavor of the school. However, it presents serious problems when public funds are concerned.[16] It should provide considerable hesitation to those who are considering whether or not to extend public funding to religious schools, and it should also lead to considerable hesitation on the part of religious educators who are thinking of requesting such funding. Were religious schools to be publicly funded, then pressure to require open hiring on the basis of academic qualifications would surely materialize.

Frequently those who wish support for religious schools are not happy about the public monitoring that such support entails, and express concern that professional standards limit religious diversity.[17] Yet this begs the question about what to do about illiberal private and religious schools that, should support to some religious schools be advanced, would likely argue that support for one religious school but not another is discriminatory. The answer is that the liberal state has a right to treat religious schools differently on the basis of the quality of their education and the extent to which they serve the needs and requirements of liberal democratic societies. Under this guiding principle, illiberal religious schools should not be supported by state funds.

The larger question is not that of support, but whether there may be other reasons for allowing such schools to exist. Since parents do not have a right to deny their children an autonomy developing education, they do not have a right to send their children exclusively to an autonomy retarding school. Yet the liberal state must allow parents a lot of leeway. Liberalism does not, except under extreme circumstances, allow a government agency to enter a person's home to reconstruct the politically incorrect or autonomy retarding education of their children.[18] This is not because it approves of such teachings, but because it is aware that other rights are also at stake and an overly intrusive state, even one acting in the name of one liberal principle, can threaten other liberal principles, in this instance the right to privacy. However, the school is not just an extension of the home, a mistake that some states make in terms of inadequate monitoring of parents who home-school their own children.[19] The inhibitions on state interference in parent/child relations does not mean that a parent has exclusive rights over a child's educational experience.

Because the commitment of liberalism entails a commitment to the coexistence of many different comprehensive doctrines and ways of life, the liberal state must exercise caution before it interferes with a parent's educational preferences. Schools that advance a preferred way of life must be distinguished from those that teach intolerance for any way of life other than their own. The former must be allowed; the latter should not be. When addressing religious schools a certain amount of chauvinism is to be expected and, as long as the schools are not receiving public funding, should be tolerated. According to some Christians, Jews and Muslims do not get into heaven; according to one fundamentalist teacher, Unitarians allow Hitler into their heaven; according to a Muslim teacher, Christianity is polytheistic; according to some Jews, Jews have a God-given right to Israel.[20] While these claims may seem odd to those who do not share the belief system, they do not, by themselves, constitute a threat to democratic pluralism.

While there are reasons to object to such teachings, they are part of the signature curriculum of some religious institutions, and may even serve to ease the ideological pressure on public schools.[21] Regulation of these institutions is problematic because state regulation of religious teachings is a serious problem for liberal democracies.[22] Hence, a significant burden of proof is placed on the state when it comes to monitoring religious schools, and private religious schools have often been allowed to operate outside of the social consensus.[23] This burden, however, is on the side of tolerance, not support. Whether such teachings should be interfered with is a delicate matter, but it is certainly one that should not be off the agenda of a wider public discussion.

Moreover, intensity of commitment should not be confused with indoctrination. One important test is whether students are provided with the skills required to exit a tradition should they later choose to do so. These skills involve both the academic and vocational education needed to take up work in the larger society and the capacity to evaluate different traditional practices. Policy makers need therefore to distinguish between schools that reflect parents' intensity of commitment from schools that use psychological manipulation, selected skill training, or intimidation to inhibit future adults from considering factors that might lead them to exit the tradition.

However, should such schools function to deny a minimal level of autonomy, to advance significant intolerance, or to retard the development of a reasonable capacity to exit, the presumptive right given to parents should not be sufficient to prevent the closing of the school. A less drastic measure would be to allow the school to remain open during the afternoon or weekend as a supplement to the public schools that the child would be required to attend. As Brighouse, a supporter of choice, notes: "Parents have a fundamental right to have intimate relationships with their children, which are conditional on the protection of certain of the children's interests. Failure to protect those interests amounts to forfeiture of the right, in the same way that failure to obey the laws amounts to a forfeiting of one's right to freedom of association."[24]

THE FALLACY OF RECOGNITION

One argument for religious recognition is an extension of the recent concern about cultural recognition put forth by Taylor, Kymlicka, and others. It addresses the need of the individual to have the collectivity to which he or she belongs appropriately recognized by the larger society. For Taylor, misrecognition or nonrecognition may constitute a real harm to the individual, whereas for Kymlicka it places the individual at a disadvantage when it comes to material and psychological development and flourishing. To recognize a culture is to provide special incentives to maintain or enhance it. For example, choosing as individuals alone, parents in Quebec have a strong incentive to send their children to English speaking schools given the opportunity structure of greater Canada. This incentive is present even if, everything else being equal, they would choose to send the children to French speaking schools. However, the opportunity structure means that everything else is not equal and the collective result of these individual decisions would be to erode the French language and to increase the incentive to choose English schools. Thus, noting the tendency of unchecked individual choice to bring about undesirable results, Taylor provides an argument for developing laws that give French culture a special status in Quebec.[25]

However, the case for providing incentives to promote a belief of a certain kind, such as the case with religious recognition, is much harder to make because it involves an interference with freedom of conscience of those who, not necessarily sharing the belief, are taxed to support it. Moreover, to deny such support is not an infringement of the rights of the believer. Freedom to believe is not conditioned on recognition in the thick sense that Taylor suggests for culture. Rather, it is conditioned on respect for uncoerced choices and requires a safe climate in which people may practice their religion. The state does not fail to give respect if it refuses to support a religious school. It fails to give respect if it does not assure a safe climate in which congregants can practice and express their beliefs and involve their children in them. Granted, this is a minimal conception of respect. It allows beliefs of many kinds to flourish without requiring those who do not believe in a certain way to support those beliefs. This conception of respect is consistent with the rejection of tyranny that underlies the First Amendment of the United States Constitution.

IV. The Problem of Meeting the Requirements of Non-tyranny

There are two features of tyranny that the First Amendment of the United States Constitution rejects.

First, citizens should not be taxed to support congregants or their opponents. This feature is violated under the following condition: if tax funds are provided to:

1. schools that are not accountable to the public for their instructional programs, and where;

2. instruction takes place within a positive or negative religiously charged environment, and;

3. is delivered to children in a way that will likely inhibit the development of the capacity to freely assent to a belief system, and;

4. where it is intended to and will have the likely consequence of enforcing ultimate commitment and controlling devotion by degrading other traditions.

Second, citizens should not control the beliefs of congregants. Parents have rights to freedom of speech and association and, as an extension of these rights, and as a part of the practical conditions of raising children, parents may exercise strong, although not absolute, guidance over the religious beliefs of their children.

Under many circumstances these two aspects of tyranny can be rejected simultaneously. However, there are situations in which support for one places a strong tension on the support for the other, and this is the case with many proposals for public support to religious schools, including various voucher proposals. This conflict can be seen in the problems involved in making sense of a recent Wisconsin Supreme Court ruling[26] upholding legislation that provides vouchers for parents to pay tuition to private and religious schools.

BENSON V. JACKSON AND THE VOUCHER ISSUE

In *Jackson v. Benson*, the Wisconsin State Supreme Court upheld a parental choice program in which state funds were granted to Milwaukee parents to send their children to private, including religious, schools. In doing so, the Court overruled a 2 to 1 opinion of The Wisconsin Court of Appeals against the law. A few restrictions are placed on the schools participating in the program. They have to comply with antidiscrimination provisions as well as with the health and safety codes applicable to public schools in the state. Moreover, children, upon the request of their parents, have a right to opt out of devotional services should they choose to attend a religious school. Prior to the inclusion of religious schools, the participating private schools were required to submit to performance and financial audits of the Superintendent of schools, but this requirement was dropped when the law was amended.[27]

From the Wisconsin Court's point of view the program was constitutional because: (1) Since non-sectarian private schools were also supported, in its eyes, the legislation did not favor religion over non-religion; (2) Since state monitoring was reduced to a minimum, the Court noted that the state was not interfering with the free exercise of religion; (3) Since the law required religious schools to allow any student supported by public funds to be excused from religious activity upon a written request from a parent or guardian, the Court felt that it did not violate the Establishment Clause; (4) Because the aid is restricted on the basis of income, the Court held that its primary intent is not to aid religion, but to help poor children receive a better education. (The program has an income limitation that restricts participation to students whose family income does not exceed 1.75 times the federal poverty level.)

Thus the Court found the law constitutional, arguing that it does not violate the Establishment Clause ("Congress shall make no law respecting an Establishment of religion") and is consistent with the constraints developed by the US Supreme Court—it had a "secular purpose," "will not have the primary effect of advancing religion and will not lead to excessive entanglement between the State and participating sectarian schools." The purpose of the law, the court noted, was not to advance religion, but rather "to provide low-income parents with an opportunity to have their children educated outside of the embattled Milwaukee Public School system." Thus, in the Court's eyes, the state is supporting parental choice and religious schools benefit only as an indirect consequence of that choice.

PUBLIC FUNDS WITHOUT PUBLIC CONTROL

When religious schools were added to the voucher program in 1995, the legislation eliminated the state performance evaluation and the Superintendent's authority to conduct financial or performance evaluation audits. On the traditional interpretation of the First Amendment, and the Free Exercise Clause, the elimination of these requirements enables the state to avoid interference in the activities of religious institutions. The Court cited this as one of the reasons it felt the legislation in its amended form was Constitutional, "the State is not given the authority to impose a 'comprehensive, discriminating, and continuing state surveillance' over the participating sectarian private schools."[28] In other words, the law is constitutional in the eyes of the court because the State of Wisconsin will not be able to monitor how its funds are used with regard to the performance of the children that they are intended to benefit. Yet, given the traditional interpretation of the First Amendment and the balance between non-support/non-interference, this tips the balance to the side of non-interference.

The Wisconsin Court understood correctly that were it to *require* religious schools to be monitored in the way that public schools are, it would be in danger of violating the Free Exercise Clause of the Constitution, the Clause that guarantees the right to worship without government interference. Just as we do not want government agents monitoring our churches, so we should not want them, uninvited, monitoring our children's religious education. However, the Court wrongly assumed that it is possible to disentangle academic instruction from religious instruction. Yet a religious school may have a different set of academic priorities from a public one and academic subjects will often be taught to illustrate religious messages. However, this creates a bind that seems to place the Free Exercise Clause in direct conflict with the Establishment Clause.

On the one hand, if religious schools are not subject to the same monitoring as public ones, then they are enjoying an advantage which is clearly counter to the Establishment Clause and must be corrected. They are allowed to indoctrinate children into discriminatory ideologies and to do so with the use of public funds. On the other hand, if such monitoring is not waived and government agents sit in religious classrooms, or set the standards and evaluate the outcomes, then the Free Exercise Clause is violated. Is there any way to avoid this conundrum? In responding to this question I want to go somewhat beyond the legalistic issues involved in interpreting the US Constitution, and look more deeply at the issue of tyranny that motivated the religion clauses.

V. Conditions for State Support of Religious Schools

I want to suggest that there are four conditions that have a bearing on the question of under what conditions support to religious schools is allowable in liberal democratic societies. They are as follows: (a) Growth in autonomy of the child and the primacy of the educational mission; (b) Political equality; (c) True availability of education to all; (d) System legitimacy. I treat these below.

AUTONOMY AND GROWTH AND THE PRIMACY OF THE EDUCATIONAL MISSION

Tyranny has more than one object. Forcing one person to support activities which are intended to advance the religious beliefs or non-beliefs of another is one of them, and this is especially so in the case of children who have little autonomy in the matter. Socializing children in such a way that they maintain their dependency on their parents or teachers is another. Here children's destinies are manipulated so that they have no other choice but to live the lives that their parents and teachers have laid out for them. The use of this power by parents is one reason why the case for parental rights must be a limited one. Parents may in their own mind have the best interest of the child at heart without an awareness of their own self-serving motivation for defining their child's interest in a certain way, or without an accurate understanding of what constitutes the child's best interest.

Autonomy refers to the developing capacity of a child to choose a life in accordance with her own critically developed conception of the good. Autonomy requires the ability to reflect upon one's own socialization process, and to eventually take greater control over that process. Growth refers to the capacity of a child to incorporate new information and influences into that life as her interaction with her physical and social environment becomes more deliberate and goal directed.

This growth requires adult guidance, but the aim for liberal society is to develop independence of purpose and control. A parent, for the first time, guides her toddler's hands on the computer mouse. The toddler has no idea of the parent's intent, but enjoys the physical contact and lets her hand be guided. After some months the parent can feel her intention being taken over by the child. The parent's hand plays a smaller and smaller role in controlling the mouse and the child's hand takes over more and more of the work. Soon the child goes to the computer by herself, opens up the game alone. Then, after some time has passed, she selects her own games. Later, she uses the computer to communicate with others, and even forgets the original game and the pleasure gained by contact with her parent's hand on hers as they worked to guide the mouse. In this way she becomes free from her earlier dependence on her parent's hand and intentions.

Educating children in a way that intentionally maintains the initial dependency, and reproduces uncritically the parents' goals in the child, is a type of tyranny. It is not necessarily that the child is being forced to do something against her will, as in the case of the reluctant tax-paying citizen. It is rather that the child is being denied the opportunity to develop a will of her own.[29] The citizenry of liberal democracies have a stake in discouraging this kind of tyranny because it has a stake in reproducing the subjective conditions that are essential to its own reproduction as a liberal society.

It is sometimes a judgment call whether schools that foster non-autonomy and non-growth should be allowed control over children's education, a judgment that will depend on weighing the effects of parental educational tyranny against the consequences to the child's development of governmental intervention in the parent-child relationship. However, as the earlier citation of Brighouse notes, a parent's right to educate children is not an absolute one and can be removed when it seriously harms the child.[30]

Categories such as manipulation and best interest are open textured, and standards are not easily or precisely set. It is often in the interest of children, even those whose parents are not particularly wise in the way of understanding their own motivation or their child's interest, that caution be exercised in asserting state control over a parent's authority to educate her child in a specific school. The tragedy of the education of Native American children in state run boarding schools should be sufficient evidence that the government is not necessarily wiser than a parent. However, that was a case in which the primacy of the educational mission was subordinated to a larger social goal of total assimilation, and children were removed from the nurturing home environment and placed in the total institutional environment provided by the state.

Religious schools that refuse to hire people from other religions, or that structure the school so that the viewpoints of other religions are blocked out of consideration, should be understood as schools where the educational mission is not primary. In these cases support is not warranted. However, the issue of whether a religious school of the parent's choice should be *allowed* is quite different from that of whether it should be supported. A condition for supporting religious schools in liberal democratic society is that they not subvert the subjective conditions necessary for reproducing liberal democratic citizens, and that they thus provide the educational requirements for children to grow into reflective autonomous citizens. One of these conditions is that at age appropriate times children are allowed to gain intellectual and emotional distance over the form of life with which they are most familiar, and to understand that there are many reasonable forms of life.

POLITICAL EQUALITY

One of the features of many religious schools is that they provide students with a disposition to favor those who share their devotional orientation over those who do not. The fundamentalist message that atheists and members of other religious faiths will not go to heaven; the Muslim view that Mohammed was the last and the greatest prophet with a more complete version of God's message than the others, including Moses and Jesus; the Jewish belief that Jews are God's chosen people; all are, in one way or another, exclusionary beliefs. The exclusionary effect may be even more penetrating when delivered to young children who have not yet had much contact with members of other faiths, and who do not yet comprehend the metaphorical functions of language.

Because members of the citizenry belong to many different faiths as well as to no faith, they have an interest in mitigating the effect of these exclusionary messages and enhancing the cooperative possibilities of people from different groups in the larger society. This can be done by both religious and non-religious schools. For example, regardless of the religious message, schools can advance a message of political equality in which students learn to separate their self-defined religious standing from their political standing and where they learn that their political voice, even when informed by their faith, should count no more than that of any other citizen. One might teach this in a number of ways in a religious context. In some religions it might be seen as the manifestation of the respect that arises from the moral worth of each individual. In others, it might be understood as one of the implications of self-fallibility arising from original sin. In advancing this distinction, religious educators would need to encourage students to become critically reflective of the doctrinal errors made by past leaders of the faith. For example, Southern Baptist schools might have units on their Church's erroneous defense of slavery and the belated retraction. Mormons, following lessons about their own persecution, could explore the church's failing in refusing black people membership. Catholic Schools could study the behavior of the Church during the Inquisition and the Crusades. And Jewish schools could encourage students to reflect upon the relationship between Jews and Palestinians and the issue of social justice. In all religious schools the distinction between the disposition to favor believers like oneself could be mitigated by appeals to humility and the ever present possibility that anyone, religious leaders included, can be wrong about God's will. Such programs within religious schools could go some way in furthering civic friendship. However, without such mitigating messages there is little to advance the idea of civic friendship across congregations.

Religious schools could acknowledge the humanity of everyone, believers and non-believers alike, and the obligation each of us has to enable others to participate in the determination of our collective and individual futures. Loving one's neighbor as oneself allows self and neighbor to participate together without fear or hatred in mapping their joint futures in a liberal democratic society. As one Talmudic scholar put it: "The sanctity of life is not a function of national origin, religious affiliation, or social status. In the sight of God, the humblest citizen is the equal of the person who occupies the highest office . . . 'Heaven and earth I call to witness, whether it be an Israelite or pagan, man or woman, slave or maidservant, according to the work of every human being doth the Holy Spirit rest upon him.' "[31]

Welcoming Factor

Liberal democratic societies require informed and knowledgeable people able to participate in political discussions, to listen to the point of others, and to defend and amend their own point of view when reason and wider considerations suggest they do so. Liberal democratic societies also need citizens able to participate in the economy, capable of taking advantage of the opportunities it offers, and of defining new opportunities and setting new economic priorities.

Religious schools often provide these services equally as well as, and sometimes better than, do public schools. However, there is more to the economic side of education than the services a school provides for its own students. Citizens in liberal democratic societies need to have the freedom to move from one part of their country to another, and such mobility requires that education be seen as available for their children.

Availability requires not just that a school exist in the new location but that the school is one that a child could attend without discrimination and with a reasonable expectation that she will be accepted. Given a highly mobile population, citizens in liberal societies have to assure that all areas of the country have schools that are able to provide a hospitable atmosphere for children from different backgrounds.

This requirement provides a special problem in some societies for those who wish to support religious schools. One way in which religion is used (or interpreted as being used) is as a welcoming signal for believers in a faith and a hostile signal for non-members. Thus the presence of a publicly supported religious school of only one or two denominations can serve as a signal to those from other denominations that they would have a difficult time in this place.[32]

In societies with highly dense populations, or in those with very limited possibilities for mobility, this may not pose a large problem.

Hence, The Netherlands, a small and densely populated nation, can provide many different kinds of religious schools within a small area. If a student feels unwelcome in one, she may choose to attend another. How well such an approach works depends on the reasonableness of the population and its ability to develop avenues of cooperation across religious faiths.

Larger countries with areas where the population is sparse may have more difficulty with this kind of arrangement. People in liberal societies need to be free to move wherever their situation requires or wherever they might like, and when doing so they need to have assurances that their children have available to them schools that do not discriminate because of race, creed, or color. Moreover, they need to be assured that the available schools will not assault their children's identity by requiring that they remold their lives to conform to a certain image of goodness. Gay students cannot expect to hear that we love the sinner, but hate the sin. Jewish and Muslim students must be allowed to worship without having Jesus thrust upon them in the classroom, and Catholic students should not have to listen to teachings that reject Jesus' divine status or that hold that a belief in Jesus violates the First Commandment.

When a community has only a few public schools, it is important that they signal a welcome to anyone who might have a reason to move into the community, and this is unlikely when schools carry a strong religious message. The fact that such schools may not engender significant protest is not a sufficient reason to support them, since possible protestors may have understood their presence as a message of unwelcome. This may be difficult for some countries that have been dominated by a single religious tradition. Nevertheless, full membership requires that people from many different faiths and non-faiths feel that the entire country, and not just parts of it, belong to them, and this may well require changes in the way religious schools are supported.

Legitimacy, Accountability, and Coherence

One of the critical issues in public support for religious schools does not involve individual rights, but rather the degree of social cohesion and solidarity that a nation requires in order to function. Historically this has been one of the critical reasons that some nations have given priority to one religion or another. They wanted to provide the emerging citizen with the outcome and the loyalties of the settled ones and it was assumed that connecting public schools to a religious agenda was an effective means of doing this. This is one reason why, until the latter part of the twentieth century, many schools in the United States began the day with a prayer to God and a salute to the Flag.

As global populations become increasingly mobile and as religious affiliations within any one nation widens, as questions are raised about the hegemony of the dominant group, the link between national solidarity and religious commitment cannot be taken for granted. Reducing the tie between national loyalty and religious affiliation may promote solidarity more than linking the two. Loyalty can be developed in children to the principle that the liberal state enables everyone to worship as they wish and that they can be assured that another form of belief will never be privileged over their own. This means that any support will be conditional on the promotion of the surplus loyalty required for liberal multireligious societies to continue to function.[33] Under some circumstances this might best be accomplished by providing support to religious schools. In others it might be accomplished by withholding support for them.

If religious schools are to be supported by public funds, however, then they should be accountable to a public body. This would require some changes in the way in which we conceptualize the distinction between the public and the private, and the boundaries between the religious and the non-religious. In the United States, for example, the two clauses of the First Amendment are designed to give maximum freedom to religious bodies in conducting their own affairs and educating children into the faith. However, the price of such freedom has been the absence of government support. If this were to change, and greater support provided, then some groups might well experience a curtailment of freedom as their educational practices would become a matter for public consideration. The problem would be to find ways to accomplish this while still maintaining the uniqueness of different religious orientations.

There are at least four possible ways in which this might be accomplished: (1) Standardized tests to assure that achievement meets minimal standards; (2) Providing funds to support that part of education that is secular, while requiring the religious congregation to support that part that is devotional and sectarian; (3) Require participating schools to include members of the general public on their governing board. This possibility can be interpreted in two ways—the outsiders could be appointed by the congregants or they could be appointed by the citizenry; (4) Providing inspection and accreditation teams drawn from the larger society. These alternatives are not mutually exclusive, but some are preferable to others.

Before exploring these different possibilities, one important qualification needs to be addressed. In the discussion below I am addressing the issue of religious schools that might choose to participate in such a scheme. However, I want to leave open the possibility that some religious schools may not want to adopt the controls that public accountability requires. For example, imagine a school that held that standardized tests fostered unhealthy competition and pitted student against student in a way that was disruptive to the entire community. If such a school wishes to remain self-supporting and to also opt out of state assessment, then the state has a burden to show why it should not do so or to provide less competitive means for assessing student achievement. If, however, the school wishes to be supported by public funds the state could decide that standardized tests are a condition for such support. Given this qualification, I turn to the different ways in which educational accountability of the congregant to the citizenry might develop.

As we have seen, a number of people argue that standardized tests in a few basic subjects are sufficient to evaluate the merits of an individual school, whether public or private. I have already addressed this view in my critique of the minimum. Moreover, while standardized tests have become more common as states exert greater control over schools, they tell us only a very little about the climate of the school and its merits or demerits. To the extent that standardized tests provide some guidance in evaluating the success of a school in preparing students for the world of work, they have a certain usefulness. The burden will be on any individual school that wishes to disregard them to show: (1) either that some other purpose is defensible and that standardized tests hinder this purpose; or (2) that the school has a better way of assessing the qualities that standardized tests claim to measure.

The second possibility, supporting only that part of education within a religious school that has a secular purpose, presents similar problems, for in many devotional schools it is not possible to separate the devotional from the secular because the entire climate of the school is intended to encourage commitment to a certain faith. Hence when children read math books, they read them in a classroom that has a large cross on the wall or in front of a teacher wearing a yarmulke, or with the boys separated from the girls according to Islamic tradition. Lessons in English may concentrate on religious virtues, and social studies may emphasize the importance of certain religious heroes, while much of the taken for granted discourse of the school assumes a certain religious orientation as the following examples from a Catholic school in Ireland indicate:

> I sent my four year old to the local school for one year. Unfortunately, the responsibility lay with me to remove the child from the school during the daily "religion" class, [which she did not want him to attend and from which the law allows removal] This would have meant someone going to school at noon hour every day to take him out . . . And when it came to issues such as trips to Church, which occurred outside of regular religion class, I was not informed.[34]

Religious schools carry with them certain expectations. They form the premises from which other discussions flow. For example: "A priest came into my . . . son's class and stated, 'I presume everybody is going to be confirmed.' At this point some pupils jokingly pointed to my son saying that he wasn't religious. The priest asked him why he was not being confirmed. My son said that he didn't do religion. 'Why not?' asked the priest. 'That's none of your business and I don't wish to answer any more questions.' There was a long and stony silence."[35]

Thiessen, one of the strongest proponents of Christian education, criticizes McLaughlin, a more liberal advocate, for failing to understand that "every part of the curriculum will serve a religious end within a Christian school."[36] The difficult task then is to provide a system of accountability in which the inner workings of the school can maintain its religious character in a way that does not subtly discriminate against those who may, for whatever reason, wish to attend the school, but do not share its religious orientation.

VI. Public and Private Reconsidered

Part of the problem arises because of the way in which we continue to conceptualize public and private as two completely separate spaces with a strong boundary between them. Thus on one side are public schools, supported by public funds, with administrators accountable to an elected body and funding dependent on the will of the electorate. On the other side of the boundary are private schools, many of which are religious, in which the state has only a minimal interest in their activity. Here safety and other minimum regulatory requirements must be met, but beyond that they are free to go their own way. The state neither supports nor encourages them. The need to minimize state intrusion in religious affairs may leave little choice but to allow wide freedom to religious schools.

Where states believe that it is desirable to provide some support to religious schools, they could develop public bodies to which participating religious schools could voluntarily submit themselves for continuous monitoring and on-site inspection. Participating schools might be provided the opportunity to appoint, perhaps on a rotating basis, a reasonable portion of the supervising body, while the rest would be appointed by elected representatives of the citizenry at large. Schools that chose to participate would then be granted a certain degree of state support and it would be understood that the schools are allowed to express their religious identity in non-discriminatory ways. The body might want to provide certain incentives for maintaining a religiously plural teaching staff, but where religious schools are supported, participating schools should be allowed to hire people who will advance a given orientation. However, schools would be required to admit students from other religious and non-religious orientations, and would be required to hire teachers in non-religious courses on the basis of their subject matter competence, allowing that they are not hostile toward the religious orientation of the group. Religious instruction and devotional activities would be supported by the denomination itself.

Schools that did not wish to participate in such a program would be subject to minimum certification requirements, would receive no state support, and would have no representation on the body that supervised state supported schools. They would be allowed to maintain independent status as long as students showed evidence of sufficient factual knowledge and skills to make informed judgments about their lives. The difference between the supported and the non-supported schools would be largely a difference in the burden of proof. To maintain their support religious schools would be expected to demonstrate that they serve to advance democracy and autonomy, and monitoring procedures would be in place to assure that they did so. In order to close down a non-supported school the state would have the burden to show that it actively promotes anti-democratic means.

Glenn suggests that peer review could serve as an adequate accountability measure and I tend to agree with him.[37] However, he is unclear about who should constitute a group of peers and, given his enthusiasm for religious schools, it is likely that he would exclude representatives from outside a denominational group. However, such exclusion should be unacceptable if it would provide public funds without any effective public controls. Another possibility, one that is more promising, would include representatives of other viewpoints—both religious and non-religious—on such review teams.

In my own view such reviews should never be a condition for a school's existence, but it should be a condition for any public support to instructional programs. Schools that do not wish such support should be able to opt out of this inspection process, except where evidence exists that they are violating the law. This should reduce any concerns about violation of the Free Exercise Clause in the United States.

Glenn largely objects to this kind of arrangement, arguing that it leads to compromise and to a reduction in the distinctly religious flavor of the school, and would prefer support with minimum controls. Yet his attempt to ease temptation and to make religious education easy only addresses the autonomy requirements of the school. It does not address the autonomy requirement for the child and fails to address the education required for reproducing the practices and understandings required in liberal pluralistic societies. Religious schools that wish to receive state support should be willing to have their programs monitored by groups that represent the public, and members of those groups must also be appraised of the religious nature of the school.

Conclusion

I have argued in this essay that congregants who wish to pass on their beliefs, practices, and understandings to children through religious schools have a right to do so. However, liberalism provides no inherent right to demand that the state support such schools. The state only has an obligation to assure that there is a safe and secure environment for religious beliefs to be expressed and taught to others. However, to argue that congregants do not have a right to demand public support for religious education is not to say that public support for religious education is inherently undemocratic or that it need be avoided at all costs. A number of liberal democratic states do support religious schools without seeming to compromise their liberal democratic character.

Nevertheless, liberal democratic societies do have a stake in reproducing the intersubjective understandings and practices that will assure their continuation across generations, and should a state find reason to support religious schools, it also has an obligation to monitor those schools in terms of democratic pluralistic values. Non-supported schools should be provided considerably more freedom from state control than ones supported by public funds.

Acknowledgments

Appreciation to Kevin McDonough, Harry Brighouse, Tyll Van Geel, Jason Odeshoo, King Alexander, Larry Parker, Nick Burbules, Meira Levinson, and the students in my seminar on Religious Educational Policy for their comments on earlier drafts.

19

An Assessment of Arguments for Teaching Religion in Public Schools in the United States

Some people believe that to introduce the subject of religion in public schools is unconstitutional and hence they wrongly hold that schools cannot teach Bible or world religion without breaking the law. In fact, the Supreme Court has only ruled unconstitutional devotional religious teaching. The landmark 1963 Supreme Court decision, *Abington v. Schempp*, which deemed devotional reading of the Bible in public schools to be unconstitutional, had already made this quite clear:

"Nothing we have said here indicates that such study of the Bible or of religion, when presented objectively as part of a secular program of education, may not be effected consistently with the First Amendment" (*Abington Township v. Schempp* 374 U.S. 203 at 225, 1963).

Indeed, not only is religion allowed by the Court, as explained in the same decision: "One's education is not complete without a study of comparative religion or the history of religion and its relationship to the advancement of civilization. It certainly may be said that the Bible is worthy of study for its literary and historic qualities" (*Abington Township v. Schempp* 374 U.S. 203 at 225, 1963). Despite the fact that Abington allowed teaching about religion to take place in public schools, controversy continues about the merits of doing so, and indeed even those who agree among themselves that Bible courses should be taught often disagree intensely among themselves about how to teach it (Feinberg and Layton 2014).

Controversy is not a sufficient reason for rejecting an important subject but it does suggest that a more robust discussion of educational aims is needed. To allow the spectra of these conflicts to haunt the present discussion suggests a lack of imagination where both sides assume, one in positive tones, the other in negative, that instruction about religion must inevitably involve indoctrination. The resolution requires an understanding of the unique role that public education should be expected to play in a liberal, democratic society.

Most arguments for introducing religion courses into the public schools fail to consider its unique mission and thus set the stage for the educational, if not the legal, abuse of these courses. Public education is not served by making the schools an adjunct to any church or set of beliefs or non-beliefs. Without a robust discussion about the distinctive role of education decisions will often be directed by the exercise of political power rather than by the educational needs of the students, the demands of the subject matter, and the informed consideration of educators. Nevertheless given these conflicts it is not surprising that many public school educators are gun shy about teaching anything that smacks of religion. Still, America's recent religious revival permeates all aspects of public life and has been especially prominent in debates about the place of religion in public schools. The need for clarity on the place of religion in public education is intensified by recent educational innovations such as charter schools. These schools allow like-minded parents to join together to form a tax-supported school and to hire teachers who reflect their values and commitments.

Five Arguments for Teaching Religion in Public Schools: An Evaluation

There are five common reasons given in favor of teaching religion in public schools. I will call these (1) The Patriotic Argument, (2) The Moral Argument, (3) The Constitutional Argument, (4) The Literacy Argument, and (5) The Academic Argument. These five arguments boil down to the following:

1. *Patriotic Argument*: The United States is a Christian nation, founded on Christian principles and thus to fail to teach religion is to threaten the basic fabric of our country.

An Assessment of Arguments for Teaching Religion | 375

2. *Moral Argument:* The Bible is an important source for character development and hence should be a critical component of moral education.

3. *Constitutional Argument:* The absence of religion in the schools advantages non-belief over belief, creating an anti-religious climate and hence violating the First Amendment of the Constitution.

4. *Religious Literacy Argument:* Students need religion courses to address rampant illiteracy as revealed by the failure of many students to correctly answer the simplest question about the content of the Bible.

5. *Academic Argument:* Courses in religion and, especially the Bible, help students academically by introducing them to many of the references found in great literature, such as Shakespeare.

Some of these arguments are clearly wrong, some because of factual errors and others because of conceptual ones, but all make the mistake of assuming that a reasonable argument for teaching religion is also a reasonable argument for teaching religion in *the public* schools.

Let's look briefly at each of these arguments.

The Patriotic argument is really two sub-arguments. The first sub-argument holds that because the majority of Americans are Christians, this is a Christian country, and concludes that public schools have a responsibility to maintain this identity across generations. The second sub-argument is that because the Founding Fathers were Christian that they intended this to be a Christian nation where the Bible is honored in public institutions like schools.

The problem with the first sub-argument is that while it is true that a majority of Americans come from a Christian background, it is not true that the sum of individual identities always a collective identity make. A thought experiment can test this argument. Imagine that tomorrow the vast majority of Americans were to convert to Islam, or become atheists. This would not automatically make the United States an Islamic or an atheistic country. This is the conceptual error. The problem with the second sub-argument is simply that the American creed—life, liberty and the pursuit of happiness, the moral basis of the country—derives more from the Enlightenment than from the Bible.

The Moral argument holds that the Bible provides role models for character education. Those who use this argument often have in mind the quality of obedience and loyalty: For example, one teacher tells his students:

> God will dwell among them [sc. Israel], give them guidance, give them counsel, give them advice, but it all hinges on their obedience. Obeying Moses, obeying the Ten Commandments, obeying the Leviticus law. . . . In other words, God's telling them, "You do things my way and I've got your back." . . . So there are rewards if they obey, but there is punishment if they disobey—The people are told if they disobey and they have some of this stuff happen—sudden terror, enemies coming up, wild beasts—if the people come back and say, "You know what, we really goofed, we really made a big mistake, our bad," then God would forgive them, and he would remember the covenant, and they would be restored back to the way it was before they disobeyed. So, that is the belief on the part of the Israelites. If we do good, we get good; if we do bad, bad things will happen. If we slip up and do bad, we can come back. There's a way back. (as reported in Feinberg and Layton 2014, 29–30)

The teacher then likens the behavior of the Israelites to that of the students and what befalls them if they disobey school rules.

There are two problems with this argument as exemplified by the above quote. First, obedience—even where forgiveness is one of its features—can serve to magnify vice as well as virtue, and can, in some circumstances, be an inappropriate "virtue" for life in a democratic society.

The second problem is that the argument is actually incomplete and that a more adequate argument would provide an important role for deliberation and debate. In fact the Bible sanctions different types of moral behavior only some of which are appropriate for today, some not. The wanton murder of the Egyptian First born sons by a God who kept "hardening Pharos's heart" or the genocide found in Samuel I, the anti-Jewishness of Paul in the New Testament are moral abominations by today's standards and yet they seem to be condoned by the Bible.

A closer look would suggest that there are other, more promising educational examples for meaningful moral discussion in a democratic society, such as Abraham successfully arguing with God over the fate of Sodom, or the lament of Job who does good, obeys God but is *rewarded* with pain and suffering but still does not despair. Yet many who promote Bible classes in public schools avoid pointing out tensions in what the Bible counts as moral. For example, Ecclesiastes—"the race is not to the swift, nor the battle to the strong, neither yet bread to the wise, nor yet riches to men of understanding, nor yet favour to men of skill; but time and chance happeneth to them all" (*The Holy Scriptures: According to the Masoretic Text*, Philadelphia: The Jewish Publication Society of America, 1917, Ecclesiastes, 11) suggests that obeying God does not automatically trigger favorable consequences.

The problem with the moral argument then is not that it is essentially wrong, but that it is often implemented in a simplistic and distorting way. Instead of mining the Bible for a rich and complex understanding of morality there is a one-dimensional view that the Bible is a clear recipe for *correct* behavior. As one teacher put it in defending his simplistic teaching: it's best not to over-analyze the text." Yet this clearly shortchanges the potential richness of the Bible as a source of reflective character development (as developed in Feinberg and Layton 2014).

The Constitutional argument rightly points to the fact that various interpretations of the First Amendment hold that the Constitution requires that schools must not favor one religion over another or religion over non-religion or, *non-religion over religion*. However, the Constitutional argument goes further and wrongly concludes that to neglect the religious point of view violates the First Amendment by disfavoring religion. Hence the argument continues: when public schools fail to present a religious point of view they are promoting an unconstitutional anti-religious one (Nord 2010).

The problem with this argument is that it wrongly assumes an equivalency between non-religion and anti-religion, and it wrongly assumes too that to not treat a religious point of view is the same as being anti-religious. If one were to accept this argument there would be a number of additional complications. For example, if a school decided to address the Moslem and Christian religions, would that mean that it was anti-Hindu and Anti-Jewish? Or, is the assumption that all religions are essentially the same—an assumption that most religious would reject.

The argument involves a conceptual mistake in its assumption that not treating something in school is the same as being opposed to that thing. This equivalence makes some sense in restricted cases, but only under certain conditions that do not apply in this case. For example, in a homophobic climate, to fail to address gay issues in a school would be rightly seen as supporting a homophobic agenda. Yet this is clearly not the case with religion, and it is especially not the case with Christianity. The social environment in which schools are imbedded is more often than not a religious, if not a Christian one. Religion is not rejected when, say, biology class does not treat creationism. This is a topic for a Sunday school class, not a *public* school science class, and if biology is taught correctly in a public school the teaching should represent the consensus of biologists, not theologians. Besides the fundamental conceptual error, the argument is also problematic because it distorts "religion" and assumes that there is but one religious point of view.

The Religious Literacy argument claims that Americans students do not know basic facts about religion, such as what did Moses bring down from the Mountain? Or who gave the Sermon on the Mount? According to this view American students are religious illiterates, and public schools should correct this.

There are two parts to this argument, a factual claim and a moral conclusion about the school's responsibility. Assuming the factual claim is correct—a big assumption given the anecdotal nature of the evidence—the moral issue is problematic. Why, one may ask, given a comprehensive list of complaints about student illiteracy, from psychological illiteracy, to economic illiteracy, to emotional illiteracy, to historical and international illiteracy, to cultural illiteracy, to critical illiteracy and so on, what is so special about religious illiteracy? And why should Bible or religious courses jump in front of all others for inclusion in a crowded public school curriculum? Besides, there is a long tradition in the United States of family and church providing religious education if that is what they want. Why change that now?

The Academic argument holds that knowledge of the Bible can be very helpful in aiding students' understanding of classical texts such as Shakespeare. Hence knowledge of the Bible will give any student who strives to get into a good college an advantage.

The problem is not that the argument is false: there are many direct and indirect references to the Bible in Shakespeare, but it is surely an inefficient way of teaching. If students needs to be familiar with a certain

Biblical reference in order to understand a passage in *Hamlet*, the teacher could just tell them about the meaning of the Biblical reference, where it is to be found, and then let the student go on with reading *Hamlet*.

While some of these arguments will work in limited circumstances—for example, some may want to make a case that Biblical illiteracy deserves to be corrected before, say economic or psychological illiteracy, the common mistake is the view that any reasonable case for teaching religion or Bible is an adequate case for teaching Bible or religion courses in *public* schools. In the following I want to address this error in two ways. The first is to suggest the kind of ideal argument that would be adequate, given well-trained teachers and appropriate teaching methods. The second is to sketch a set of minimum requirements that even under less than ideal circumstances need to be in place if these courses are to be considered.

The Liberal Argument for Teaching Religion

The term "liberal" can mean many things and has undergone a number of iterations (e.g., classical, contemporary). However, its basic meaning refers to respect for the individual and for the individual's right to pursue a rich and happy life on his or her own terms. For public education the realization of this right means that public schools have a responsibility to provide their students with the skills, outlook, and perspective required to choose and revise their own conception of the good, both as an individual and as a part of the larger collective (see Brighouse 2000).

From the point of view of liberal theory there are two potential justifications for introducing religion courses into the public schools. The first is that courses about religion might be important for the development of student autonomy and the second is that such courses could help improve the quality of civic participation. The first justification follows from the understanding of autonomy, as the capacity to choose and to revise one's conception of the good, and from the facts that autonomy must not only be respected but also developed. Children must be educated into autonomy.

Education for autonomy requires three things. First, an understanding of the traditions out of which prevalent conceptions of the good arise. Second, an openness to the influence one or more of these traditions has had on one's own development. Third, a developed capacity to recognize and reflect upon one's inherited conception of the good. Educational philosophers have traditionally held that a good education must avoid manipulating students' beliefs and, in so far as possible, must avoid indoctrinating them (see Snook 1972). But this is only a negative injunction, telling schools what they must not do, assuming that autonomy will develop by itself. Schools that aim to *promote* or *facilitate* autonomy need to do more. They must provide the logical skills and the information necessary to assess different conceptions of the good (Brighouse 2000).

Religion *is* an important source of people's conception of the good, and to neglect to teach students about religion is to fail to provide them with the material they need to intelligently revise their own conception of the good. The failure of many public schools to offer courses in religion can be traced to two impulses. First, some religious conservatives hold that religious instruction should be the exclusive domain of the family and second, many progressives fear that religion classes will be used to indoctrinate students. Certainly problems can arise when religion is taught in a public school in such a way as to make it difficult for students to evaluate the conceptions of the good that it offers—when they are in subtle or not so subtle ways indoctrinated and manipulated. However, it need not be taught in this way.

The second liberal argument for teaching religion involves the requirements of a democratic public in the postmodern age. A democratic civic public arises when people from different traditions engage with one another in the construction of meaning and the building of a common future, and, as I have argued elsewhere, it is the unique role of a *public* school to create such a public (Feinberg 2012, 36). At a time when different religions are playing such an important role in civic life, both in the United States and globally, informed public participation requires a greater understanding of the role religion plays in people's lives. As part of their unique mission public schools have a responsibility to provide this understanding.

A public education at its best should be a process where future citizens learn to recognize strangers as inheriting a shared fate and as co-agents in building a common future (Allen 2004). Despite the many difficulties that religion courses present, they could serve important civic ends and contribute to the construction of a democratic civic public where people from different traditions would engage with one another in the construction of meaning and the building of a common future. Although often an arena for sectarian interests, religion courses, taught by well-trained teachers and as a part of the public school humanities curriculum, could serve this civic role, but alas, too often they do not.

Nevertheless, given the importance of religion in both American and international culture, given the many misconceptions perpetrated about certain faith traditions, and given the difficulty that many people have in rationally discussing differences of faith and commitment, while often deeply problematic, these courses have the potential to make a unique and positive contribution to the civic role of public education.

Religion and the Role of the Humanities

The humanities, where religion courses should be firmly situated, serve to awaken students to the significance of interpretive, analytic, and reflective skills. Here students become aware of their own interpretive framework and the way it influences their understanding of texts and practices. Because autonomy must both be respected as well as developed, the proper aim of this awakening for religion courses in public schools is not to change belief, nor to encourage students to believe that all religions are of equal worth (although some students may conclude that they are). Rather, the aim of the humanities from a civic standpoint is to promote civic skills by preparing the ground for engaging different points of view in civically constructive ways (see Wexler 2002, 43).

This is precisely what the humanities do in good literature or history courses where students learn to distinguish a primary text from its subsequent reception, and to entertain competing interpretations. From this, they can learn to acknowledge the contested nature of many claims, to draw tentative hypotheses about meaning, to differentiate the various functions texts fill for different audiences and then to engage the shifting horizons of the different audiences. The entire process requires that students develop the capacity to reflect on their own understanding as they learn to engage each other through texts in more complex and refined ways. While few religion courses now fully reach this stage, the subject itself has tremendous potential for contributing to a reflective civic and civil discourse, and thus it has great potential for enhancing autonomy by providing students with an understanding of different interpretive possibilities that exist both within and between different communities.

Nevertheless, while religion courses have the potential to advance individual growth and civic engagement, any endorsement of actual religion courses must be reserved and tentative. Few teachers are trained to teach religion and even fewer to teach it in ways that promote autonomy and enhance civic discourse among religious strangers. It is not then hard to understand why some schools are reluctant to teach religion courses and why many that do teach them do not do so in a way that enhances the civic discourse.

Nevertheless, the failure to teach religion is not due to a lack of interest on the part of students. As Noddings suggests there is certainly intense student concern about religious questions (1993). Nor is it likely that most high school students are not mature enough or intellectual enough to engage religious issues. Teachers report that many students who are slow in other areas shine in their religion courses (see Feinberg and Layton 2014). Nor is the topic of religion unimportant in an increasingly globalizing world (see Nord and Haynes 1998). Nor is there a lack of ideas about how to teach religion in a professionally competent way (Nash and Bishop 2009).[1]

Guidelines for Teaching Religion

Still, one of the most telling paradoxes of American education is the reluctance of many schools to teach the most canonical of all books in the Western traditions, the Bible. Neither the Hebrew Bible nor the "New Testament," to say nothing of the Koran, is a common source material in most schools. This reluctance is partly due to the absence of teachers who are adequately trained to teach Bible courses that are appropriate for a public school setting where fear of religious indoctrination must be taken into account. What might such training look like? The following are some minimum guidelines that my colleague, Richard Layton, and I have proposed (see Feinberg and Layton 2014):

1. Respect: Respect requires that teachers take students' ideas and beliefs seriously, that they are willing to give them reasonable consideration, even if they disagree with them and that they refrain from taking advantage of their greater authority to undermine or manipulate them.

2. Inclusiveness: Inclusiveness involves respecting communities of belief and non-belief.

3. Academic Integrity: Academic integrity requires that schools not design courses to appeal to specific segments of a community if that appeal involves manipulating the material or its manner of presentation in order to favor one set of beliefs over another or to discourage open student inquiry.

Conclusion

At a minimum, as long as a division of labor between home and school is respected, religion courses could have a role to play in public education. Religion can be taught in the public schools as a part of the human experience and as a way for students to understand their own traditions and those of others. It is the task of the parents, should they choose, to initiate their children into a religion and to teach them to worship in a particular tradition. It is also their right to not do this. Public schools have no legal or educational business in the worship business, and they step over important educational and legal boundaries when they advance one religion over another or religion over non-religion. Nevertheless, religion is a vital part of the human experience, and while many parents can engage their children in their own religious tradition, few have the knowledge or the interest to place that tradition in a wider context of traditions and interpretations, a context which is one of the critical dividing points between teaching religion as a devotional act and teaching it as a humanistic subject.

Acknowledgments

My appreciation to the Spencer Foundation for supporting this research and to the Religious Education Association for inviting me to present this material at its 2013 meeting in Waltham, Massachusetts. The article draws on work that was done with my colleague, Richard Layton.

20

Toward a New Progressive Educational Movement

> When I say that the first object of a renascent liberalism is education, I mean that its task is to aid in producing the habits of mind and character, the intellectual and moral patterns, that are somewhat near even with the actual movement of events.
>
> —John Dewey, *Liberalism and Social Action*[1]

In this chapter, I address the question Dewey raised in his book *Liberalism and Social Action* and ask just what are the habits of mind and character, the intellectual and moral patterns that would be somewhat near the actual movement of events as we are experiencing them today in the first quarter of the twenty-first century. I also suggest ways in which a renascent progressive education could contribute to the construction of those habits of mind and character.

The Social Imaginary of Optimism

A social imaginary, according to Charles Taylor, is an implicit worldview that people draw upon in understanding and communicating to one another. It delineates collective expectations and aspirations and shapes their normative standards.

In 1944, Gunnar Myrdal, the Swedish economist, captured much of this idea of imaginary by his description of the "American Creed" as a commitment to the "essential dignity of the individual human being, of the fundamental equality of all men, and of certain inalienable rights to freedom, justice, and a fair opportunity."[2] In addition to this set of beliefs, the imaginary of optimism and trust also presupposed that things are moving in the right direction—in this case, toward that "more perfect union." Pragmatism's promotion of science as the engine of desirable social change belongs to this imaginary. Dewey's understanding of progressive education and his faith that schools could produce the requisite habits of mind, character, intellect and morality that this creed required was also part of this imaginary.

Myrdal, quoting Ralph Bunch, the African American political scientist, diplomat and future Nobel Peace Prize winner, captures the prevalence of this Creed. "Every man in the street, white, black, red or yellow, knows that this is 'the land of the free,' 'the land of opportunity,' 'the cradle of liberty,' 'the home of democracy,' that the American flag symbolizes the 'equality of all men' and guarantees to us all 'the protection of life, liberty and property,' freedom of speech, freedom of religion and racial tolerance."[3]

I doubt that every man in the street *knew* that this "was the land of the free." Nevertheless, the very fact that, without a hint of irony, Myrdal quotes Bunch, who, despite his accomplishments, would have been confined to the back of the train or, worse, lynched for approaching a white woman as an equal anywhere below the Mason-Dixon line, illustrates just how pervasive was this Creed. It served, though, not as a picture of the real world, but rather as an aspiration about what that world could and might become.

Dewey and the Imaginary of Trust and Optimism

Dewey's educational philosophy both drew on an imaginary of trust, hope and optimism and contributed to it. His goal was to promote the qualities of mind and the character traits required by both scientific inquiry and a democratic society. Students would develop the skills and dispositions required to examine competing courses of action and the capacities required to cooperatively solve scientific, social and environmental problems. A *democratic education would help children learn* to work together to shape a social and natural environment where human growth would be the norm.

For Dewey, a democratic education enlarges meaning and expands community. It draws on the active interests of individual students and connects them to the larger historical community. It helps students develop the skills they will need to shape their futures and to actively participate in shaping the direction of society. A democratic education provides future citizens with multiple points of connections with each other. It enables them to develop new interests and association. An autocratic authority, whether practiced in traditional schools or in paternalistic families, Dewey thought was anathema to this ideal.

Dewey on the Meaning of Americanization

Dewey was an advocate of educational diversity long before the word entered the politically correct lexicon. He argued that individual and social growth depended on novelty, on the extension of existing interests and on the development of new ones. Diversity of interest, environment and individual talent introduced novelty and thus was a condition of individual and communal growth. However, his emphasis was not on ethnic or gender diversity—although he likely would have supported both—as much as it was on economic diversity. He believed that the largest impediment to diverse educational experiences was the rigid class lines that prevented "the adequate interplay of experience."[4] He saw this rigidity as a trademark of classical capitalism as currently practiced in the United States.

In fact, progressives differed on what should be done about ethnic diversity. Dewey occupied a middle ground between two poles. The first pole was represented by President Woodrow Wilson, a political progressive as defined at the time, who held that there should be one single American identity that overrode any other allegiance. The other pole was represented by cultural progressives like Horace Kallen (1882–1974), a Jewish American philosopher. In contrast to Wilson, Kallen held that American pluralism must acknowledge the uniqueness of each individual culture. He believed that each national immigrant group had its own distinctive emotional register and its own aesthetic forms, which he felt were most genuinely expressed in their own unique language. (African American philosophers like Alain Locke and W. E. B. Du Bois, both of whom explored the particular experience and contribution of black culture, also developed the idea that the experience and values of each individual culture were unique and should be encouraged.) Kallen felt that whereas in Europe, these differences often resulted in national conflict, he argued that America provided an environment where each culture could add its voice to the other in a peaceful way, thus maintaining their own unique identity.

Dewey sympathized with Kallen's views but was skeptical of the idea that immigrant group members, many of whom had been antagonists to each other in Europe, could exist peacefully in America without significant educational intervention. Left to their own devices, he believed that these groups would reproduce their European conflicts in America and would maintain antagonistic relations and reinforce old autocratic habits. He also feared that such habits would lead to the exploitation of the newest immigrants both by members of their own group and by unscrupulous native politicians. Dewey saw progressive schooling to be a prerequisite for individual growth and social harmony and a democratic America.

For Dewey, the flourishing of the individual and the flourishing of a democracy required the same things: novelty, diversity, reflection and experimentation. Individuals grow when old habits are challenged by new conditions. Societies grow when they are able to intelligently adapt to a changing environment and to direct it in productive ways through reflection, inquiry and science. Communities grow when their members can freely intermingle with members of other communities. Dewey observed that every aspect of the environment—natural, physical, technological, social and cultural—was undergoing a profound change, and he believed that change required new modes of control and development if it were to proceed in a humane and productive way. He believed that cultural groups were valuable and that working together, they could participate in the co-construction of an emerging cultural identity.

Limitations

Dewey's educational ideas have always been controversial. The criticisms include the friendly assessment by the philosopher Israel Scheffler, who contended that subject matter can generate its own interest without attaching itself to an already present interest that students brings with them to the subject. Scheffler believed that intellectual problems embedded in complex theory can be sufficient to generate an interest in some students where none had existed before. In other words, teaching students complex theory does not always require a preexisting interest that needs to be corralled into learning a worthwhile subject.[5] I believe that Scheffler is quite right and that Dewey overemphasizes the need to colonize a preexisting interest.

Another criticism offered by E. D. Hirsch, Jr. is that progressive education is inefficient and that students often can learn more efficiently by direct instruction where the teacher lays out the larger ideas, concepts or methods that need to be learned and where learning is then reinforced by practice, which might include drill, recitation, and memorization. Hirsch also has a point, although he fails to see the important connection Dewey makes between the how—or method of instruction- and the what—or the subject that is learned. The criticism of Dewey also includes more hostile critics from the political right, who irrationally blame Dewey for the decline of the national moral character and for misunderstanding the educational prerequisites of philosophy.[6]

A few theologians, such as Reinhold Niebuhr, rightly questioned Dewey's core optimism, and the journalist Walter Lippmann challenged Dewey's faith in *open and transparent* inquiry. However, for the most part, Dewey's belief that the scientific method, extended to social affairs, could resolve even the most intransient of human problems fit nicely with the social imaginary of the times and was consistent with the growth of the social sciences. From the 1920s through the 1950s, Dewey's ideas were at the forefront of American liberal political thought.

This changed dramatically in the late 1960s and early 1970s as then newly named "old left"—i.e., Dewey's liberals—gave way to a less positive "new left." This change was more than generational—"Don't trust anyone over 30," the cry of the new left in 1970—it was also intellectual, marking a challenge to both political authority and to intellectual authority, including that of Dewey.

From a Social Imaginary of Optimism to a Social Imaginary of Suspicion

The educational philosopher, George Counts, delivered his famous "Dare the Schools Build a New Social Order" speech in 1931, before the Progressive Education Association. In it, he expressed the optimism that schools could be a significant agent of progressive change even in the midst of the worst economic depression in history. Of course, there were different responses at the time, but these were largely about the merits of indoctrinating students into the new social order as opposed to finding ways to letting them come to the *right* conclusion by themselves, conclusions that many progressives confidently professed to know. Even the Communist party in New York thought that a voice in the schools was sufficiently important that they contested with more liberal members, including Dewey, for control of the union.

It is the response to Counts's question "Can the school build a new social order?" that divided the 1930 educational progressives from the New Left of the 1970s. By the 1970s, the imaginary of the left had changed from one of basic trust that the schools could be a force for progressive change to one of deep distrust. The change is illustrated by contrasting the hope generated after the *Brown v. Board of Education* decision in 1954 which ended legal segregation to the white reaction against bussing in the late 1960s and early 70s in such "liberal" enclaves as my hometown, Boston. All of this had an impact on my own work and the way I began to read Dewey in the late 1960s and early 1970s.

Some Background

I was born almost eighty years after Dewey. He was still alive and actively engaged in politics, education and philosophy when I was learning to walk. He was witness to the Great Depression from its beginning. I was born just before it ended. We both were alive, he, eighty-six, me, eight, when the atomic bombs were dropped and the Second World War ended. He died when the Korean War (1950–1953) was at its height and when my own political awareness was beginning to waken and just as Richard Nixon was coming into national prominence. By the time television brought the Army McCarthy hearings into my home in 1954, Dewey had passed away. In that same year, *Brown v. Board of Education* was decided, and segregated schools were ruled unconstitutional.

Growing up in Boston in the 1940s and 50s, it was not too hard to condemn the legally segregated conditions of the South as a violation of the basic idea of equal opportunity, an idea that Dewey had championed throughout his life. It was a lot harder for me to realize just how normalized segregation and inequality was in the North. There were no African American students in my *legally* unsegregated grade school.

When my high school asked for volunteers to house the single African American band member from another school, my family was the only one to volunteer. But these were only the outer trappings of informal apartheid; the inner ones were more difficult to identify until they hit you in the face. And so my surprise was palpable when a Boston department store in the mid-1960s finally put a black manikin in its display window. It was also palpable a few years later in Champaign when I had to bring our young daughter to the emergency room and I mistook the black female emergency room *doctor* for the nurse and the white male *nurse* for the doctor.

Dewey did not likely experience the full impact of these changes, allowing his generation—at least those of white European origin—to take the idea of American exceptionalism for granted. For my own family, some of whom had come to America to escape the pogroms in Russia and some others who would have been murdered in the Holocaust had they remained in Europe, America was, for all its many faults, exceptional. But this was not true for everyone. The story of slavery, of Native American genocide, of the takeover of Mexican land was told, if told at all, from the point of view of slave owners and conquerors. The Vietnam War, the Civil Rights movement, the assassinations of President Kennedy, Malcolm X, Dr. King, Medgar Evers and Robert Kennedy, the Watergate hearings, all marked a change in the dominant social imaginary and the consciousness of my generation. At stake was the very idea of American exceptionalism and of progress itself.

This was the real dividing point between Dewey's generation and those that followed mine. I was in the middle, having internalized much that Dewey had also internalized—the promise of public education for a more inclusive, more democratic society, and yet I was also standing outside of Dewey's generation and questioning much that it took for granted—including the belief that schooling could achieve greater equality by itself.

This change was consistent with the development of a new social imaginary, suspicion and distrust, born of the violence that met civil rights workers and of the slaughter of the Vietnam War. Vietnam was more than a tragic mistake. The over three million Vietnamese and 58,000 American deaths terminated whatever remained of America's self-congratulatory innocence. The lesson of Watergate was not just that the government makes mistakes, which Dewey certainly knew, but that it lies and that it does so systematically and impartially by Democrats and

Republics alike. Watergate and Vietnam reframed the social imaginary from optimism and trust to suspicion and distrust.

The Struggle on Campus

At the time in the late 1960s and early 1970s, the faculty of the University of Illinois Urbana Champaign College of Education was divided between young Turks, like myself, and the older, more established faculty members. One of my senior colleagues, a Dewey scholar, loudly called me a traitor at a party because of my opposition to the War in Vietnam, and he later chalked a Swastika on my office door. After the murders of students at Kent and Jackson State, I, and others, spoke in favor of a resolution for a campus boycott to protest the war. A day or so after the resolution was passed, a top administrator called me into his office to tell me that if I wanted to change the world, the university was no place for me. I later found out that he gave the same message to other protesting faculty. After Watergate and after the government duplicity became undeniable, it seemed to me that both the colleague who thought me a traitor and the administrator who questioned my place in the university, along with much of the nation itself, softened their opposition to the resistance, with some joining it.

The Changing Social Imaginary

Behind these charges and counter charges were two competing views about the proper relationship between power and intelligence, interpreted then as the politician and the intellectual. The old left held that intelligence could still be linked to power to serve the public good, even though some eventually came to question the wisdom of the Vietnam War. The new left held that power corrupted intelligence and that resistance was the only viable form of effective action. The slogan "don't trust anybody over 30," popular at the time, implied that power corrupts, older people are prone to cooptation by power and only distrust and resistance, qualities of the young, purify. The Watergate scandal was not alone in convincing many people, even some over thirty, that engagement with the government corrupts. It was reinforced by earlier revelations about the cooperation between academics—psychologists, anthropologists, economists—and the

Department of Defense to overthrow democratically elected regimes in other countries and promote a pro-American business policy.

The conflict was about both legitimacy and meaning. To illustrate this, consider the two closely related terms—cooperation and cooptation—and their implication. The first, of course, is essential to Dewey's political and educational philosophy and is foundational to his ideas about both democracy and *democratic* education. It relies on the social imaginary of trust and optimism. When you decide to cooperate with someone else, you assume that the conditions for true cooperation are present, trust, good will, transparency and a reasonably equal balance of power. Cooptation holds that these conditions are not present and that the call for cooperation is bogus.

When these conditions are thought to be absent, then calls for cooperation will be rightly taken as an attempt at cooptation. Here, the imaginary of trust turns into the imaginary of suspicion and mistrust. The charge of cooptation is not the same as a charge of insincerity. The call for cooperation may be a perfectly sincere one, but if the system itself is corrupt, an otherwise sincere but uniformed call for cooperation will be taken as an attempt at cooptation. This is how things looked to many people in the late 1960s and 70s.

Reading Dewey Under the Imaginary of Suspicion

It was in the context of this shift in the social imaginary that Dewey's Polish Study was brought to my attention by Ron Szoke, my then–research assistant. Dewey had performed the research on a Polish group living in Philadelphia with graduate students and in 1917–18 and submitted the eighty-page report as a confidential document to the War Department in 1918—today the Department of Defense—on the attitudes of this group. A few years before the study when I was writing my dissertation, Dewey's involvement with the Polish Community and the War Department had not been a topic for Dewey scholars, and I, like most other Dewey scholars, had completely overlooked it. I simply criticized his technical philosophy for failing to address potential conflicts between community and science.

In hindsight, my failure to see the significance of the Polish Study and Dewey's support for the American involvement in the First World War reveals something about my own mindset and about the social imaginary to which it was attuned. I was focused on Dewey's formal *philosophy* and ignored much else. So even though Dewey's study of the Polish Community was marked "confidential" for the War Department in 1918, by 1965, when I finished my dissertation, it was a secret only in the sense that no one had paid any attention to its content, even though it was available to anyone who might be interested and was described fully on pages 52–54 in the then definitive bibliography of Dewey's works.[7]

Given the social imaginary of the early 1970s, the political relevance of the Polish Study to my earlier observation about the tension between intelligence and community in Dewey's thought was now apparent. Dewey had cooperated with the War Department and used social science inquiry to question the loyalty of members of the Polish community. A-hah! Science over community! My criticism was now more than strictly a matter of logic, as it had been in the dissertation; it had become a matter of the meaning of democracy. Or, to put it in terms of the 60s and 70s, Dewey was coopted by the War Department to promote the "cooperation" of the Polish community in advancing American interests as defined again by the War Department.

Some of Dewey's former colleagues, such as Jane Addams and Randolph Bourne, remained faithful to their pacifist ideas throughout the war and lamented the extent to which American intellectuals, including Dewey, had supported the war and aided the propaganda supporting it.[8] Addams notes that any opposition during the war was largely silenced by government propaganda, public pressure and by the intellectuals who supported the war. She would likely have had Dewey in mind when she made this remark. He not only came to support the war shortly after it was declared but found a number of occasions to argue against its critics.

Deconstructing the Social Imaginary

A word of clarification about my use of the term social imaginary is in order. The idea of a social imaginary helps us understand the ways in which people make collective sense of their world and the expectations that they share as normal and justifiable. It does not *explain* social change, but is useful in recognizing and labeling it. Nor does it capture the nuances of change, as if we go suddenly from one social imaginary to the next. Certainly there was much distrust in the 1930s, and a lot of people in the 1970s continued to believe that cooperation between academics and government was, on balance, a force for good. The idea of a social imaginary captures a certain tone that pervades discourse and decision-making. It does not explain that change, nor does it weigh how many consciously ascribe to it.

Nor does a change in the social imaginary signal a change in all its parts. The change from the old left to the new was not a rejection of the American Creed as much as it was suspicion about whether it could be achieved under existing conditions. Similarly, the later suspicion and repudiation of the male domination of the new left by feminism drew upon the rhetoric of the new left for equality pointing out how inconsistent it was with its own sexist practices and opening the way for a new set of critiques.

The Social Imaginary, then, is not some massive beast that turns on its parents and devours them whole. It can be deconstructed, its pieces rearranged and then reconstructed. The imaginary of trust was not overthrown completely by the imaginary of suspicion. There was not for example, a wholesale rejection of the American Creed as a worthy ideal to strive for. Rather, rejected was the idea that it could be achieved by relying on good will alone and reform from above. Dr. King, Rosa Parks, Saul Alinsky, Daniel Ellsberg and, later, Harvey Milk demonstrated the necessity of different forms of non-violent resistance to obtuse, intransigent leaders. Cornell West relates this to Dewey and a limitation in his idea of social change. "His gradualism is principally pedagogical in content, and his reformism is primarily dialogical in character. He shuns confrontational politics and agitational social struggle" for education and continuous discussion.[9]

The problem is not with education and discussion as such. However, these become problems under conditions of oppression, intransigence and unequal power. Under these conditions, the call for cooperation is to be seen as a ploy to disguise cooptation. And this is what guided much of my own reaction to Dewey's educational writings in the 1970s when I noted his silence on critical race issues such as lynching[10] and segregated schools.[11] The difference was partly about the framework through which subordination was to be understood and whether race had a status independent of social class. But the difference was also about tactics, and the most effective way to promote desirable social change. King, Parks and Alinsky made Dewey's slower, more discursive method less than promising in situations of oppression. As Dr. King put it in his "Letter From a Birmingham Jail":

> I must make two honest confessions to you, my Christian and Jewish brothers. First, I must confess that over the past few years I have been gravely disappointed with the white moderate. I have almost reached the regrettable conclusion that the Negro's great stumbling block in his stride toward freedom is not the White Citizen's Counciler or the Ku Klux Klanner, but the white moderate, who is more devoted to "order" than to justice; who prefers a negative peace which is the absence of tension to a positive peace which is the presence of justice; who constantly says: "I agree with you in the goal that you seek, but I cannot agree with your methods of direct action"; who paternalistically believes he can set the timetable for another man's freedom; who lives by a mythical concept of time and who constantly advises the Negro to wait for a "more convenient season." Shallow understanding from people of good will is more frustrating than absolute misunderstanding from people of ill will. Lukewarm acceptance is much more bewildering than outright rejection.[12]

King certainly agreed with Dewey about the unity of thought and action, but King's non-violent protest had overtaken Dewey's more cautious, more scientifically inflected approach to change. "In any nonviolent campaign there are four basic steps: collection of the facts to determine whether injustices exist; negotiation; self purification; and direct action. We have gone through all these steps in Birmingham. There can be no gainsaying the fact that racial injustice engulfs this community. Birmingham is probably the most thoroughly segregated city in the United States. Its ugly record of brutality is widely known. This tactical difference was also a moral difference." To put it differently, King's words and actions set the social imaginary to a different register—one where inquiry was about tactics and should be a handmaiden to justified protest and resistance. Certainly the difference between King and the liberal moderates was a tactical one, but, as he insisted, it was a moral one as well. Collective power was one ingredient that Dewey underestimated in his call for progressive education.

The Reconstruction of Dewey's Ideas in the Post Modern World: A Fourth Leg for Democratic Education

My criticism of Dewey is itself a part of the pragmatic tradition. It aims to bring together our deepest understanding of democracy with the facts of social life as we experience them. Clearly, the post-Civil War social imaginary had restricted Dewey's consideration of the centrality of race in American life. Like most white progressives at the time, for Dewey, racial issues were addressed largely as problems of class. As Glaude remarks: "race and racism remained marginal intellectual categories despite the long, looming shadow of slavery that framed their (James and Dewey) extraordinary lives."[13]

This should not be surprising, given that the very concept of *racism* was largely shaped in the Twentieth Century.[14] Even Dr. King's "March on Washington" was a march for jobs, not just race, and he hoped to include blacks and whites in the struggle for social justice—not an irrational hope. Dewey was not, of course, oblivious to the treatment of blacks, as his role in the formation of the NAACP attests, but he greatly feared categorizing people in any way that suggested essentialism. He rightly believed that any individual was potentially more than any one classification could encompass, but this belief obscured the very special concerns of subordinated racial populations.

Yet the experience of race as it was revealed to white Americans during the Civil Rights era stripped away the collective myth of American innocence and American perfectibility. And it opened up the possibility of different readings of the American experience—and the need for different voices to be heard through fluid categories of identity, and counter narratives. It also raised the question of power, of who has it and how it is and should be distributed. This suggested a much messier project than that promoted by post-Civil War narratives of national unity or by the older progressive idea of consensus through education and science.

Toward a New Progressive Education

Let's return to the questions I raised (with Dewey) at the beginning of this essay: What are the habits of mind and character, the intellectual and moral patterns that would be somewhat near the actual movement of events as we are experiencing them today in the first quarter of the twenty-first century, and how might a new form of progressive education contribute to the reconstruction of those habits of mind and character? Dewey believed that the scientific method could be used to advance a progressive agenda, yet he underestimated the extent to which unequal power would be used to distribute the methods and benefits of science unequally.

A new progressive education would recognize structural and systematic inequality and promote more equitable distribution of power. The idea of a new progressive education has three interrelated dimensions. First, it has a political dimension. Students would understand the ways in which benefits are developed and distributed in American society. Second, it has a creative dimension. Students would develop the ethical and aesthetic capacity to imagine alternative realities. Third, it has an academic dimension. Students would develop the scientific, communicative and the *political* skills that promote agency and fulfillment. Here are a few random examples of some of these dimensions.

Recognition of Collective Agency

In the early 1970s, just about the time I read Dewey's Polish Study, I developed a curriculum unit that was centered on the bus boycott that happened in Montgomery in 1955–56 and that spirited Dr. King to national prominence. The unit was inspired by the progressive idea, but had a stronger political content. With the help of a local grade school teacher in a standard elementary school classroom, we developed a group project that required the students to duplicate the boycott using materials we provided and to simulate the problems of the boycott leaders. In doing so, students had to consult demographic materials and to decide effective ways to communicate the boycott to members of the population that could not read newspapers. They had to use maps, news clippings and primary sources to determine where people lived and worked and to then develop car pool routes to take people from their home to their workplace. They also had to figure out how to communicate the boycott to the black population, and, thus, they had to get an idea of how many people could read posters and other notices. For the sizable number of black people in Montgomery who, at the time, had trouble reading, they had to figure out other modes of communication, such as radio broadcasts and church sermons. They then wrote sermons and developed artwork that promoted the boycott. In the process, students learned map-reading skills, communication skills and organization skills as they learned the role that everyday citizens could play in social change. They also learn a lot about history as they learned about the long history of Civil Rights. With more time or with older students, they might have learned about how textbooks reconstruct history by comparing, say, Rosa Parks's long training at Highlander school to the picture of history text of the tired lady who one day simply decided not to move to the back of the bus. In this unit, students were learning about local efforts to develop collective political agency, but in addition, they were improving basic skills such as literacy, map reading, historical understanding communication and cooperative planning.

Development of Skills of Civic Engagement

The development of communicative and political skills and historical understanding are critical if what Meira Levinson calls the "civic empowerment gap" is to be closed. Civic empowerment involves the knowledge, skills and dispositions that are required to be politically engaged in effective ways. The empowerment gap describes how students differ according to racial, social class and ethnic factors. Levinson argues that racially segregated schools may require a different approach to civic education than do more integrated ones. Empowerment for minority students involves learning and navigating the routes to power within the dominant culture, something more privileged students often learn at home. She believes that effective collective action requires students to learn the ways of the dominant power structure even as they embrace their own traditions. Levinson suggests a number of experiential civic education projects, such as mock trials, community organizing, voter registration drives, collective action about contentious community issues, such as street repair, snow removal and garbage pick-up,[15] that can be used to enhance community engagement and civic empowerment.

Developing a Vision of Renewal

Environmental issues present additional opportunities for students to develop the habits of civic engagement and the moral character that extends beyond any single ethnic identity. One example is the work of

Harbor High School in New York. The school, located in Manhattan, is described by its advertising as helping to revitalize the sea life in the harbor by seeding the return of the oyster to New York. Oysters were once abundant in the harbor but became essentially extinct as the water, and much of the ecosystem that sustained sea life, became polluted. Today students at Harbor High and other schools are working with the project to bring the oyster back, and in the process, they are learning the history and ecology of the bay and using the bay to develop place-based science and math curricula that meet state standards and are also applicable to the work of restoring the oyster beds. In learning about the oyster and its role in the development of New York—once, but no longer, one of the largest oyster exporters in the world—the students learn valuable lessons about ecological history, science and math, and they learn too about the effects of human activity on the global as well as the local environment. The opportunity for students from different schools and different communities within a district to come together around a civil concern provides opportunities for multicultural, multi-racial and religious cooperation.

Using New Tools to Extend Identity Beyond the Local and National Communities

Finally, the Internet and the World Wide Web make it possible for students to develop interests that transcend local and national boundaries and address issues of global concern. One example at the University of Illinois is the use of the Internet by my colleague, Linda Herrera, to develop a global studies unit on peace education (one of Dewey's major concerns). She was fortunate to be able to draw on two exceptional resources, Raj Gandhi, journalist and a grandson of Mahatma Gandhi, and Mohamed El Baradei, a nuclear weapons inspector and past Egyptian vice president. Both were teaching at the University of Illinois at the time, and both are internationally known for their work on democracy and peace.[16] Herrera was teaching an online course at the time with students enrolled from many different countries. With Gandhi and El Baradei's guidance, the students created a webpage on international and peace issues, and then the students translated it into their different languages, Chinese, Arabic, Korean and Urdu, for others around the world to take advantage of.

Label Warning

We should be cautious about using the labels "progressive education" or "new progressive education," as if they indicated something very different from education pure and simple.[17] The idea of education pure and simple always involves the same things: teach students to be mindful of their environment—natural and social; help students develop respect for each other; encourage them to understand the world that they will inherit as the past's legacy to them and to contribute to the legacy that they will build for future generations. Finally, provide them with the critical intellectual tools that will help them make sound judgments.

There is nothing either uniquely progressive or uniquely traditional about this list, and as Dewey fully appreciated, any education worthy of the name will include both traditional and progressive elements. The ingredients of good teaching are pretty straightforward. Understand your students, their backgrounds, needs, their interests and their specific talents; understand the subject sufficiently well so that you can teach the requisite skills and engage your students in a critical discussion of inherited points of view; encourage students to test their ideas out and revise them if necessary; and encourage them to become active and engaged members of a community. In addition, as a teacher, learn about the community so that you can communicate with parents and community members about your goals and their children's needs.

As with all lists, this one too is incomplete, but that incompleteness is a mark of any education—progressive, new progressive, traditional—open for revision.

Notes

Chapter 1

1. Feinberg himself continues to contribute. See his book *Educating for Democracy* (Cambridge: Cambridge University Press, 2023).

Chapter 2

1. John Dewey, reference letter for Kenneth Benne, University of Illinois Archives, Benne file.
2. Walter Feinberg, *Hegel's Conception of Property*, Unpublished Master's Thesis, Boston University, 1962.
3. Walter Feinberg. *A Comparative Study of the Social Philosophies of John Dewey and Bernard Bosanquet*, unpublished Doctoral Dissertation, Boston University, 1965.
4. Walter Feinberg, *Reason and Rhetoric: The Intellectual Foundations of Twentieth Century Liberal Educational Reform* (New York: John Wiley), 1974.
5. John Dewey, "Confidential Report: Conditions Among the Poles in the United States," Washington: 1918.
6. Milton Halsey Thomas, *John Dewey: A Centennial Bibliography* (Chicago: University of Chicago Press, 1962).
7. W. Feinberg, "The Conflict between Intelligence and Community in Dewey's Educational Philosophy," *Educational Theory* 19, no. 3 (Summer 1969): 236–48.
8. Walter Feinberg and Kevin McDonough, "Liberalism and the Dilemma of Public Education in Multicultural Societies," in *Citizenship and Education in Liberal-Democratic Societies: Teaching for Cosmopolitan Values and Collective Identities*, ed. Kevin McDonough and Walter Feinberg (Oxford: Oxford University Press, 2003), 1–22.
9. C. D. Hardie, *Truth & Fallacy in Educational Theory* (New York: Bureau of Publications, Teachers College, Columbia University), 1942/1962.

10. R. S. Peters, *Ethics and Education* (USA: Scott Foresman, 1967).

11. Walter Feinberg, *Understanding Education: Toward a Reconstruction of Educational Inquiry* (Cambridge: Cambridge University Press, 1982).

12. Eric Bredo and Walter Feinberg, *Knowledge and Values in Social and Educational Research* (Philadelphia: Temple University Press, 1982).

13. Walter Feinberg and Suzanne R. Langner, "The Other Face of Competition," in *Money, Power and Health Care*, ed. Evan M. Melhado, Walter Feinberg and Harold M. Swartz (Ann Arbor, Michigan: Health Administration Press, 1988).

14. Walter Feinberg, *On Higher Ground: Education and the Case for Affirmative Action* (New York: Teachers College Press, 1988); A. Belden Fields and Walter Feinberg, *Education and Democratic Theory: Finding a Place for Community Participation in Public School Reform* (Albany: State University of New York Press, 2001).

15. Walter Feinberg, *Japan and the Pursuit of A New American Identity: Work and Education in A Multicultural Age* (New York: Routledge, 1993).

16. Walter Feinberg, "Philosophical Ethnography: Or How Philosophy and Ethnography Can Live Together in the World of Educational Research," in *Educational Studies in Japan: International Yearbook*, No. 1, 2006 (Japan: Japanese Educational Research Association, 2006), 5–14.

17. Walter Feinberg, *For Goodness Sake: Religious Schools and Education for Democratic Citizenry* (New York: Routledge, 2006).

18. Walter Feinberg, "Culture, Class and Nation: An Educator's Reconstruction," Unpublished Butts Lecture: American Educational Studies Association, Charlottesville, VA, November 2005.

19. Walter Feinberg, *On Higher Ground: Education and the Case for Affirmative Action* (New York, Teachers College Press, 1998).

20. Walter Feinberg, *Common Schools, Uncommon Identities: National Unity and Cultural Difference* (New Haven: Yale University Press, 1998).

21. Walter Feinberg, "The Dialectic of Parental Rights and Social Obligation," in *School Choice Policies and Outcomes: Empirical and Philosophical Perspectives*, ed. Walter Feinberg and Christopher Lubienski (Albany: State University of New York Press, 2008).

Chapter 3

1. See Sol Cohen, "The History of the History of American Education, 1900–1976: The Uses of the Past," *Harvard Educational Review* 46, no. 3 (1976): 298–330, for a close approximation of this statement.

2. See, for example, Paul Hirst, "Liberal Education and the Nature of Knowledge," in Reginald Archambault, ed., *Philosophical Analysis and Education* (Humanities Press, 1972).

3. Samuel Bowles and Herbert Gintis, *Schooling in Capitalist America: Educational Reform and the Contradictions of Economic Life* (New York: Basic Books, 1976).

4. See Walter Feinberg, "I.Q., Intelligence and the Distribution of Knowledge," *Boston Studies in Philosophy of Science*, forthcoming.

5. See Paul Willis, *Learning to Labour: How Working Class Kids Get Working Class Jobs* (England: Saxon House, 1977).

6. I am indebted to comments by W. O. Stanley for this example.

7. I am indebted here to discussions with Peter Goldstone.

Chapter 4

1. Appreciation to Willard Boyd, President of the Field Museum for this insight.

2. Walter Feinberg, *Understanding Education: Toward a Reconstruction of Educational Inquiry* (Cambridge: Cambridge University Press, 1983), 147–74.

3. Ibid.

4. Because schools and other educative institutions exist within a network of supporting institutions and practices, the scope of Philosophy of Education is wide ranging, encompassing critiques of popular culture, media, and economic practices as they impinge upon the education of the young.

5. For a most useful history of this organization see James M. Giarelli and J. J. Chambliss, "The Foundations of Professionalism: Fifty Years of the Philosophy of Education Society in Retrospect," *Educational Theory* 41, no. 3 (Summer 1991): 265–74.

6. As quoted in Giarelli and Chambliss, 268.

7. In referring to deconstruction I am not speaking of its use strictly as a literary method in, say the work of Barbara Johnston. I am addressing its limitation when used as a devise for social criticism. The extreme of this, of course, would be in the work of Paul DeMan.

8. It is important to see the opposition between principled and relational thinking that has recently been made to characterize the difference between male and female thinking, not as a logical opposition, but as built into genderized practices that could be otherwise.

Chapter 5

1. Liza Dalby, *Geisha* (New York: Vintage, 1985), 108, 159–60.

2. Ibid., 170–71.

3. Takeo Doi, *The Anatomy of Dependency* (Tokyo: Kodansha International, 1973), 11–12.

4. Alasdair MacIntyre, *Relativism, Power and Philosophy: Proceedings and Addresses of the American Philosophical Association* (Newark, DE: The American Philosophical Association, 1985), 13.

5. Ibid., 18.

6. Colin M. Turnbull, *The Mountain People* (New York: Simon & Schuster, 1972), 11.

7. Ibid., 12.

8. Ibid., 32.

9. Ibid.

10. Ibid., 287–95.

11. Sawako Ayiyoshi, *The Doctor's Wife* (Tokyo: Kodansha International, 1978).

Chapter 6

1. While this may seem less true of Lakatos who allows that personal ambition may motivate the scientific enterprise, he understand values largely as nonrational motivators rather than factors in the scientific process itself.

2. To the extent that the policy was based on an assumption that closing schools would improve test scores recent survey research has shown that except for a very few students who were sent to high performing schools, most of the students who were displaced did not improve their test scores. Cf. Torre and Gwynne 2009.

3. The pragmatist would understand that background understanding would determine the legitimacy of the question and the first question could well lead to an important insight if asked by someone unfamiliar with the situation. In other words, the extreme spike in the death rate could, given an unknowing investigator, lead to questions about causation. For an already knowledgeable investigator to speak only of deaths and not murder would be a cover up.

4. It is worth noting that traditional positivism draws on both with analytic truth having the character of "T" truth (without the *divine* guarantee) and synthetic truth enjoying only the little "t."

5. Granted this requires a commonsense understanding of "heart and mind" "in-here," and "subjective," which a strict positivist would question.

6. These are my terms.

7. An example of the rejection of potentially useful research findings occurred after WW II when the allies sealed the research of the notorious Nazi Doctor, Joseph Mengele.

8. Such change in standards is often a theme of literary works. See, for example, Coetze 2000, a book that explores how a reevaluation of the colonial experience in South Africa paralyzes any action based on previous moral expectations. Also see Ishiguro 1989.

9. My appreciation to Fred Lighthall who is writing a book on this episode.

10. I use the term suspicion here to indicate a certain response to modernity, and, in Bourdieu's case, toward the possibility of education to advance human well-being. While both are powerful instruments in shedding light on particular form of oppression in Bourdieu's case the suspicion is built into his very definition of terms and in Foucault's into his methodology itself.

Chapter 7

1. John Dewey, *Theory of Valuation*, in *International Encyclopedia of Unified Sciences*, ed. Otto Neurath, vols. 1 and II (Chicago: University of Chicago Press, 1939), 11.
2. Ibid., 12.
3. Ibid., 13.
4. Ibid., 33.
5. Ibid., 34.
6. John Dewey, *Individualism Old and New* (New York: Capricorn Books, 1962), 46.
7. John Dewey, *Theory of Valuation*, 31–32.
8. Ibid., 49–50.
9. This dual choice is quite consistent with many of Dewey's ideas on the nature of ends. It is consistent with the idea that the function of an end is to re-establish activity. Thus to choose an end is to choose the kind of activity, i.e., the means, to achieve it; it is also consistent with the idea that without a consideration of means, that which could have been an end is but a mere dream or fantasy. "It 'becomes an aim or end only when it is worked out in terms of concrete conditions available for its realization, that is in terms of 'means.'" *Human Nature and Conduct* (New York: Modern Library, 1957), 234.
10. Dewey and Tufts, *Ethics* (rev. ed.; New York: Holt, Rinehart and Winston, 1936), 181.
11. John Dewey, *Philosophy and Civilization* (New York: Capricorn Books, 1903), 77.
12. Ibid., 78.

Chapter 8

1. The first view is the one that James took. The second belongs more to Peirce. In my reading Dewey failed to come to grips with the difference and vacillated between them.
2. My appreciation to Terri Wilson for pointing this out in this way.

Chapter 9

1. The National Commission on Excellence in Education, *A Nation at Risk: The Imperative for Educational Reform* (Washington, DC: U.S. Government Printing Office, 1983; John Goodlad, *A Place Called School: Prospects for the Future* (New York: McGraw-Hill, 1983). See also Mortimer Adler, *The Paideia Proposal: An Educational Manifesto* (New York: MacMillan, 1982).

2. It is instructive to remember that in the 1970's, even President Nixon was advocating a national health insurance bill. A recent survey by Arthur D. Little Inc., of 125 experts in health care (as reported in *The Champaign-Urbana New Gazette*, Saturday, June 1, 1985), found a shared belief that the public would shortly abandon its goal of equal health care.

3. The National Science Board/The National Science Foundation, *Today's Problems, Tomorrow's Crises* (Washington, DC: National Science Board, 1982).

4. *Making the Grade. Report of the Twentieth Century Fund Task Force on Federal Elementary and Secondary Educational Policy* (New York: Twentieth Century Fund. 1983), 3.

5. *Nation at Risk*, 17.

6. For others who claim the same link, see, for example. National Science Board, *Today's Problems*; Twentieth Century Fund, *Making the Grade*; and Business-Higher Education Forum, *America's Competitive Challenge: The Need for a National Response* (Washington, DC, 1983). The last of these deals largely with post-secondary education.

7. These interviews took place in December 1984.

8. This is a body appointed by the Prime Minister and has a somewhat analogous function to that of our National Commission on Excellence in Education.

9. High school education is not compulsory in Japan. However, Japanese schools actually graduate a significantly higher percentage of high school aged students than do schools in the United States. Somewhere over 90 percent of high school-age children attend school in Japan and, of these, about 97 percent graduate, according to Hindenuri Fujita, "A Crisis of Legitimacy in Japanese Education: Meritocracy and Cohesiveness" (paper presented at the annual meeting of the Comparative and International Education Society, 22 March 1984 at Houston, TX).

10. Ibid., 14.

11. For a critical analysis of these schools and the role that they play in the Japanese economy, see Michio Morishima, *Why has Japan 'Succeeded'? Western Technology and the Japanese Ethos* (Cambridge: Cambridge University Press, 1984), 184–93.

12. In Korea, the penalty for tutoring is for the child, expulsion from school, for the father, loss of any government job. and, for the tutor, six months in jail.

13. Rokuro Hidaka, *The Price of Affluence: Dilemmas of Contemporary Japan* (Tokyo: Kodansha International, 1984), 107.
14. *Making the Grade*, 6.
15. Paul E. Peterson, "Background Paper," in *Making the Grade*, 157.
16. Ibid., 158.
17. Ibid., 118.
18. Ibid., 157.
19. Ibid., 6.
20. Ibid., 14 (note).
21. Henry M. Levin and Russell W. Rumberger. *The Educational Implications of High Technology* (Stanford: Institute for Research on Educational Finance and Governance, 1983).
22. See *Making the Grade*, 11.
23. Mortimer J. Adler, *The Paideia Proposal: An Educational Manifesto* (New York: Macmillan, 1982).
24. *The Paideia Program: An Educational Syllabus* (New York: Macmillan, 1984).
25. *Paideia Proposal*, 23–24.
26. Ibid., 16–17.
27. These include Ernest Boyer and Theodore Sizer.
28. In November 1983, I chaired a panel with Adler and a number of his critics for the annual meeting of the American Educational Studies Association. The substance of much of this criticism was that Adler's proposal did not take into account individual differences. His response, as I recall it, was essentially that he recognized that there were different limits to the speed and the amount that different children could learn. However, there are some essentially humanizing experiences and to deny children the opportunity to participate in these is truly discriminatory.
29. For those who are concerned that Adler would neglect craft work, driver's education, and other such areas, they should be reassured that Adler's school will find a place for many of these areas including automobile repair, driver's education, metalworking, sewing, cooking, and typing. See *The Paideia Proposal*, 33.
30. Goodlad, *A Place Called School*.
31. Theodore R. Sizer, *Horace's Compromise: The Dilemma of the American High School* (Boston: Houghton Mifflin Co., 1984).
32. Ernest L. Boyer, *High School: A Report on Secondary Education in America* (New York: Harper and Row, 1983).
33. Goodlad, 140.
34. Boyer, 5.
35. Sizer, 6.
36. Goodlad, 146–47.

37. Ibid., 149.
38. Ibid., 160.
39. Ibid., 161.
40. Ibid., 150.
41. Ibid., 161.
42. I suspect that the practice of firing both non-tenured and tenured teachers at the end of the year in order to meet budgetary constraints, together with a decline in purchasing power, has been one of the major reasons for the decline in the attractiveness of the teaching profession.
43. Sizer, 28.

Chapter 10

1. I am indebted to Ruth Jonathan for this observation.
2. A. MacIntyre, "The Idea of an Educated Public," in *Education and Values: The Richard Peters Lectures*, ed. G. Haydon (London: Institute of Education, 1987).
3. Ibid., 25.
4. Ibid., 18.
5. Ibid., 19.
6. Ibid., 28.
7. A. MacIntyre, "Is Patriotism a Virtue? The Lindley Lecture," Department of Philosophy, University of Kansas, 1984.
8. Ibid., 8.
9. Ibid., 8.
10. Ibid., 9.
11. Ibid., 9.
12. Ibid., 13.
13. Ibid., 10.
14. J. Haldane, "Religious Education in a Pluralist Society: A Philosophical Examination," *British Journal of Educational Studies* 34, no. 2 (1986): 161–81. https://doi.org/10.1080/00071005.1986.9973734.
15. A. MacIntyre, *Whose Justice? Which Rationality?* (Notre Dame, IN: University of Notre Dame Press, 1988), 394.
16. I am indebted to Ruth Jonathan for raising this issue.

Chapter 11

1. This needs to be amended as referring to an ideal since Aristotle also observed that the character of education would depend on the character of the constitution of a given state.

Chapter 12

1. This is one reason why Bourdieu and Passeron 1977 is innovative as social theory but insufficient as an educational theory.

2. It is an interesting aspect of this flattening that Said (1978) does not emphasize for balance the images of the West present in "oriental societies."

3. My appreciation to Mark Halstead for his helpful comments. A version of this paper was delivered as the Butts Lecture before the American Educational Studies Association in 2005. Appreciation also to the Spencer Foundation for its support.

Chapter 13

1. *Wisconsin v. Yoder*, 406 U.S. 205 (1972).

2. *Mozert v. Hawkins County Board of Education*, 827 F.2d 1058 (1987).

3. *Mozert* parents wanted schools to provide alternative material for their children, but the main issue was whether the children should be required to read material to which their parents objected.

4. I am drawing on David Miller's definition of multiculturalism; see David Miller, *On Nationality* (Oxford: Oxford University Press, 1995), 131.

5. Think, for example, of the shock registered in the film *The Crying Game* when the male lead discovers that his beautiful lover has a penis. Since nothing else has changed, some extraterrestrial observer might wonder why this has precipitated such a large emotional change. The only thing that makes it understandable is our knowledge that men are supposed to love women and that women are not supposed to have penises.

6. I believe that this is the birth order that is supposed to signal a faith healer.

7. I use quotation marks to indicate that both need and culture are in contention in this dispute.

8. Harlan Lane, *The Mask of Benevolence* (New York: Knopf, 1992), 267.

9. Ibid., 12.

10. Ibid., 142.

11. Ibid., 93.

12. See Will Kymlicka, *Multicultural Citizenship* (Oxford: Clarendon, 1995), 7.

13. For an insightful treatment of the problem of standing, see Judith N. Shklar, *American Citizenship: The Quest for Inclusion* (Cambridge: Harvard University Press, 1991); Walter Feinberg, "Affirmative Action and Beyond: A Defense of Race- and Gender-Based Affirmative Action," *Teachers College Record* (Spring 1996): 362–99.

14. Molefi Kete Asante, *The Afrocentric Idea* (Philadelphia: Temple University Press, 1987).

15. I am not denying here that some other cultures may have been violated as severely. The culture of traditional immigrant groups, however, does not generally fit this mold.

Chapter 14

1. As things presently stand, white males can bring antidiscrimination lawsuits. Moreover, affirmative action as a policy to promote the advancement of underrepresented groups often serves to increase fairness for white men. For example, the requirement that universities must advertise widely for new positions instead of relying on the old boys' network has enabled many white male Ph.D.'s to become viable candidates for academic positions that otherwise would have been closed to them.

2. There are exceptions, and some white men have sued their companies on grounds of systematic discrimination.

3. *Chicago Tribune*, August 24, 1995, section 1, 1.

4. Ibid., August 21, 1995, 8.

5. Dinesh D'Souza, *Illiberal Education: The Politics of Race and Sex on Campus* (New York: The Free Press, 1991), 251–53.

6. Richard Allen Epstein, *Simple Rules for a Complex World* (Cambridge: Harvard University Press, 1995).

7. Andrew Hacker, "Who Should Go to College," *The New York Review of Books*, May 11, 1995, 38.

8. For not only would one have to subtract from the pool those African-American students who would lose seats because of the turn from race to need, but one would also have to subtract those who, having completed undergraduate college, would not compete successfully for professional places under less flexible guidelines. This is illustrated by the admissions policies of the University of Texas that came under scrutiny in *Hopwood v. Texas*. In order to correct the lingering effects of past discrimination, the University of Texas law school decided to admit African and Mexican Americans in proportion to their graduation rates from Texas colleges—approximately 10 percent Mexican-American and 5 percent black. To achieve this goal, however, the law school has adjusted its standards significantly and the university lawyers conceded that without racial preferences very few of the targeted group would have been successful. Although an admissions policy that reached further into the white working class, as NBAA preferences would presumably do, would probably reveal many more whites with lower scores, it would also dilute the number of successful applicants from some of the now targeted groups. Just how much dilution would occur at this second phase is difficult to say since the change in policy would limit spaces in undergraduate school to blacks who are more competitive.

9. Richard Kahlenberg, "Class, Not Race," *The New Republic*, April 3, 1995.

10. Ibid.

11. Nathan Glazer, "The Emergence of an American Ethnic Pattern," in *From Different Shores: Perspectives on Race and Ethnicity in America*, ed. Ronald Takaki (New York: Oxford University Press, 1994), 11–23.

12. Alan H. Goldman, "Affirmative Action," in *Equality and Preferential Treatment: A Philosophy and Public Affairs reader*, ed. Marshall Cohen, Thomas Nagel, and Thomas Scanlon (Princeton: Princeton University Press, 1977), 204–5.

13. Ta-Nehisi Coates, "The Case for Reparations," *The Atlantic*, June 2014.

14. Ibid., 202.

15. For example, in my interviews with the talent scout for a new Japanese automobile factory in the United States, I was told that mechanical ability tests were scored differently for men and women on the grounds that women were simply less likely to have had much experience with mechanical work, but that there was also little reason to think that those hired would not be able to learn the skills needed. See Walter Feinberg, *Japan and the Pursuit of a New American Identity: Work and Education in a Multicultural Age* (New York: Routledge, 1993). Much of the same can be said of admission to professional schools. In medicine, for example, I have been told by the admissions director of a highly considered medical school that each year the school must turn down the equivalent of one fully qualified (on technical grounds) class.

16. Cohesion often develops for other reasons as well. For example, persecution may lead to a strong identity between people who otherwise disagree about many matters but who share a common enemy who denies them rights that are otherwise granted to members of the preferred group.

17. For a very good discussion of this see Will Kymlicka, *Multicultural Citizenship* (Oxford: Oxford University Press, 1995).

18. As quoted by Michael Walzer, "What Does It Mean to Be an 'American'?," *Social Research 51* (Fall 1990): 609.

19. Stokely Carmichael and Charles Hamilton, *Black Power* (New York: Random House, 1967).

20. Ronald Dworkin, "Why Bakke Has No Case," *The New York Review of Books*, November 10, 1977, 12.

21. Ibid., 14.

22. Ibid., 12.

23. In *Regents of the University of California v. Bakke* 438 U.S. 265 1978 the court avoided addressing this issue in the consensus decision by Justice Powell.

24. Antonin Scalia, "Commentary—The Disease as Cure," quoted in Ronald J. Fiscus, *The Constitutional Logic of Affirmative Action* (Durham: Duke University Press, 1992), 12.

25. Suppose, for example, that just prior to Kristallnacht a group of young German Jews, not believing the evidence and not wanting to leave Germany,

were kidnapped by the Jewish authorities in Jerusalem with the intent of saving them from what was coming and that, as a result, they were saved. I do not believe the State of Israel would now owe them special consideration because they were forced to leave Germany. This is obviously an extreme case, but it is for this reason that I am reluctant to allow the fact of force alone to always be decisive.

26. Incidentally, it is immaterial to this point whether slave labor was the most efficient way to develop the country, a point that some economic historians like to dispute. If a more efficient alternative were available, then probably more people would have immigrated. The fruits of slave labor were, however, sufficient for those who actually did immigrate and it is the descendants of these people to whom the issue of the debt is relevant for addressing Scalia's claim. If a more efficient alternative had been utilized, we can assume that additional people would have taken advantage of it and immigrated. What is important is that slave labor was an efficient enough wealth producer to entice those who did immigrate to do so.

27. I am, of course providing a variation of John Rawls's original position here (A *Theory of Justice* [Cambridge: Harvard University Press, 1971]). Nevertheless, one might counter that the year of immigration is also blindly and randomly assigned and, allowing that as the year of emancipation recedes, and more generations are added to our random assignments, the chances of falling into a generation that permitted slavery and then of falling into one of the slave positions decreases, certainly it is possible that some brave souls might take their chances and make the wager for freedom—hoping for either a good position or a safe year. And they might do so reasoning that if they do not escape slavery, at least their children will be free. Yet if they also knew that their children and their children would, if they happened to be descended from slaves, remain stigmatized as a result of their ancestry, the wager would lose its appeal.

28. Oscar Handlin, *The Uprooted: The Epic Story of the Great Migrations That Made the American People* (New York: Grosset and Dunlap, 1951), 37–63. Granted, in many instances the choice was extremely limited given conditions at home, but it was a move that many saw as an opportunity.

29. Judith Sklar, *American Citizenship: The Quest for Inclusion* (Cambridge: Harvard University Press, 1991), 3.

30. The reduced quality of everyday life is reflected in greater difficulty in renting and buying a home, higher prices asked for automobiles, slower service in stores, greater surveillance on the street, more frequent rejection of qualified job applicants. For a graphic depiction of this see Diane Sawyer's documentary "True Colors," "Prime Time Live." ABC, September 26, 1991.

31. See James Anderson et al., *Brief of Amici Curiae, State of Missouri v. Jenkins*, no. 93–1823, in the Supreme Court of the United States, October

1994, for a view of some of the continuing effects of such discrimination on school performance.

32. Blue-collar trade and service jobs and much less so in professional fields. See *USA Today*, February 23, 1995, 8A.

33. One exception to this is where companies have begun to correct a history of past discrimination and where seniority policies would result in layoffs for minorities who were recently hired to correct this history.

34. There are many ways to do this, but a general surtax on incomes over a certain minimum aimed at creating more professional programs and general support services for African Americans and members of other groups that meet certain criteria would certainly be a useful addition to existing policy and would distribute the burden more equitably.

35. Fiscus, *Constitutional Logic of Affirmative Action*.

36. Ibid., 10.

37. Ibid.

38. Ibid.

39. Ibid., 13.

40. Ibid.

41. To hold this one must also hold the reasonably sound view that IQ scores do not measure intelligence in any hard-wired way. See Walter Feinberg, *Understanding Education* (Cambridge: Cambridge University Press, 1983).

42. Of course it is not irrelevant in Fiscus's terms for accounting for our present difference in attitude, but it is irrelevant in terms of describing the injustice of our situation.

43. Dworkin, "Why Bakke Has No Case."

44. I owe this example to my colleague Jefferson McMahan. Also, George Sher, "Ancient Wrongs and Modern Rights," *Philosophy and Public Affairs* 10 (1980): 3–17, makes the same point with regard to immigrants.

45. Ibid.

46. Fiscus, *Constitutional Logic of Affirmative Action*.

47. I am not denying here that some other cultures may have been violated as severely. For example, the culture of Native American groups was violated in a different way, but perhaps no less severely. However, the culture of traditional immigrant groups does not fit this mold.

48. "Would be" because the concept of theft, at least for the slave, did not apply in the legal sense and it is this that is the larger affront to morality than mere theft.

49. My appreciation to Jefferson McMahan for raising this consideration.

50. For example, an important complement to affirmative action policies in higher education might include the establishment of extended funding programs based on financial need. At a time when the main cause of declining

black enrollment in and graduation from higher education is economic, affirmative action policies that fail to consider financial factors are by themselves insufficient. See Niara Sudarkasa, "Black Enrollment in Higher Education: The Unfulfilled Promise of Equality," in *The State of Black America*, ed. Janet Dewart (New York: National Urban League, 1988), 7–22.

51. For example, structural changes that have taken place over the better part of this century have served to reduce the opportunities for intergenerational mobility for the children of unskilled and semiskilled laborers, many of whom are recent immigrants. These structural changes, if not addressed, may well serve to create many of the same conditions that the present affirmative action policy has been designed to address, such as the mobility deadlock caused by the way in which lack of educational and economic opportunities reinforces certain social definitions and cultural practices that then serve to constrain motivation and opportunities, which in turn reduces educational and economic opportunities. Unlike the case of African Americans, there may not always be a strong argument that a historical debt is owed here and unlike women, members of these groups may not be spread among the different economic classes. However, to the extent that mobility for members of all groups is important, need is important. It is not a substitute for race and gender, but it is still a consideration.

Furthermore, affirmative action should be but one relatively small piece in addressing a much larger problem, a problem that included the considerable mobility that capital has gained within the last two decades and the relative immobility of labor, especially at the lower, less skilled levels. These are factors in the concerns that affirmative action seeks to address, and in the way in which affirmative action is received. Yet these problems require solutions that are international in scope and even harder to obtain.

Chapter 15

1. Martha C. Nussbaum, *Cultivating Humanity: A Classical Defense of Reform in Liberal Education* (Cambridge: Harvard University Press, 1997), 28–29.

2. Charles S. Peirce, "The Fixation of Belief," *Popular Science Monthly* 12 (November 1877): 1–15.

3. This term was used by John Dewey to express a conception of pragmatic truth.

4. Charles Peirce called this process "abduction." See Jürgen Habermas, *Knowledge and Human Interest*, trans. Jeremy J. Shapiro (Boston: Beacon, 1968), 114.

5. Amy Gutmann, *Democratic Education* (Princeton: Princeton University Press, 1987).

6. Richard M. Hare, "Adolescents into Adults," in *Aims in Education: The Philosophical Approach*, ed. H. B. Hollins (Manchester, UK: Manchester

University Press, 1964), 47–70; John Wilson, "Education and Indoctrination," in Hollins, 24–46; Anthony Flew, "What Is Indoctrination?," *Studies in Philosophy and Education* 4 (1966): 273–83; and Ivan Snook, "Indoctrination and the Teaching of Religion" (Ph.D. diss., University of Illinois at Urbana, 1968).

7. Alan Peshkin, *God's Choice: The Total World of a Fundamentalist Christian School* (Chicago: University of Chicago Press, 1986); and James G. Dwyer, *Religious Schools v. Children's Rights* (Ithaca: Cornell University Press, 2001).

8. Alasdair C. MacIntyre, *After Virtue: A Study in Moral Theory*, 2nd ed. (Notre Dame: University of Notre Dame Press, 1984).

9. Ibid.

10. Shelly Burtt, "Comprehensive Educations and the Liberal Understanding of Autonomy," in *Citizenship and Education in Liberal-Democratic Societies: Teaching for Cosmopolitan Values and Collective Identities*, ed. K. McDonough and W. Feinberg (Oxford: Oxford University Press, 2003), 179–207.

11. The classic works on this are A. J. Ayer, *Language, Truth, and Logic* (New York: Dover, 1952); and Karl Popper, *The Logic of Scientific Discovery* (New York: Basic, 1959).

12. The point here is not that these may be the activity of religiously sponsored schools. Historically this would be wrong, since until a U.S. Supreme Court decision in the early 1960s, children in most public schools prayed. The point is that this feature of education, whether performed in private or public schools, is a religious feature.

13. While there is a similar ceremony for girls, the readings are often shorter.

14. This is almost by definition the case. A school that had a religious affiliation but did not give a high priority to prayer might best be called a *religiously sponsored school* rather than a *religious school*.

15. There is a sense in which my self-identity is tied to my extended identity and that had, say, I been adopted at birth by a Mexican family, in some sense I would be a different person than the one I am.

16. Paul Willis, *Learning to Labor: How Working Class Kids Get Working Class Jobs* (Westmead, UK: Saxon, 1977). Willis certainly valorized resistance, but he was well aware of its limitations when it was both blocked by and served to block alternative visions.

Chapter 16

1. There are, of course other arguments, but these two are designed to appeal beyond the religious community and to be persuasive to those who are neutral regarding religion. Because both arguments appeal to the preference given to public education they appeal to those who find private as well as religious schools attractive alternatives to public ones. There is one argument that is specific to religious education that I do not address and that is the claim that

there is a causal relationship between a religious education and a morally correct person. This claim has some obvious problems. It is vague (what are we to count as moral behavior?), and given this vagueness and the many different flavors of religious education it is difficult to establish empirically. Catholic schools seem to do a good job of emphasizing wider communal needs. See Anthony S. Bryk, Valerie E. Lee, and Peter B. Holland, *Catholic Schools and the Common Good* (Cambridge, MA: Harvard University Press, 1993). But others religious schools provide their students with an education that narrows their vision, and promotes intolerance of other religions. See Alan Peshkin, *God's Choice: The Total World of a Fundamentalist Christian School* (Chicago: University of Chicago Press, 1986) and James G. Dwyer, *Religious Schools v. Children's Rights* (Ithaca, NY: Cornell University Press, 1998).

    2. I am indebted to King Alexander for this observation.

    3. *Pierce v. Society of Sisters*, 268 U.S. 510 (1925).

    4. *Cochran v. Louisiana State Board of Education*, 281 U.S. 370 (1930).

    5. *Everson v. Board of Education of Ewing Township*, 330 U.S. 1 (1947).

    6. *Board of Education v. Allen*, 392 U.S. 236 (1968).

    7. Joseph P. Viteritti, "Blaine's Wake: School Choice, the First Amendment, and State Constitutional Law," *Harvard Journal of Law and Public Policy* 21, no. 3 (1998) (through Lexis/Nexis).

    8. Paul E. Peterson and Bryan C. Hassel, eds., *Learning from School Choice* (Washington, DC: Brookings, 1998).

    9. John E. Chubb and Terry M. Moe, *Politics, Markets and America's Schools* (Washington, DC: Brookings Institute, 1990), 55.

    10. James S. Liebman, "Voice, Not Choice," *Yale Law Review*, 101 (1991): 259–314.

    11. James G. Dwyer, *Religious Schools v. Children's Rights* (Ithaca, NY: Cornell University Press, 1998).

    12. Joseph P. Viteritti, "Blaine's Wake."

    13. Ibid.

    14. I say "ironically" because few religions would see their education as just a consumer good.

    15. Chubb and Moe, *Politics, Markets and America's Schools*.

    16. Charles L. Glenn, *Choice of Schools in Six Nations* (Washington: U.S. Government, 1989), 47–81.

    17. *West Virginia Board of Education v. Barnette*, 319 U.S. 624 (1943).

    18. *Tinker v. Des Moines Independent Community School District*, 393 U.S. 503 (1969).

    19. *Mozert v. Hawkins County Board of Education*, 827 F. 2d 1058, 1067 (6th Cir. 1987), cert. denied, 484 U.S. 1066 (1988).

    20. Joel Feinberg, *Freedom and Fulfillment* (Princeton, NJ: Princeton University Press, 1992), 76–97.

    21. Ibid., 23.

22. *Runyon v. McCrary*, 427 U.S. 160, 176 (1976).

23. I emphasize *right* because such a waiver does not necessarily mean such support is unconstitutional on other grounds.

24. William L. Galston, "Two Conceptions of Liberalism," *Ethics* 105 (April 1995): 516–34.

25. For an argument along these lines see Dwyer's criticism of religious education.

26. Milton Friedman, *Capitalism and Greedom* (Chicago: University of Chicago Press, 1962).

27. Eamonn Callan, *Creating Citizens: Political Education and Liberal Democracy* (Oxford: Oxford University Press, 1997). Walter Feinberg, *Common Schools/ Uncommon Identities: National Unity and Cultural Difference* (New Haven, CT: Yale University Press, 1998).

28. Bryk et al., *Catholic Schools and the Common Good*.

29. Granted, there are many challenges to this autonomy in the form of standardized tests and increased accountability. However, with a few exceptions, markets are actually likely to intensify accountability to test scores as the primary currency for evaluating market-driven schools.

30. The Illinois legislature has passed such a tax. It benefits people who can afford to pay $2,500 or more in tuition by providing a $500 tax deduction.

31. Liebman, *Voice Not Choice*.

32. For a useful critique of this metaphor see Jeffrey R. Henig, *Rethinking School Choice: Limits of the Market Metaphor* (Princeton, NJ: Princeton University Press, 1994).

Chapter 17

1. Walter Feinberg, *For Goodness Sake* (New York: Routledge, 2006).

2. Erazim Kohak, *The Embers and the Stars: A Philosophical Inquiry into the Moral Sense of Nature* (Chicago: University of Chicago Press, 1984), 45.

Chapter 18

1. Walter Feinberg, *Understanding Education* (Cambridge University Press, 1982) and Amy Gutmann, *Democratic Education* (Princeton: Princeton University Press, 1987).

2. Jonathan Glover, *I: The Philosophy and Psychology of Personal Identity* (London: Penguin, 1991), 197.

3. This argument is sometimes given by those who argue that orthodoxy gives children rules to rebel against or to reconsider, as opposed to what they see as wishy-washy liberalism.

4. Charles L. Glenn, *The Ambiguous Embrace: Government and Faith-Based Schools and Social Agencies* (Princeton: Princeton University Press, 2000).

5. There are notable exceptions to this. In one of her comments on this chapter Meira Levinson noted that very few Friends or Episcopal schools take religious affiliation into account in student selection, and less than half of these schools rated religious development as one of their three most important goals. However, my own interviews with Muslim, Jewish, Catholic, and Lutheran educators all expressed a strong preference for teachers of their own faith.

6. This is not to suggest that public schools do not turn out students who are also scientifically misinformed. The issue is whether standardized tests are adequate to address teaching that is intentionally biased against evolution.

7. Some Evangelical Christians have begun to understand this issue and a few have begun to argue that rejection of evolution in its scientific Darwinian form is not only harmful to their cause, but also wrong and, indeed, ungodly. See Mark A. Noll, *The Scandal of the Evangelical Mind* (Grand Rapids: William B. Eerdmans, 1995).

8. Warren A. Nord, *Religion and American Education: Rethinking a National Dilemma* (Chapel Hill: University of North Carolina Press, 1995), 138–60.

9. Noll, *The Scandal of the Evangelical Mind*, 177–210.

10. *Tinker v. Des Moines Independent School District*, 393 U.S. 503 (1969).

11. *West Virginia State Board of Education v. Barnett*, 319 U.S. 624 (1943).

12. Appreciation to Meira Levinson for these examples. See *Cole v. Oroville Union High Sch. Dist.*, 228 F.3d 1092 (9th Cir. 2000) and *Santa Fe Independent School District v. Doe*, 530 U.S. 290 (2000).

13. Levinson considers an option like this in Meira Levinson, *The Demands of Liberal Education* (Oxford: Oxford University Press, 1999). Levinson, however, largely focuses on the development of individual autonomy, and pays considerably less attention to the need to reproduce democratic practices and institutions.

14. Harry Brighouse, *School Choice and Social Justice* (Oxford: Oxford University Press, 2000), 92. Walter Feinberg, "On Public Support for Religious Schools," *Teachers College Record* (August 2000).

15. My ongoing research in religious schools supports this observation. Interviews with administrators in eight separate schools involving four major religious groups—Muslim, Lutheran, Catholic, and Jewish—all expressed a preference to hire their own and usually did so. Given two similarly qualified people, strong preferences were shown for those in the same religion, regardless of the subject.

16. Glenn deals with many of these issues in detail and believes that there are ways to protect the specific character of the school while also providing government funds. However, his belief that this should be done with a minimum of government oversight would favor religious schools over non-religious ones.

17. Glenn, *The Ambiguous Embrace*.

18. This observation needs to be modified in the case of home schooling which, if such practices are to be allowed, needs to be predicated on parents giving up some of this authority to allow the state the same monitoring privileges that it assumes for any school.

19. See the opinion in *Runyon v. McGrary*, 427 U.S. 160 (1976) where, even though the Court denied that the practice of excluding racial minorities was protected by the Constitution as Freedom of Association, it allowed that parents have a right to send their children to schools that advance the belief that racial segregation is desirable. The opinion neglects to consider the role that schools have in reproducing the subjective conditions of democracy, and to other groups.

20. These are all beliefs that I have heard expressed by religious educators in my ongoing research.

21. Alan Peshkin, *God's Choice* (Chicago: University of Chicago Press, 1986).

22. Brighouse believes that by providing public support for such institutions they can be brought under greater public control. Yet this is an empirical issue and will likely differ from country to country depending on historical and cultural factors. Nevertheless, as I argue later, the possibility for such control should certainly be a factor when considering whether public funds should go to support religious schools. See Harry Brighouse, *School Choice and Social Justice* (Oxford: Oxford University Press, 2000).

23. David Blacker, "Fanaticism and Schooling in the Democratic State," *American Journal of Education*, 106, no. 2 (1998), 241–72.

24. Brighouse, *School Choice and Social Justice*, 17.

25. Charles Taylor, *Multiculturalism*, ed. A. Gutmann (Princeton: Princeton University Press, 1994), 52–72.

26. At this moment, the US Supreme Court has refused to review the Wisconsin decision hence allowing it to stand, at least for the time being. Both supporters and critics believe that the Wisconsin decision may serve to open the floodgates for vouchers. However, there are at least three obstacles that stand in the way of this happening immediately. The first is the US Supreme Court, which will eventually rule on some voucher case, and which is rather evenly divided at this time. The second is individual state constitutions which differ considerably in their attitude toward public support for religious and private schools, with some explicitly forbidding it. The third is the view of political and educational leaders about whether such support is politically sound and educationally wise. Whether the decision in Wisconsin leads the nation down the path to choice, or whether it turns out to be a legislative and judicial dead end, will depend on just how well the implications of choice are understood, both for the relationship between church and state and for the improvement of education.

27. The Supreme Court of Wisconsin, case No. 97-0270, *Jackson v. Benson*, June 10, 1998, www://courts.wi.us/html/sc/97/0270.htmp. p. 11 of 46.

28. *Jackson v. Benson*, 22.

29. See Jessica Benjamin, *The Bonds of Love* (New York: Pantheon, 1988), 11–50.

30. Brighouse, *School Choice and Social Justice*.

31. Bokser and Bokser, "Introduction: The Spirituality of the Talmud," in *The Talmud: Selected Writings*, 7 (1989), 30–31. Quoted in Michael Perry, *Love and Power* (New York: Oxford University Press, 1991), 40.

32. While non-religious public schools would continue to exist in most urban areas, it should not be assumed that this would be the case in smaller towns where religion pervades all activities. See, for example, "School Prayer: A Community at War," *Frontline*. PBS.

33. Feinberg Walter, *Common Schools/Uncommon Identities* (New Haven: Yale University Press, 1998).

34. David Alvey, *Irish Education: The Case for Secular Reform* (Dublin: Church and State Books, 1991), 16.

35. Ibid., 15–16. It should be mentioned that not all the incidents are so negative. One very religious teacher used the taunting of a non-religious boy to teach the class how fortunate they were to have a child who was different from them in the classroom. While there is a positive message in this episode, we should not forget the climate that promotes such taunting nor its effects when an enlightened teacher is not present (Ibid., 16).

36. Elmer John Thiessen, *Teaching for Commitment: Liberal Education, Indoctrination and Christian Nurture* (Montreal: McGill-Queens University Press, 1993).

37. Glenn, *The Ambiguous Embrace*, 279.

Chapter 19

1. It is true that there could be more curricular material, but the Pluralism Project at Harvard has been working to correct this deficit and its Web page could be of great help to interested teachers: The Pluralism Project (http://pluralism.org/resources/ tradition/index.php?trad=3).

Chapter 20

1. *The Later Works*, 1935–1937 V. 11, *Liberalism and Social Action* (Carbondale: Southern Illinois University Press, 2008), 45.

2. Gunnar Myrdal, *An American Dilemma: The Negro in a White America*, vol. 1 (New York: Harper Row, 1944/1964), 4.

3. Ibid., 4.

4. John Dewey, *Democracy and Education* (New York: Free Press, 1916), 85.

5. Israel Scheffler, *In Praise of the Cognitive Emotions* (New York: Routledge, 1991), 151.

6. See James Scott Johnston, "The Dewey-Hutchins Debate: A Dispute over Moral Teleology," *Educational Theory* 61 (February 2011): 1–16.

7. Milton Halsey Thomas, *John Dewey: A Centennial Bibliography* (Chicago: University of Chicago Press, 1929, 1957, 1962), 52–54.

8. Jane Addams, *Peace and Bread in Times of War* (Urbana: University of Illinois Press, 2002), 36–37.

9. Cornell West, *The American Evasion of Philosophy: A Genealogy of Pragmatism* (Madison: University of Wisconsin Press, 1989), 102.

10. Paul C. Taylor, "Silence and Sympathy: Dewey's Whiteness," in *What White Looks Like: African-American Philosophers on the Whiteness Question*, ed. George Yancy (New York: Routledge, 2004), 227–42.

11. Walter Feinberg, *Reason and Rhetoric, the Intellectual Foundations of Twentieth Century Educational Reform* (New York: John Wiley, 1974), 109–10.

12. Martin Luther King, "Letter from a Birmingham Jail," April 16, 1863.

13. Eddie S. Glaude Jr., *In A Shade of Blue: Pragmatism and the Politics of Black America* (Chicago: University of Chicago Press, 2007), 1, parentheses mine.

14. Walter Feinberg, *What Is a Public Education and Why We Need It: A Philosophical Inquiry into Self-Development, Cultural Commitment, and Public Engagement* (Lanham: Lexington Books, 2016), 95–112.

15. These are my examples.

16. Gandhi is a grandson of Mahatma Gandhi and is prominent Indian journalist and peace activist in his own right, and Mohamed El Baradei had served as Director of the International Atomic Energy Administration and in that role had refuted the Bush Administration's claim that Iraq had weapons of mass destruction, the rationale used to justify the American invasion of Iraq. Later, during the Egyptian Spring, El Baradei also served, albeit briefly, as his country's vice president.

17. For a lovely exploration of this phrase from a Deweyan point of view see Philip W. Jackson, *What is Education?* (Chicago: University of Chicago Press, 2012).

Reference Bibliography

Abu-Lughod, L. 1991. "Writing Against Culture." In *Recapturing Anthropology: Working in the Present*, ed. R. G. Fox. Santa Fe, NM: School of American Research Press.
Allen, D. 2004. *Talking to Strangers: Anxiety of Citizenship since Brown v. Board of Education*. Chicago: University of Chicago Press.
Anderson, B. 1983. *Imagined Communities*. London: Verso.
Anderson E. 1993. *Values in Ethics and Economics*. Cambridge: Harvard University Press.
Apple, M. W. 1982. *Education and Power*. Boston: Routledge and Kegan Paul.
Aristotle. (1953) 1956. *The Ethics of Aristotle*. Translated by J. A. K. Thomson. London: Penguin.
———. (1948) 1957. *The Politics of Aristotle*. Translated by E. Barker. Oxford: Oxford University Press.
Ayer, A. J. 1936. *Language, Truth and Logic*. New York: Dover.
Behar, R., and D. A. Gordon, eds. 1995. *Women Writing Culture*. Berkeley: University of California Press.
Biesta, G. J. J., and N. C. Burbules. 2003. *Pragmatism and Educational Research*. Lanham: Rowman & Littlefield.
Bohman, J. 1996. *Public Deliberation: Pluralism, Complexity, and Democracy*. Cambridge: MIT Press.
Bourdieu, P., and J. C. Passeron. 1977. *Reproduction in Education, Society and Culture*. London: Sage.
Bredo, E. 2009. "Getting Over the Methodology Wars: Comments on Howe." *Educational Researcher* 38 (3): 441–48.
———, and W. Feinberg. 1982. *Knowledge and Values in Social and Educational Research*. Philadelphia: Temple University Press.
Brighouse, H. 2000. *School Choice and Social Justice*. Oxford: Oxford University Press.
Callan, E. 1997. *Creating Citizens: Public Education and Liberal Democracy*. Oxford: Oxford University Press.

———. 2004. "Citizenship and Education." *Annual Review of Political Science* 7: 71–90.
Chomsky, N. 1959. "A Review of B. F. Skinner's *Verbal Behavior*." *Language* 35 (1): 26–58.
Coetze, J. M. 2000. *Disgrace*. New York: Penguin.
Davis, M. 1998. *Thinking Like an Engineer: Studies in the Ethics of a Profession*. New York: Oxford University Press.
Delaney, J. J. 2005. "Jean-Jacques Rousseau (1712–1778)." *Internet Encyclopedia of Philosophy*.
Dewey, J. (1938) 1984. *Logic: The Theory of Inquiry, The Later Works of J. Dewey, 1925–53*. Vol. 12 (LW 12). Edited by J. A. Boydston. Carbondale: Southern Illinois University Press.
———. (1939) 1984. *Theory of Valuation, The Later Works of J. Dewey, 1925–53*. Vol. 13 (LW 13). Edited by J. A. Boydston. Carbondale: Southern Illinois University Press.
———. (1949) 1984. *Knowing and the Known, The Later Works of J. Dewey, 1925–53*. Vol. 16 (LW 16). Edited by J. A. Boydston. Carbondale: Southern Illinois University Press.
———. 1910. *How We Think*. Boston: D. C. Heath.
———. 1925. *Experience and Nature*. Chicago: Open Court.
———. (1916) 1944. *Democracy and Education: An Introduction to Philosophy of Education*. New York: Free Press.
———. 1988. *Human Nature and Conduct: 1922*. Carbondale: Southern Illinois University Press.
———. (1927) 1988. *The Public and Its Problems*. Athens: Ohio University Press.
Dolby, N., and G. Dimitriadis, with P. Willis. 2004. *Learning to Labour in New Times*. New York: Routledge Falmer.
Feinberg, W. 1975. *Reason and Rhetoric: The Intellectual Foundations of 20th Century Liberal Educational Policy*. New York: John Wiley.
———. 2006. *For Goodness Sake*. New York: Routledge, Taylor & Francis Group.
———. 1962. "Hegel's Conception of Property." Unpublished Master's Thesis, Boston University.
———. 1965. "A Comparative Study of the Social Philosophies of John Dewey and Bernard Bosanquet." Unpublished Doctoral Dissertation, Boston University.
———. 1969. "The Conflict between Intelligence and Community in Dewey's Educational Philosophy." *Educational Theory* 19, no. 3 (Summer): 236–48.
———. 1982. *Understanding Education: Toward a Reconstruction of Educational Inquiry*. Cambridge: Cambridge University Press.
———. 1993. *Japan and the Pursuit of a New American Identity: Work and Education in a Multicultural Age*. New York: Routledge.
———. 1998. *Common Schools/Uncommon Identities: National Unity/Cultural Difference*. New Haven, CT: Yale University Press.

―――. 1998. *On Higher Ground: Education and the Case for Affirmative Action*. New York: Teachers College Press.

―――. 2006. "Philosophical Ethnography: Or How Philosophy and Ethnography Can Live Together in the World of Educational Research." In *Educational Studies in Japan: International Yearbook, No. 1, 2006*, 5–14. Japan: Japanese Educational Research Association.

―――. 2008. "The Dialectic of Parental Rights and Social Obligation: Constraining Educational Choice." In *School Choice: Policies and Outcomes*, edited by C. Lubienski and W. Feinberg, 219–36. Albany: State University of New York Press.

―――. 2012. "Critical Pragmatism: The Reconstruction of Science and Values in Educational Research." *European Journal of Pragmatism and American Philosophy* 4 (1): 222–40.

―――. 2008. "The Dialectics of Parental Rights and Social Responsibility." In *School Choice Policies and Outcomes: Empirical and Philosophical Perspectives*, edited by W. Feinberg and C. Lubienski. Albany: State University of New York Press.

―――. 2012. "The Idea of a Public Education." *Review of Research in Education* 36: 1–22.

―――, and S. R. Langner. 1988. "The Other Face of Competition." In *Money, Power and Health Care*, edited by Evan M. Melhado, Walter Feinberg, and Harold M. Swartz. Ann Arbor, MI: Health Administration Press.

―――, and K. McDonough. 2003. "Liberalism and the Dilemma of Public Education in Multicultural Societies." In *Citizenship and Education in Liberal-Democratic Societies: Teaching for Cosmopolitan Values and Collective Identities*, edited by Kevin McDonough and Walter Feinberg, 1–22. Oxford: Oxford University Press.

―――, and J. Odeshoo. 2000. "Educational Theory in the Fifties: The Beginning of a Conversation." *Educational Theory* 50 (3): 289–307.

―――, and R. Layton. 2014. *For the Civic Good: The Liberal Case for Teaching Religion in Public Schools*. Ann Arbor: University of Michigan Press.

―――. 2014. "Teaching Bible in Public High Schools: Toward a Conception of Educational Legitimacy." *American Educational Research Journal* 50 (6): 1279–1307.

Fields, A. B., and W. Feinberg. 2001. *Education and Democratic Theory: Finding a Place for Community Participation in Public School Reform*. Albany: State University of New York Press.

Foucault, M. 1965. *Madness and Civilization: A History of Insanity in the Age of Reason*. New York: Vintage.

―――. 1970. *The Order of Things: An Archeology of the Human Sciences*. New York: Vintage.

―――. 1979. *Discipline and Punish: The Birth of the Prison*. New York: Vintage.

Fraser, N. 1997. *Justice Interruptus: Critical Reflections on the "Postsocialist" Condition*. New York: Routledge.
Fredrickson, G. M. 2002. *Racism: A Short History*. Princeton, NJ: Princeton University Press.
Freire, P. 1968. *Pedagogy of the Oppressed*. New York: Herder and Herder.
Friedman, M. 1955. "The Role of Government in Education." In *Economics and the Public Interest*, edited by R. A. Solo, 123–44. New Brunswick, NJ: Rutgers University Press.
Geertz, C. 2000. *Available Light: Anthropological Reflections on Philosophical Topics*. Princeton, NJ: Princeton University Press.
Gilligan, C. 1982. *In a Different Voice: Psychological Theory and Women's Development*. Cambridge, MA: Harvard University Press.
Glaude, E. S. Jr. 2007. *In a Shade of Blue: Pragmatism and the Politics of Black America*. Chicago: University of Chicago Press.
Glover, J. 1991. *I: The Philosophy and Psychology of Personal Identity*. London: Penguin.
Gutmann, A. 1987. *Democratic Education*. Princeton, NJ: Princeton University Press.
———, and D. Thompson. 1996. *Democracy and Disagreement: Why Moral Conflict Cannot Be Avoided in Politics and What Should Be Done About It*. Cambridge, MA: Harvard University Press.
Habermas, J. 1971. *Knowledge and Human Interest*. Translated by J. J. Shapiro. Boston: Beacon Press.
Hardie, C. D. 1942/1962. *Truth & Fallacy in Educational Theory*. New York: Bureau of Publications, Teachers College, Columbia University.
Hirsch, E. D. 1987. *Cultural Literacy: What Every American Needs to Know*. Boston: Houghton Mifflin.
Huntington, S. P. 2004. *Who Are We? The Challenges to America's National Identity*. New York: Simon and Schuster.
Ishiguro, K. 1989. *Remains of the Day*. New York: Vintage.
Jaeger, W. (1939) 1967. *Paideia: The Ideals of Greek Culture: Vol. 1. Archaic Greece—The Mind of Athens*. Translated by G. Highet. Oxford: Oxford University Press.
Jefferson, T. 1805. Letter to Littleton Waller Tazewell, 5 January. Special Collections Department, University of Virginia Library, Charlottesville. http://etext.virginia.edu/etcbin/toccer-new2?id=Jef1Gri.sgm&images=images/modeng&data=/texts/ english/modeng/parsed&tag=public&part=1&division=divl.
Kohak, E. 1984. *The Ember and the Stars: A Philosophical Inquiry into the Moral Sense of Nature*. Chicago: University of Chicago Press.
Kymlicka, W. 1995. *Multicultural Citizenship*. Oxford, England: Clarendon Press.
Lakatos, I. 1970. "Falsification and the Methodology of Scientific Research Programmes." In *Criticism and the Growth of Knowledge*, edited by I. Lakatos and A. Musgrave, 91–196. Cambridge: Cambridge University Press.

Lippmann, W. 1955. *The Public Philosophy: On the Decline and Revival of Western Society*. Boston, MA: Atlantic Monthly Press.

MacIntyre, A. 1981. *After Virtue*. Notre Dame, IN: University of Notre Dame Press.

———. 1987. "The Idea of an Educated Public." In *Educational Values: The Richard Peters Lectures*, edited by G. Haydon, 15–36. London: University of London.

———. 1988. *Whose Justice? Which Rationality?* Notre Dame, IN: University of Notre Dame Press.

MacKinnon, C. A. 1989. *Toward a Feminist Theory of the State*. Cambridge: Harvard University Press.

Mann, H. 1957. "Annual Reports." In *The Republic and the School: Horace Mann on the Education of Free Men*, edited by L. Cremin. New York: Teachers College Press.

Mansbridge, J. 1980. *Beyond Adversarial Democracy*. Chicago: University of Chicago Press.

McDermott, R. 1993. "The Acquisition of a Child by a Learning Disability." In *Understanding Practice*, edited by S. Chaiklin and J. Lave. New York: Cambridge University Press.

———. 1997. "Achieving School Failure: An Anthropological Approach to Illiteracy and Social Stratification." In *Education and Cultural Process*, edited by G. Spindler. Prospect Heights, IL: Waveland Press.

McEwan, I. 2007. *On Chesil Beach*. London: Vintage.

Milgram, S. 1963. "Behavioural Study of Obedience." *Journal of Abnormal and Social Psychology* 67 (4): 371–78.

Mosteller, F., and R. Boruch, eds. 2002. *Evidence Matters: Randomized Trials in Education Research*. Washington, DC: Brookings Institution Press.

Musgrave, A., ed. 1970. *Criticism and the Growth of Knowledge*. Cambridge: Cambridge University Press.

Nagel, T. 1996. *The View from Nowhere*. Oxford: Oxford University Press.

Nash, R., and P. Bishop. 2009. *Teaching Adolescents Religious Literacy in a Post-9/11 World*. Charlotte, NC: Information Age Press.

National Education Association of the United States and Commission on the Reorganization of Secondary Education. 1918. *Cardinal Principles of Secondary Education*. Washington, DC: U.S. Bureau of Education.

National Research Council. 2002. *Scientific Research in Education*. Edited by R. J. Shavelson and L. Towne. Washington, DC: National Academy Press.

Noddings, N. 1993. *Educating for Intelligent Belief or Unbelief*. New York: Teachers College Press.

Nord, W. 2010. *Does God Make A Difference?: Taking Religion Seriously in Our Schools and Universities*. Oxford: Oxford University Press.

———, and C. Haynes. 1998. *Taking Religion Seriously Across the Curriculum*. Nashville: First Amendment Center.

Pippin, R. B. 2010. *Nietzsche, Psychology, and First Philosophy*. Chicago: University of Chicago Press.
Plato. (1945) 1964. *The Republic*. Translated by E. M. Cornford. New York: Oxford University Press.
———. 1986. *The Dialogues of Plato*. With an introduction by E. Segal. New York: Bantam Books.
Popper, K. 1959. *The Logic of Scientific Discovery*. London: Hutchinson.
Putnam, H. 2002. *The Collapse of the Fact/Value Dichotomy and Other Essays*. Cambridge: Harvard University Press.
Quine, W. V. 1960. *Word and Object*. Cambridge: MIT Press.
———. 1993. *From a Logical Point of View*. New York: Harper.
Rawls, J. 1971. *A Theory of Justice* (5). Cambridge, MA: Harvard University Press.
———. 1993. *Political Liberalism* (9). New York: Columbia University Press.
Reich, R. 2008. Common Schooling and Educational Choice. In *School Choice: Policies and Outcomes*, edited by C. Lubienski and W. Feinberg, 21–40. Albany: State University of New York Press.
Rousseau, J. J. (1762) 1957. *The Social Contract*. Translated by C. Frankel. New York: Hafner.
Sabine, G. H. 1958. *A History of Political Theory*. New York: Henry Holt.
Said, E. 1978. *Orientalism*. New York: Pantheon.
Satz, D. 2010. *Why Some Things Should Not Be for Sale: The Moral Limits of Markets*. Oxford: Oxford University Press.
Snook, I. A. 1972. *Concepts of Indoctrination: Philosophical Essays*. London: Routledge.
Taylor, C. 1992. *The Ethics of Authenticity*. Cambridge, MA: Harvard University Press.
Thomas, M. H. 1962. *John Dewey, a Centennial Bibliography*. Chicago: University of Chicago Press.
Torre, M., and J. Gwynne. 2009. *When Schools Close: Effects on Displaced Students in Chicago Public Schools*. Chicago, Consortium on Chicago School Research at The University of Chicago Urban Education Institute, October.
Wexler, J. D. 2002. "Preparing for the Clothed Public Square: Teaching About Religion, Civic Education and the Constitution." *William and Mary Law Review* 43 (3): 1159–1262.
Williams, M. S. 2003. "Citizenship as Identity, Citizenship as Shared Fate, and the Functions of Multicultural Education." In *Citizenship and Education in Liberal-Democratic Societies: Teaching for Cosmopolitan Values and Collective Identities*, edited by K. McDonough and W. Feinberg, 208–47. Oxford: Oxford University Press.
Willis, P. 1978. *Learning to Labour: How Working Class Kids Get Working Class Jobs*. Farnborough: Saxon House.
Wolfe, J. 2012. "Does Pragmatism Have a Theory of Power?" *European Journal of Pragmatism and American Philosophy* 4 (1): 120–37.

Index

Abington v. Schempp, 373
abortion, 185, 186
absolutism: in intercultural research, 77–94; and pragmatism, 102–105, 106; in religious education, 315. See also objectivity; relativism
accountability of private/religious schools, 16–17, 335–336, 345–348, 354–355, 359–360, 365–371
activity (concept), 128–129, 132, 135
Addams, Jane, 394
Adler, Mortimer, 151, 154, 164–165
affirmative action, 265–302; conservative v. liberal approaches to, 270–276, 277–278; defined, 267–268; and equality of opportunity, 268–269; and Feinberg's faculty position, 33; as group right, 279–286, 293–298; need- v. race-based, 14, 265–266, 276–279, 301–302; and reparations, 286–301; weakening of, 152, 162, 163–164. See also gender; race
African-Americans, 67, 248–249, 262–263, 271–272, 287–301. See also affirmative action; race
agency, 215, 226, 227, 398–399
The Agora, 192, 195–196, 214
aims of education: critical reflection on, 314; and culture, 223, 246; renewing a public, 215; in study of education, 53–54, 62, 70–71, 147–148
amae (concept), 79–81, 87, 89, 91–94
American Educational Studies Association, 46
American Philosophical Association (APA), 82
Amish culture, 229, 239–241, 258
analytic philosophy, 37–38, 95
Anderson, Elizabeth, 118
anthropology, 40, 82–89, 96
Arendt, Hannah, 66
Arian Creed, 306, 311
Aristotle, 193–195, 202, 207–208
Ariyoshi, Sawako, 85–86
assimilation, 114, 220–221, 362
authenticity, 153, 195
autonomy: as condition for funding, 360–362; conflicting values with, 89, 92, 341–342; development of, 345–346; education for, 314, 321, 354–355, 379–380, 381; overview, 13–14

belief. See faith
Benne, Kenneth, 25, 27, 28, 29, 33
The Bible, 375, 376–377, 378–379

bilingual education, 161, 162–164, 172, 249
Bloom, Alan, 184
Bosanquet, Bernard, 7, 31, 34
Boston University, 23–31
Bowles, Samuel, 51
Boyer, Ernest, 166–167, 170–171, 172
Brown v. Board of Education, 18, 390
Bunch, Ralph, 386

Case, Harold C., 26, 27, 28
Catholicism, 104–105, 143–147, 305–311, 315–316, 317–319, 343. *See also* religion
choice. *See* school choice
Christianity, 184–185, 375–376
citizen/citizenship: education for, 19–20, 338–340, 349–350; vs. members of a public, 208–209; mentioned, 361–369. *See also* public, concept of a
civic education, 198, 379–382, 399
civil rights. *See* affirmative action
class, social, 198, 232–235, 242
code switching, 146–147
colonialism, 85, 220–221, 225–226, 228
common schools: historical context of, 220–221, 235–236; role of, 12–13, 219; teaching of culture in, 221–229, 237–238
common sense, 112–113, 114–117, 138
communication. *See* deliberation
community, 121–136, 235–236, 316–319. *See also* culture; identity; individualism
compensatory justice. *See* reparations
Conant, James, 150, 151
congregants, 348–350
consciousness, reproduction of, 55–56. *See also* reproductive role of education
corporations, 170–171

Counts, George, 389–390
creationism, 188, 189, 228
critical inquiry/reflection, 303–324; and conceptions of rationality, 311–313, 315–316; discomfort from, 319–322; and faith, 304–311; and identity, 322–323; in non/religious traditions, 314–315; overview, 303–304, 324; and religious partiality, 316–319. *See also* deliberation; reason
critical pragmatism. *See under* pragmatism
cultural relativism, 77–94
cultural reproduction. *See* reproductive role of education
culture, 219–238, 239–263; and class, 232–235, 274; as culturing, 229–237; and deaf education, 249–255; for educational purpose, 224–229; endangered, 255–257; forms of recognition of, 246–249; and group rights, 257–263 (*See also* group rights); hierarchies of, 220–224; and identity, 235–237, 241–244; and research, 77–94; schools' responsibilities toward, 13–15, 237–238, 239–241, 244–256
curriculum, 149, 150, 164–165, 166, 350–351

deaf education, 249–255, 256–257
debate. *See* deliberation
deconstruction, 65–67, 71–73
Delaney, James, 196
deliberation, 192–196, 199–202, 207–210, 238. *See also* critical inquiry/reflection
dependency, 80–81, 86–87, 89, 93
Derrida, Jacques, 66, 72–73
de-schooling, 68
desires, 125–129, 132–133, 195, 196, 205–206

Dewey, John, 121–136; and community/culture, 238; and critical pragmatism, 113–114, 137; on democratic education, 385–389, 393, 397; and objectivity of values, 109; Polish study by, 7–8, 18, 31, 34–36, 40–41, 393–394; and a public, 197–198, 200; on research, 69, 97, 98; and truth claims, 103–104

disciplines of education. *See* educational studies, discipline of; philosophy of education, discipline of; science

discourse, 65–75, 187–188

discrimination. *See* affirmative action; equality/inequality

distributive justice, 294–295

diversity, 387–388

dogma, 146–147

Doi, Takeo, 79–81, 89, 91–93

Dworkin, Ronald, 284–286, 295

ebonics, 248–249

economic need, 259–260, 261

educational reform, 149–173; conclusions about, 171–173; and inequality, 160–164, 167–171; reports on, 11, 149–160, 166–167; for unified culture, 164–165

educational reports: alternatives to, 166–167; *Making the Grade*, 160–164; *A Nation at Risk*, 150, 154–157, 167, 171–172; overviews of, 149, 150, 151–152, 154; *The Paideia Proposal*, 164–165

educational resources: culture's claims on, 241, 245, 249, 257–259; and economic need, 259–260, 261; and historical injustice, 262–263; and standing, 260–261. *See also* religious schools, funding of; school choice

educational studies, discipline of, 45–63; foundationist viewpoints on, 46–47, 48, 49, 59, 62–63; and history of education, 47–50; integrated nature of, 59–62; research in, 9–10, 97–102. *See also* philosophy of education, discipline of

ends and means, 129–132

The Enlightenment, 180–181

epistemology. *See* knowledge

equality/inequality: and critical pragmatism, 113–117, 139; and cultural hierarchies, 220–221, 236; and educational quality, 160–164; *vs.* efficiency, 152; evaluations of, 166–167; in Japanese education, 157; of opportunity, 268–269; and schools, 161, 167–171, 349, 362–364

ethnocentrism. *See* relativism

ethnography, 5–6, 40, 137–148

euthanasia, 104–105

evolution, 177, 188, 228, 350–351

experience, 103–104

expert v. local knowledge, 100–102, 111, 114, 139

exploitation, 78, 80, 85–87

fact/value dichotomy, 10, 99–102, 107–108, 110–113

faith: and conceptions of rationality, 311–316; and identity/community, 316–319, 322–323; *vs.* reason, 304–311

false consciousness, 78, 80

feminist theory, 71–72, 73, 94

Fiscus, Ronald, 293–296, 298, 301

foundationists, 46–47, 48, 49, 59, 62–63

frames, 55, 57–58

freedom, 205–207, 349

free school movement, 153

Freire, Paulo, 91, 115, 138, 142
friendship, 194, 212–213, 214
funding. See educational resources; religious schools, funding of; school choice

gender, 74–75, 113, 115–117, 210–211, 242, 260. See also affirmative action
Gintis, Herbert, 51
Glazer, Nathan, 276–277
Glenn, Charles, 369–370
globalization, 41–42, 236, 270
Glover, Jonathan, 226–227, 237
Goldman, Alan, 277
good, conception of the, 17–18, 182–183, 184–185, 314, 334, 379–380
Goodlad, John, 166–167, 168–171, 172
Greene, Maxine, 65–67, 71–73
group rights, 257–263, 276–277, 279–286, 293–298
growth (concept), 197–198, 237–238, 360–362

Habermas, Jurgen, 201
Haldane, John, 184–185
Hardie, Charles Dunn, 37
Harris, W.T., 238
Hegel, Georg Wilhelm Friedrich, 30
higher education, 160, 267, 271–273
high schools, 149, 171
Hirsch, E. D., Jr., 389
historical injustice, 14–15, 262–263, 267–269, 275–276, 277–278, 286–301
history of education, 7, 14, 47–50
Hortas, Carlos, 163
humanities, 6–7, 381–382

identity: common national, 13–15, 164, 179–180, 195, 235–237, 245; created through a public, 12, 192, 202, 212–214; and critical reflection, 322–323; cultural (See culture); multiple, 241–244. See also community
immigrants, 287–292, 296–301
inclusivity, 222–223, 382
independence, 80–81, 86–87, 89, 93
individualism, 127–128. See also community; identity
indoctrination, 314, 355–356, 374, 382
inequality. See equality/inequality
injustice. See historical injustice
inquiry. See critical inquiry/reflection
institutions, study of, 68–70, 75
integration of schools, 161, 390–392, 399
intelligence, 8, 121–136, 392–393
intercultural research, 77–94
intergenerational reproduction. See reproductive role of education

Jackson v. Benson, 328, 358–360
Jaeger, Werner, 192
Japanese culture, 77–94 *passim*
Japanese schools, 11, 40, 78–79, 155–160
justice. See historical injustice

Kahlenberg, Richard, 272, 273
Kallan, Horace, 387–388
King, Martin Luther, Jr., 25, 33, 395–396
knowledge: codes, 9, 56–59; of expert v. local actors, 100–102, 111, 114, 139; moral, 104–105; public, 213–214; and reproductive role of education, 53–59; treatment of in research, 50
Kuhn, Thomas, 58
Kymlicka, Will, 257–258, 356

lack, 129, 132–136. *See also* desires
Lakatos, Imre, 96
Lane, Harlan, 252–253, 254, 256–257
language: and culture, 227–228, 250–251, 356; ebonics, 248–249; and moral judgment, 108–109; systems, 82–83
Levinson, Meira, 399
liberal education, 151, 164
liberalism: and concept of a public, 195, 196, 197, 202; and critical reflection, 324; and pluralism, 15, 341–344; and religious education, 355, 379–381; and rights, 239–240
Lippmann, Walter, 199, 202, 203
literacy, 172
local v. expert knowledge, 100–102, 111, 114, 139
logic, 105–108, 115–117, 121

MacIntyre, Alasdair: and absolutism/relativism, 82–83, 102–103, 106; and a public, 181–187, 198–200, 202, 203, 207
Making the Grade, 160–165
markets, 203, 270–271, 329–330, 332–335, 338
Marx, Karl, 45–46, 63
McDermott, Ray, 112, 141–142, 143
McEwan, Ian, 206–207
means and ends, 129–132
medical education, 109–110, 115–117, 283
merit, 274–275
Merleau-Ponty, Maurice, 66
Milgram, Stanley, 110
minority groups, 257–263, 276–277, 279–286, 293–298. *See also* affirmative action; culture; *specific groups*
moral education, 183–184

moral invention, 104–105, 110, 210
Mozert v. Hawkins County Board of Education, 239–241, 258, 330
multicultural education, 3–4, 241, 244–246
Myrdal, Gunnar, 385–386

Nagel, Thomas, 98
national defense, 152, 154, 155, 156
A Nation at Risk, 150, 154–157, 167, 171–172
Native Americans, 220, 228, 262–263, 362
neighborhood effects, 202–207
neo positivism, 110–113. *See also* positivism
Newton, Isaac, 107
Nicene Creed, 305–311, 315–316
Nietzsche, Friedrich, 207
No Child Left Behind, 98
norms, 108, 139, 140–145, 206, 207, 210–212
Nussbaum, Martha, 303–304, 312

Oakland University, 31–32
objectivity, 108–110. *See also* absolutism; relativism

The Paideia Proposal, 154, 164–165
parents: rights of, 17, 239–241, 331, 354–355; and school choice, 203–207, 215–217, 325–326, 329–330, 332–338 (*See also* school choice); and the teaching of culture, 228
patriotism, 183–184, 236
pedagogy, 25–26, 28–29, 35, 305–311, 321–322
Peirce, Charles Sanders, 104
Peters, R.S., 38
Peterson, Paul, 161
philosophy: *vs.* anthropology, 82–89; ethnography as tool for, 138–140;

philosophy *(continued)*
  vs. philosophy of education, 10, 69–71; public, 199, 202
philosophy of education, discipline of, 77–94; and analytic movement, 37–38; discourses of, 65–75; and ethnography, 137–148; Feinberg's approach to, 4–11, 19–21; future of, 41–42; and intercultural research, 77–94, 115; *vs.* philosophy, 10, 69–71; practice v. theory in, 46–47, 71, 89; and relativism-absolutism debate, 78–79, 88–89; role of, 38–50, 65–69. *See also* educational studies, discipline of
Philosophy of Education Society (PES), 37, 68, 69
philosophy of science. *See* science
Pierce v. Society of Sisters, 327
Plato, 192–194
pluralism: and concept of a public, 185, 202; and critical reflection, 312, 313, 324; and diversity, 387–388; and liberalism, 15–16, 341–344, 355; and role of schools, 12–13, 18
positionality, 223
positivism: basic tenets of, 95–96; and fact/value dichotomy, 99–102, 109, 110–113; neo, 110–113; post-, 96–97, 111; and pragmatism, 105–106
post modernism, 142, 181
poverty, 11, 14, 261
pragmatism, 95–119, 137–148; *vs.* absolutism and relativism, 102–105; critical, 9–10, 19, 113–115, 137–148; and rationality, 311–313; and religious education, 16; and research, 9–10, 97–102; as temperament, 117–118; and values, 95–96, 100–115

prayer, 305, 317–318
presentism, 47–48
private schools, 216, 353, 368–370. *See also* religious schools
professional education, 111
public, concept of a, 177–190, 191–217; communication in, 207–210, 212–214; contemporary, 198–202; defined, 191; Dewey on, 197–198; education's role in, 12, 177–181, 187–190, 214–215; historical context, 192–197; MacIntyre's views on, 181–187; and norm setting, 210–212; and religious schools, 15–18, 330–332, 335–338; and school choice, 202–207, 215–217. *See also* citizen/citizenship
Putnam, Hilary, 108–110

Quine, Willard Van Orman, 96

race: and Feinberg's early tenure, 33–34; and historical injustice, 14–15, 262–263, 267–269, 275–276, 277–278, 286–301; and identity, 242–243; and integration of schools, 161, 390–392, 399; and John Dewey, 391, 395–397. *See also* affirmative action
racism, 210–212, 282–283
rationality, 304, 311–313, 315–316. *See also* reason
Raup, R. Bruce, 69
Rawls, John, 201
reading education, 112, 141–142
Reagan, Ronald, 153
reason, 192–194, 304–311. *See also* critical inquiry/reflection
recognition (concept), 14, 246–263, 356–357
reflection. *See* critical inquiry/reflection
reform. *See* educational reform

relativism, 6, 77–94, 102–105. *See also* absolutism; objectivity
religion: and evolution, 177, 188, 228, 350–351; exclusionary attitudes of, 342–344, 355, 363–364; and publics, 15–18, 177, 186; teaching of in public schools, 17–18, 373–383. *See also* religious education; religious schools; *specific religions*
religious education: and conceptions of the good, 184–185; funding of (*See* religious schools, funding of); in liberal democratic societies, 345–350, 370–371; liberalism and pluralism in, 15, 341–344; *vs.* public education, 216; in public schools, 373–383. *See also* religion; religious schools
religious schools: accountability of, 16–17, 335–336, 345–348, 354–355, 359–360, 365–371; aims of, 346–347, 349; critical reflection in, 314–316, 322–323; funding (*See* religious schools, funding of); and pragmatism, 16; *vs.* public schools, 368–370; teaching faith and reason in, 305–311. *See also* private schools; religious education
religious schools, funding of, 325–340; and citizenship, 338–339; and conceptions of a public, 330–332, 335–338; conditions for, 360–368; fallacies about, 350–357; market considerations in, 329–330, 332–335; and non-tyranny, 357–360; overview of, 325–328, 339–340, 370–371. *See also* religious schools; school choice
reparations, 14–15, 262–263, 267–269, 275–276, 277–278, 286–301
reports. *See* educational reports
reproductive role of education: and cultural groups, 240, 244, 253; as domain of educational studies, 9, 50–54, 59, 62, 67; and formation of a public, 191, 212–214, 216; and inequality, 167–171; and knowledge, 53–59
research in education. *See* educational studies, discipline of; ethnography; history of education; philosophy of education, discipline of
respect, 89–94, 214, 246–247, 357, 382
rights: of children, 353–354; discourse, 65, 74–75; education accountable for, 180–181; of groups, 257–263, 276–277, 279–286, 293–298; intergenerational, 300–301; of parents, 17, 203–204, 239–241, 354–355; in research, 49
Rorty, Richard, 103
Rousseau, Jean-Jacques, 196–197

Saito, Hisao, 158
Scalia, Antonin, 287–293
Scheffler, Israel, 388–389
school choice: and concept of a public, 215–217, 335–338; and the market, 329–330, 332–335; stakeholders in, 352–353; and values, 202–207; voucher programs, 358–359. *See also* religious schools, funding of
school closings, 98
science, 96–102, 106–113
secondary schools, 149, 171
secular humanism, 351–352
segregation of schools, 161, 390–392, 399
self, nature of, 130–131
sexism, 210–212
silencing in schools, 74–75
simultaneity, 281–284
Sizer, Theodore, 166–168, 171, 172

skilled clusters, 53, 54–56
slavery, 289–301. See also reparations
social imaginaries, 18–19, 385–387, 389–390, 392–396
social reproduction. See reproductive role of education
Socratic ideal, 303–304, 312
specialists v. local actors, 100–102
speech community, 201
synthetic statements, 95

talent, 294–295
taxes. See religious schools, funding of
Taylor, Charles, 356–357
teacher education, 34, 147–148
teachers, 17, 170, 189, 354, 369
teacher unions, 161–162
teaching. See pedagogy
testing: and accountability, 350–351, 366–367; and affirmative action, 271, 273, 284–285; and American vs. Japanese students, 155–156, 157–160; and pragmatism/positivism, 98–99, 100
threshold levels, 110
tracking, 169
trust, 212–213, 386–387, 393–394
Turnbull, Colin, 84–85

tyranny, 351–352, 357–368

universities. See higher education
University of Illinois, 33–36, 392, 400

valuation, process of, 122, 123–132
values, 94–119; absolutist and relativist perspectives on, 102–104; Dewey's theories on, 122, 123–128, 132; in ethnographic research, 141–142; vs. facts, 10, 99–102, 107–108, 110–113; and historical research, 48; and ideology, 153; objectivity of, 108–110; and positivism, 94–99, 110–113; and pragmatism, 105–106, 110–117; public, 202–207, 210–212
Vietnam War, 35–36, 153, 391–392
vocational education, 149–150, 151
voting, 209–210
vouchers. See religious schools, funding of; school choice

Wartofsky, Marx, 26–28, 30
Wisconsin v. Yoder, 229, 239–241, 258

Zeno's paradox, 105

www.ingramcontent.com/pod-product-compliance
Lightning Source LLC
Chambersburg PA
CBHW032008220426
43664CB00006B/178